Letter from Washington
1863–1865

Letter from Washington
1863–1865
BY LOIS BRYAN ADAMS

Edited with an Introduction by

Evelyn Leasher

Wayne State University Press   Detroit

Great Lakes Books

A complete listing of the books in this series can be found at the back of this volume.

Philip P. Mason, Editor
Department of History, Wayne State University

Dr. Charles K. Hyde, Associate Editor
Department of History, Wayne State University

Copyright © 1999 by Wayne State University Press,
Detroit, Michigan 48201. All rights are reserved.
No part of this book may be reproduced without formal permission.
Manufactured in the United States of America.

03 02 01 00 99   5 4 3 2 1

Library of Congress Cataloging-in-Publication Data

L (L. B. Adams)
    Letter from Washington, 1863–1865 / by Lois Bryan Adams ; edited with an introduction by Evelyn Leasher.
       p. cm. — (Great Lakes books)
    Excerpts from the author's newspaper column which originally appeared in the Detroit advertiser and tribune.
    Includes bibliographical references and index.
    ISBN 0-8143-2798-2 (alk. paper)
    1. United States—History—Civil War, 1861–1865—Personal narratives. 2. United States—History—Civil War, 1861–1865—Women. 3. United States—History—Civil War, 1861–1865—War work—Washington (D.C.) 4. L (L. B. Adams) 5. Women journalists—Michigan—Detroit—Biography. 6. United States. Dept. of Agriculture—Biography. I. Leasher, Evelyn M. II. Title. III. Series.
E628.L25   1999
973.7'81—dc21
                                                        98-46253

DESIGNER S. R. TENENBAUM

Grateful acknowledgment is made to the Mary Dickey Masterton Fund for financial assistance in the publication of this volume.

Contents

List of Illustrations   7

Introduction   9

PART 1 1 8 6 3   31

PART 2 1 8 6 4   53

PART 3 1 8 6 5   221

Glossary   345

Bibliography for Glossary   363

Index   365

ILLUSTRATIONS

1. *Michigan Farmer* cover, 1860	14
2. East front of the capitol	44
3. U.S. Patent Office	56
4. President's house	79
5. Scene in the house	110
6. Armory Square Hospital	151
7. Hospital scene	154
8. First reading of the Emancipation Proclamation	180
9. Colors of the Second Michigan Infantry	197
10. Michigan State Relief Association ministering to wounded at White House, Virginia	211
11. Office of the United States Christian Commission in Washington	214
12. The Sanitary Commission a success	216
13. Lady clerks leaving the Treasury Department at Washington	218
14. Tin-Tin Malikin by John Mix Stanley	229
15. President Lincoln taking the oath at his second inauguration, March 4, 1865	243
16. President Lincoln's funeral procession in Washington City	257
17. John Wilkes Booth	260
18. Grand review in Washington	264
19. Miss Mary Harris	284

Introduction

"Washington has its peculiarities aside from being the national capital, which entitle it to the notice of correspondents," wrote Lois Bryan Adams, special correspondent to the *Detroit Advertiser and Tribune*.[1] In her column, Adams wrote about such topics as everyday life in Washington, the U.S. Department of Agriculture, government clerks, politics, war news, President Abraham Lincoln, hospitals and the stories of the men in them, African-American events, women's issues, Reconstruction, fashion, and the natural history of the capital district. From October 1863 to December 1865 Adams reported on the nation's capital to the people of Michigan. Adams was one of the first women in the federal civil service, one of the first employees of the United States Department of Agriculture, and a woman newspaper correspondent in an interesting place who wrote for a regional audience, and wrote well.

Her columns reflect contemporary opinions from the point of view of a woman, an ardently pro-Union Republican, and a middle-class northerner. Her commentaries reflect the popular northern sentiment of the day. She was an observer or a participant in many of the events she wrote about and she provided firsthand information about a place few of her readers had visited.

As one of the first women in the federal civil service, her comments on the work and on her fellow employees document the great social change involved in having men and women working in the same office. This experiment changed the way the business world operated and there are few firsthand accounts from early participants.

The U.S. Department of Agriculture separated from the Patent Office in 1862. Few early records of its personnel and their work exist. Thus, Adams's accounts of the work of the department are a valuable source of information about the first few years of the department. Adams used her columns to promote the idea of the department among Michigan farmers, and especially to introduce them to the practical benefits of scientific agriculture.

Life in Washington, D.C., during the Civil War was a topic of immediate concern to Adams and she discussed it frequently in her columns. The city's population swelled during the war as the government increased in size and function. New government employees, wounded soldiers, escaping and freed blacks, and civilian refugees swelled the city's size and strained public services. The new arrivals found a middle-border city with few amenities. Housing was in short supply and rents high. Adams was also a sensitive observer of the city's passing scene—its social life, politics, weather, and people. Although life in the national capital could be hard and squalid, it could also be beautiful and stirring, especially to a strong Union sympathizer who rubbed shoulders everyday with the leaders of her cause.

The sick and wounded soldiers in Washington's hospitals were of deep concern to Adams. She volunteered as a hospital visitor with the Michigan Soldiers Relief Association and served as a link between Michigan and Michigan soldiers in the hospitals. She was well aware of being an important source of information to the people of Michigan and did her best to provide timely and accurate information to those at home as well as comfort to those in the hospitals. Through her columns, she sought to mobilize the people of Michigan to support the relief organizations and charities that were struggling to bring comfort to the tide of sick and wounded soldiers that during the bloody battles of 1864 seemed almost endless.

Newspaper reporting was not exclusively a male occupation in Adams's day, but women newspaper columnists were the exception. Adams was not a pioneer in her reporting, but she was a professional. She had been writing for publication for over twenty years and knew how to write and knew her audience.

Adams signed all her columns "L" and was never identified by name in the *Detroit Advertiser and Tribune,* not even when the letters were called "admirable" by the editor.[2] Readers of the day would have known that "L" was Lois Bryan Adams, as she was a prominent literary figure in the state. She was readily identifiable by her initial, which she had used as a pseudonym for some time.

That Adams was well known to contemporary readers is evidenced by the entries in biographical dictionaries of the era. For example, an entry in *Irish Celts,* a book in which Celts of all nations and ages are given brief biographical notice, noted:

Adams, Mrs. L. B., a talented writer in prose and verse, whose maiden name was Bryan, was born of Irish parents in New York in 1818, and came with them to Michigan when but an infant. She taught school for awhile, but afterwards became a writer for the press, contributing regularly to the *Michigan Farmer* and Detroit *Advertiser,* the former of which she edited for some time, first as associate of R. F. Johnstone, and was a valued correspondent of the N.Y. *Tribune.* She is the

Introduction

author of some exquisite little poems, and was a writer of much grace and finish. She died in Washington in 1870.³

In the *Red Book of Michigan,* she is one of four women to rate a mention in the biographical section:

Adams, L. B.—She was the daughter of John Bryan who emigrated to Michigan from New York in 1823, and was born in the latter state in 1818. Her early education was obtained through private tutors. She was married in 1841 to James R. Adams, who was an editor at White Pigeon and Kalamazoo, and died in 1847; in 1848 she went to Kentucky as a teacher, where she remained three years, and then returned to Michigan, and was for several years a regular writer for the press, especially the *Detroit Advertiser* and the *Michigan Farmer,* and also for the *New York Tribune.* Finding that her literary labors were injuring her health, she obtained a position in the Museum of the Agricultural Department in Washington, where she was associated with Isaac Newton and Horace Capron, and Professor Townsend Glover, all of whom highly appreciated her services, and she died in Washington city on the 29th of June, 1870, deeply lamented. She was a writer of graceful verse, and many of her poetic productions were associated with her much loved Michigan and the valley of the St. Joseph.⁴

Lois Bryan Adams was recognized in her day but needs an introduction for the modern reader. An explanation of Adams's life and career before her Washington years helps put her columns in perspective. They evolved from her life and previous experience as an author and editor, as well as from the particular time and place she wrote about.

Lois Bryan came to Michigan with her family in 1823.⁵ The family migrated from Whitestown, N.Y., and were one of the first five families to settle in what is now the Ypsilanti area. When they moved to the Michigan frontier in 1823, the family consisted of John and Sarah Bryan and their five children, with Lois being the second child. Her mother, Sarah, kept a journal and recorded the trip from New York and the family's first days in Michigan. She wrote:

We left Geneseo October 7th, 1823, for our new home—arrived in Detroit in ten days; put up at the Widow Hubbard's who kept a sort of boarding house.... After a wearisome and almost indescribable journey of four days through thick woods, my husband cutting the road before us with an axe, we came, the night of October 23rd to the beautiful Huron shores. We had the privilege of staying in a log cabin till we could build one of our own, which we moved into the last day of December. Eight weeks after this, February 27th, 1824, Alpha was born; we called him Alpha Washtenaw the latter being given in honor of the county, and the former on account of his being the first white child born in the county.⁶

John Bryan was a carpenter by trade and found work readily available in Michigan's rapidly growing towns. His work often took him away from home and, in those days of few roads and little mail service, these absences could lead to hardship and worry for the family. In October 1824, he left to take a three-week job in Monroe. His wife reported in her diary:

> The three weeks passed; a good supply of potatoes was nearly all the provisions we had left, and I began to look with great anxiety for my husband. . . . Two months passed, and brought cold December for me and my little ones, but brought no news from him whose duty it was to provide for us. . . . It was now the 23rd of December. . . . I returned home and stood in our log cabin door, thinking about what to do next, when my husband rode up, and put an end to my fears. He had written several letters, which were delayed in Detroit, and never reached me. Finding wages high, and the roads very bad, he had concluded to remain, supposing I was well provided for.[7]

When the Bryan family moved to Michigan Territory it was still sparsely settled with few roads and fewer settlements. The 1820 census for Michigan listed 8,765 residents (and that included areas that are now Wisconsin and Minnesota). Most of the residents were in the southern part of the state. Agriculture was the mainstay as food was grown for household and farm animals. Skilled craftsmen such as John Bryan with his carpentry skills were much in demand in the towns and cities, but often purchased land and raised crops in addition to practicing their trade.

Schools were rare. To educate their children, interested pioneers banded together to hire a teacher and provide lessons. The Bryans wanted their children to have a good education so they appropriated a room in their house for the school and began lessons. In "this we soon grew to be quite independent, establishing a little district of our own, setting apart what was intended for the 'best room,' when the house should be finished, as a school room, and installing our eldest sister as teacher. There in our little domestic academy we pursued the studies we had commenced at institutions of more pretension, varying our exercises by taking turns week about at the housework with our mother."[8]

In the weeks of doing housework other skills were learned which were needed if the family were to be self-sufficient.

> All those boys must be clothed from the products of our own wheel and loom. Labor-saving machinery was not so common then as now. Our mother had been brought up after the old-fashioned way, and was quite familiar with all the mysteries of spinning, dying, weaving, and making up clothing for her household, and it was her custom for years to have all this done under her own roof—much of it, indeed, by her own hands. We had no silks or jewels to display, but I remember being very proud of the smooth-pressed, home-made plaids made up into dresses and cloaks for our winter wear at the district school. We had neither piano, melodeon, guitar, nor even an accordion, but the wheel and loom and churn instead; and we were far more familiar with the care of lambs and calves and chickens than with the heroes and heroines of any novel, old or new.[9]

In 1835, the Bryan family moved from the Ypsilanti area to the Constantine,

Introduction 13

Michigan, area with their ten children. It took five days to move the family and household goods 150 miles to their new home on the banks of the St. Joseph River.

In 1839, Lois attended the White Pigeon Academy, a short-lived branch of the University of Michigan.[10] At that time, women were not admitted to the University of Michigan in Ann Arbor, but the branch academies admitted them to study in Ladies' Departments, where they received separate instruction in classical learning, English literature, and teacher education.

In 1841, Lois Bryan married James R. Adams, a newspaper editor. At the time of their marriage he was editor of the *White Pigeon Republican*. From White Pigeon they moved to Centerville, where he published the *Centerville Democrat*. In 1845, they moved to Kalamazoo, where he published the *Kalamazoo Gazette*. Lois Adams described the problems a newspaper publisher in a small town faced:

> In a printing office in one of the most prosperous villages in the State, a man is standing at the case; there is no copy before him, he sets in type the thoughts of his busy brain, he has no time to write them out. Editor, proprietor, and chief compositor, he is always there, day and night, except the few hours when he takes his troubled sleep, or goes to his home at meal time under pretense of dining, but in reality to comfort the patient little wife waiting him there, with the assurance that prospects are brightening, that so many promises must eventually result in something, and that so much hard labor, self-denial, and suffering must meet with its reward; that reward they both hope will be in the shape of a few dollars wherewith they can purchase comfortable food and clothing. They share a scanty loaf between them, laying by enough, no, not enough, but what will answer for them, for supper, and trusting in Providence for the next day, the printer goes back to his work—the Paper must go on.... The paper must go on, pay or no pay, for the villagers want the news of town and country, and to see what new tale or poem the editor's wife has written, while she, in a rusty, faded dress, the only thing like a decent one she has, sits in her lonely room, patching her husband's threadbare shirt, thinking of the crust laid by for her supper, and trying, but, alas, in vain, to see one gleam of brightness in the dark and dreary future.[11]

Adams left the newspaper business and bought a sawmill in the Kalamazoo area. He was successful in this business and "for many months there was not among the birds of the forest a brighter pair than the printer-sawyer and his wife."[12]

Unfortunately, this happiness and prosperity did not last. James Adams died of consumption in the summer of 1848. Lois Adams, needing to support herself, moved to Kentucky and taught school there for three years. She continued to write and publish that writing in Michigan, including in the byline her address in Kentucky, which indicates she was in Lafayette County at "Bryan's Station."[13]

In 1851, Adams moved back to Michigan and began contributing to the *Michigan Farmer*, the state's leading agricultural periodical. She also wrote for the *Detroit Advertiser*. In addition to her literary work she was an assistant principal at Paw Paw Union school.

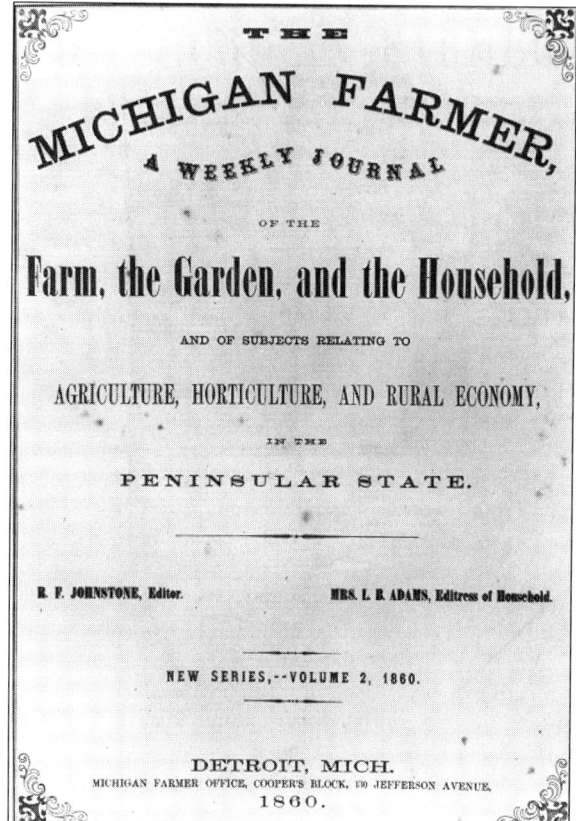

Michigan Farmer cover, 1860.

In 1853, while visiting her sister in Aurora, Illinois, she wrote a series of letters that were published in the *New York Tribune*. She wrote: "You have, I perceive, no regular correspondent in this section of the Union—no letter of little news, or reporter of progress of those great principles which are working such great revolutions in the East. There are many things transpiring almost daily in this remote area which would not only be interesting but encouraging to the friends of progress and reform everywhere."[14]

That year, Adams began working in the Detroit office of the *Michigan Farmer*, published by Robert F. Johnstone and W. S. Duncklee.[15] She moved to Detroit and boarded with the Johnstones.[16] Johnstone described her qualifications for the position:

> Her experience with her husband, who had been a printer . . . and her own literary tastes and aspirations, had made her well acquainted with the routine of a newspaper, and she undertook the work of attending to proofs, the mails, the literary and household departments of the *Michigan Farmer*. After a year's work

Introduction

of this kind, Mr. Dunckee made her an offer of his share of the *Farmer*, which she accepted, and she became joint proprietor, publisher and editor.[17]

At the same time she also did considerable office work on the *Democrat and Inquirer*, and subsequently on the *Detroit Advertiser*.[18]

Adams was not the only woman who became the editor for an agricultural periodical in the 1850s.[19] Several women took over the Household or Ladies' Departments of agricultural periodicals about this time. In many cases the women who began these specialized departments were wives of the editors. When establishing a journal, the editors often promised items of interest to women, but most found they lacked the knowledge and expertise needed for the job. "These articles constituted a highly specialized field and the editors' lack of training was obvious—especially to the editors themselves. This feeling was well expressed by the editor of the *American Agriculturist*, when he wrote in 1844, 'We wish someone would volunteer to make us a Ladies' Department . . . for we feel totally inadequate to attempt anything of the kind—yet the farmers' wives and daughters ought not to be neglected.' "[20]

In the February 1856 issue of the *Michigan Farmer*, the "Household Department" was initiated with the byline "Edited by Mrs. L. B. Adams." The motto of the new department was, "She looketh well to the ways of her household, and eateth not the bread of idleness" (a quotation from Proverbs 32:27). In her first column Adams commented on her hopes for the department.

> The household is a little kingdom by itself. It occupies but a small part of the world, yet within that little space how many interests are centered! Home is called woman's peculiar sphere, and so it may be, but it is not hers alone. She has parents, husband, brothers, sons, to share its privileges and blessings with her, and her labors, whether performed with household implements, or with the pen, must have their happiness and welfare in view, or half the object of her life is lost. She was given for a help-meet for man, and where, or how can she better help him than by looking well to the ways of her household, informing and improving her own mind, and making home, what every man's home should be, the most attractive place on earth for him?[21]

In the Household Department, Adams's format was usually a poem, often by herself, an editorial about an issue of current interest, a letter or two from readers, recipes, and a puzzle or two for children. In these columns, Adams, in common with other women editors of her time, worked to achieve a response from her readers, to establish a friendly tone that would make her readers feel they were acquainted with the editor and also make them wish to become better acquainted.

In the December 1856 issue, she made this editorial position clear:

> Ourselves—permit us to drop the pompous plural for a time, and pretend to no more than we are—a single unit—I. It is well enough on ordinary occasions

for a woman to adopt the custom of editors generally, and keep the potent "we" between herself and readers but now I wish to come a little nearer, to sit down beside you, my *Farmer* household friends, and feel free to talk with you concerning our mutual interests. It is common, and very natural to us all, to feel more interest with those in the course of life with ourselves, and more interest and confidence in those who have had experience in the things of which they write, than in those who write from theory only, or from a distant view of the life they profess to describe.[22]

Adams did not discuss politics in her columns, as the agriculture papers of the day were generally silent on this subject, but she did comment on social issues of the day, especially those pertaining to education and work for women. One of the questions she received and answered was about her views on women in the workplace. As one of those women working to support herself, she had a clear answer:

Our ideas in the matter are simply these: that not sex, but ability and inclination, governed by a prudent regard for the proprieties of life, should alone limit the question of fitness for any position connected with business to which women may be called. If circumstances seem to make it necessary that a woman employ other implements than those in her kitchen or parlor, she ought at least to have the privilege of making a trial, and if she proves capable, and does the work as well as a man could, why is it not as well as if a man had done it? As to engaging in any of the public professions, such as the law, the ministry, or the practice of medicine, we consider that a personal matter to be decided by the wishes and abilities of the individuals themselves, though for our own part we should never care to see a woman in the pulpit or at the bar; as physicians we should be glad to have them multiplied.[23]

This attitude toward women's position in society was not uncommon at the time. "The early women's rights movement showed little interest in getting the vote. . . . Of more immediate concern were control of property, earnings (not the same thing by any means), guardianship, divorce, opportunity for education and employment, lack of legal status (women still could not sue or bear witness), and the whole concept of female inferiority perpetuated by established religion."[24]

Adams's work at the *Michigan Farmer* involved her in its day-to-day operations in her role as business manager. She was in charge of keeping the accounts and knew that income often fell behind expenditures. One of her duties was to collect the price of subscriptions. The common system in those days was to bill after receipt of the paper with special prices offered for subscribers who acted as agent for the paper by having several papers go to their address, which they in turn distributed and collected for. This system led to many problems, and even though the *Michigan Farmer* had as many as 12,000 subscribers, they were not all paid up to date. In the fall of 1858, Adams traveled throughout the state to collect for overdue subscriptions. She noted her travels through the countryside and her various adventures in meeting subscribers in several of her columns that fall. That she had doubts about her role as collection agent she made clear early in the series of articles:

> Our traveling Agent was ill in a distant part of the State, our Editor . . . must stay in town . . . and there was nothing left but for the Household to come forward and take an active part in out-of-door business—in other words we must make out bills for our delinquent subscribers, and go and present them in person (we had tried it by mail till satisfied that our postage was thrown away). Not being of the strong-minded class, we ventured out with fear and trembling, yet not without strong faith in our ultimate success, based on the confidence we had in the honor of those to whom we had to appeal. . . . Brief as these calls necessarily were, they have left in our mind many pleasing recollections and delightful pictures of rural life, and introduced us to many persons and families whose warm-hearted friendship was received as gratefully as it was cordially given.[25]

In 1859, the monthly *Michigan Farmer* became a weekly journal. Adams took on even more responsibility for the publication when her co-owner and co-editor, Robert Johnstone, accepted a position as General Superintendent of the Agricultural Farm at the newly organized College of Agriculture in Lansing. He remained editor, but Adams had charge of the day-to-day operation of the paper. In explaining the changes Johnstone wrote: "The duties which have been assumed, of course, will oblige us to be at Lansing, but during our absence, the business department of the office will be attended to by Mrs. L. B. Adams, who as Proprietor and Associate, has had charge of it for the past three years."[26]

The *Michigan Farmer* met with hard times with the coming of the Civil War. In 1861, Adams and Johnstone sold the newspaper because it cost more to put out than they were taking in. Both Adams and Johnstone continued to write for the *Michigan Farmer* as the paper changed hands several times during the Civil War years. When the owner moved the publication to Chicago, merged it with another agricultural journal, and changed its name, their involvement ended. After the war, Johnstone brought the *Michigan Farmer* back to Detroit and published it with another partner. Adams did not again participate in its ownership or management.

While working for the *Michigan Farmer* Adams continued to write and publish poetry and prose for other periodicals. In 1860, her poetry was recognized by William Coggeshall in *Poets and Poetry of the West.*[27] She was one of five Michigan poets selected for inclusion in the book which included 97 men and 55 women. Four pages of her poetry and a brief biographical sketch are included in the book.

In 1862, Adams's published *Sybelle and Other Poems* (New York: Carleton) as "L." The book was listed in the Recent Publications section of the *Atlantic Monthly* of May 1862, and cost 50 cents. The title poem, "Sybelle," is about 80 pages long. The book also included as assortment of shorter poems, many of which had been printed in the *Michigan Farmer.*

Sybelle is a young, western, country girl in tune with nature and the world around her, whose view of life is changed by an encounter with a young gentleman from the city who comes to the area where she lives to regain his health. They fall in love, but he has to return to the city and his betrothed. For the rest of his life he remembers her and works to live up to her expectations of him. She remembers their time together and wishes him well in his worldly ventures. The poem contains many passages on the natural beauty of the countryside where the lovers meet and part.

The Detroit newspapers printed glowing reviews of the work. "We have read 'Sybelle,' and pronounce it one of the most impassioned works of art that has been given to the reading world from a woman's pen; for 'L.' is a woman gifted evidently with more than ordinary genius."[28] "Sybelle is an honest, self-reliant, American poem, borrowing nothing from the classics, drawing its inspiration from nature, and not from what others have written, and is a decided addition to our national literature."[29] The book was offered as a subscription premium for the *Michigan Farmer* in 1863 and the name of the author was made clear in the advertisement. One could receive 200 strawberry plants, two grapevines, "or a copy of Mrs. L. B. Adams beautiful book, entitled 'SYBELLE, and other poems' for five subscriptions."[30]

In 1863, Adams received an appointment as clerk in the newly organized U.S. Department of Agriculture, and moved from Detroit to Washington, D.C. Appointments to the federal civil service in the 1860s were based on recommendations from the state's representatives and senators. There were no entry tests or qualifications. Adams was recommended by both Michigan senators, Zachariah Chandler and Jacob Howard, and by Representative Rowland Trowbridge, who was a member of the House Committee on Agriculture.

The Detroit Adams left was the largest city in Michigan with a population of 45,169—more than double the 1850 population of 21,019. According to Appleton's Travel Guide:

> Detroit is one of the great commercial depots of the West. . . . It is pleasantly situated upon the Detroit River, a link in the chain of waters which unite Lake Huron and Lake Erie. Detroit occupies a position admirable for business activity, being directly in the way of the flood of travel and transportation from the Atlantic to the Mississippi, and great railways and steamers , with their freights, necessarily pay it tribute. Not only is the city thus commercially alive, but it is distinguished also for its manufactories of many kinds.[31]

Modern conveniences were also appearing in Detroit by the 1860s. Gas or kerosene lights replaced candlelight in homes and businesses. Water was piped into homes, replacing open wells and hand pumps. Stoves replaced fireplaces for heating and cooking. Ice was available for refrigeration. There were several newspapers and journals published there. Detroit was not yet considered among the first rank of cities in the United States, but it was growing fast.[32]

Introduction

When Adams went to Washington, D.C., she went to a city in the midst of great change.

> The war brought unparalleled growth, bustle and problems. The city's population quadrupled from 41,000 in 1860 to 160,000 at its wartime peak. With the advent of northerners, the city's distinctive antebellum Southern atmosphere changed to that of a thriving city, riding the crest of a wartime wave. Besides the regiments of soldiers who daily marched through the streets, throngs of lobbyists, speculators, inventors, and job seekers poured in, each looking for a share of the money to be made in the wartime economy.[33]

The federal civil service had employed few women workers before the Civil War.[34] In 1854, the Patent Office hired three women copyists, one of whom was Clara Barton, and allowed them to work in the office rather than take the work home. In 1855, Secretary of the Interior George B. McClelland stopped the office work for the women. He wrote: "I have no objection to the employment of the females by the Patent Office, or any other of the Bureaus of the Department, in the performance of such duties as they are competent to discharge, and which may be executed by them at their private residences, but there is such an obvious impropriety in the mixing of the sexes within the walls of a public office, that I determined to arrest the practice."[35]

In 1861, Frances Spinner, of the U.S. Treasury Department, was authorized to hire one woman to clip currency. When that clerk did more work in one day than any of the male clerks, other female clerks were hired. In 1862, Congress authorized the hiring of women in the federal civil service at a salary of $600 a year, exactly half the starting salary of a male clerk.

Even $600 a year, with paid vacation and sick leave, was more than most jobs for women paid in the 1860s. Many women applied for these jobs and for most it was their first venture into the workplace. For many of their male co-workers it was their first experience with females in the workplace. There were adjustments on both sides, but the experiment succeeded in getting the work done. This mixing of the sexes within the walls of public offices in Washington helped open the doors of office employment for women in other places.

In a study of these pioneering civil service workers, Aron noted several characteristics they had in common:

> These pioneering female clerks came from native-born, white, middle-class families; they were the daughters, widows and wives of doctors, lawyers, ministers, and other government clerks. . . . Forty three percent of female clerks who assumed their positions between 1862 and 1890 lived someplace other than Washington prior to taking their government jobs. . . . Federal women clerks had been well educated, most having enjoyed the advantage of a secondary education.[36]

The 1862/63 Official Register of Officers and Agents listed 176 women clerks employed by the federal government, making Adams one of the pioneers in this field. In many ways she was better prepared than the average new woman civil servant, having already gained experience working in the offices of the *Michigan Farmer*.

Adams wrote about the work of the government clerks in her columns. Her views on the inequalities in salary, the political games necessary to the service, the routine nature of some of the work, and the threatened strike by the clerks offer a contemporary insight into the way the government worked during the war years.

Adams worked in the United States Department of Agriculture, which was formed in 1862 by President Abraham Lincoln, the new department taking over responsibilities which had been in the Patent Office.[37] The mission of the new department as stated in the enabling act was "to acquire and to diffuse among the people of the United States useful knowledge on subjects connected with agriculture . . . and to procure, propagate, and distribute among the people new and valuable seeds and plants."[38] The first commissioner of the department was Isaac Newton, a friend of Lincoln and former Pennsylvania dairy farmer who had been in charge of the agriculture section of the Patent Office before the new department was formed. He started the department with a small staff in a cramped office space in the basement of the Patent Office building. Adams was one of the first employees on his staff. In 1864, the budget for the department, as published in the *Detroit Advertiser and Tribune,* contained a list of employee positions which included the commissioner, chief clerk, one clerk of the fourth class, four clerks of the third class, four clerks of the second class, six clerks of the first class, an entomologist, a chemist, an assistant chemist, a draughtsman, a translator, two messengers, and two laborers.[39] This small staff had to do all the work mandated in the establishment of the department. Since the records of the Department of Agriculture are negligible for the Civil War years, Adams's account of the work of the department's first years of work are significant.[40]

Mary Clemmer Ames toured the government departments and in her book *Ten Years in Washington* described the work of many of the women civil-service employees. She found that the Agriculture Department

> affords temporary employment for numbers of women, two or three months a year, and two have permanent positions there. The temporary work is the putting up of seeds for universal distribution, and occasionally copying is given out. Of the two ladies who find constant employment there, one is the assistant of Professor [Townsend] Glover, in taking charge of the Museum. She is the widow of a western editor, and at one time had exclusive control of a public journal (an agricultural one) herself. She is a woman of large intelligence, a proficient in botany and natural history, which fact gave her, her present position, and enabled her to fill it with credit to herself. The other lady employee is a taxidermist, who prepares the birds and insects for the Museum.[41]

Further evidence of Adams's involvement with the department is found in the *Report of the Commissioner of Agriculture for the Year 1863*, where may be found "Farmers' Boys" by Adams, a piece she rewrote from one of her *Michigan Farmer* articles. It includes this advice: "Boys on the farm, as well as in college, have a future before them, and should be educated in reference to the place in that future which their natural abilities entitle them to fill. Parents who do not act on this principle, but simply drive their boys like horses or oxen to the plough, will find their farm improvements paid for at a dear rate, and need not wonder at finding themselves deserted and left to a lonely old age."[42]

In addition to her paid position in the Agriculture Department Adams found time to be a volunteer for the Michigan Soldiers Relief Association.[43] The association was composed of people from Michigan residing in Washington and included members of Congress as well as government clerks. Anyone from Michigan was welcome as a member of the association, whose aim was to provide relief and comfort to Michigan soldiers and sailors in the Washington, D.C. area. Someone from the association visited every hospital in Washington, Georgetown, and Alexandria at least twice a week, and whenever a major battle occurred agents were sent to the scene with supplies and food. The agents of the Michigan Soldiers Relief Association were, for the most part, unpaid volunteers. Agents took treats, wrote letters, and acted as friendly visitors, an important role as family lived far away and it was difficult for relatives to come to Washington.

> While the lady visitor operated entirely outside hospital regulations and with no specific nursing functions, she nevertheless appropriated to herself all the responsibilities of a relative. She read and wrote letters, sat with the dying, brought in food sometimes in defiance of doctors' orders, listened sympathetically to all complaints, and in every conflict of authority or personality invariably took the side of the soldier patient.[44]

After the war the wounded soldiers remembered the lady visitors in the hospitals. One tribute from a Michigan soldier reads:

> Once after a long march in the scorching August days I found myself in a hospital in Washington. . . . The brightest memory I took away with me was that of the face and voice of a beautiful lady who came several times while I was there. Her presence was like a gleam of sunlight in a darkened room. Courage and cheerfulness, strength and healing, seemed to follow in her train. She brought me some little delicacies to eat and drink, but better than that, she would sit down by the side of my cot and talk about home and mother, and the great cause in which we were engaged. That lady put new life into my veins, and I believe now that but for her I never would have left that hospital alive.[45]

The Letter Book of the Michigan Soldiers' Relief Association mentions Adams's work on several occasions. For example, on May 19, 1864 it was noted: "Mrs. Plumb of Ypsilanti and Mrs. Adams of Detroit are working with our Association among the Michigan wounded in hospitals of this city, Alexandria and Georgetown." On June 30, 1864, the letter book noted: "At the present time the following ladies and gentlemen are laboring under the auspices of the Association and devoting their whole time to the care of the wounded: In the hospitals of Washington and vicinity: Mrs. Brainard of Lapeer, Mrs. Plumb of Ypsilanti, Mrs. Adams, and Miss Moore of Detroit."[46]

Adams was one of many men and women who volunteered their time in the hospitals or with the relief organizations. Walt Whitman, the poet, spent time as a volunteer in Washington hospitals and wrote several pieces about his experiences there. Louisa May Alcott served as a nurse for a time in a Washington hospital and wrote *Hospital Sketches* about her experience. Clara Barton, who later founded the American Red Cross, worked with the wounded soldiers in the field and brought medical supplies to doctors near the battlefields. Many other women and men devoted time and effort to the work of helping the soldiers. The United States Sanitary Commission and the United States Christian Commission were massive organizations with volunteers in all the states working to provide needed supplies to soldiers. In addition, every state had its own relief organization in Washington that endeavored to help soldiers and their visitors from their own area.

Adams's account of her work as a hospital visitor has an immediacy not found in the accounts written after the war was over. She listed the wounded she knew of in her columns in an effort to let family members and friends know as soon as possible about their loved ones. She also used her column to promote the work of the relief organizations.

Adams remained in Washington at the Department of Agriculture after the war. When Congress authorized a pay raise for women workers she was promoted and given the higher rate of pay. She witnessed the growth of the department in the postwar years including a move into a new building in 1868. She had health problems, perhaps because of her work in the hospitals. In May 1870, Adams came back to Michigan for a vacation. After her return to Washington in June she became ill of inflammation of the lungs, and died June 28, 1870, at age fifty-two. Her body was returned to Michigan to be buried near her father in Constantine.

Adams's columns reflect her experience in Michigan as well as her life in Washington. In particular, the voice she chose in the Household Department as friend and sister is carried over into these columns. This voice was not unusual for the over six hundred women periodical editors of the nineteenth century, according to Patricia Okker.

> In periodicals edited by and for women, the editors often used the rhetoric of intimate female relations, creating what I call the sisterly editorial voice. This voice is characterized by a relative informality and an assumed equal and personal relationship between editor and reader. Just as some editors referred

to other women editors as "sisters," so too did they invoke the informality of expression such as "old friends" and "sisters" when referring to readers. Consider, for example, the opening of an editorial titled "Ourselves," written by Lois Bryan Adams for the *Michigan Farmer* in 1856. Though the periodical itself targeted both men and women, the Household Department in which this editorial appeared was assumed to be for and by women. . . . While male editors sometimes also chose to drop the editorial *we,* Adams's association with her choice of *I* with her identity as a woman fits well with the sisterly editorial voice generally. Here she assumes a friendly, even intimate relationship with her readers who share 'mutual interests' . . . the sisterly editorial voice, while informal, was not without authority. In contrast to the strategies of denial and self-effacement sometimes noted in the works of nineteenth century American women writers, confidence in their public authority as editors generally characterized the women who used the sisterly editorial voice.[47]

The columns Adams wrote from Washington, D.C., continued the use of the "sisterly" voice she found useful in her *Michigan Farmer* column. This voice allowed her to continue to write for her friends in an easy conversation about her new life in Washington. She noted in her December 1, 1863, column:

Aside from news, or matters connected with the war, Washington has objects of interest to the public at large—objects which thousands will never see, and of which they can know nothing except through the medium of correspondents for the local press. The war, it is true, has brought thousands here who would otherwise never have known Washington . . . but the "loved ones at home" would also like to have some definite idea of what the wanderers have seen, and in what pleasant paths their feet have trod.

Most of the reporters of the war, whether in Washington or in the field with the troops, were men. The larger East Coast newspapers kept a large staff of reporters busy reporting the political and war news. Use of the telegram to report the news increased greatly as editors challenged their reporters to get them the latest news, preferably before a rival newspaper could print it. Many of these reporters were headquartered in Washington, D.C.

From the beginning of the war until its very end the national capital was the focal point of press interest, not simply because it was the seat of the national government but also because Washington got the first reports from the eastern war theater and transmitted them by telegraph to all parts of the country. . . . In recognition of the importance of the national capital as a center of war news, the press sent its ablest men there.[48]

These men were reporting political and war news, not providing commentary. Adams, by contrast, commented on news her readers had already heard. These reporters were working with the telegraph system and their news would reach their papers the same day, unlike Adams's column which was mailed to the newspaper and appeared when the editor chose to use it.

Other women besides Adams were newspaper correspondents in Washington during the war years. Jane Grey Swisshelm was often identified with her Washington reporting.[49] Swisshelm, a newspaper publisher and reporter from Minnesota, prided herself on her strong stands on issues and on righting the wrongs she saw around her. Swisshelm did not have a regular column but contributed her pieces to the *New York Herald* and to the *St. Cloud Democrat,* in Minnesota. Swisshelm, like Adams, had a civil service position, volunteered in the hospitals, and promoted Republican ideas. In addition, she was a friend of Mrs. Lincoln and moved in Washington society circles. An example of her style is a column written in November 1865 titled "Women Workers":

> There is a radical error in the manner of appointing women [to the civil service]. It is not every man who is fit for any pioneer movement, and to expect that all women or even a majority, are fitted for this advance post on the picket line of civilization, is expecting superhuman perfection of the feminine half of humanity. Yet such is the system, or want of system, on which this grand experiment has been inconsiderately tried. To get an appointment no qualifications are required, except influential friends. . . . Some Honorable Senator or Representative has a female friend without visible means of support. He gets her a place, and she makes her appearance, perhaps a little piece of painted impertinence, who might have been stowed away in the catacombs in the days of the Pharaohs for all one can tell of her age, but who studiously assumes the airs of a miss of sixteen. Her wrinkles are filled out with pipe clay or some other kind of light-colored mud; her eyebrows are made of black lead or lampblack, or something in that line her hair is dyed until it is dead enough to satisfy any respectable undertaker of the propriety of burial; and one wonders that she does not add a setting of green leaves to the magenta-colored roses on her thin cheeks. She comes tripping in on the toes of her infinitesimal gaiters, gets off her things, and displays a head which reminds one of a drop chandelier trimmed for a ball and undergoing the process of dusting, while her pins, chains, bracelets, frills, and other fixtures would set up a tin box peddler in trade.[50]

This column was widely reprinted, even appearing in the *Detroit Advertiser and Tribune.* Adams disagreed and responded to this column in one of her own about women and the civil service: "Mrs. S. uses no discrimination, so far as her own sex is concerned, but rates them all alike, and all of very little account because they differ from herself. . . . She has some ideas of practical good sense, which if enforced by attractive personal example, and without the accompanying termagant spirit seemingly inherent in her nature and inseparable from her name, might be of appreciable weight and influence."[51]

Another writer with a different style was Emily Briggs, who wrote as "Olivia" for the *Philadelphia Press,* beginning in 1861. She wrote four to six letters a week on Washington government and society. Briggs's husband was in the federal civil service and his political and social connections helped her find material for her columns. "Emily Briggs never hesitated to write about politics or express strong opinions on issues, but her real talents lay in her colorful descriptions, her keen eye for social and fashion trends, and her witty style of writing."[52] Briggs was not writing for hometown friends, and her tone is considerably different from that of either Adams or Swisshelm.

For all their differences in style and substance these women Washington correspondents had several things in common. Maurine Beasley, in a study of the women who were Washington newspaper correspondents found that

> a composite picture of these outstanding women journalists shows that most came from the West, where women enjoyed greater freedom than in the East. . . . All were divorcees, widows, or single women who had to earn their own livings. . . . Unlike many women of their day, as a group these early women journalists were not burdened by a large number of children. . . . In short, the nineteenth century woman Washington correspondent emerges as an independent individual of above average intelligence with a flair for words who turned to newspaper work from financial necessity.[53]

Outside of Washington there were other women correspondents and columnists.[54] Perhaps the best known of the time was Fanny Fern, the pen name of Sarah Willis Parton, who had a popular weekly column in the *New York Ledger*. Using humor, she spoke to the issues of the day, especially as they applied to women. Her columns were reprinted into best-selling books, and she earned a very respectable living from her literary work.

Sarah Josepha Hale was editor of *Godey's Lady's Book*, a periodical with a very large circulation in both the North and the South, and was one of the best-known women of her day. She wrote editorials, books, and poetry and used the sisterly or friendly voice in her columns. Hale, however, wrote for the whole country and her sisterly voice was not aimed at any one region as was that of Adams.

Adams's columns were clearly aimed at her Michigan readers. Her columns have not been noticed before this book, perhaps because she wrote for a relatively obscure newspaper. For whatever reason they were overlooked, they deserve attention because of their content and what they tell us about life for a middle-class, northern, professional woman in the middle of the nineteenth century. They also deserve attention because they contain well-written reports of interesting people and events.

Adams's report of the Washington meeting of the Ladies' National Covenant illustrates what makes her writing interesting. She was at the meeting as a reporter and a participant. She noted the different roles women took at the meeting and thought the time was long past when women had a man speak for them in a public gathering. She did not fault the man, but the notion. She admired the courage and ability of the women who did speak in public. She gave credit to all serious, sensible suggestions on any side of the issue. The reporting is first rate, the issues are clear, and the result is clearly stated. The facts are not slighted or slanted to reflect only the reporter's opinion, but the reporter's opinion is clear.

There are many other memorable moments in these columns and much first-rate reporting. Adams's colorful descriptions, her participation in interesting events, and her sisterly reporting style all contribute to this important account of the Civil War years in Washington, D.C.

These columns were transcribed from a microfilm copy of the *Detroit Advertiser and Tribune*. Occasionally the microfilm was not legible and a word or a line is missing. The missing place has brackets to indicate the material was not legible.

The date and page number at the beginning of each column indicates publishing information. The second date is the date Adams put in the piece and indicates when it was actually written. Some of these dates are missing from the original columns.

The varying titles of the column are as found in the newspaper. In some cases another column in that day's paper was called "Letter from Washington." In other cases it is not obvious why the title of the column changed.

A few paragraphs have been omitted as they added no new information. Spelling of names has been amended if it is clear an error in spelling was made. Otherwise, the transcriptions are as close as possible to the original columns. Any errors in transcription are the responsibility of the editor.

Adams referred to a variety of people, places, and events that were headline news in her day but may not be known by today's reader. She also made many literary, biblical, and mythological allusions in these columns. There is a glossary at the end of the book that provides basic information regarding those references that may not be familiar. It is possible to find whole books, and in many cases whole libraries, about almost every person and event of the Civil War years and I have not provided citations to all those sources of information. The glossary does not provide details of careers or battles, but I have attempted to provide enough information to make Adams's meaning clear. A bibliography following the glossary provides information about the sources used in compiling the glossary.

Notes

1. *Detroit Advertiser and Tribune,* March 11, 1864, 4.
2. *Detroit Advertiser and Tribune,* November 9, 1864, 2.
3. "Adams, Mrs. L. B.," in *Irish Celts: A Cyclopedia of Race History, Containing Biographical Sketches of More Than Fifteen Hundred Distinguished Celts, With a Chronological Index.* (Detroit: L. F. Kilroy, 1884).

4. "Adams, Mrs. L. B.," in *The Red Book of Michigan: A Civil, Military and Biographical History*, ed. Charles Lanman (Detroit: E. B. Smith and Co., 1871). The other women listed were Julia Wheelock, Electra Sheldon, and Caroline Kirkland.

5. The primary biographical sources used for the life and career of Adams are: "Death of Mrs. L. B. Adams," *Detroit Advertiser and Tribune*, July 2, 1870; "The Late Mrs. L. B. Adams," *Michigan Farmer*, July 9, 1870; and "Memoir of Lois B. Adams—Poet, Editor, and Author" *Michigan Pioneer and Historical Collections* 18 (1891): 312–18. Unless otherwise noted the biographical information cited here is from one of these sources.

6. "Sarah Bryan," in *The Pioneer Women of the West*, ed. Elizabeth F. Ellet (Philadelphia: Porter and Cortes, 1852), 361–67.

7. Ibid., 363.

8. *Michigan Farmer*, January 1857, 22.

9. *Michigan Farmer*, December 1, 1856, 370.

10. "White Pigeon Academy," *History of St. Joseph County, Michigan* (Philadelphia: L. H. Everts, 1877), 440.

11. *Michigan Farmer*, April 21, 1859, 134.

12. Ibid.

13. In the *Family Favorite and Temperance Journal* of April, July, and December 1850 articles signed Mrs. L. B. A. appeared with addresses given variously as Fayette County, Kentucky, and Bryan's Station, Kentucky.

14. "Illinois Letter," by L. B. A. appeared in the *New York Tribune*, July 13, July 25, August 17, and September 13, 1853.

15. For a publication history of the *Michigan Farmer* see Joseph George Duncan, *The Michigan Farmer: A Century of Agricultural Journalism 1843–1943* (Master's thesis, Michigan State University, 1950); and "A Sketch of the History of the 'Michigan Farmer,'" *Michigan Pioneer and Historical Collections* 7 (1884): 99–102.

16. Robert Johnstone (1816–80) was part of Adams's life from this time forward. He was born in Ireland and came to America in 1833. He apprenticed at Cambridge University Press in Massachusetts, arriving in Michigan in 1852 as commercial editor of the *Detroit Advertiser*. In addition to his connection with the *Detroit Advertiser*, he became a partner in several other publishing projects, including the *Michigan Farmer*. In 1855, he was elected secretary of the Michigan Agricultural Society, a position he held for many years. During the Civil War, after selling the *Michigan Farmer*, he worked on several newspapers in Michigan including the *Kalamazoo Gazette* and the *Detroit Free Press*. In 1869 he formed a new business partnership and revived the *Michigan Farmer*. He was editor of the *Michigan Farmer* at the time of his death on October 25, 1880, at age sixty-four. On Johnstone see "Robert F. Johnstone," *Detroit Post and Tribune*, October 26, 1880; "Robert F. Johnstone," *Michigan Pioneer and Historical Collections* 4 (1881): 436–38. Adams is listed in the 1857 Detroit City Directory as boarding at the Robert F. Johnstone home.

17. *Michigan Farmer*, July 9, 1870, 490.

18. *Detroit Advertiser and Tribune*, July 2, 1870, 2.

19. Probably the best-known woman editor of the nineteenth century was Sarah J. Hale, but there were others. Two recent books on the subject are Sherilyn Cox Bennion, *Equal to the Occasion: Women Editors of the Nineteenth Century West* (Reno: University of Nevada Press, 1990); and Patricia Okker, *Our Sister Editors: Sarah J. Hale and the Tradition of Nineteenth Century American Women Editors* (Athens: University of Georgia Press, 1995). Okker includes a list of over six hundred women editors in the nineteenth century.

20. Albert Lowther Demaree, *The American Agricultural Press 1819–1860* (1941; reprint, Philadelphia: Porcupine Press, 1974), 161.

21. *Michigan Farmer*, February 1856, 55.

22. *Michigan Farmer*, December 1856, 369–70.

23. *Michigan Farmer,* May 7, 1859, 150.

24. Eleanor Flexner, *Century of Struggle: The Woman's Rights Movement in the United States* (Cambridge, Mass.: Belknap Press of Harvard University Press, 1959), 83.

25. *Michigan Farmer,* October 1858, 309–10.

26. *Michigan Farmer,* April 16, 1859, 125.

27. William T. Coggeshall, *The Poets and Poetry of the West: With Biographical and Critical Notices* (Columbus, Ohio: Follett, Foster and Co., 1860), 328–31.

28. "New Books: Sybelle and Other Poems, by L.," *Detroit Daily Advertiser,* March 15, 1862, 4.

29. "Literacy: 'Sybelle'—A New Poem by a Michigan Authoress," *Detroit Daily Tribune,* March 29, 1862, 4.

30. Several ads for *Sybelle* appeared in the *Michigan Farmer* in 1863.

31. *Appleton's Companion Hand-Book of Travel to the United States and British Provinces* (New York: D. Appleton, 1861), 236.

32. Information about the history of Detroit and Michigan may be found in several sources, one of which is Willis Dunbar, *Michigan: A History of the Wolverine State* (Grand Rapids: W. B. Eerdmans, 1995).

33. Patricia Faust, ed., *Historical Times Illustrated Encyclopedia of the Civil War* (New York: Harper and Row, 1986), 806.

34. Information about women and men in the federal civil service may be found in Cindy Aron, " 'To Barter Their Souls for Gold': Female Clerks in Federal Government Offices, 1862–1890," *Journal of American History* 67 (March 1981): 835–53; idem, *Ladies and Gentlemen of the Civil Service: Middle-Class Workers in Victorian America* (New York: Oxford University Press, 1987).

35. Quoted in Mabel Deutrich and Virginia C. Purdy, eds., *Clio Was a Woman: Studies in the History of American Women* (Washington, D.C.: Howard University Press, 1980), 2.

36. Aron, " 'To Barter Their Souls for Gold,' " 837–38.

37. The history of the United States Department of Agriculture may be found in Wayne David Rasmussen and Gladys L. Baker, *The Department of Agriculture* (New York: Praeger, 1972). Women's roles in the department may be found in Gladys Baker, "Women in the U.S. Department of Agriculture," *Agricultural History* 50 (January 1976): 190–201.

38. Act Establishing the Department of Agriculture, May 15, 1862, paragraph 1.

39. "Department of Agriculture," *Detroit Advertiser and Tribune,* July 29, 1864, 5.

40. Kenneth Munden, *The Union: Guide to the Federal Archives, Relating to the Civil War* (Washington, D.C.: Published for the National Archives and Records Administration by the National Archives Trust Fund, 1986), 581.

41. Mary Clemmer Ames, *Ten Years in Washington: Life and Scenes in the National Capital, as a Woman Sees Them* (Hartford, Conn.: A. D. Worthington, 1874), 367.

42. Mrs. L. B. Adams, "Farmers Boys," *Report of the Commissioner of Agriculture for the Year 1863* (Washington, D.C.: Government Printing Office, 1863), 308.

43. Information about the Michigan Soldiers Relief Association may be found in several sources including L. P. Brockett and Mary C. Vaughn, *Woman's Work in the Civil War: A Record of Heroism, Patriotism and Patience. 2 volumes* (1867; reprint, Heritage Books Reprint, 1993), 2:197–203; Lanman, ed., *The Red Book of Michigan,* 197–203; Jno Robertson, *Michigan in the War* (Lansing: W. S. George and Co., 1880), 105–13; Julia Wheelock, *Our Boys in White: The Experience of a Hospital Agent In and Around Washington* (New York: Lange and Hillman, 1870); Robert Spiro, *History of the Michigan Soldiers Aid Society, 1861–1865* (Ph.D. diss., University of Michigan, 1959); and Francis Davis McTeer, "In Bonnet and Shawl: Adventures of a Michigan Relief Agent during the Civil War," in *Michigan Women in the Civil War* (Lansing: Michigan Civil War Centennial Observance Commission, 1963), 64–84.

44. McTeer, "In Bonnet and Shawl," 73.

45. Charles T. Saxton, *Woman's Relations to the War: An Address Delivered by Charles T. Saxton Before the Wayne County Veteran Soldiers' and Sailors' Association at 'Camp Hancock,' Solus Point, N.Y., August 19, 1886*, 12.

46. *Letter Book of the Michigan Soldiers Relief Association* is in the Burton Historical Collection, Detroit Public Library, Detroit, Michigan. Laura Plumb wrote of her connection with Adams in a letter to her aunt dated May 31, 1864: "I have not told you she [Adams] came to see me very soon after I came and we have been together most of the time . . . I find her a *very* pleasant lady." Laura Plumb Collection, Michigan Historical Collections, Bentley Historical Library, Ann Arbor, Michigan.

47. Okker, *Our Sister Editors*, 23, 25.

48. J. Cutler Andrews, *The North Reports the Civil War* (Pittsburgh: University of Pittsburgh Press, 1955), 48.

49. Information about Jane G. Swisshelm may be found in *Crusader and Feminist: Letters of Jane Grey Swisshelm 1858–1865*, ed. Arthur J. Larsen (St. Paul: Minnesota Historical Society, 1934); Jane G. Swisshelm, *Half a Century* (Chicago: Jansen, McClurg, and Co., 1880).

50. Larsen, *Crusader and Feminist*, 308–9.

51. *Detroit Advertiser and Tribune*, November 17, 1865.

52. Donald A. Ritchie, *Press Gallery: Congress and the Washington Correspondents* (Cambridge, Mass.: Harvard University Press, 1991), 154.

53. Maurine Hoffman Beasley, *The First Women Washington Correspondents* (Washington, D.C.: George Washington University Studies: no. 4, 1976), 23.

54. The work of various women reporters and columnists of the Civil War period may be found in several sources: F. B. Marbut, *News from the Capital: The Story of Washington Reporting* (Carbondale: Southern Illinois University Press, 1971); Donald A. Ritchie, *Press Gallery: Congress and the Washington Correspondents* (Cambridge, Mass.: Harvard University Press, 1991), 145–61; Marion Marzolf, *Up from the Footnote: A History of Women Journalists* (New York: Hastings House, 1977); Barbara Belford, *Brilliant Bylines: A Biographical Anthology of Notable Newspaperwomen in America* (New York: Columbia University Press, 1986); Andrews, *The North Reports the Civil War;* Beasley, *The First Women Washington Correspondents*.

1

1863

October 15, 1863, page 4

Life in Washington

FIRST IMPRESSIONS | THE CITY | ITS CROWDS | LIVING PRICES | CHANGES

Correspondence of the *Advertiser and Tribune*
Washington, October 9, 1863

The city is like a beehive on swarming day, all bustle, activity and apparent confusion. The streets and sidewalks are filled from wall to wall with the mixed and hurrying throng, coming and going as if life itself depended on their speed. Mixed indeed it may well be called, for surely the streets of no other city ever presented such a conglomeration of humanity as may be found in Washington just now. The shades of color are indescribable, but black and tan seem largely predominant among the side-walkers, and on the carriage-boxes. Soldiers, with every stripe and pattern of uniform known in Uncle Sam's military wardrobe, crowd the streets, singly and in squads, on foot and on horseback, lounging on the walks, swarming at the doors of restaurants and liquor shops, marching hither and thither as in quest of something to do; or galloping away, Gilpin fashion, with their heads in advance of their horses and legs and clanging sword-cases "flying all abroad." The tread of army horses and the roll of army wagons through the main thoroughfares is incessant. Long trains of them are constantly coming in, side by side with the counter-currents rolling outward, bearing supplies to the forts and encampments on the heights that encompass the city round about. Among these trains uniformed horsemen are dashing in every direction; crowded street-cars, following and passing each other on the double-tracks, glide swiftly between fearless foot passengers at the crossings, get mixed up indiscriminately with all, while timorous ones stand waiting for the ever-flowing river to pass by. The shops and stores are full, the windows and doors are full, people throng through all the highways, swarm through alleys and through by-ways; rich and poor, young and old, foul with rags, and decked with gold, the nabob and his dusky brother, once a slave, now pass each other on the freeman's level and all together conspire to make lively times in Washington. Still, all this is nothing to the crowds, the bustle and activity that will attend the convening of Congress.

There is considerable building going on in the city, as well as repairing and enlarging old houses. By some, the new impulse of activity in this direction is credited to the influx of the more energetic and enterprising Northern element which has been working its way through the sluggishness of the old *regime* since "the District" was annext to "the land of the free." But there is another element at work, as well. The love of money is not altogether confined to Yankee peddlers and their descendants. A lurking affection for base metal and its green-tinted representative has been found to exist in the breasts of human beings claiming other ancestry, and this affection is fast developing under the stimulating effect of free institutions and the consequent acknowledgment of the dignity of labor. Very tardily this acknowledgment comes, and with a very ill grace from some of the degenerate sons and daughters of the "Grand Old Gardener," but come it must, and come it does, in one way or another, from the inhabitants of every spot of earth where Freedom sets her foot. As the trade in human flesh is prohibited, other means are resorted to for making money, and as they answer the purpose, are found to be honorable. Just now the mine most diligently worked and proving most profitable is that of boarding-house keeping and room renting. For these purposes every available nook and corner, from cellar to garret, is put in requisition. Bedrooms large enough to turn round twice and lie down in, are rented for twenty, twenty-five, and even thirty dollars a month, and board is furnished at an extra charge of four, six, or eight dollars per week, according to quality. Many gentlemen, and even gentlemen and their wives, who rent rooms in private houses at the above prices, go out for their meals to hotels or restaurants. The high prices of everything in market, and the great number of people obliged to eat in order to live, give a coloring of justice to these exorbitant rates and householders having the advantage of possession, hold boarders and room-renters at their mercy. Hotel rates are still higher.

"Going to market" here is an expression of some significance; among other things it means paying for a pound of table butter 40 cents; for a dozen of eggs, 25 cents; for a pound of beef steak, 25 cents; for fresh pork $12\frac{1}{2}$ cents; for Irish potatoes, $1.25 per bushel; sweet potatoes, $1.60; fresh shelled beans, 25 cents a quart; tomatoes, 15 cents a quarter of a peck; corn meal, 32 cents a peck; and flour, at the rate of $11.00 a barrel. Melons have been selling at 15 to 20 cents apiece, and chestnuts are offered at the street corners for the slight consideration of 30 cents for a half pint—only $1.20 per quart.

For the past few weeks the weather here has been delightful—sometimes a little chilly, and now and then a rain storm—but ever again glowing with the golden Indian summer sunshine, or wrapped in the dreamy blue autumn haze. There has been no frost of consequence yet; roses and other flowers are yet blooming in the open air, and trees and shrubbery look almost as fresh as in June. It is these bright and charming days, with their fresh, exhilarating air, that have kept the streets so full of life and gaiety; for there is life and joy and prosperity in our land yet, in spite of the bloody war we are waging—it might almost be said in consequence of it, for are not these the rewards of well-doing and the fruits of a faithful adherence to the cause of truth and right?

Brilliant autumn fashions are rapidly taking the place of summer colors on the pavements. Scarlet is struggling hard of predominance; a few daring innovators have ventured to sport the color in cloaks and bonnets, and more have mounted feathers of the fiery tint; but except for children or young misses it is scarcely looked upon with favor.

The colored Odd Fellows are having a grand procession and celebration in this city to day. They make a fine appearance in their showy regalia, with bands of music playing as they march, bearing wreaths and decorated mottoes, with the Stars and Stripes floating over them along the whole line of their advance.

L.

November 2, 1863, page 2

Life in Washington

HOMELINESS OF THE CITY | FILTHY STREETS | PROSPECT OF IMPROVEMENT | SPECIMEN OF PRO-SLAVERY UNIONIST

From Our Own Correspondent
Washington, October 26, 1863

As a city, Washington is yet in its infancy, or, more properly speaking in its misshapen, unformed, straggling childhood. Like a great lubberly lout in clothes much too large for its body and limbs, it lies spreading about in all directions, showing more or less evidence of life in its extremities, but chiefly conscious of vitality along the direct line extending from its head to its heels, or down Pennsylvania Avenue from above the White House to the Capitol and the railroad depot. Its buildings, like its population, present a most incongruous medley; from the sublime to the ridiculous. Beauty and deformity are grouped together—with a great preponderance of the latter. Everything seems either dilapidated or unfinished, and about the whole city there is a behind-the-time aspect so peculiar to all Southern towns—all that are, or have been recently, under the shadow of the great national curse. There has been a want of energy, a lack of enterprise, in perfect keeping with the condition of the masses and the standard of education in the surrounding country. It has been simply a convenience for the assembling of Congress and, aside from that, and being the place where the President undergoes his four or eight years of ostracism, Washington seems to have been of no particular consequence as a city either to the few permanent residents here or to the country at large. So long as it answered the general purpose in a slip shod sort of way, and the inhabitants could manage to live through from one session of Congress to another, no further improvement seemed necessary. In this jog trot manner the Capitol itself has been lagging for years in its tedious progress towards completion, and is still apparently light years from that desired end. The beautiful dome is still disfigured by the rough scaffolding at the top, and the colossal bronze statue of the Goddess of Liberty, which is destined some day to take its place, lies in half a dozen pieces in a little board pen on the ground at the bottom of the building. Emblematic of the times some may say; and perhaps it is. At least it is emblematic and characteristic of the place and the people. In the private dwellings the general style of architecture varies from plainness to uncouthness, real ugliness outside and inconvenience within being the chief features. They are built with basements, and, for the convenience of having the back door in front, clumsy looking stairways are constructed on the outside under which the basement doors open upon the street, and at the top of which ingress is found to the first floor. Looking down a street with all these staircases and kitchen doors in full view, gives one the idea that the houses have been torn inside out and "hind side foremost." They look ungainly and outlandish enough. The streets themselves are in keeping with the houses appearing to have been turned upside down by some convulsion of nature and not yet settled into the staid and proper deportment streets in a civilized city are expected to assume. Very few of them have yet been paved; in some that interesting operation is now going on, with all the delightful accessories of stone and sand piles blockading the sidewalks.

DIRT

Speaking of sidewalks, an idea prevails in most Northern towns that the flagged or paved spaces, so called, lying between the building and the curbstone, are intended for the accommodation of foot passengers; and they are generally appropriated for that use. It is different here. Let a lady set out for a walk down any of the business streets, and she will have to run a gauntlet of dozens of negroes in front of ironmongers' stores, attacking regiments of stoves with brooms and brushes regardless of passers-by among whom the blacking flieth where it listeth; whole groceries are turned out upon the pavement as if to air themselves, mackerel barrels tilted edgewise, with the dripping fish hanging over the rims against which, and other greasy and floury commodities, her blacking spattered silks must rustle if she would pass; boxes bristling with vicious nails catch at her dress and tear it, dirty feet in the crowding throng trample it into the offal of long lines of filthy livery stables she is compelled to pass; she must sweep it over piles of coal and drag it through heaps of straw and the accumulated debris in front of shops and stores and worse than all, trail it through a hundred or more little runnels brimming with kitchen and chamber slops which cross the pavement from every house corner, emptying into the street gutters; all these, with the dust ankle deep in dry weather or subsiding into pronounced mortar bed in wet, conspire to give a lady's dress—to say nothing of herself—somewhat of demoralized appearance by the time she reaches Pennsylvania Avenue. For sidewalk obstructions, and all manner of street uncleanliness, Washington just now may take the prize. Street sweepers and scavengers are institutions yet apparently unknown here. Some allowance must of course be made for "war time," but too many of these defects and blemishes are palpably chronic and have come down from past generations. The war did not lay these shabby pavements nor channel them with their filthy water courses. The commonest bricked or flagged sidewalk in Detroit is neater laid and smoother than the best here, and the dirtiest streets in that city can boast of nothing like these slop bearing runnels channeled across the pavements every few paces. If a Yankee were obliged to have them running from the corners of his house, he would bridge them with whittlings before he would see them lying thus to the disgust of all decency.

A CHANGE WORKING

Aside from its public buildings, none of which seem yet to be finished, but will be beautiful when they are, Washington is shabby-looking and a very dirty city. And, judging by the past, there is little prospect that it will improve in any great degree till the character of the population is entirely changed. Just now it may be considered as in a transition state. The old Rip Van Winkle drowsiness has been terribly broken in upon and disturbed by the invasion and innovations of more energetic and restless elements. There will be chaos for a while—moral, social, and physical chaos—but it needs no prophet to foretell what the result will be when the land is once more at peace. Already many of the old rotten pillars that sustained its tottering social fabric are gone. Scarcely a day passes that does not strip from one or more the false colors they have drawn about them, to protect from confiscation the wealth they have amassed, and there follow the red flag and the auctioneer's hammer, and after them new faces at the windows, and new phases of social life. It is notorious that at the beginning of our national difficulties a great majority of the old settlers were secessionist at heart; some threw off their disguise and joined the enemies of the Government at once; others have worn the mask of friendliness with more or less success; some wear it still, but they feel that it is growing more and more transparent, and that they are standing on very slippery places. One by one they must inevitably go down and when they are gone it only remains to be seen whether better or worse will fill their places. Worse can scarcely be; therefore Washington may "wait in hope."

A SOUTHERN UNIONIST

As a specimen of the sham loyalty that prevails to a considerable extent, especially among the ladies here, take the following: The speaker's husband is in

Government employ; she is a Virginian, and of course one of the first of her race, though, as will be seen, rather awkward in her attempts to propitiate the long despised Goddess whose head it is hoped will soon be visible as she rises to her grand pedestal on Capitol Hill.

"O I'm very much in favor of the Union indeed I am; I don't know what the country would do without it, but then you know, we Virginians have such a prejudice against the Yankees. It is dreadful! Dear me! But we can't help it. We know all they want is to get our land from us, and then they think we will have to work as hard as they do. That is all they are fighting for, just to get our land and here they come right into Virginia and take it from us. They want to bring us down to their own level by getting our niggers away. I don't wonder we hate them, though it is a dreadful thing to have this war, and I think the Union ought to be saved—I'm sure I hope it will be. We'd think a great deal more of it if Union people did not pester themselves about the niggers so much."

Being asked what she thought of the principle of slavery in itself she replied: "O really I don't know—there are so many different opinions—it is thought there is a heap of wrong comes of it in many ways; and I'm sure if it will save the Union I ought to be willing to have it done away with. But I think it was God's work in the first place. We know slavery is a divine institution—we get it from the Bible. Some pretend that the institutions of the Old Testament ought to be done away with, and I believe most of them ought to be; but you know there is a *little* about slavery in the New Testament—at least servants are spoken of. I believe it is God's work bringing them over from the old country in the first place to have them civilized and made so they would know how to be happy. In Virginia we live with them just as we do with our families and think as much of them. If these abolition Yankees get them free now they ought to be made to take every one of them to the North and take care of them. But they won't do it, you'll see. They are only jealous of our ease and comfort, and have got up this war to bring us down to their own level. They want to make us work—that is all they care for. I hate these abolitionists and Yankees—but then I am for the Union, and hope it will be saved. If God's design in bringing the niggers over here has been accomplished, we ought to be willing to let them go though I think it is mean that the one's who are trying to get them from us can't be made to take them home and take care of them, as we have had to do. My husband is true to the Government and so am I, of course, and we both hope it will be able to save the Union."

That is one specimen.

L.

November 24, 1863, page 4

Life in Washington

A VISIT IN GEORGETOWN | MRS. SOUTHWORTH, THE AUTHORESS

Correspondence of the *Advertiser and Tribune*

Georgetown is not exactly Washington, but so near it that the little I have to say about it at present can come under the same head. It stands in about the same relation to the Capital city that Springwells does to Detroit, or East and West Ypsilanti to each other, or Upper and Lower town at Ann Arbor, Middle and Lower town at Lansing, etc. In fact, though separate cities, they have grown together like the Siamese twins, with the street railroad for the binding ligament, and they have a community of interest which makes them almost one. The dividing line is a deep ravine, bridged, at the bottom of which runs a little thread of a stream called Rock Creek. Washington contains the Government buildings, the residences of Government officials, and is the center of business for the District, as the Nation. Georgetown has its College, and its Convent, an old institution where large numbers of young girls are educated, both Protestant and Catholic; and it has streets as shabby and filthy as any Washington can boast, and is full of ancient, dilapidated houses, quaint old structures with moss-grown roofs and crumbling walls. The city seems originally to have been built on a series of ridges, and these have in many instances been graded down to level the streets, some of the houses are left in rather precarious positions perched on the edges of crumbling banks, while others appear to have gone down cellar with little prospect of ever getting up again. But there are some very handsome old residences here and there about the city, though it is not so much the houses that are handsome as the situation, the grounds and the stately trees by which they are surrounded. All is so still and picture like about them, and so ancient, they look as if they might have stepped out of some quaint old romance written a hundred years ago and sat down here to see what the present generation are about. They do not seem to belong to this age and especially to this warring part of the world.

From the embankment of the water works near the north limits of the city a fine view toward the south and east may be had of the two cities, the broad, sweeping Potomac and the fortified heights both on the Virginia and Maryland side. On a clear day the city of Alexandria eight or ten miles below can be distinctly seen. Signal officers are stationed on this embankment where, by the aid of glasses, they have command of the river, and of the forts both to the north and south, to a great distance.

A small but very beautiful "City of the Dead," called Oak Hill Cemetery, is near. This lovely spot detains many wandering feet besides those which "go no more out forever." There is a romantic little chapel with roof and windows of stained glass, and walls completely hidden by heavy masses of old English Ivy; the terraced slopes and hills are as green and fresh now as in June and a great profusion of roses and chrysanthemums of every color are in full bloom among the still and white memorials of the dead. On almost every grave were wreaths, vases of flowers and bouquets, all fresh as if just placed there by loving hands. The old oaks from which the places takes its name are thickly scattered all over the grounds.

But it is not particularly to see Georgetown, to get the views, or to visit its pretty cemetery that I spent the day of November 13th, 1863, a day full of golden sunshine, and soft blue haze, and warm, sweet Southern airs. It was to see one whose name is so public that the man, woman or child who does not know it must be benighted indeed, and yet who is herself so quiet, so unpretending, so little known personally out of the circle of friends, that even for me to speak of her here seems almost like an intrusion upon domestic privacy. But if she knew, as I do, how glad her thousands of readers and admirers would be for a sight of her face or even a glimpse of the little bird's-nest cottage where she lives, she would forgive me the liberty I take. Plainly, then, I went to Georgetown to see Mrs. Southworth. Once before I had met her accidentally, and this was a mere brief call to be succeeded soon I trust by a more satisfactory visit. At the upper end of a long, dreary street, and just across the road leading down to the great aqueduct bridge, entirely by itself stands the house in which Mrs. Southworth, our noted romance writer lives—a small wooden house, a story and a half above the basement, painted dark brown, and trimmed with white. It clings, as it were, to the side of a steep bank, the level road being in front and a deep ravine behind. The view from the little porch on the river side is very beautiful, commanding a long stretch of the Cumberland canal, a broad sweep of the Potomac, including the island once the home of the traitor Mason, now the camping ground of Federal troops, and a long line of heights on the Virginia side from almost every eminence of which rises a flagstaff giving the Stars and Stripes to the breeze. The great canal is so near, you might almost throw a pebble into it from the cottage door.

Within the cottage all seems so quiet, one would never suspect it of being the birth place of the wild exciting romances that enthrall her hundred thousand readers and keeps curiosity on tiptoe by the year; still less would one suspect that plain, pale, and sad-looking woman in black, of being their author. The first floor of the cottage contains three rooms, two in front, the first of which is the family parlor and general reception room, and the next the authoress' own room, where her writing desk is, and where she sits from Monday morning until Friday noon, week after week, before that desk by the little window, working out the characters now figuring in the *New York Ledger,* under the title of "Self-Made." Forty-one large manuscript pages were just completed and put up for the mail, besides several columns of proof for her publisher in London, England, for whom she is also writing. This quiet little room contains three pretty book cases, well filled, a center-table, a few chairs, and some fine pictures. The most perfect order and neatness is everywhere manifest. The authoress is a widow, perhaps at middle age, certainly not past it, and the mother of two children, a son and daughter. She has thoughtful blue-gray eyes, and in her black dress, with her dark hair bound plainly around her head, looks as unlike her spirited, dashing heroines as one could well imagine. Her voice is mild and pleasant, and in conversation she is genial, earnest, and sincere; and, what will endear her still more to her many admirers, she is a true patriot. Her devotion to the welfare of the soldiers in hospital here very near cost her life.

Of the character and tendency of Mrs. Southworth's writings it is neither necessary nor in place to speak here. I have simply endeavored to give her location and personality, not for the mere gratification of an idle public curiosity, but because I know how much more interest we all take in the writings of an author for whom we have a personal regard, or of whom we have personal knowledge, than we do of a stranger whose "local habitation and name," are mere myths and fancies. A touch of humanity makes all the world kind, it is said, and, if I mistake not the knowledge that Mrs. Southworth is a real, living woman, like the rest of us, working for her daily bread and for the support of her family, will add a new interest to her stories, and bind her with a stronger tie than ever to those who linger over the pages of her wild romances.

L.

December 1, 1863, page 2

Life in Washington

The Public Institutions | The Capitol | The Public Gardens | The Tea Plant Experiment | The Smithsonian Institute

Correspondence of the *Advertiser and Tribune*
Washington, November 25, 1863

Aside from news, or matters connected with the war, Washington has objects of interest to the public at large—objects which thousands will never see, and of which they can know nothing except through the medium of correspondents for the local press. The war, it is true, has brought thousands here who would otherwise never have known Washington, except as a name, connected with an indistinct idea of its being the capital of the United States, and the place where Congress met and the President lived; but the "loved ones at home" would also like to have some definite idea of what the wanderers have seen, and in what pleasant paths their feet have trod. They, in their far and quiet woodland homes, little dream of the many grand and beautiful things our beneficent Uncle Sam keeps at this, his headquarters, for the benefit and amusement of all his wandering nephews and nieces; and the beauty of it is that it is all free, and everybody is welcome. The poorest and the richest can enjoy alike, and the common soldier, weather-worn and shabby though he be, can walk side by side with the gold-bedizened officer through marble halls, and gaze his fill on works of art, magnificent paintings and groups of statuary, or spend hours among the wonders of the museum, or ramble through the public gardens and green-houses, smelling the fragrance of strange and rare blossoms, and refreshing his eyes with the sight of wonderful tropical plants and trees, the bread-fruit tree, the palm, the monstrous-leaved banana, and many others. Or he can walk in the delightful groves, all so nicely trimmed and kept, and recline at his leisure on the seats fixed under the shady trees.

THE CAPITOL

There are so many resorts, and all so full of interest, it is difficult to say which is the favorite. But let us begin at the Capitol, the grand and beautiful structure which has been so many years, forty or more, I believe, growing to its present state of perfection, and through many of whose arches, halls and winding galleries the chisel and hammer of workmen yet resound. This temple of Liberty, as in reality it should be if it has not always been heretofore, is placed on the brow of a low hill, and has two fronts, one to the east and one to the west. The west front is towards the city, and commands a most beautiful view of the broad basin where Washington and Georgetown lie, surrounded by the low rim of sand hills called Georgetown Heights on the right, and the far off Arlington Heights on the left beyond the Potomac. The river lies in the distance like a broad band of silver, dazzling bright in the sunshine but so far that not a ripple or sparkle is visible, only smooth, silvery gleam, as from a solid surface. The Capitol grounds at the west front are very beautiful; they cover several acres, in the form of a semicircle, sloping from the Capitol to the streets of the city, and are laid in winding walks, with rows and groups of stately trees, patches of flowers, fountains, and so forth, around and among which are arranged seats where the weary may rest and where friends and lovers may hold pleasant *tete a tetes*. These seats are always more or less occupied when the weather is fine. Some days a hundred or more people may be seen, singly, or in two and threes, seated there, some reading, some writing, some talking, and some only idly lounging in the sunshine. Several flights of broad stone steps lead up the terraced hill, past a large fountain and basin filled with gold fish, and into the Capitol. The basement or ground floor seems to be a bewildering maze of vast pillared spaces, far reaching aisles and sounding galleries where the dim twilight is here and there broken by a twinkling gas burner, and from which unexpected doors open into passages where dusky staircases are visible on one hand, or on the other into brilliantly lighted rooms, where the glitter of glass may be seen and where men "look upon the wine when it is red, and it giveth its color in the cup." Happy if they were content with *only looking*. Somewhere here below too, is the great furnace, the fiery heart that sends the warm breath through all the great building.

THE ROTUNDA

But let us go higher. From the west front door two flights of steps take us straight up to the Rotunda, the grand center of the whole. This is a circular room ninety-six feet in diameter, and is lighted by almost innumerable windows in the center of the dome, which rises above it to the height of nearly three hundred feet. The lower portion of the rotunda wall is divided into eight large square compartments, each filled with immense paintings of a historical character, such as the Embarkation of the Pilgrims, the Baptism of Pocahontas, Surrender of Cornwallis, Declaration of Independence, and others. All around the room, over the doors and in niches for the purpose, are groups of statuary. From this grand center you may wander north and south, east and west, over nearly four acres of marble halls and place-rooms, and colonnaded vestibules and corridors, and up and down broad winding flights of marble stairs with paintings or statuary greeting you at almost every turn, and everywhere you tread on painted tiles that look like porcelain, laid in beautiful mosaic patterns after choice Pompeian and modern designs. It is useless here to attempt a particular description of either the inside or outside of this splendid edifice, almost every part of which, as we gaze upon it, seems more beautiful than the other, over which hundreds of people, and a majority of them soldiers, are every day rambling.

THE LIBRARY

But it will not do to forget the library room. This occupys the front of the second story, and contains the Congressional Library. The room is eighty-one feet long, thirty-four wide, and thirty-eight feet high. Around the sides and in the galleries above are deep recesses filled with books, numbering nearly one hundred thousand volumes. The center of the room is furnished with tables, chairs, sofas, and globes. There, Tuesdays, Thursdays, and Saturdays, when Congress is not in session, and every day when it is, everybody may come, select the books they like, and sit down and read to their heart's content; or, if they would write, the attentive librarians will furnish the necessary materials, and the tables are at their service. Every day these chairs, sofas, and tables are occupied; people come and read and write and go their way, so much the richer and happier, and nothing to pay.

THE GROUNDS

The grounds enclosing the Capitol contain 35 acres, and both to the east and west are handsomely laid out with paved and graveled walks, and well furnished

East front of the capitol. From *Bohn's Handbook of Washington*, 1860.

with seats under the large and thickly planted trees. In the center of the eastern grounds is a colossal statue of Washington, on a broad pedestal of granite twelve feet high. Within the iron railing which incloses it have been planted a number of rose bushes, and the one immediately in front of the statue is now, the 25th of November, bending under the weight of full-bloom, blood red roses. Others have paler and white ones in bloom.

Across the street in front of the west Capitol grounds, is one of the public gardens. The garden is a broad, barren looking tract of land, anything but inviting to the passerby. The large green house standing in the center, however, attracts many visitors, and it is well worth a visit to see the perfection to which tropical plants and trees are brought here. The bread-fruit, banana, and various species of the palm, are conspicuous for their singular and beautiful foliage. Further still towards the west is another garden, about as barren in appearance as the first. Here are two greenhouses filled with plants from almost every part of the world, but none so large in size as in the former. It is in this garden that experiments have been made with the Chinese tea plant. These foreign shrubs are now of some four years' growth, and are about the size our currant bushes would be at that age. One has been left out in the open grounds for two winters past, and seems as hardy as any evergreen, preserving its foliage unfaded through the season. It is in blossom now. The flower is white, about the size of a syringa or a mandrake blossom, and, without any stem to speak of, seems to be stuck on singly along the stalks and the ends of the branches. I have one of the blossoms, and a sprig of the Chinaman. Both of these gardens are free to the public, and are much visited.

THE SMITHSONIAN INSTITUTE

Still west are the extensive and beautiful grounds of the Smithsonian Institute, with their broad gravel walks and carriage drives, and in the center the noble building itself with its nine towers lifting up an invitation for all to enter and see the wonders within. What is within it would take pages to describe. Imagine in the extensive museum all the wonders of animal, vegetable, and mineral creation; specimens of everything gathered from the realms of ocean and air, as well as from the earth, and all in the most life-like perfection of beauty or hideousness given by nature, and you will doubtless find them here. Every animal that walks or has walked the earth, within reach of man to get, is here, perfect as in life, all but the breath and power to move. Birds of the air, from the mighty condor and albatross down to the tiniest humming-bird are here, and their nests and eggs too. The most beautiful and monstrous shells and sprays and trees of coral from the ocean with all manner of animals that inhabit the "briny deep," snakes and all creeping things, minerals from the "bowels of the earth," horrid Egyptian mummies, skeletons and skulls of men and beasts and birds, manufactured curiosities from all lands, hideous stone and wooden deities from the far off Pacific Islands; indeed, more wonders than we can enumerate, are here daily gazed at by hundreds of delighted visitors, all free to come and go and stay as long as they please. One large room is devoted to paintings, another to paintings and statuary, another is a laboratory stocked with scientific and mathematical instruments. And yet another is a large public library, where, as at the Congressional, everybody is welcome to read and write and enjoy themselves. This library, however, is not so extensive as the other, being mostly confined to works of a scientific nature.

Having already exceeded the limits of a letter, and seeing still before so many places of public interest that deserve more than a passing notice, I must defer mention of them to another time.

L.

December 23, 1863, page 3

Life in Washington

A Visit to the Patent Offices | The Hall of Relics | Foreign Gifts

Special Correspondent of the *Advertiser and Tribune*
Washington, December 17, 1863

The Patent Office in Washington is another of the free public institutions which has its daily crowd of visitors. The building is of white marble, three stories high, and extends around the four sides of an open court. The first and second stories are occupied mostly by offices connected with the Department of the Interior, and the third might truly be called Uncle Sam's curiosity shop. There are three immense halls, one three hundred feet long, and each of the others four hundred feet, fitted up with double rows of large glass cases, in which are deposited models for patents of all the inventions imaginable, from a steam engine to a clothes pin. Fertile as we know the brains of our nation to be, the endless variety of ingenious devices here collected is almost past belief. Not only are the floors of the two longest halls filled, but double rows of galleries running the same length above them are fitted up in the same manner, and nearly all the cases more or less crowded with exquisitely made and neatly labeled models. The hall on the fourth side of the building is yet unfinished and unoccupied. Repairs are also being made in the one running parallel to this, by newly plastering the arches and repairing the long rows of pillars that support them. This is the hall first entered by visitors as they ascend the broad, winding stone staircase from the second floor, and it is here that they linger longest. And after rambling through the others, return and linger still, and look reverently and speak low, as if in these central receptacles were something more sacred than works devised by cunning brains and wrought by skillful hands. And so there is.

Here are collected and treasured as national heirlooms the relics of the one man of America whose memory is without stain. Several large glass cases in this department are filled with the army equipment, furniture, clothing and other articles once belonging to George Washington. In one may be seen two old-fashioned bow-backed chairs and a handsome dressing bureau, and some of his clothes in the half-opened drawers, which were brought from Arlington since the beginning of the war, and deposited here for safe keeping. Another contains the table furniture used by him. Here are piles of china plates and platters, blue and white, many of them cracked, some with pieces broken out and some carefully mended. There are parts of a lighter and finer set which was presented to Mrs. Martha Washington by Lafayette, and two curious and beautiful glass candelabra with heavy glass drops the gift of Count Rochambeau to Gen. Washington. This case also contains a curious, narrow three story washstand, with a dressing glass at the top; a large china punch bowl, and other glass and china vessels of various kinds, besides the great hall lectern from Mount Vernon, an immense leathern portmanteau containing his marquee, a small iron "treasure chest," and a roll of blankets, a center table and other articles; and two sides are partially draped with the tent used by him in the army. In another are the tent poles carefully preserved, with all the camp equipage used by Washington in the Revolution. Quaintly shaped coffee and tea urns of copper, standing upon feet for the convenience of placing heating lamps under them, a copper pitcher, old style camp kettles' with wooden handles, a little gridiron, little black handled knives with their two-tined companions, a camp chest open to show its interior economy of departments, the tumblers he drank from, and the very bellows to blow his fire, are all here. In an upper part of the same case may be seen his war sword, his writing case used in the Revolution, the black knotted cane, with gold head, willed to him by Dr. Franklin, and the vest, britches and coat worn by him when he resigned his commission at Annapolis in 1783. There is also here a curious-painted copper-plate pannel from the stage coach used by him when President. Accompanying this pannel is the following verbatim description:

"The coach boddy was whitish, or a cream colour, the pannels being ornamented with the four seasons and painted by Capriana, a famous painter of his time. The panel was presented to John Varden by Mrs. Mary Dunlop, of Georgetown, D.C."

Mr. Varden deposited it here among other relics of the great and good man.

The vest and breeches of Washington are of light cream color, and the coat a fine dark blue, faced with white, and ornamented with gilt buttons.

Beside the bundle of tent poles in the bottom of this case is the old, well worn war saddle used by the brave Baron DeKalb.

There are two full-size statues of Washington in this department. The most beautifully chiseled one is by Powers, and was brought from Baton Rouge about a year ago, when the building in which it was there deposited was destroyed through the agency of the war. It is the first object that greets the eye as one enters the hall, and few go out without turning to take one more look at that well-known form and face.

A little to the right as you go in, alone in its tall narrow glass receptacle, is another object that commands almost equal reverence with any yet mentioned, and certainly excites more wondering curiosity, and that is the identical printing press on which Benjamin Franklin worked nearly one hundred and twenty years ago. But for the label upon it I imagine few of the rising generation would ever guess for what this clumsy wooden frame, with it queerly contrived fixtures, was made. But there it stands, with its sturdy ink-smeared posts, and well-worn rounce and screw, an infant embodiment, as it were of an idea that in so short a time has grown to the almost omnipotent power now ruling and swaying the world at its will. It looks like some hideous little genii lost out of the long past ages and prisoned here to measure the strides of the giant progress by.

There are some people who do not believe the world progresses; they should be at once sent on a pilgrimage to Washington, to see the Franklin printing press.

Near here are several large cases devoted to foreign curiosities. One contains, hanging by their necks and partially stuffed to show their shapelessness, fifteen silk robes of Japanese make and fashion. These royal garments are cut goring, the waists being about as large round as a barrel, and growing wider at the bottom of the skirt; the skirt body and sleeve are all one piece, the latter being merely large, baggy openings for the arms, and the body as nearly shapeless as it can be as a connecting link between them and the skirt. The material seems rich and heavy; some are of plain white, some figured white, some heavily flowered with great flaunting vines and leaves, and others plaided; but in all the ground work is white. They hang there like so many Mrs. Blue Beards in bridal array, fifteen all headless in a row.

Beneath these are a number of beautiful large screens of bamboo work, hung together on hinges in sets, so that they may be spread open, or closed like doors. These are also specimens of Japanese ingenuity.

In another case may be seen a complete set of most curiously wrought Japanese armor, and some of their implements of warfare. And here is a magnificent article, bridle and all the trappings for a fully caparisoned horse. The saddle is of white embossed and flowered leather, and the caparisons of purple and white silk, and heavy crimson fringed head and breast gear. The stirrups are very heavy, and are about as like to our idea of that article as an Indian dug-out would be. These are also from Japan.

A little way from this, looking through a glass cover we see on a broad shelf beneath, various manuscript pages and large sheet of parchment spread out, and written over in unknown languages. These are the original treaties of foreign nations, among which are the Turkish, Persian, Russian, and so forth. Here is also a large collection of coins and medals, and farther along, among other things are packages of Persian shawls, and spoons and forks in imitation of gold from Hommooe. In the bottom of this case is a Persian carpet 30 feet long by 15 wide, which was presented to Mr. Van Buren when President, by the Imman of Muscat.

Here, and all through these immense halls and galleries, are thousands of curiosities impossible to enumerate in a letter. I have only attempted to mention a few which are of peculiar interest from their personal associations.

Here every day, from nine in the morning till three in the afternoon, may be seen hundreds of visitors of all ages; a majority of them are soldiers whom the war has given this opportunity of seeing the treasures of the national capital.

L.

December 29, 1863, page 4

Life in Washington

Fine Art Criticisms at the Capitol | Street Scenes

Special Correspondence *Advertiser and Tribune*

Funny things do sometimes happen even in Washington. It is amusing to go the rounds of the Capitol, and hear the remarks of the uninitiated on the works of art there to be seen. In the library the other day a middle-aged, well-dressed couple undertook an inspection of the globes. Walking confidently up to the great sphere representing the celestial worlds, they began turning it on its axis and spelling out the mythological names of the constellations. It was evidently a new view of creation to them. After blundering through Microscopium, Apparatus Sulptoris, Scutum Sobeski, and stumbling over Sagittarius, Serpentarius, Monoceres and Ursa Major, the man turned to his companion and said:

"Well, I don't see no place here that I ever knowed or heard on. This is all in furrin parts I reckon."

"Yes; let us look on the other one," said the lady.

After spelling out several hard names on the terrestrial globe, the lady's eye caught the familiar word "Hudson."

"O, here now," said she, placing her finger on the great bay bearing that name, "here is the Hudson—now we can find New York. It must be close by; I was there onst you know, and I should know it in a minute."

But a patient search through the polar regions, and around the margin, and over the waters of Hudson's Bay failed to develop anything that the lady could recognize as the city of New York.

"Well, 'taint no matter now," said the gentleman; "let's go and find the picters and sculpings."

Believing that there would be some fun in the "picters and sculpings," with such critics in company, I was ready to go and help find them. The strangers, glad to be noticed, readily accepted my escort to that grand pannel painting by Leutze, facing the great staircase leading to the galleries of the House of Representatives. How grand it is, no none who has not seen it can imagine. It is an illustration of the motto wreathed in the scroll above it, "Westward the course of Empire takes it way." In a vast wilderness of mountain scenery a large caravan of emigrants is brought to a stand-still by finding the narrow defile through which they are to pass blocked up by fallen trees. While two or three of their number set to work with axes to remove the obstructions, the others are depicted in the various attitudes they might be supposed to assume on such an occasion. Some are sitting in their wagons, some on horseback, some on rocks, some standing, and nearly all with eager eyes looking in the direction their guide is pointing, far beyond the mountain pass, to still wilder and apparently interminable ranges of mountain peaks and shadowy deities, that yet lie between them and their destined home. Few can look upon some of the faces there without feeling those deep emotions which move to tears, and I have seen the eyes of strong men grow dim, and heard a tremulous tenderness in their tones, as they pointed out to a companion one of the central figures of the group, a woman seated on a mule, with a babe in her arms. In that true woman's face, what a struggle is there between hope and despair; how the home-sickness of the heart, kept down through weeks of weary journeyings, swells up into the single tear on her cheek as she holds the babe to her bosom, and strives to summon to her lips the wonted smile, to sweeten the expected kiss. She cannot smile. Her heart is too full. There are no kisses on her lips just now, only the passing agony of an unutterable sorrow. But behind all is the true woman's soul, which we know will be patient, enduring, and uncomplaining to the end. It is a face that brings moisture to many eyes.

But I need not linger over particulars, especially when I know that pages of description could not do justice to this grandly conceived and executed work of art. It is a picture to be seen and studied by weeks instead of moments, but our friends merely glanced over the prominent figures in the foreground, remarking that they looked like hunters, with their guns and dogs, and that the white-nosed oxen were "as like as life." Then the man pointed to the mountain peaks in the background, to the topmost heights of which one man has climbed, and is waving his hat, while another on a ledge of rock just below is reaching up to him a flagstaff with the stars and stripes to plant on the lofty battlements.

"There!" exclaimed our friend, "I knew I had seen all this somewhere! Now, that I as I see that are man, it comes to me, all but the name—let's see, what was his name? We read all about him in a book last winter, how he climb up the rocks—O, pshaw, now, don't you remember the fellow's name? He was the first man that ever climb so high with the flag?"

I suggested Frémont.

"Yes, yes; that's him—that's the very place where he climb up now, ain't it? and what's all these people doing? They ain't hunters, Susan; for see, there's women and babies along, and besides I don't reckon he had his family along when he climb up the rocks that time."

"O, I'll tell you," said the lady. "It's war time, and these people are running away from the war. See the camp-fires over yonder," pointing to some volcanic peaks in the distance, "and how they've got so fur away they feel safe and are going to put the flag up."

"No, it's that feller I told you of that climb the rocks. I knew quick as I looked at it, as well as if I'd seen it all afore."

"Well, now, I know I *have* seen something just like it somewhere," said the lady, and turning to me, "Where did the man get it from to paint? He must have took it from something, for I know I've seen it. O, yes, now I remember? it was in Harper's Magazine! yes, I know that's just where it was taken from, for I've seen it there."

"Well, may be he did, part of it," said her companion; "but, I know the man with the flag is the one I read of in that book, for he is the only one that climb up them rocks, that I know."

And so, between Fremont and Harper, the artist and his design was quite crushed.

The "sculpings" next claimed attention; but nothing of interest occurred till we came to where Franklin, the calm philosopher, in his niche, at the foot of the Senate staircase, his form almost of colossal size, chiseled to almost breathing life, stands with one elbow resting on the stumps of a lightning splintered tree. Two men were passing it at the moment we came up and one remarked, "There's old Dr. Franklin who taught us how to handle the lightning; see where it struck that tree!" "Dear me! dear me!" exclaimed our rustic friend, "it struck the tree while he was so close by it, and yet never hurt him! well, I never!"

NATIVES VS. CONTRABANDS

Some of the tinctured natives of Washington affect great disgust towards their more pure blooded, but less aristocratic contraband brethren and sisters. A little ochre-tinted native was sitting on the end of a dirty log the other day, digging her toes vigorously into the mud, and slandering with all the bitterness her tongue was capable of, an ebony-hued contraband of the other sex who chanced to be passing and turned as if to speak to her.

"Go 'long wid ye; don't ye open yer mouf har, you no 'count contraban' puppy dog nigger! Reckon yer marsa has done catcher yer mammy wat makes ye grin so. Go 'long wid ye! I wouldn't be seen speakin' to a poor, misable, puppy dog, contraban' nigger, no how. Go long! Ise a regular Washington nigger, I is; an' non o' yer misable black conterbans'."

L.

2
1864

January 30, 1864, page 4

Our Washington Letter

THE DEPARTMENT OF AGRICULTURE | DESCRIPTION OF THE COMMISSIONER'S OFFICE, ETC.

From Our Own Correspondent
Washington, January 20, 1864

Last Saturday, a bright, genial day, was taken advantage of by the Congressional Committee on Agriculture to pay a visit of inspection to the public gardens, the offices, seed room, etc., now under the special charge of the Department of Agriculture. This Department, it will be remembered, is of quite recent origin as a distinct, independent institution under Government, it having, up to the passage of the act erecting it into a separate department in the spring of 1862, been combined with the Patent Office Bureau, in which connection it had lingered and languished for years, a sinecure to some of the officers and managers, but of comparatively little utility to the class of community it should benefit most—the tillers of the soil in new and distant States. The position it then occupied was a subordinate one; whereas, by its merits and interests, it should in reality stand first among the departments under the special care of the Government.

The zealous and energetic officers of this new department have had much to contend with since its organization, but they are the kind of men who grow strong in defending a good cause, men who seem to have at heart the principles of doing the greatest good to the greatest number, and have set themselves about organizing and perfecting a system whereby farmers in all parts of our vast country can be supplied not only with the elements of future crops for their fields, but also a harvest of knowledge, gathered from widespread and diversified experiences. While they are importing the choicest and rarest seeds from foreign lands, to scatter broadcast over our own, they are gathering in month by month each year, records of the results of experiments, details of farm management, the causes why and wherefore the successes and failures of improvements and innovations, and indeed, knowledge of all kinds affecting the farmers' interests. This is embodied in a handsome volume, made still more attractive by illustrations, and sent again, like the seeds, cereals, and plants, broadcast through the country, there to germinate and bring forth

U.S. Patent Office. From *Bohn's Handbook of Washington*, 1860.

knowledge of still higher excellence for the succeeding years. The report of the Commissioner of Agriculture for the first year of the independent existence of the department, 1862, forms a very able introduction to a volume replete with interest on almost every subject connected with farming. It is a volume which will not be laid on the shelf to be covered with dust and eaten with mildew, but will be read as a household book, for its wholesome home truths, its practical suggestions, and able essays on the various branches of farm economy. These papers, once read by the farmers, will stimulate inquiry, encourage experiments and lead to a still higher development of the resources of the soil, the results of which will aid to form volumes of still greater excellence.

This department is as yet too new to have its labors and the full scope of its designs well understood and appreciated by the country at large, and the difficulties under which it was organized, and with which it is yet struggling, have hindered to a degree the efficiency of the efforts made to extend and multiply its benefits. Still it has done a great work, of which the distribution through the country of 1,200,000 packages of seeds, cereals, etc., is a small part. The correspondence it has called forth, and the information thereby gathered for wider dissemination in the future, is of the greatest value. Another fact to the credit of its present officers should be remembered, that now the seeds sent out give universal satisfaction as to their purity, their germinating qualities, and their utility. The greatest care is taken to procure only the best. Large importations are constantly being made of such seeds, cereals, and plants as are in the greatest demand, especially for the increasing and ever spreading population of the Northwest. The Commissioner's report shows that in no section of the country have his efforts been so well appreciated and so ably seconded by prompt responses and returns of knowledge and experience in exchange for seeds, as in the West.

Now, how does the reader think all this great labor of this most important department is carried on? In what splendid room of State does our Commissioner sit, with his array of secretaries and his little army of clerks about him? What museums, laboratories, and libraries are at his command, from which to draw replies, by investigations or experiments, for the hundreds of letters of anxious inquiry that daily pour in upon him? What spacious suites of rooms has he in which to store the thousand and one specimens of agricultural products that are sent to him, not only from all parts of our own country, but from lands beyond the sea; yea, even from the "uttermost parts of the earth?" And where is his vast storehouse from which the packages of seeds come forth by millions? Under what vaulted roof are the marble granaries into which he dips his hand to dispense these blessings to the world? Come and let us see.

Here, about in the center of the city of Washington, is that beautiful marble structure called the Patent Office, the galleries and museum department of which were partially described in a former letter. In that letter, however, no mention was made of the basement part of the building. Now, instead of going up that lofty flight of granite steps leading through those double rows of fluted columns to the grand halls above, let us pass through this little iron gate and enter the narrow, dirty door opening on a level with the ground. Far in front of us reaches a long dim hall, on each side of which are offices of some of the different bureaus connected with the Department of Interior; but here, at the left, we turn into a longer, dimmer, dirtier passage, which we follow towards the glimmer of daylight faintly visible some three hundred feet in advance. Sometimes the darkness and dirt are made more distinct by the sickly flickering of a faint gas light in the misty region overhead. But let us go on. Open these heavy banging doors which lead us into a still darker passage, and now, by a yellow glare of gas light on a door at the left, the words, "COMMISSIONER OF AGRICULTURE. NO ADMITTANCE." Knock gently, and though the watchful guardian at the next door may tell us we cannot get in, the Commissioner is engaged, we must come into the waiting room and take our turn with the many already before us, the chances are ten to one that the Commissioner himself, yielding to the first impulse of his kindly nature, will rise, reach forth his hand and open the door for us, for, from the center of room where he sits, he can almost reach it without rising. When once he sees us we are safely in. Here is a room no larger than a comfortable, good-sized bedroom should be; that chair in the center, before that little table piled with letters, books, and papers, is the Commissioner's special seat, which he graces with his portly form, above which smiles his benignant face, set off by bushy eyebrows, whiskers and hair, all white as snow. Directly behind him, so near that he can almost touch it, is a broad, temporary shelf, or table, on which are piled the offerings of Ceres, the strange and curious products of the soil, from various climes and many lands. There is no room or chance for arrangement or classification; grasses, grains, leaves, bulbs, seeds, and indeed samples of almost everything that grows, may be found in this medley, and much as the confusion may irritate the organ of order, there is no help for it; every inch of the room is occupied; there are piles of bottled grains and seeds in one corner, the great iron safe in another; tables and writing desks in every place where tables and desks can stand, and the stove between the two low windows, opening almost upon the ground. The waiting-room beyond is equally crowded with desks and tables, and always more or less with those working for the Department, or waiting to ask for work. Still beyond this is what is called the Library, a small room, with two or three sides lined with books, but the center so filled with the inevitable desks and tables, and their busy occupants, that it is difficult to get at them. Across the hall are two small, gloomy rooms, occupied by clerks, and this is all the space granted to this important department in all that building covering over 100,000 feet of ground. But here, untiring, and full of zeal and energy for the great cause in which all their energies are enlisted, the undaunted Commissioner and his able chief clerk have labored on, intent to perform to the utmost the duties imposed upon them by the law which established the department.

In another letter will be given a description of the great storehouse for seeds, the working of the machinery which grinds out and sends abroad its million packages yearly; and also some further elaboration of the works performed in the Commissioner's special domain.

L.

February 1, 1864, page 1

Our Washington Letter

THE STOREHOUSE OF THE AGRICULTURE DEPARTMENT

From Our Own Correspondent

At an inconvenient distance from the offices occupied by the Commissioner of the Department of Agriculture, is an old, low building situated in the immediate vicinity of stables and filthy back alleys, a building that a well-to-do farmer of Michigan, or of any other respectable State, would be ashamed to own as a barn, but might consider tolerable as a shelter for his Berkshire, Suffolk, or White Chesters; and here are the government seed rooms; this is the great storehouse from which the 1,200,000 packages of seeds have been sent forth during the past year to enrich and beautify so many homes. Let us go in.

Following the footsteps of the honorable Committee on Agriculture, as they come down from that marble temple, goddess-crowned, on Capitol Hill, we cross this muddy vacant lot, picking our way carefully by stepping on bits of board and broken bricks, to escape the attractions of the soft, tenacious clay beneath, and, opening the only door that presents itself, find ourselves at once on the field of action—if action that can be called where one can scarcely move hand or foot without trespassing on the grounds or rights of his neighbor. Stop a moment, and survey the scene. So the honorable Committee did. The room is, perhaps, twenty-five feet by thirty; in the center are two large tables surrounded by men, young and old, so busily at work putting up and packing seeds for distribution that scarcely an eye is raised to look at the intruders. (Perhaps it is because there is not room enough to raise them—you would think they could hardly find space to wink without going out doors.) In the corner at our right, two or three tiers deep, are piled sacks of cotton seed reaching almost to the ceiling; across the end at the left are loaded shelves and rows upon rows of barrels, boxes, and parcels, almost blocking up the way to the Superintendent's little cramped up den, called by courtesy his office; on the opposite side of the room are more boxes, more parcels and more men at work. The stove is somewhere in that vicinity, too, judging from the direction of the pipe overhead, but the tables and an opaque mass of humanity are between us and it; let us, after dipping our hands into these sacks of golden wheat, turning over on our palms the plump Victoria peas, sniffing, as with a foretaste of future quids and aromatic vapors, at the infinitesimal tobacco seed just imported from Cuba, and smiling benignly over bags of pink-eyed beans, as the committee did, turn into this narrow passage between the piled-up barrels at our left, and ascend, by a short flight, to the regions above. When once our heads are well above the floor we may as well stop, see what is to be seen, and retire. To advance here would be among the impossibilities. Before us is a room 50 feet long by 25 wide; down the center nearly the whole length extends a table, on each side of which sit women and girls, forty in number, gray-haired, middle-aged, and youth scarcely past childhood, all closely crowded together, and bent over the work of filling and stitching up the piles of little seed bags before them. Between these busy workers and the wall, on either side, in rows three deep, stand casks and barrels, and piled upon these are other barrels, sacks, and boxes, containing seed prepared, or to be prepared, for distribution by mail or express to country homes far away.

Think of it, you to whom these little packages come, you who own the broad, fair fields and blooming gardens, to be made richer and more beautiful by the tireless efforts of the Commissioner of Agriculture, and all his zealous co-workers here—think if, comparing the good that has been and might be done by this Department, with others under the Government, even half justice has been done, or half the fostering care extended to it that should have been. Cramped for want of room, and crippled for want of means, it has still suffered no relaxation of effort. Watchful of the great interest committed to its care, it is quick to learn and prompt to supply, to the extent of its ability, the growing and diversified wants of the country. It has brought flax seed from California, tobacco seed from Cuba, and hundreds of bushels of choicest wheat and other cereal grains from the old world, together with several thousand dollars' worth of the most valuable seeds for field and garden culture, and not forgetting to combine beauty with utility, has added to these a large collection of flower seeds, all of which, with the best varieties of grains and vegetable seeds grown in our country, have been spread abroad with a lavish hand.

Within the last year 1,500 bushels of cotton seed have been procured, packed and distributed, principally among the farmers of the West. By the one item of tobacco seed alone it has increased the wealth of our Northern, Middle and Western States by millions of dollars. And who shall estimate the amount of satisfaction and happiness conferred on thousands of homes in the distant and sparsely settled West, by the rich additions this Department has already made to the wealth and beauty of their newly-broken yard and garden grounds? This is one of the results that can only be appreciated by the recipients of the favors, and by the officers of the Department to whom their satisfaction is expressed in the warmest terms of gratitude. Over half a million of the packages distributed have been sent directly or given to those applying for them, and, that the results might be known as facts, and not mere guess work, circulars of inquiry were addressed to some thousands of recipients, and in almost every instance the replies were of the most satisfactory and gratifying nature. This has convinced the Commissioner, and should convince all, that, in the words of his last report, "In no department of this government, does the expenditure of a like sum confer upon so large a proportion of the people anything like the same amount of pleasure and substantial enjoyment."

When we come, in another letter, to speak of the labors and benefits of this Department in other ways, aside from the mere distribution of seeds, it will be seen that this is comparatively a small part of the work undertaken and the good designed to be accomplished. But referring now to this division of its labor alone, let any sensible farmer ask himself if it is right, that while all the other wheels of this vast and intricate machinery of government run smoothly on gleaming golden axles, this, the great balance wheel of all, should be allowed to grate and grind on rusty iron? As he desires improvement and progress among the class of community of which he is a member, by far the largest and most important class of citizens in our country, let him ask why this one interest has been so disregarded and neglected, while millions have been appropriated to others of a secondary nature. Let him ask these questions and require his representatives in the capitol yonder to answer, when they take up the modest petition of the commissioner for $130,000 to carry on his labors through the present fiscal year. They will appropriate twice that amount, and think it a small matter, to fit up a vessel to lie at her leisure among the Atlantic billows idly watching the blockade runners carrying their contraband goods into Wilmington harbor; they could throw away millions in experiments with the useless monster mortars that line the banks of the Mississippi, or in a thousand other extravagances of war or of speculation, and must the pittance asked for this, the most humane and most beneficent of all causes, because underlying and securing the prosperity of all other, be granted grudgingly or not at all? Art and science and literature have temples fitted for the offices of their high priests and for the reception of the offerings of their devotees, but what has agriculture? Where are the priests of Ceres and Pomona found, and where is the treasure house of their offerings? We have shown them to you faithfully and truly pictured.

What, it may be asked, were the thoughts of the honorable Brutus J. Clay, Chairman of the House Committee, on this subject, as he led his honorable brother members along that dismal basement passage and ushered them into an apartment looking, with its contents, more like a common gardener's storeroom than the office and reception room of his honor the Commissioner of Agriculture? And what of those who followed him? Did any idea of the inappropriateness of the place and the interests there enter their brains? Fresh from the forest like cornfields and fragrant hemp and tobacco plantations of Kentucky, from the luxuriant and varied harvests of the central and northern States, and from the broad grain fields and blushing orchards of the West, did the thought cross their minds that the interests they represented could here find no room for such development as the state of the country required? And, when, emerging from the crowded seed room, and brushing the dust of bags and barrels from the congressional broadcloth, did they turn to the pages of the Commissioner's report, read again the record of the great work done, and resolve that henceforth his hands should be unbound and room and means given him according to his desire to accomplish good. Let us hope so.

L.

February 3, 1864, page 4

Our Washington Letter

THE AGRICULTURAL DEPARTMENT AGAIN

From Our Own Correspondent
Washington, January 26, 1864

It is far too common a thing for farmers themselves to say, and for legislators to think, that agriculture can take care of itself. Indeed, farmers, as a class, have always been noted as being more heedless in regard to the rights and wants of their profession, less desirous of advancement in it as an art, and slower to accept the aid offered them by science, than any other division of community. Thanks to the light that has been forced upon them from every surrounding with which they come in contact, they are gradually growing into the belief that there may be progression even in the tilling of the soil, the culture of crops, the raising of stock, and the growth and perfection of fruit. They find that science can help them, and law also, and are beginning to make their claims felt in both of these directions. What science has done for them it is not our province now to speak of, but simply to show what law or government has attempted. Every thinking man will attest the truth of the following observation of the Commissioner in his last report. "If we examine the history of those foreign countries which have attained the highest agricultural prosperity, it will be found that every one of them was generously aided by the Government; and on the contrary, where legislators have neglected the interest of agriculture, their countries are backward in wealth, intelligence and prosperity. Indeed the above remark is true in regard to the various States of our republic where legislative aid has been extended or refused."

Thoroughly impressed with the importance of these facts, and believing that the cause was worthy of a department of its own, the friends of agriculture, in the spring of 1862, succeeded in disentangling it from the wheels and pulleys and intricate engineering manipulations of the Patent Office, and set it apart to be specially cared for and fostered by the Government. They asked, and justly too, why this most important of all our national interests should be placed second to any other, and especially why it should be committed to those whose legitimate business unfitted them for the practical knowledge of matters that concerned it most. What has the making out and filing of patents to do with the cultivation of the farm and the securing of crops? It may be said that many of these patents were for agricultural implements, designed for the special benefit of the farmer. Well, and if they were; after securing the patent-right to the inventor, and placing the carefully-wrought model in its appropriate case of glass in some one of the long, arched halls and galleries devoted to these specimens of mechanical ingenuity, how much more capable would the Commissioner of Patents, or his assistants, be of advising with regard to its use on the farm? Because they could distinguish between a harrow and a spinning wheel, were they therefore competent to discuss the merits of Morgan horses, the draining of marsh lands, and the best mode of keeping cabbage? A man might hold the office of Land Commissioner all his life, and yet not know the difference between clay soil and quicksand, or between Indian corn and a barley corn; still, by virtue of the apparent verbal connection of his occupation with the material that farms are made of, it would seen more rational to intrust the interest of agriculture to his hands than to those who have heretofore, in the name of government, controlled them. Each in his own sphere may be all that is required or desired, but the cause of agriculture required something more than either could perform. The awakening intelligence of farmers, the new and fast multiplying wants of the country, and the consciousness, growing out of this season of our nation's trial, that upon the progress and prosperity of agriculture depended mainly the success of our armies, and the permanence of our government, demanded that it should be in hands untrammeled by other interests, under the care of men who understood and loved it, and would devote, with zeal, their time and energies to its advancement.

The Department was established. The act of Congress specially creating it, says: "The general designs and duties of this Department shall be to acquire and to diffuse among the people of the United States useful information on subjects connected with agriculture, in the most general and comprehensive sense of that word, and to procure, propagate, and distribute among the people new and valuable seeds and plants."

It is made "the duty of the Commissioner of Agriculture to acquire and preserve in his department all information concerning agriculture, which he can obtain by means of books and correspondence, and by practical and scientific experiments (accurate records of which experiments shall be kept in his office) by the collection of statistics, and by any other appropriate means in his power, to collect, as he may be able, new and valuable seeds and plants, to test by cultivation the value of such of them as may require such tests; to propagate such as may be worthy of propagation, and to distribute them among agriculturists."

He is also to employ "chemists, botanists, entomologists, and other persons skilled in natural science pertaining to agriculture," who are to analyze, botanize and anatomize for the benefit of farmers, and the results of whose labors are to be preserved in the Commissioner's Department.

Beginnings have been made with more or less promise of successful advancement in all these various divisions of labor; but as yet, for want of room and means to carry them on to any great extent, the main efforts of the department have been devoted to collecting, importing and distributing seeds, and compiling, publishing and sending forth through the country as liberally as possible, the most valuable agricultural information that could be obtained. This season alone, they are furnishing an assortment of seeds to over a thousand agricultural societies and clubs, besides the thousands distributed through members of Congress, and tens of thousands through private applications and individuals.

Of the value of the information already sent abroad, reference need only be made to the first annual report—a volume of over 600 pages—every one of which is replete with interest and useful knowledge, not for farmers only, but for every citizen, every patriot, and every statesman. Let every one who can get it, read at least the introductory paper. If it does not awaken the farmer's pride in his calling, and excite in him an ambition to excel, then he has no pride to be awakened, and no ambition worthy of the name. Its grand truths will call forth the wonder and admiration of the citizen, the gratitude of the patriot, and stimulate the true statesman to a noble zeal for the protection and advancement of the cause to which our country owes so much, and on the prosperity of which so much of its future greatness depends.

The collection of statistics purely agricultural, that may be found towards the close of the volume, shows that a wonderful amount of careful work has been done in that division of the department. Of this work, the way in which it is done, the object and utility of it, mention will be made in a future letter; and also some description of the entomologist's labors and designs, the attempts at a pomological museum, the propagating garden, greenhouses, etc.

Look now at the labors required by law of this Department, and compare them with the facilities provided for their accomplishment. A more bitter satire on the whole thing could hardly be penned than the reply of the chief clerk, when asked by your correspondent to be shown through the Department. "Why," said he, "there is nothing to see! nothing but these two or three rooms where there is hardly room to turn round, one or two gloomy ones across the hall where the clerks are, and the crowded shell of a seed room over on the other square—that is all. There is nothing to see."

Could the same be said with regard to any other department under government, however subordinate to this, or inferior to it in importance? But we went quietly about, saw what there was *not* to be seen, and your readers have it before them.

L.

February 5, 1864, page 4

Our Washington Letter
The Government Propagating Garden

From Our Own Correspondent
Washington, January 28, 1864

Every one at all conversant with the popular agricultural journals of this country during the last three or four years has heard more or less about the Government propagating garden at Washington. What they have heard or experienced in regard to its utility, however, has been rather less than more. In a former letter mention was made of two public or Government gardens; there are two, both public, both belonging to the Government, but only one is under the control of the Department of Agriculture, or has in any way a claim to the title of the Government propagating garden. The other may more appropriately be called the Congressional flower garden, as its principal object is to furnish members of Congress and their ladies with bouquets, and to propagate for their special benefit and gratification a miscellaneous variety of greenhouse and other flowering plants and shrubs, of which each member, if he chooses, can claim his "quota," make his selection, and have it sent to his own home at Uncle Sam's expense.

The garden, or collection of plants, has been in existence and accumulating for something more than twenty years, and previous to the secession of the Southern States was almost entirely under their control, all the packages of seeds and plants from it being distributed in that direction, while they in return voted yearly appropriations of eight or ten thousand dollars for its benefit, incidentally their own. It was originally begun by the botanist, Mr. Breckenridge, with the design of making a complete botanical collection, and while under his charge was enriched with many rare and curious foreign and tropical plants. At the death of Mr. A. J. Downing, Mr. B. took charge of the Smithsonian grounds, gradually neglecting his own, and finally resigning it altogether into other hands.

The real Government propagating garden had its origin only about four years ago, and was designed then principally for the cultivation of the China tea plant. For this purpose two glass structures were erected, each 100 feet long by 25 wide, in which a great number of the plants were propagated. The result of the great experiment, about which so much noise was made throughout the country, proved, however, nothing more than was already known, namely, that the plant would grow in this climate, and that, comparing the value of labor here and in China, we could not compete with the Celestials in the manufacture of tea, so long as they were content to work for a penny a day. In view of this last fact, there was little inducement for the Government to prosecute the tea business to any great extent—the impracticable Orientals were consigned to less expensive apartments, and the glass houses were devoted to the cultivation of flowers. Attempts were also made to establish an experimental garden, where various kinds of plants, shrubs, and fruits could be tested, and then distributed through the country. But for want of system, or knowledge, or proper management, or all together, little or nothing of account had been done up to the time when, by act of Congress, the garden, with its "fixtures and property," came into the hands of the officers of the new Department of Agriculture.

From the disorder consequent upon former neglect and incompetency the garden has not yet time to recover, but traces of the skillful hand under whose management it now is are fast becoming visible. The Commissioner, at great pains and expense, succeeded in securing as Superintendent the services of Mr. William Saunders, a gentleman well known to the horticultural world by his valuable writings which have appeared in every journal devoted to that interest for many years past. In fruit culture Mr. Saunders is a practical experimentalist, and has given to the world much accurate and important information on that subject. He is also an accomplished florist, draughtsman, and landscape gardener, having an eye for the beauty as well as the utility of his art in all its various applications. When Mr. Saunders came to Washington to accept his position, but a little more than a year ago, he found the "propagating garden," aside from the greenhouses, scarcely more than a common grass plat, with winding graveled walks cutting the sod here and there into fantastic shapes, but on that dead level, and without the relief of shrub or tree, producing no artistic effect whatever. Some attempts had been made for the formation of a complete collection of improved varieties of native grapes, but Mr. Saunders found them nearly all either misnamed or with no names at all; so that no reliance could be placed upon them; they were consequently destroyed by burning, and an entire new collection commenced. The results of the efforts of his predecessors in other directions were mostly considered worthy of the same honor, for Mr. Saunders is strictly of the David Crockett persuasion, especially where fruit is concerned, and believes in being "right" before he goes "ahead."

This piece of ground, comprising only five acres, is far too small for the purposes designed, but till more can be obtained, efforts are being made to turn every foot of it to practical use. The design of the Government propagating garden is not to benefit or bring revenue to the Government directly, but, like the other divisions of this department, to scatter benefits gratuitously among the people at large. Here are to be made experiments whose results are to be published in the annual reports, and here are to be grown all the varieties of flowers, fruits, shrubs, etc., that can be obtained, or may be thought worthy either for beauty or utility, and from these, seeds, cuttings, bulbs, and plants are to be distributed freely to those applying for them. Already the Superintendent reports that during the past year some 25,750 articles, as above named, have been sent from this garden, about one-half of them through members of Congress, and the remainder to agricultural and other rural associations, to be disseminated by them in their several communities.

A very intensive correspondence has been entered into with our Ministers, Consuls, and missionaries in foreign countries for the purpose of obtaining through them such seeds, plants, bulbs, or cuttings as may be thought valuable for trial here; and also efforts are made to collect the same from all parts of our own country, that their relative merits, their hardiness, and adaptation to climate may be tested and known. Mr. Saunders has opened books in which are recorded all his transactions in this relation. The names of all seeds and plants sent to him, where from, the names of the donors, the conditions of such seeds and plants at the time of reception, the date of their being sown and planted, and the results, are all briefly but intelligently registered. Also, the date of sending away any package, and to whom sent. Besides this, he keeps daily and weekly records of the appearance, growth, and maturity of such plants and fruits as are considered worthy of this attention. Thus he has, since accepting his position here, collected and planted over one hundred varieties of grapes, all of which he can vouch for as being true to their names; these are planted side by side, and every change in the perfection and ripening of the fruit is daily noted, so that when cuttings of them are sent to any locality, a correct description of their value and qualities may be had with them. The same course is pursued with pears; a dwarfed and standard of each sort being planted side by side, and their progress and conduct in fruit-bearing carefully noted.

Pomologists will at once appreciate the value of such a course as this, and when they come to get their trees and vines, will have the satisfaction of reading the record, and of knowing that they have the precise quality of fruit they ask for.

Mr. Saunders' designs pay special attention to the diseases of fruits and fruit trees—the blight, the mildew, the blistering of leaves, the withering of trees, the spotting of fruit, and various other evils of that sort, which make such ravages in orchards, graperies and gardens. His researches in this direction, assisted by the skill of the entomologist, will be of great value, especially to many inexperienced fruit-growers of the great Northwest. He is also testing the availability of various shrubs for the purpose of hedges, having samples of each, so that those desiring them can see and judge of their utility.

It is also the design of the Department, as soon as means and grounds for the purpose can be obtained, to establish a botanical garden, and museum of native plants. Extended conservation is needed, so that some sort of classification of plants may be had—the merely ornamental or florist's collection in one, the medicinal in another, the textile in another, and so on. One can readily conceive what an addition this would be to the usefulness of the Government garden.

Indeed, the object of a garden like this, the full scope of the design of which can only be hinted at in so brief a letter, when considered in all its bearings, must be acknowledged as one of the most noble, important, and universally beneficial character. It will be the great wholesale storehouse of just such information as a rapidly growing country like ours needs. Especially will it be found of incalculable benefit to emigrants coming from other lands to make new homes in this. The system now begun, well developed and keeping pace with the wants of the country and the demands of the times, will save years of vexation and disappointment to inexperienced foreigners, and, in fact, to thousands of the inexperienced of our own country as well.

Application has been made for land and means to establish orchards and vineyards for testing fruit, and fields for testing grains, grasses, and vegetables, that when proved good they may be sent abroad correctly named and described. Congress could hardly confer a greater blessing upon our whole land than by granting this petition.

L.

February 8, 1864, page 4

Our Washington Letter

THE STATISTICAL BUREAU OF THE AGRICULTURAL DEPARTMENT

Correspondence of the *Advertiser and Tribune*
Washington, January 30, 1864

Reference has been made in a former letter to the labors of the statistical division of the Department of Agriculture. Let us glance briefly at the manner in which these labors are performed, their value to the farmer, and the means by which their beneficial results may be greatly increased.

By consulting the report of this Department for 1862, it will be seen that great difficulties were in the way of getting at the knowledge required to base a system of agricultural statistics upon. The census returns were found to be very imperfect, and at best unsatisfactory for this purpose, as they attempted nothing more than an inventory of the leading crops, and of the chief items of agricultural investment; whereas, the object aimed at by this Department was, to ascertain the amount of our principal crops; their yield per acre; the average sown or planted; the average prices in each State; and their total value in the States where raised—not as represented in New York, or other commercial seaport towns, with all the costs of storage and freightage added to their original value. If by any means a true statement of the above facts could be had for one year, or even an approximation to a true statement, it will at once be seen that a basis would be found, by means of which, from year to year, the precise condition of the agriculture of the country could be ascertained. Comparisons would show whether the number of cultivated acres was increasing, or the yield per acre decreasing, or the contrary; and also whether the immense crops annually raised were at the expense of the soil, or in consequence of improved systems of farming. In this way, too, would be unfolded the vast internal commerce of our country, by showing what crops are peculiar to the different sections, the cost of transportation, and where the crops are consumed. Other objects of the plan sought were to show "at what expense to the farmer his crops are produced; at what cost to the soil; and what are the errors of our agriculture, its difficulties, its hardships and its wrongs."

In instituting researches for the above objects, the Commissioner had an efficient aid in the clerk of the statistical bureau, Mr. L. Bollman, of Indiana, a man practically acquainted with the different phases of agriculture, and for some years the agricultural correspondent of the *Cincinnati Gazette.*

Circulars were last winter sent to every county in the loyal States, making such inquiries as would lead to the results desired. Others were issued during the summer and fall months to ascertain the monthly condition of the crops, their amounts, value, etc. From the returns received in answer to these inquiries, monthly reports were made out and largely distributed to the public. Over 2,000 correspondents were engaged in furnishing this information, at what expense to the Department may be calculated, when it is known that pre-paid envelopes had to be forwarded to all for the returns, instead of franked ones; that privilege having been taken from the Commissioner by the Post-office law passed at the last session of Congress.

Facing all these difficulties the work went on; an immense amount of valuable information was monthly gathered in, and as often compiled, published in pamphlet form, and scattered abroad, again at the rate of from 15,000 to 20,000 pamphlets per month. Now, as farmers are beginning to see what is being done, and to understand the object and utility of these circulars and reports, so great is the demand for them that it would exhaust an issue of 50,000 a month. Wherever they go they prove perfect "exterminators" of those "speculators," whose success in "fleecing" the farmer is based on his ignorance and consequent credulity. By these reports the farmer sees at once the state of the various crops throughout the country, and, as the condition and prospects of foreign crops and markets are also given, a little intelligence as to the relations of supply and demand will make him as wise as the speculator.

Extensive correspondence has been entered into with our Consuls in every part of the globe, and with the most satisfactory results. As soon as the system is perfected, regular returns will be received from them in regard to the crops and markets of all countries with which we have commercial relations, and the weights, measures, and currency of which will be reduced to the American standard, so that they may be as readily understood by our farmers as the reports of our own country papers are.

When their reports for last September appeared, there was an instant rise in the price of corn, because a glance at those eloquent statistical tables showed accurately the amount of injury done to it by the frost in every State; and happy was the farmer who had the knowledge before the speculator had him! In these circulars and reports every branch of farming interest is considered—cattle, horses, hogs, wool, etc., receiving the same attention as the immediate products of the soil—altogether forming a most complete synopsis of the agricultural history of our country.

It is not necessary here, interesting though it might be, to explain the formation of these valuable statistical tables, the basis on which the calculations are founded, or the method by which their accurate results are reached. These are fully explained in the Commissioner's report before referred to, and will be found as plain and simple as they are satisfactory.

There is a certain class of farmers, the race is happily dying out, but is not yet quite extinct, who are slow to believe that a man with intelligence enough to hold a pen or write an article for the press, can by any possibility be their friend or have a wish to promote their interest. Too ignorant, and often willfully so, to appreciate the dignity of their calling, they are suspicious of intellect in any shape, but more especially so when it appears in "book form," or tries to approach them through the columns of a newspaper. There are some such men in Michigan, or were a few years ago, who welcomed the wool speculator and quietly allowed him to blind their eyes with one hand while he took off their fleeces with the other, against the urgent protest and remonstrance of a paper earnestly devoted to their interest. Doubtless the same men, if living, would pursue the same course now, and be as distrustful of the efforts of this department for their benefit, as they were of their own State advocate; and reap in the end, as they did then, the satisfaction of being able to say they had their own way and would show that they were not to be driven or coaxed out of it by any of the book-farming gentry. These men, however, will soon kill themselves, or by force of circumstances gradually emerge from their chrysalis shell into a more enlightened state of existence.

Farmers who are worthy of the name are fast taking rank with not only the intelligent, but the intellectual and accomplished men of the age. With such no word need be wasted in pointing out the peculiar local as well as the general benefits that must accrue to the country from a system like that now initiated by the statistical bureau of the Department of Agriculture. It is not claimed to be perfect yet, but is determinedly working its way to perfection; and even in its present state, with limited facilities, and with difficulties to encounter which cannot be enumerated here, the results already reached, in the amount of information gathered in, and the accuracy of the calculation based upon that information are gratifying and satisfactory beyond all anticipations of its originators.

Now it only remains with the farmers to help the work on, and this they may do with all courage and confidence, being assured that they have men here who are working for and with them hopefully and heartily. Do they ask what is to be done first? The reply is, in the words of your flaming advertisements, "Send for a circular."

When you answer the inquiries in the circular, send in also such other information connected with them as you may think will be of either local or general value; thousands of others will do the same from their several localities, and a condensed report of all will come back to you—not a bulky volume of book-worm theories and visionary speculations—but a neat pamphlet in clear type, every page of which will bear evidence of its origin among working and thinking men like yourselves. In the words of the report for November last: "The aim of the Department has been and will be to aid the farmers of the country in the advancement of their business, and to give them greater information of the productions and resources of this great country." Sustain it, then, and co-operate with it if you would honor your calling and have it keep pace with the progress of the rest of the world.

L.

Note.—The Department, having ascertained that to publish their report monthly does not give time for the returns of correspondents to come in, will hereafter issue it only once in two months. Too many and too important interests now demand attention to prevent their being properly prepared in so short a time as heretofore. The circulars will be issued at the beginning of the month, and be returned near the close of it, to give time to obtain all desired information.

February 9, 1864, page 4

Our Washington Letter

The Museum of the Department of Agriculture

From Our Own Correspondent
Washington, February 1, 1864

One of the most interesting features of the present organization of the Department of Agriculture, and one closely connected with the interests to be promoted by the experimental garden, is the collection of entomological plates and facsimile fruits, now being placed on exhibition in the rooms.

The reader, remembering the description given of these rooms in the first letter of this series, may well ask where, in their limited space, and among the desks, tables, and crowded clerks, place for such an exhibition, or for the visitors who will inevitably be attracted by it, can be found. The plates hanging against the wall of course occupy but little space that would be available for other purposes, but for the purpose designed, they are far from being advantageously placed, most of them being so high, and the light so bad, that it is difficult to distinguish a grasshopper from a butterfly, and quite impossible, without the aid of a microscope, or some sort of glasses, of very high magnifying power, to read the reference figures and explanations.

To find room for the long and necessarily cumbrous cases, containing the artificial fruits and other articles, is a much more troublesome business. This collection is but just now being brought in, but a small portion of the whole being yet on exhibition. Tables, desks, clerks, and piles of books, have been crowded into more compact masses than was thought possible, and the little space thus cleared is now occupied by cases, through the glazed sash covers of which the artist's beautiful imitations of nature can be seen. As for the visitors "coming to see," they must find room where they can.

As a knowledge of the science of entomology is becoming as necessary to successful fruit growing as the science of grafting or budding, it is the design of the Department to gather here all the information possible on the subject, and to have this division superintended by a practical entomologist who shall be on hand to answer all questions, whether verbal or written, in regard to the name, nature and habits of insects injurious to fruit or vegetation, and the best means for their extirpation. For this purpose the services of Mr. Townsend Glover, late of the Maryland Agricultural College, have been secured. Mr. Glover seems to be on the most familiar terms with nature, is well acquainted with all her moods and phases as developed in her various creations; is a naturalist of the most natural order; an entomologist by instinct; an accomplished botanist, and withal is gifted with the exquisite artistical taste and mechanical genius by which he can so closely imitate her works as to deceive even the most observing. Among other evidences of his art here, are manufactured toads, frogs, turtles, fishes, etc., perfect to the life, even to the peculiar crook of the toad's leg, the number and color of the warts upon his back, and the curves of his toe nails. People looking at them almost universally pronounce them perfection, or preserved specimens of the real animal.

But for the farmers, and those more especially interested in fruit-raising, the most valuable portions of this collection will be the entomological plates, with their explanations, and the beautiful specimens of facsimile fruits and vegetables. These last, ornamental and attractive as they are, have in view a higher object than the mere display of the artist's skill, in showing the degrees of perfection to which nature brings her work. The fruits, particularly, when all brought together, will be so classified and arranged that one may see at a glance the changes produced upon the same species by difference of climate and soil, and the various modes of cultivation. For instance, there is a perfect specimen of the Baldwin apple, as it grows in Massachusetts, another showing the change it undergoes on the banks of the Hudson, and a third showing a still greater change by its cultivation in the orchards of Indiana. Every variety of apple known finds its representative here, perfect in size, shape, color, and weight. From originals gathered from every part of the country where apples grow, Mr. Glover has made these exact copies, and so far as the space allowed him will permit, has them systematically arranged, numbered, named, and labeled.

The same order, with the same object in view, has been observed with all other kinds of fruit grown in this country. His collections of pears and plums is especially beautiful. The pears look in truth as if they would melt in your mouth—they are so perfect in every hue and tint and speck; the texture, stem and eye all persuading you that they have but this moment been gathered from the tree. The plums have the delicate bloom yet upon them, only broken here and there by the tips of the fingers that took them from the branches. And so with the examples of all other fruits, each being perfect according to the pattern given by nature.

These fruits are not wrought out of wax and having a regard only to the outward appearance of similarity; they are made of a composition prepared by the artist for the purpose and cast in molds of which the fruits themselves have formed the perfect pattern. They are made the exact weight of the fruit they represent, and are tinted to life by the most delicate touches of art.

Not only perfect specimens, but imperfect ones are here—apples with knots and spots, disfigured plums, and pears cut open to show how they rot at the core. It is intended to investigate the diseases, as well as to show the beauty and variety of these productions. The diseases of the trees also receive attention—and by specimens of barks and branches of injured or unhealthy ones, efforts will be made to show the nature of the injury or disease, and, if possible, point to a remedy.

Utility is on every page of the book from which this Department takes its lessons, and, in obedience to the teachings of which, it is striving to do its part towards making the world wiser and better. With the very limited means at its command, it has already laid a broad foundation for future usefulness. It has surveyed the ground and scattered some seed. That even this had been imperfectly done, perhaps none are better aware than the officers themselves, but they have the consciousness of knowing that, considering all things, they have done the best they could, and with even better results, in many respects, than could have been anticipated.

It is their design, as soon as sufficient room for their purpose can be obtained, to establish a complete fruit and vegetable museum, where specimens of all can be seen in their different stages of growth and development, as affected by change of soil, climate or cultivation. Such a collection of fruits alone, correctly named, would be of incalculable value to the pomologists of our country. Those now on exhibition are private property, belonging to the artist who made and has charge of them, but who, it is understood, proposes to sell them to the Government.

In connection with this fruit and vegetable museum, it is designed to have on hand seeds, plants, or cuttings of all the perfect ones, for public distribution. Thus, a man, by stating the nature of the climate he lives in, and the soil he wishes to cultivate, can see at once to what degree of perfection the plants or trees he desires will attain there, and can make his selection of such as are most suitable.

It is proposed also to have an ornithological museum, containing specimens of all birds in any way related to the farming or fruit interests of the country, either by the good or the harm they do, attached to the above named collection. Mr. Glover is already engaged in gathering and preparing birds for this purpose.

Thus, having stated as definitely as a limited personal observation and a brief acquaintance with the Department would permit, its present condition, its prospects, desires, and aims, it is proposed to conclude this series of letters by giving in the next a brief personal sketch of the men to whose care all these great interests are confided.

L.

February 13, 1864, page 4

Our Washington Letter

The Department of Agriculture | Pen Portraits of Its Principal Officials

From Our Own Correspondent
Washington, February 5, 1864

Aside from the intrinsic merits of any great enterprise, nothing perhaps conduces more to a general interest in its workings and success than a general knowledge of those who have it in charge. And next to having seen a man one's self, is as good a description of him as can be had from those who have seen him. The outlines here given of the chief officers of the Department of Agriculture may not convey a very definite idea of their personal appearance in regard to features, etc.; the sketches must necessarily be brief, and the design is merely to show what sections of the country they represent, and what manner of spirit they are of.

Hon. Isaac Newton, Commissioner of this Department, is as seems very appropriate, a representative of the Keystone State—a sturdy Pennsylvania farmer, earnest, zealous, and untiring in his efforts to perform to the utmost the duties imposed upon him by the position he occupies. He is intimately identified with the origin of the Department, and its friends may be sure that his best endeavors will be used to promote its success. He is a worker himself, and has shown excellent practical judgment in selecting working men for his assistants in office. Mr. Newton is a man of mature years, of portly form, benignant countenance and fatherly presence; showing, withal, in the compressed lips and frequent contraction of the shaggy eyebrows, no small share of determination, and a disposition to adhere with peculiar tenacity to his own views of right.

Mr. James S. Grennell, Chief Clerk, is from Massachusetts. He is an able representative of the intelligence, industry and adaptability of the genuine New Englander. Though a lawyer by profession, he is perfectly at home in all the details and tactics of farm management and economy, having pursued that business successfully for some years in his native State. He was, from its organization up to the time of accepting his position here, a member of the Massachusetts State Board of Agriculture, and for a number of years Secretary of a county agricultural society. By these facts it will be seen that he has been educated for the place he fills as right-hand man, first counselor, and adviser to the Commissioner in all matters pertaining to the interests of the Department. Active, prompt, and energetic, yet quiet in all his hurry about the press of business before and around him, he manages to accomplish an amount of brain work of which few would be capable in such a place, so cramped for room, and with crowds of people every day coming in, all of whom he must see, and distribute to them choice seeds or reports or advice, as their wants may be.

Mr. Grennell is a slender man, apparently in the prime of life, with dark hair and whiskers, and quick, blue eyes. His ease of manner and knowledge of the world, together with his frank and genial temperament, peculiarly fit him for the position he holds.

Mr. Lewis Bollman, chief of the statistical Bureau of the department represents a still farther western interest. He is from Indiana. His knowledge of what a farmer needs is based on his own experience in that business. He was a farmer himself, and furthermore a devout believer in the power of the press, and in the necessity of having that power used for the benefit of those of his own profession. For several years he has been engaged as agricultural correspondent for Cincinnati papers, and seems well posted in facts and figures developing the relations of commerce, manufactures and agriculture.

In personal appearance Mr. Bollman, at first sight, strikes one of being very like his columns of figures and long statistical tables. You look at those lines of figures without an idea of their meaning, and you see no beauty there that you should desire to know more of them; but let their exponent run his fingers along the columns, by a few simple statements making them as eloquent as the keys of a piano under an artist's hand, and you forget at once their wiry stiffness and unpromising "first impression." As of the figures, so of the man.

Mr. J. R. Dodge, corresponding clerk and editor, comes from Ohio. He was for some time editor of the *American Ruralist,* published at Springfield in that State. He is a practical printer, and an accomplished writer, having had much experience as a Congressional reporter, and writer for the public in many ways. The volume of the report for 1862, of this Department, contains several able papers from his pen. One is a comprehensive treatise on sheep husbandry; one an article on cotton, others on flax, flax-cotton, agricultural exports, etc. He has been connected with the Department since its origin, and is one of its most active and zealous officers.

Either from the nature of his name or his occupation, it has been found difficult to get a view of Mr. Dodge, long enough to fix his portrait with any degree of definiteness. There is only an indistinct outline of a "medium height," fair complexioned, fair haired, sandy whiskered man, a little inclined toward the future as if in earnest pursuit of some good thing soon to be caught and given to the public; but it is enough to show that he may be classed among the workers in the good cause, and a very efficient one too.

Mr. Townsend Glover, the entomologist and naturalist is, as his profession entitles him to be, a thorough cosmopolite, at home in every part of the world, and on the best of terms with the insect and vegetable creations in all quarters of the globe. He was born in Brazil, South America, of English parents; was taken to England in his youth, educated in France and Germany, and has since spent many years in traveling, gathering and preparing the valuable collections he has now on exhibition in the Department. Recently he has been Professor of Entomology and Natural History in the Maryland Farmers' College, but has now taken his place permanently as one of the Department corps. Something of the value of his beautiful collection of facsimile fruits and his entomological plates may be understood when it is known that this Government several years since appropriated $10,000 for their purchase, but the money was squandered for political and other purposes before it came to Mr. Glover's hands, and he was obliged to receive the property back again. The whole should be owned by the Government and form a part of the museum by which this rather now dry Department of Agriculture will some day be illustrated.

Imagine a rather small, restless, dark, rough-bearded man, a little careless, may be, of his outward appearance, but full of genuine politeness in his address, watching with eager eyes the interest you take in what he is telling you of the nature and history of the works of his art you are admiring so, and you have as near as pen can give it the exterior of this embodiment of genius and enthusiasm. Mr. Glover is an enthusiast in his art, and seems to live and breathe through the strange and beautiful creations with which he surrounds himself. You can listen to him, but look at them.

Mr. William Saunders, Superintendent of the Experimental Garden, is a Scotchman by birth, but an American, naturalized and acclimated, and thoroughly identified with the fruit and flower-growing interests all over our country; for where are fruits or flowers grown that words of instruction from him have not also found their way? He is well known everywhere by his contributions to public journals, and by volumes he has published in relation to the above subjects. His home is at Germantown, near Philadelphia. Though well known as a writer, it is not probably so well understood by the public at large that his accomplishments as a draughtsman and landscape gardener have won for him a very high reputation. His success in this line secured for him the honor of being chosen by the Governors of the several States, interested in that memorial to patriotism, as the artist to design and lay out the grounds for the National Cemetery at Gettysburg. With State and other cemeteries of less note, his name was already associated; with this it will be honored by a nation's gratitude for the beauty his genius has thrown around that dark Aceldama, where their best and bravest sleep. Mr. Saunders, like our entomologist, is evidently all devoted to his art. Of middle age and stature, strong-limbed and strongly built, he has the appearance of a working man, and you may expect to find him with his coat off at his grape trellises, or with pen or pencil in hand, bent over his paper or draughting-board, on the little table by his office window. His complexion and voice have tinge of the old country vigor and accent, his eyes are a bluish grey, and his address and manners easy, communicative and agreeable.

L.

February 16, 1864, page 4

Life in Washington

A Lady's First Day at the Presidents

Correspondence of the *Advertiser and Tribune*
Washington, February 8, 1864

Saturdays are public reception days at the White House. From 11 till 3 o'clock all who choose can go and pay their respects to the President and his lady, pass through the room and conservatories and go on their way.

One mile west of the Capitol, directly through the heart of the city, stands the Presidential mansion. It is Saturday, the 6th of February, a chilly, cloudy day, with a lowering sky threatening rain; but let us go. Standing at the Seventh street crossing we turn our face to the east, up Pennsylvania Avenue. Look a moment; does it seem possible that we can ever work our way through that thronging, crowding mass, pouring down the broad pavement in one incessant stream? You say no, and look toward the street cars passing each way every two or three minutes, but they are full, too—crowded to suffocation; the sidewalk will be better; there, at least, one may breathe more of Heaven's breath than of their neighbors.

We are on the fashionable, north side of the avenue; but glance across—the other side is nearly as crowded as this and all the broad space between is thronged with double lines of heavy army wagons drawn by four or six mules each, and seemingly endless in each direction; squads and companies of cavalry are passing, some one way and some another; state and private carriages, rattling hacks, omnibuses, street cars and every sort of vehicle imaginable seem mixed up in inextricable confusion; the noise is deafening and the ground trembles; but everybody is hurrying on; let us pass too, if pass we may.

Soldiers are here too, in companies and singly, in every style of uniform, and most uniformly gathered in knots and platoons about the hotel and restaurant doors. There, tearing along through the crowd, come 30 or 40 little negro bootblacks, following the rattling music of a fifer and drummer who are beating up recruits for some low theater tonight; and here are elegantly dressed ladies and gentlemen, and young misses and children, with their jaunty hats and showy scarlet plumes—crowds of everybody, going and coming, and standing at corners gathered about the handsome show windows of the stores and shops. We press on, following close upon the train of those rustling silks that sweep across and dip into the filthy gutters at every crossing, and draw little waving lines of wet dust from every brimming runnel of slop-water running down from back yards and alleys. These silks are going to the President's.

Ah, now, the way is uphill, and growing tiresome. We are passing Willards, and rounding the corner of the Treasury, that immense marble caudle-cup, whose recesses we hope to explore some day, and explain to the public how that wonderful "pap" is made, on which so many Government pets get full. Now the silks have taken themselves into the cars. We go north past the Treasury, and its grounds, and then turn again to the west. All around this square on either side of the avenue the pavement is plastered with sticky mud some inches deep; but passing this we come in front of the President's grounds and find ourselves on broad, dry, granite flagstones clean and white. The avenue here runs east and west again, and the White House is on the south side some little distance from it. Between the house and the street is a semi-circular park planted with evergreens and other trees, and having a bronze statue of Gen. Lafayette in the center. Around this little park sweeps the broad graveled carriage drive, bordered on the outer side by the wide granite footwalk and passing directly under the deep colored porch of the mansion. The park and drive are surrounded and protected by high iron palings. Iron gates lead into the drive and walk which are nearly always open.

Today guards armed with swords, mounted on handsome black horses, sit facing each other just within the gates at each end of the drive, and two more are stationed directly in front of the house. Between these guards the carriages freighted with their brocades and velvets and plumes make their entrance and exit. Foot guards are at all times pacing up and down the pavement before the house. Let us go up the steps and enter the open doors. Here is a mother plainly dressed, leading her little boy of ten to whom she is telling the story of Abraham Lincoln's youth. In the vestibule a waiter stands, motioning with his hand the way for visitors to go.

President's house. From *Bohn's Handbook of Washington,* 1860.

The mother and child pass on; we follow. There is no crowd, nobody going in just now but us. Just inside the door of the blue room stands the President between two young men, and a plump, round-faced, smiling man stands opposite him. Between these two the mother leads her boy. The President takes her hand in one of his, places the other on the boy's brown curls, says some kindly words to both, and they pass on.

The same hand takes mine, the eyes look down as kindly; he bows low and says, "How do you do?" in a tone that seems to demand a friendly reply. But no reply comes. My heart is on my lips, but there is no shape or sound of words. In one glance at that worn yet kindly face I read a history that crushes all power of speech, and before I am fairly conscious that I have touched the hand and looked into the eyes of our honored Father Abraham, I find myself on the opposite side of the room. Doubtless if he had a thought about me it was, "What a stupid creature! who does not know enough to give a name or answer a civil question!"

Six months had I been in Washington without seeing the President. Six months of anxious waiting for friends whose long-promised "some day" never seemed to draw any nearer, till at last, tired of patience and friends together, I went alone. And that was the way I met him. I, who had honored him from the first moment he put his hand so firmly to the helm of our mighty ship of state, to steer her through the perilous sea of blood and strife; I, who could have knelt to touch the hand that first swept the curse from the nation's capitol, and then proclaimed freedom to all, in the name of God and humanity; I, the child of a State so loyal and true to her very heart's core that her veteran troops, almost to a man, have re-pledged themselves to stand by him till the fiery ordeal is past; I, who had sung for him, knowing he had not time to sing for himself, and had longed for the day to come when I might speak to him as well as for him—that was the way I did it!

It is late, for it has taken at least two hours' walking on the streets, to say nothing of numerous advances and retreats up and down the sweep of the semi-circle, to get resolution up to the point of accomplishing even this. There is but time to glance about us and then retire with the already departing crowd.

The blue room is a circular apartment, papered, draped, and furnished with the color from which it takes it's name. In the center, under the massive chandelier, is a white marble table, supporting a vase of rare flowers, and beside it stands Mrs. Lincoln, now in animated conversation with the ladies and gentlemen gathered about her. We need not speak to her—she will never know we have been in the room—many others come in the same way, only to look and go. Another time we shall have confidence to pay her the respect due to her station.

It is a general remark that Mrs. Lincoln, at her receptions and parties, is always dressed with the most perfect taste—always richly and elegantly, and never overdressed. Today she was robed in purple velvet; she wears a postilion basque, waist or body of the same, made high at the throat, and relieved by an elegant point lace collar, fastened by a knot of some dainty white material, in the center of which glistens a single diamond. The seams of the basque and skirt are corded in white, and the skirt, basque, and full open sleeves all richly trimmed with a heavy fringe of white chenille. The delicate head-dress is of purple and white to match the dress. It is all very becoming, and she is looking exceedingly well, receiving and dismissing her guests with much apparent ease and grace. Mrs. Lincoln is short in stature, plump, and round favored, with a very pleasant countenance.

But the President with his attendants has already left the room; the guests are fast departing; the conservatory doors are closed; we pass out with the rest, and pass a resolution to make better use of the next reception day at the White House.
L.

February 22, 1864, page 4

Sketches in Washington
THE GOVERNMENT PRINTING OFFICE

> From Our Own Correspondent
> *Washington, February 16, 1864*

Away near the northeast corner of the city of Washington stands an old brick building, about as handsome and attractive in its outward appearance as a country jail usually is, with no enclosure, and with unpainted and weather-stained walls, and long rows of dingy, gloomy looking windows, it is the last place one would be likely to visit, either to seek for pleasure or to gratify curiosity. The only signs of life apparent about the place, looking at it from the street, are the quick, incessant jets of steam puffing from the little pipes along the roof; but as you draw near the tremble, the buzz, and roll of heavy machinery may be felt and heard. The building is 280 feet long, 60 feet wide and four stories high. It is an unpromising subject, viewed outwardly. On the north side are two small doors, some distance apart. We enter one, and having found the superintendent, J. D. Defrees, Esq., and assured him that we are not applicants for work, he is at our service with the most devoted attention, for a survey and explanation of the institution under his charge.

Nearly the whole ground floor of this great building is used for a press room, only a small apartment being partitioned off at one end, where the drying frames and hydraulic presses are, and a corner stairway in another, leading to the regions above.

In this large room are 42 printing presses, all at work, and throwing off the printed sheets with all the rapidity that steam can communicate through the countless belts and wheels and gearings, which make the ceiling literally alive with their whirring and buzzing. Down one side of the room are Hoe's cylinder presses, ranged as close as they can stand; down the other are Adams' presses, and between these rows, and in corners, wherever they find room, are little jobbing presses, but at the west end is the king of them all—Hoe's four-cylinder book press, which is, excepting for the one used by the *Harpers* of New York, the only one of the kind in operation in the world. This press was constructed expressly for the government, and on it the stereotyped book work is done, the stereotype plates being formed to fit the cylinders, and four impressions coming off at each revolution, or about twenty-five thousand as a day's work of ten hours.

All the presses are fed by girls. There is a foreman who has charge of the room, and one is employed for every two presses, but all the feeding is all done by girls— one to each Adams' press, two to each of the common cylinders, and four sit at the king's feet to wait upon him. They are paid by the week, $7 each.

On the floor above is the compositors' room, occupying the same space as the press room, small apartments being partioned off at one end for the superintendent's office, clerks, and proofreaders. Here, from 175 to 200 compositors are constantly employed, and the whole space of the great room is occupied by them and their stands, cases and various etceteras belonging to the trade. No women or girls are to be seen in this department.

On the third floor is the folding room. Here the work is mostly done by women. Long double rows of them are seated at low tables, busy with the piles of printed sheets before them, many of them wearing long leather gauntlet gloves and having queer newspaper caps on their heads. A number of folding machines worked by steam and attended by girls, are also in use here, and the whole broad chamber is like a beehive with its crowded and busy occupants and machinery.

Still above this is the bindery, where the folded sheets go through all the processes necessary to fit them for the library. There are machines for cutting the book covers, and machines for trimming, lettering, ruling and many other operations. But few girls are employed in this room. The work is mostly heavy and requires strong and steady hands.

The steam boiler, fire works, and so forth are in a small building apart from the main one, the steam for the machinery and for warming the rooms being communicated through pipes. Attached to the main building, in the rear, is the storeroom for paper where immense packages are piled up or in process of preparation for the press. Near this is the workroom with furnace and fixtures for repairing any part of the presses or machinery of the establishment that may be broken or out of order; and in a small room above, the stereotyping is done. The apparatus for this last, however, does not belong to the government, but is only employed when required, which is not to any great extent. For engraving, lithographing, electrotyping, and some other processes incident to book printing, no provision has yet been made here, and such work is done by contract in Philadelphia, and other Eastern cities. All the paper used here is furnished by contractors from the Eastern and Northern States.

Six hundred hands are in constant employ in this establishment, 250 of whom are girls. Of these last, those who do other work than feeding the presses are paid by the piece, or according to what they earn. Ten hours is a day's work, but often the whole building is lighted up and the machinery in motion till 12 and 1 o'clock at night.

It is not three years yet till the 4th of March next, since the present system of doing the public printing was adopted. Before that, as is generally known, this work was all let out by contract, and very fat jobs the contractors made of it, putting hundreds of thousands into their own pockets for which no equivalent was rendered to Government.

The law making the change was passed during the last session of Congress before the present administration, and in March 1861, the Government took the whole business into its own hands, purchased the building, appointed a Superintendent, and set men and machinery to work under him. The result has been, as shown by the Superintendent's report, an annual saving to the Government of about $200,000.

Since the beginning of the war the amount of public printing has increased enormously, and the building and fixtures, though occupied to their utmost extent, are too limited in capacity and power to do all that is required.

The character of the printing and binding, in material and workmanship, is superior to that furnished under any system which has preceded the present; and the experiment of the Government doing its own work, both as regards its quality and the economy of its cost, may be regarded as completely successful.

L.

February 29, 1864, page 4

From Washington

Opening of the Great Fair at the Patent Office

From Our Own Correspondent
Washington, February 23, 1864

Washington celebrated the birthday of its great namesake in a very appropriate manner. The 22nd was the day set apart for the inauguration of the grand Fair got up by the ladies for the benefit of the Christian Commission and the families of the District volunteers. Although quite a little army of soldiers, clerks, and others, officered by the lady managers had been at work on the decorations of the hall, all was not yet quite complete when the hour for admitting the public arrived, but amid the blaze of splendor that everywhere met the eye, these little deficiencies were quite unnoticed.

The hall itself is the grandest place that could have been selected for such an exhibition. It is in the third story of the Patent Office building, on the partially finished and unoccupied north side, and is 300 feet in length by 75 feet wide, and high in proportion. The floor is of marble, and the walls, though yet unplastered, have been so wreathed and draped with evergreens and the national colors, that scarcely a blemish is visible. Down the center and along each side, stands, booths, bowers, and fairy-like arbors are ranged, all brilliant with the "red, white, and blue," draped, festooned, and bound and blended with the twining wreaths of evergreen. These booths and bowers all bear appropriate mottoes, and are all filled with the beautiful and tempting things that Fairs are made of, with pleasant-faced ladies adding still stronger temptations for visitors to invest in the great charity scheme. The hall is warmed by registers, and well lighted with gas, and presents by night a scene of bewildering beauty and dazzling splendor.

At the extreme west of the hall a handsome stage is built up, at the back of which is a large brazen shield, from which spears and lances radiate like sunbeams, bearing on their points small crimson pennons, while behind them flash the everywhere present stars and stripes. The front of this stage is handsomely draped and festooned, like everything else, with red, white and blue, and evergreens fashioned in various symbolic forms. On each side of the front is a splendid stand of arms, surmounted by armor and an ancient plumed helmet, and intertwined with evergreens.

It was expected that Edward Everett would have been here to deliver the opening address, but he did not come, and his place was very happily supplied by the Hon. L. E. Chittenden. The vast hall was crowded almost to suffocation long before the speaker was announced, and the passing time was somewhat enlivened by the martial music of the band present.

A little before eight, a general buzz and clapping of hands went through the crowd, and it was whispered that the President was coming up the hall. Very soon, accompanied by his son Robert, the Rev. Mr. Sunderland, Hon. B. B. French, and other gentlemen, he passed through to the rear of the stage, came upon it and quietly took his seat on a sofa in one corner, with his son beside him. Prayer was offered by Mr. Sunderland in a most fervent and patriotic spirit, after which Mr. Chittenden was introduced. His address was of considerable length, but so earnest, patriotic, and eloquent, that it was listened to throughout with rapt attention, the audience frequently showing their hearty approval by sincere and merited applause. After the address, the Hon. B. B. French, Commissioner of Public Buildings, read an original poem on the occasion of the present gathering and exhibition. It was also radically patriotic and anti-slavery in its tone, and was loudly applauded by the audience.

When Mr. French retired there was a universal clapping of hands for the President to come forward. It continued so long and so earnest that several gentlemen on the stage went to him to persuade him to gratify the general desire; but it was some moments before he would allow himself to be moved at all, and when he did rise and come forward, it was evidently with very great reluctance. He was looking extremely pale and worn, but smiled good-naturedly as he remarked that he thought the Committee who had invited him to be present had practiced a little fraud upon him, as no intimation had been given that he would be expected to say a word. He was unprepared for a speech, and felt that after the eloquent address and poem to which the audience had listened, any attempt of his would be a failure; besides, from the position he occupied everything that he said necessarily went into print, therefore, it was advisable that he should say nothing foolish. (Laughter and applause, and a voice, "Nothing foolish ever comes from our President.") It was very difficult to say sensible things. In speaking without preparation he might make some bad mistake, which, if published, would do both the nation and himself harm. Therefore, he would only say that he thanked the managers of the fair for the persevering manner in which they had prosecuted the enterprise for so good an object, and with this expression of his gratitude, he hoped they would accept his apology and excuse him from speaking.

He then retired to his seat amidst the hearty applause of the multitude. Soon after this the benediction was pronounced, and the President and his party withdrew. There was music by the band, and some singing on the stage afterward, and the hall was filled till midnight and after by the crowds who on this first day of opening came more to see than to buy.

One of the most attractive features among the decorations at this fair, is a miniature representation of Gen. U. S. Grant's headquarters at Chattanooga. Near the center of the hall a space some 14 feet square is inclosed, and within are built up two little mountains of rock work, mosses, and branches of evergreen. On the top of one mountain is a fort, with soldiers, cannon, and everything complete; on the other a lookout; a rustic bridge spans the gorge between them, and at the bottom of the gorge is a small body of water with a boat and ducks on its surface; and along its banks and scattered among the rocks are turtles, cattle, goats, and birds, as like as life. A winding gravel road runs from the fort to the lookout, and heavily laden wagons are ascending the heights of each mountain. On the low ground beneath the foot and protected by it, is a rustic building, with the name "U. S. Grant" over the door. Around the whole enclosure slender columns with evergreens springing up, from the tops of which light arches meet over the center, forming a sort of airy dome. Altogether it is very beautiful and draws crowds of admirers.

As a sort of side scene some enterprising ladies have got up a representation of a New England kitchen a hundred years ago. Here several hoopless dames may be seen in petticoat and short gown, with high-crowned cambric caps and other evidences of antiquity; one is spinning at the big wheel, another at the little one; one winding yarn from old-time swifts, one carding; young girls churning, knitting and paring apples; visitors coming in with their antique calash sunbonnets; the fortune-teller in her red cloak and hood, the circulating snuff-box, strings of dried apples along the wall, the wooden mortar and pestle and iron candlesticks on the chimney-piece, old-fashioned pitchers and pewter dishes on the dresser—all are there, and the identical old fire-place, that some of us may remember, with the pot hanging from the crane, and the fore-stick burned in two. It all seems very well done except the talking. When people here attempt Yankee talk, they slide down at once into the negro slang, which is quite another thing. However, the New England kitchen at the Washington fair promises to be a very attractive and remunerative feature.

L.

March 11, 1864, page 4

Life at the Capital

WASHINGTON DUST | A DUSTY VIEW FROM THE CAPITOL | STREET SCENES ON GAL(E)A DAYS

From Our Own Correspondent
Washington, March 1864

Washington has peculiarities aside from being the National Capital, which entitle it to the notice of correspondents. The one which often presents itself most palpably to the senses is the dust. It may be thought that this is no peculiarity; that dust is common wherever earth and wind are; and so it may be, but not Washington dust. This is a specialty; an article manufactured expressly for the latitude, longitude, altitude, and possibly, the turpitude of Washington. It is a dust that no sprinkling can lay, and no pavements can bury from sight; only a general down-pouring from the floodgates of heaven can unite the warring, rebellious particles into that boundless and bottomless conglomeration called mud, which here is also a specialty, no other city producing it to such an extent, and of such remarkable tenacity as Washington.

The dust of Washington is no invisible, impalpable, unsmellable, tasteless, noiseless creation, born of the coquettish dallyings of vagrant zephyrs with the fragile daughters of mother earth, lingering at street corners and in by-paths of unfrequented parks. No, indeed; it is the full-grown, boisterous offspring of that old stormer Boreas and mother Earth herself; and never before did child "take after" both parents in such a remarkable manner. You have only to shut your eyes, and it is the king of storms himself, sweeping down his mighty pathway with sounding wings, invisible to mortals; open them, and it is earth rising up boldly to meet you, rubbing her gritty cheeks against your own, pouring her very being into yours through nostrils, eyes, and ears, penetrating through all your garments, filling your hair and all the pores of your skin till you are literally a living exemplification of the poet's image, "Earth to earth and dust to dust." You look and feel more like a walking molehill than a man.

Washington people do not pretend to recognize each other on dusty days. Senators, contrabands, and the civilized classes are all on an equality then; all apparently made of the same material—clay, and common, yellow, potter's clay at that; all look, and smell, and feel of the earth, earthy. It is said that at such times many housekeepers have in their halls a servant standing ready with a basin of suds and scrubbing-brush and towel, and that all who enter must submit their faces to the ordeal of soap and water before they can be recognized or allowed to go into the presence of the family.

But to have what a Yankee would call "a realizing sense" of what a dusty day in Washington is, one should go to the Capitol and take a view from one of the highest western windows overlooking the whole city and Georgetown and the heights beyond. As the wind comes sweeping over these heights and down the Georgetown streets, it is gathering an immense volume of dusky blackness, which swiftly rolls up mountain high, stretching its threatening wings far around the rim of the broad basin in which Washington lies, and then instantly swooping down upon the doomed city, burying every vestige of it from sight as completely as if it had never been. It is a mingling of earth and heaven; the whole blue space to the very zenith is choked up, the sun is blinded and the sky lost to sight. But the furious winds will not let it rest; they sway and swirl, and toss, and scatter it till dim outlines of steeples and chimneys at the right, the towers of the Smithsonian and the spectral form of the great monument at the left become visible; and lo, as you are looking to see where the streets shall appear, what wrecks these warring elements have made in them, another sahara, higher, darker, and swayed and torn by fiercer winds, comes pouring down, literally burying every vestige of man and his works from sight. And thus they come, hour after hour through the whole twenty-four, and some times forty-eight, without a breathing place between.

And what do you think the poor mortals down below and in the midst of all this blinding storm are doing? Will they shut themselves within doors till it is past? Why should they? The wind and dust are within as well as without. Through loosely hung doors and rattling windows they pour, and revel on velvet carpets and among lace and silken draperies. From basement to garret, from the gritty dishes on the dinner table to the dust covered pillow on which you would lay your head, it is all about the same, in doors and out, dust, dust, dust.

No; Washington does not shut itself up and fold its hands just because the wind blows and the dust flies. It goes on with its business the same as ever, though comical disarrangements are sometimes made in its affairs. There are twistings of spires, uprooting of houses and inappropriate changing of side-boards. Here is a shanty converted into kindling wood, and there two fine hacks, with horses attached, are taken up bodily and thrown bottom side upwards in the gutters; here is a woman struggling to double a street corner in the face of the gales, her crinoline catches the wind, or, rather, the winds catches the crinoline, pulls and strains and wrings it, till the fastenings give way, when lo, a skeleton falls to the ground, and the relieved lady goes on her way rejoicing, while a sable contraband of the masculine persuasion steps into the patent spiral, draws it up carefully, fastens it about his waist, and marches on solemnly behind her.

Exhibitions of this sort are not infrequent at any time of the year, and though winter is usually regarded as the gay season, Washington has its gal(e)a days the whole year round. People who have had experience of a few of these days can easily understand why Congressmen are so unequal sighted—sometimes clear and discerning, and at others so blind as to run their heads against the great pillars of the capitol as if they were straws to be pushed out of the way, in their own ambitious zeal to reach the highest pinnacle. Blinded by Washington dust, they might run a tilt against the Goddess of Liberty herself, and could scarcely be charged with "malice aforethought" if found on her pedestal when the storm was over, and she prostrate at its foot with broken neck. Doubtless the verdict of a Coroner's jury, in case of such an event, would be, "Died of Washington dust."

L.

March 22, 1864, page 4

Life at the Capital

RELICS OF THE OLDEN TIME

    Correspondence of the *Advertiser and Tribune*
    Washington, March 17, 1864

Among the ancient laws yet in force in the nation's capital is one which gives a landlord the right of seizure upon any goods or chattels to whomsoever belonging, that may chance to be found in the house occupied by a tenant neglecting or refusing to pay rent. This law in a city where a great majority of the inhabitants are tenants and boarders or lodgers, and where rents are so enormously high and tenants somewhat of a transient class and not always responsible, is the occasion of some curious serio-comic acts in the various dramas of domestic life. An innocent couple quite oblivious to the risk, established themselves in handsome rooms without making any inquiries into their host's title to the premises. They have come to Washington "for the season," and of course had a well assorted wardrobe. Returning from a pleasure excursion one day they found their rooms with all the contents in possession of officers, and their well-filled trunks, wardrobe and all, went at auction to pay a delinquent and absconding tenant's rent.

    In another instance, unfurnished rooms were taken and handsomely fitted up with carpets, pictures, and other etceteras to make a cheerful home for a newly appointed $1,200 clerk and his wife and daughter. The latter, in anticipation of "coming out" while the city was thronged with fashionables, was provided with an outfit for the occasion; and altogether rather an expensive style of living was entered upon, considering that all available capital at command was invested in preparations, and only the meager monthly salary remained for future contingencies. The house was in possession of a female sharper who had by some means evaded paying her rent regularly; and at length, having secured the first month's pay of her lodgers, besides receiving considerable sums from transient boarders, she was missing, and all the furniture and finery of the unfortunate clerk and his family went to pay his rent bill. The descent to more humble lodgings and fare was rather sudden, and the grand coming out has been deferred to another season, but a lesson was learned in regard to the ways of the world at Washington, that will probably not be soon forgotten.

It is not an unfrequent sight to see boarders and lodgers who are sharp enough to suspect or discover when all is not right, suddenly packing trunks and transferring them together with other loose property to some neighbor's rooms until the danger of confiscation is passed. This law is a relic of English supremacy in the old colonial days, and like many other fossil relics is preserved among the archives at the national capital.

In the matter of currency, too, Washington still clings to the old fashioned "levy," a contraction for eleven pence, and sells its groceries and dry goods for so many "levies" the pound or yard. In many respects it might be called the fossil city, so pertinaciously does it cling to old customs and ways of living and doing. Very little of the beauty or convenience of architecture as adapted to the wants of a progressive age in modern cities, can be found here. Dwellings that were built under the slave dynasty were constructed especially with a view to giving full play to nerve and sinew, and developing to the utmost the muscular power of the chattels on whose shoulders the housework fell. Kitchens were made as far as possible from where the results of the labors performed were wanted, and everything needed in the kitchen was most ingeniously stored as far from it as the limits of the owner's possessions would allow. Water for household uses was not to be had short of a half hour's journey to some distant hydrant or street pump, from whence it was "toted" in buckets borne upon the chattel's head, that being the only use it was supposed could be made of its brains.

Since the annexation of the District of Columbia to the republic of the United States, and the consequent influx of the civilized races of the North and West, the premises of the aforesaid chattels being made vacant by law, the former owners have shrunk into them and now gather their revenue from their rent-roll and the pockets of boarders and lodgers, instead of from the multiplication of pickannies as aforetime. All the inconveniences of their ill-arranged quarters bear upon their own shoulders now, but instead of seeing it in a proper light and with the will to remedy former errors, they blame it all upon the "Lincoln Administration," and claim that this meddling with their domestic affairs was small business for the President and his Cabinet. They are stout believers in the "let alone" policy, and feel their chivalrous pride terribly shocked at having to conform in any measure to the wills of these Northern innovators. They love their pride, but they love money better; so they soothe the irritation of the former by abundant salvings of the latter. Green salve has long been noted for its superior soothing qualities, and is peculiarly efficacious when applied to proud flesh of the sort here found.

One man, who had large possessions in Ethiopia, and many personal investments therein, of various tints and hues, foresmelling the rat that was to eat his malt, if kept in that shape, ran them to the Southern market, and soon transformed the price they brought into houses and lands in Washington. He is now the owner of some 50 houses, all of which are rented, and bring him in from $50 to $75 and $100 per month each, some even more. Yet so resolute is he not to submit to have hired help in the place of slaves, that he shuts himself and his wife into the back rooms of their house, makes her do all their work, will receive no company because he can have no slaves to wait upon them, and sanctifies to himself his sordid misery and exclusion from the world by piling curses on the unsuspecting heads of the powers that be. The "one great war of life" with him now is, that the street pump is out of his wife's reach. He has still too much of the old chivalric pride to send her with a bucket some two or three streets away for water, and too much of the fossilized nature to go himself, or with his vast wealth provide a way for having it brought to his own door; yet water they must have, so his shivering, shriveled form may often be seen at corners where he stands to hail unemployed urchins, and chaffer them down from two pennies to one on the bucket full to be brought.

Others, a little less exclusive, and more gracious, quietly retire to kitchens and back parlors, and give up the other rooms to lodgers, not, as they modestly aver, that they have any need of the revenue therefrom, but simply because having no slaves, and being unable to find other help that may be depended upon they cannot entertain the company that would otherwise throng their house. In genuine pity to friends, they turn them into the street, and fill their room with strangers.

Thus, what was once "high life" here, goes "below stairs" of its own accord, and probably may vanish away altogether, under pressure of the stronger, truer life, that is pouring in with its work-day energy, and fearless, self-sustained individuality.
L.

March 25, 1864, page 4

Life at the Capital

A Lament For The Past | Common People | Our Modern Hercules | Southern Fine-Ladyism Illustrated | The Change Progressing | Spirit of the Day

From Our Own Correspondent
Washington, March 21, 1864

No better evidence of the progressive regeneration of the capital need be asked for than is found in the pitiful lamentations of that class who in heart still cling to the ancient regime—the few, comparatively, who yet remain to bewail the downfall of Southern supremacy at Washington.

"Ah," said one of these lady Jeremiahs the other day, "It is so sad and humiliating to compare Washington now with what it was in the days of some of our former Presidents! How gay and brilliant society was in the times of Pierce and Buchanan, and others who had those aristocratic Southerners in their Cabinets, and in other high official positions here. They were such elegant men—so accomplished and gentlemanly, and their wives and daughters dressed so splendidly, and were such perfect ladies! We see nothing now of that high refinement, that grace and ease of manner, and elegance of dress that distinguished Washington society when the wives and daughters of Southern Congressmen were here. Everybody is so common-looking now. From the President down, both men and women are common, ordinary people." "Yes," said another, "how we miss the elegant toilettes and queenly graces of those Southern ladies at our receptions and on the streets. Washington does not seem itself at all. It is just overrun with the commonest kind of people, these Northern Yankees and Western rail-splitters and clodhoppers with their families, who seem to fancy that the world belongs to them, and that the White House and Pennsylvania Avenue are graced and honored by their presence. I don't suppose we shall ever have society again here as it was before the war. What a pity it is!"

Yes, indeed; what a pity it is that so much elegance and finery should have to give way before the onward march of a higher and purer civilization. What a pity that this wonderful power which wrought the work of a century in a day, which cleansed a worse than Augean stable by a single sweep of the pen, and changed the polluted ground of the national slave mart into free and happy homesteads, could not have come to the capitol in velvet drapery and satin slippers! But it is not in such garments that our Hercules wrought. He had seen too many yielding Sampsons shorn of their strength by the white-handed Delilahs they sought to propitiate. With feet that crushed the flimsy barriers set up by a false aristocracy, he measured his course to the capital, and with bare and brawny arms opened the way for the living tide that is now pouring through its heart. He seems not to have chosen his counselors for the "elegant accomplishments," and the "ease and grace of manner," which distinguished the Floyds and Thompsons of former cabinets. The "queenly ladies," who flattered and fooled and bought over to the slaveholders' interests the men in whose hands the nation had trusted its life and liberties, have gone where their luring toilets and artful blandishments are, perhaps, better appreciated than they would be among the stern, hard-handed workers and thinkers who crowd the capital now.

It is but a few years since one of these very accomplished ladies whom the forlorn toadies so tenderly yearn for, exerted her wiles to draw a Northern Senator into a snare where all her husband's threats could not drive nor all his golden baits lure him—and she succeeded. A Northern lady who knew the facts, and would have prevented the Senator's sacrifice, remonstrated with the Southern dame against such an outrage of womanly dignity and violation of principle.

"You innocent creature," was the reply; "my dignity will not suffer in the least; and, whatever I may do, we must have his vote. You understand that. As for principle, that is all nonsense; as far as I am concerned I shall use nothing stronger than flattery; your Northern Senators like that—we can lead them anywhere with it. I fancy they get very little at home, as they are so easily intoxicated by it here. They will sell their souls and seal their nation's doom for a smile. The Southern ladies do not come to Washington to display our charms and our handsome dresses to each other; and if we are gracious to your husbands and brothers, it is not without a motive. They like flattery, and we are none the worse for petting them a little, my dear."

This is a specimen of the class who have given place to the "common looking, ordinary people," the Northern Yankees and Western rail-splitters, who have so offended the eyes and ears of poor toadies yet lingering in slaveless kitchens and gloomy back parlors.

Yes, Washington is changed, or, rather, changing; for its regeneration, though well begun, is still far from complete. Let us hope the present will bequeath to the future some nobler standard of merit than mere elegance of dress. The vigorous life concentrating here has power, if rightly organized, to make this the nation's intellectual as well as political metropolis. Socially and politically, it can never again be the Washington of four years ago, or even three. Then it was politically Southern, and socially slave-ridden. Now it is politically the vital portion of our almost redeemed republic, and socially absolved from the hideous bonds that cursed it mentally, morally, and physically.

Once, and not very long since, it would have been as much as an anti-slavery man's life was worth if he dared express his sentiments openly. Now it is almost impossible for Congressional rules and etiquette to keep the galleries quiet when a senator or member advocates the constitutional doctrine that *"All* men are born free and equal"; there is an involuntary lifting of hands and a thrill of approval felt and seen as if applause were hard to restrain. In the churches where christian ministers preside, the most radical anti-slavery doctrines meet with hearty amen, and in the crowded League rooms and public halls where the once proscribed abolitionists are now welcomed, thronging multitudes shout the downfall of slavery.

On Saturday night last an immense crowd gathered at the Union League rooms in expectation of being addressed by Gen. Neal Dow, recently from the Libby prison; but as he left for the North on the evening train, Vice President Hamlin and Senator Morrill, of Maine were called to the platform. Senator Morrill made a most telling speech on the condition of the country, past, present, and prospective. His denunciation of slavery and demand for its utter extinction, were echoed with hearty shouts of approval, and the mention of the name Abraham Lincoln in connection with the coming Presidential campaign sent the whole audience wild with excitement and enthusiasm. Cheer after cheer went up, with the swinging of hats, the clapping of hands and stamping of feet, till it seemed as if the floor and walls of the building must give way to make room for the growing spirit of liberty demanding expression.

All these things are significant of the change that is being wrought by the "common people" who overrun Washington.

L.

March 28, 1864, page 4

From Washington

The Supreme Court | Portraits of the Justices | An Incident | Andrew Johnson of Tennessee

From Our Own Correspondent
Washington, March 1864

The Supreme Court is in session at the capitol. What was once the old Senate Chamber was, after the completion of the north wing and the removal of the Senatorial body, with its attendant offices, to that part of the building, converted into a court room, by dividing the larger east portion from what which forms the passage-way to the new wing. This room is oval in shape, and lighted by circular windows set in a high dome. We enter through double sets of doors, each attended by a colored porter, and find ourselves facing the dais or raised platform upon which their Honors, the Justices, will soon appear, which extends across the eastern side of the room, and is separated from the center by double railings, hung with crimson drapery. Behind the upper railing, which runs along the edge of the dais, are the 10 large chairs waiting for their occupants. Behind these chairs is a row of columns of variegated marble, with plain white Grecian capitals supporting a gallery, which today is without occupants. The center of the room is enclosed by railings, also hung with drapery, and is filled with chairs, desks and tables, for the use of those having business with the court, lawyers pleading, and so forth. Without this space, on either hand, are two rows of semi-circular, crimson-covered seats, for spectators. The wall on this side is relieved by plasters of variegated marble, and decorated with busts of the former Chief Justices, Oliver Ellsworth, John Jay, Rutledge, and Marshall. The floor throughout is handsomely carpeted. We turn to the right and take seats. As the hand of the clock over the door points eleven, the crier of the court takes his place at a desk at the south end of the Justice's platform, and the clerk, Mr. Middleton, appears at the opposite end. Lawyers and others are filling up the center space. The Patent Lock case is to argued today, and Mr. Bakewell, of Pittsburgh, has his table covered with locks of various patterns, which he is rubbing up and preparing for illustrations. Suddenly all in the room rise to their feet, and all eyes are turned towards the door at the far north end of the dais. Slowly and in stately order the venerable Justices, in their flowing black silk gowns, enter and proceed to the front of the platform; when, all standing, the crier says:

"O-yea, O-yea, O-yea; if your honors please, the court will now open."

Seats are at once resumed, and court is open for the day. While Mr. Bakewell is defending his client's rights, let us take a brief outline sketch of the *personelle* of the honorable Judges in attendance.

Hon. Roger C. Taney, Chief Justice, is too ill to be present, and his place is filled by Justice Wayne of Louisiana.

Mr. Wayne occupies a seat near the center, with three of his honorable brethren on his right, and five on his left. He is an elderly man, tall and erect; with an intellectual face, rather long-featured, and somewhat severe looking. His hair is quite gray and rolls in short curls around his head. He bends forward listening earnestly to the case before him.

Justice Nelson of New York, is next on the right. He is an old man, with hair nearly white and worn in long straight locks hanging about his neck and shoulders. His face is smooth, with rather short features and high cheek bones. He is busy with the pens and papers on the desk before him.

Justice Clifford of Maine is in the next seat. He is the youngest looking one among the nine. He is short and fat, with smooth face and dark hair, and is lying back lazily in his chair, stretching his legs, and squinting over his puffy cheeks with half-open, sleepy looking eyes. Yet he looks as if there were strength in him that could be roused if occasion required.

Justice Miller of Iowa occupies the seat on the extreme right. He is apparently a middle aged man. His face is thin and pale; he is slightly built, has dark hair and dark whiskers cut short under the chin. He is busily engaged in writing.

Judge Catron of Tennessee occupies the first chair on the left of presiding Justice Wayne. He is an elderly man, large and broad-shouldered, with a clear, good-natured face, short features, and grayish hair parted smooth and brushed till it shines with glossiness. He, too, is writing.

Justice Grier of Pennsylvania is next. He is a man of years, rather tall and large, with thin white hair above an angular and severe face. He has a pamphlet in his hand, but is bent forward listening earnestly.

Justice Swain of Ohio is next in order, a middle-aged gentleman, of medium size, with smooth, angular face, and short black hair. He is writing.

Justice Davis of Illinois is a large man with dark brown hair, and whiskers showing a slight touch of age. His attention is given to the speaker of the locks.

Justice Field of California is seated at the extreme left. He is tall, and the top of his head from front to back is entirely bald; the side hair and whiskers are dark, and he has a massive forehead and heavy brows. He seems to have no concern about what is being said, but is closely bent over his writing.

As the case before the court is not one of special interest to spectators, none care to stay beyond the opening ceremonies. We leave their Honors to their dignity, and go wandering with a friend through the handsome rooms of the Chief Clerk and Secretaries of the Senate. Here we are introduced to ex-Postmaster Bowen who relates a pleasing incident that has just transpired in connection with the great fair now being held in this city. Mr. Bowen was in the Managers' room, when a young soldier came in with a small and exquisitely modeled steam engine made by himself, and which he wished to have placed in the exhibition hall. As all articles made by soldiers and placed there are sold for their personal benefit, his name was asked in order that the proceeds of this might be reserved for him. He replied that though he had refused $120 for it, he offered it as a donation to the fair, and at the same time modestly expressed a wish that he could be transferred from the army to the navy service which would be more congenial to his tastes. Bowen at once took the model to Secretary Welles, and in a very short time the brave and ingenious young soldier received his transfer and an appointment as second engineer in the department for which his peculiar talents filled him. The model was made while in camp, of such materials as old gun-barrels and other disabled weapons of war might furnish, and is a specimen of most artistic and finished workmanship.

In the room of the Chief Clerk we have a momentary view of the patriot statesman of Tennessee, Andrew Johnson. He is a very different man, physically, from what "our fancy painted him," being only of medium stature, but well and strongly built, and younger-looking than we had supposed. May he live to see his noble State redeemed from the political and social wrongs that have oppressed it so long.

L.

March 29, 1864, page 4

From Washington

In the Senate | A Voice From Virginia | Squirming Among the Copperheads | Senator Salisbury on "Gentlemanly Instincts"

From Our Own Correspondent
Washington, March 22, 1864

Quite a stir was made among the Copperheads in the Senate today by the speech of Senator Willey, of Western Virginia. It was announced and expected that Hon. Jacob M. Howard would have the floor today for his great speech, but Mr. Willey asked the privilege of occupying an hour; Mr. Howard gave way, and the hour was extended to two and a quarter by the Virginian, which made it too late for Mr. Howard to speak, consequently he has deferred till tomorrow.

Senator Willey's seat chances to be on the Copperhead side of the house, and the heavy blows he dealt right and left soon cleared the space around him. One after another the honorable members slid away, till only Saulsbury, of Delaware, was left, and even he could not keep his seat. He paced back and forth in the space outside the semi-circular row of desks, with short, angry steps, held both hands tightly clenched under his coat-tails, and looked unutterable scorn at the back of the unconscious Senator who had the floor.

Senator Willey is not an easy speaker; he has nothing of grace of manner and eloquence of language which would attract the attention of the crowd. He is a slender man, standing rather tall and stiffly, with the sheets on which his thoughts are written held in his left hand, and his right one giving emphasis to what he says by sudden, angular strokes up and down and around about him. His speech is low but terribly earnest. He is defining his position politically, and showing why, though a Southerner, he is in favor of free institutions, free labor, and the immediate and utter extinction of slavery. Once as a slave holder he had thought the business proper enough, and had denounced any interference with or discussion of the subject as meddling officiousness; but this rebellion had opened his eyes as it had a great many others. Now he saw the opposite sections of our country in their true light—the one under free labor growing and extending its boundaries and multiplying its blessings as no other country had ever done, encouraging, and honoring mechanical genius, art, science, and literature, which in return crowned it with honor and prosperity; and the other degrading labor, cursed by a spurious aristocracy, feeding on its own vitals, brutalizing its entire population and preparing for them a heritage of perpetual degradation and shame. To substantiate his statement he quotes the opinion of such men as Washington, Patrick Henry, John Randolph, Thomas Jefferson, and others.

He described vividly, as a converted slave-holder might, the brutalizing effects of negro slavery upon the white race, reading extracts from *DeBow's Review, The Southern Literary Messenger,* and other exponents of Southern principles and practice, some of which were exceedingly classic in their expression of naked facts as well as of naked truths. This public unveiling of the image was too much for the refined sensibilities of admirers of "the chivalry," and very soon there were only empty seats on that side of the House. Powell and his friends have sought some more congenial atmosphere, Garret Davis is in close consultation with Reverdy Johnson, and Saulsbury, weary perhaps with his rapid walking, and finding that his clenched fists and angry glances are unappreciated, throws himself into his chair with his hands clasped over his head and an expression on his face that would, if it could, annihilate the still unconscious Senator before him.

The beauties of the slave-pen and the auction block were laid bare by the hand of one who knows in what their charms and attractions consist; in short, the proud descendants of "the cavaliers" had full justice done to them and their pet institution. It was a speech worthy of the young spirit of Freedom, which has already risen to such majority and strength in Western Virginia.

The subject of prejudice against color has been a good deal agitated in the Senate of late. In perfecting and getting through a bill for organizing a company for a new line of street railroads in the city, it was a serious question as to whether colored people should be permitted to use the cars in common with white people. Some quite warm discussions took place, and among others Mr. Spaulding violently opposed the admission of the colored race to the privileges of the whites. He said: "As to occupying the same seats with them, all the gentlemanly instincts of the superior race rise up in utter abhorrence of such an idea."

Senator Morrill of Maine replied to him, and after some eloquent remarks, in which he quoted the Delaware gentleman's words as often as possible, he went into statistics, giving the total number of slaves in the States, and showing how far the mulattoes and those of lighter tint outnumber the real negroes, and summed up by saying: "These facts show which way the gentlemanly instincts of the superior race are inclined." Senator Saulsbury wilted.

L.

March 31, 1864, page 4

An Incident

A WOMAN OF THE RIGHT STAMP

From Our Own Correspondent
Washington, March 26, 1864

Mrs. _____, wife of a Commissioner of one of the Government Departments in this city, was recently coming home from Baltimore, when she was accosted on the cars by a man who claimed to be a gentleman, and an acquaintance of some former member of her family. She received his overtures of friendship civilly, and entered into a conversation with him, which soon turned upon the political topics of the day. When the question of the next Presidency came up, the gentleman expressed himself strongly in favor of Gen. McClellan, and said, in very emphatic terms:

"I would give $20,000 to see McClellan our next President, and another $20,000 to defeat the Lincolnites."

This was too much for the loyalty and patriotism of the lady.

"Sir," said she, "out of respect to my friends whom you knew, I have tried to treat you politely, but now you have forfeited all claims to any such consideration. I shall not only not invite you to call upon me in Washington, but will assure you that if you venture to set your foot in my house without an invitation, my husband will kick you into the street."

The man, like a true Copperhead, then proposed conciliation, compromise, apologies, anything for peace. But no; the lady knew no such thing as conciliation or compromise with treason; and as for apologies, nothing that he could say now would have the least weight with her—he need not waste his breath, for she would accept of no apology from him. A deliberate, self-acknowledged traitor has no claims to the common courtesies of life from loyal people; and as for one who could go so far as to propose a traitor for the Chief Magistrate of the nation, she knew of no words capable of expressing her abhorrence and contempt.

The conductor and many passengers were deeply interested spectators of this little impromptu drama, and the poor Copperhead took advantage of the first opportunity to slink away out of sight and hearing. He will probably be a little more cautious in the future in advocating the claims of the heir apparent of the Democratic party. The lady should receive the thanks of all loyal people.

L.

April 12, 1864, page 4

Letter from the Capital

"Winter Lingering in the Lap of Spring" | Washington Weather | The Crocus Blossoms | Inundated Streets | Landscape Gardening | The Rainbow of Promise | Sunlight on the Flag | A Beautiful Omen.

From Our Own Correspondent
Washington, April 5, 1864

I have dated my letter, as may be seen almost in the middle of spring, away here on the border of the Southern land—the very words, Washington, April 5th, seem as though they should bear to your Northern clime bright wafts of sunshine and sweet smells of flowers; but, alas, the winds that bear you them, will have to come from deeper depths of Dixie than any that have reached us yet. Sunshine and flowers! The almanac promised them long ago, yet we have only rain, rain, rain above and all around, and mud, mud, below. Day after day through dreary March the leaden skies poured down their streams mingled with sleet and snow, only alternating now and then with drearier days when the dry hurricanes ran riot through the streets, blowing and whirling everything all ways at once. These cold, sharp, obstinate winds, meeting one like a buffet on the face when kisses are looked for, are terrible. There has been nothing like spring here yet, since the few warm days we had in February—only sour-looking, watery skies pouring down their tornadoes of wind and torrents of rain.

The crocuses in the capital grounds, poor little things, thought it was spring a month ago, and came out all gay in orange and purple and white. I went past them a few days since and they were standing up to their eyes in snow, nothing visible but a faint purple and orange glow bordering the great star-shaped beds that lay white and cold as if in the depths of a Northern winter. The poplars and maples thought spring was coming too, and put on their reception dresses of crimson and silver gray, but as if jealous winter had reached back his hand to blight them again, they stand stripped and stark, while their velvet tassels and crimson blossoms are crushed and trampled on the drenched pavements. Drenched, yes, indeed; what is there in Washington that is not drenched with this pouring rain that has been coming down day and night, night and day, as if the windows of heaven were opened and the fountains of the great deep broken up once more! The paved streets are like rivers, the unpaved ones are bottomless, sidewalks are flooded, and cellars at a discount with their floating capital of provision barrels, boxes, and drowned rats.

Today, in defiance of inundated streets and streaming elements, I went to the capitol—went out, in the first place, because floods of rain and depths of mud are preferable to the blinding smoke that contrary winds pressed down instead of drawing up the chimney of my little room; and went to the capitol because there only, in all this dreariness, are to be found glimpses of the bow of promise for better and brighter days. There, in the broad and well-kept grounds, steadily and cheerily looking upward through all this chill deluge, stand the sturdy little crocus blossoms, like rays of living light, shooting out of the dark mould; and there, in the great halls of the nation's capitol, stand steadily and true the men who, with firm courage and quiet daring, are still pointing upwards, and guiding the nation onward through the sulphurous storm clouds and bloody rain of this struggling dawn, to the perfect midsummer day of human freedom and human rights. Other gardens have their little patches of early bloom, and other hearts have hope and courage; but they are private property; these belong to the public, to all men and women, and even children, to look upon, and take heart of courage from.

What matter if the rain is pouring from the clouds, and streaming from the low-branched, leafless trees, and rushing like a river down the slant granite flagging beneath my feet? Let it pour, and stream, and rush; it is still pleasant standing here, in these western grounds, halfway from the avenue gate to the green-terraced slope from which yon marble temple rises. Under this overgrown brown parasol, and within this long, gray "water-proof," all is dry; Goodyear's patent is protection against the clear, cold element, that ripples and frets around my feet, the only obstruction it meets in its rapid descent to the street below, for the grounds and all their pleasant walks are deserted now. There is not a lounger on all the hundred seats scattered among the trees bordering the broad granite aisles; not an eye but mine looking at the steaming, sodden grass, the dripping shrubbery, and the brown star-beds, with their triple-hued rays of purple, orange, and white.

Let made-up sentimentalism sneer as it will at the formality of regular walks and primly-kept grounds, and vent its hypocritical sighs in counterfeited longings for nature, a word it does not know even the dictionary definition of; let it bewail in drawing-room phrase, and with cultivated whine, the absence of "sweet surprises," of the "natural effect" of river, rock, and forest, and simper out its silly criticisms on city made bouquets and their luckless bearers. It is well that those who can sneer at nature in any form, whether guided and trained by art or not, can command the scent and scintillations of coal and gas light when other inspirations fail. Let us have flowers if we can from whatever source, nor quarrel with them though they do come from a trim garden or a green-house instead of from western prairies or

New England's rocky slopes. Let us have them, fresh, blooming, pure, at balls, at receptions, at levees, at lectures; yes, and at the theaters. And who shall say that any place pure enough for woman to enter, can give taint or blight to the purest flower? Let those who can enjoy the wild rambles among rocks and woody dells, in search of early spring flowers. As we cannot have mountain gorges, riverside meadows, and wooded hills in our streets, let us at least have gardens, and parks, and pleasure grounds, all as well kept and well furnished as may be, with trees, and flowers, and walks, and seats, and ever-spread carpets of green.

Cast-iron seats! sneers your sentimentalist. Yes; and what would you have better? How long, think you, would rustic benches last under the experimenting knives of the many thousands of whittling Yankees strolling and lounging here through the year? No; Uncle Samuel knew too well the boys for whom he was preparing these playgrounds, to put any such temptations to vandalism in their way. They may bring their everlasting sticks here and whittle them; they may eat their oranges and peanuts here; they may lie on their backs here with their heels higher than their heads and read the newspapers; or they may sit with both hands thrust to the elbows in their trouser pockets, and "calculate" the probable difference of time between the end of the world and the finishing off of the Capitol. All these they may do, and have done for years, and the seats are intact; while, had they been of any possible whittling material, not a chip would have been left as a relic for the next generation.

How steadily the streaming rain pours down! The wind is rising, and driving in fitful gusts through the whistling branches. This shrill, wild, driving north wind! How it rolls up the heavy masses of gray rain-clouds, and hurls them over on the southern horizon! Legion after legion they rise and spread their banners in the zenith, showering down as they go the drops that are awakening earth to new life; and legion after legion pressing on to mingle in the final conflict, the great clearing-up storm of nature's and the nation's equinox. Blow on, O wild north wind, and clear the heaven above us once again! Blow, though the towers of ambition strew thy path with ruins, and the monuments of earth's once mighty ones sink and lie buried in their own dust! Yonder, above the domes on either wing of the capitol, our flag is flying—above the Senate, where fearless men and true are pressing to its final issue the question of human rights—above the House, still thrilling with the earnest eloquence of Lovejoy's silent lips—high above both, the rainbow banner floats. Not once in all this day of storms has it drooped; nor once wavered earthward; straight out from the quivering staff the north wind holds it toward the South—and lo, a sun-break in the clouds, a flash of light through all this dropping rain, God's radiant banner of the skies, ours multiplied a thousand times and translated into immortality, spans for an instant the darkened heaven, and North and South are one again! Shall we accept the omen and bless the storm through which it came?

L.

April 15, 1864, page 1

Letter from Washington

IN THE SENATE | REVERDY JOHNSON | GEORGE THOMPSON AT THE CAPITOL | AMENDMENT OF THE CONSTITUTION | SCENE IN THE SENATE

From Our Own Correspondent
Washington, April 9, 1864

The first week of April has been an eventful one at the capital. It was led off in the Senate by the Hon. Reverdy Johnson of Maryland in a noble and thoroughly anti-slavery speech; followed up in the House by the reception and speech of George Thompson of England and crowned in the Senate by the passage of a vote to amend the Constitution by inserting a clause abolishing slavery and prohibiting it in the United States henceforth and forever.

Mr. Johnson's speech was one of peculiar interest, and was listened to with more than usual attention by the Senate. It was in explanation and justification of the vote he intended to give on the amendment of the Constitution. He carefully reviewed and refuted the theories advanced by some that the power to abolish slavery lay with the Chief Executive of the nation, or that Congress had the power of enacting laws for the purpose. Neither proclamation nor acts of Congress, he said, could affect slaves not actually under the jurisdiction of the laws of the United States. Except as a war measure, Congress and the President could not move in the matter at all, and the war power conferred upon them could not be exerted against loyal States; therefore, Maryland, Kentucky, and Missouri would be slave states still, though the institution were abolished in all others. He said that whatever his previous opinions had been, he was now convinced that no permanent peace could be established without the utter extinction of slavery. Involuntary servitude and a republican government were totally incompatible; if we would save the one we must destroy the other. It was a clear, calm, logical, and truly patriotic speech, one that it did the hearts of the Republican Senators good to hear, and the stern, incontrovertible truths of which fell heavily on the heads of the few hapless Copperheads present.

Mr. Johnson is an old man with thin white hair, but with a goodly plumpness of body, a freshness of complexion and a depth and strength of voice betokening anything but feebleness, of either mind or body. His face is of an oval cast, guiltless of beard or mustache, and his eyes are remarkably prominent, in fact "pop-eyed" is the only word that can properly describe them. The expression of his face is rather sour and forbidding; he seldom smiles, or appears to let himself down upon a common social level with other mortals, preserving, apparently, a sort of stoical dignity of indifference which seems always to be saying "I am the Honorable Reverdy Johnson, of Maryland." But whether this is only in appearance or not, it is very certain the world can afford to let him look as he pleases, so long as he will give it such hopeful, encouraging words as fell from his lips on Tuesday last.

The announcement that the House of Representatives had voted the use of their hall for Wednesday evening to the noted abolition lecturer, George Thompson of England was a terrible shock to the failing and sensitive nerves of the District slave aristocracy. Alas, they said, what is Washington coming to! Not only are the rail-splitters of the West and the mudsills of the East in our White House, and in our halls of legislation, thronging our Department and swarming our streets, but here they have invited to speak in our capitol, and against our institutions, that, to us, most odious of all human compounds, an Anglo-American Abolitionist. Not many years ago he was mobbed and beaten, and driven from one city to another, and finally from the country; now he is welcomed back, toasted and honored, and taken into the capitol to consummate his triumph.

Yes, it was a triumph, and as such the friends of freedom and free speech felt it. Mr. Thompson's welcome was most enthusiastic. The lecture was given under the auspices of the Washington Young Men's Association, and though the tickets for floor seats were one dollar each, and for the galleries 50 cents, both floor and galleries were early crowded to their utmost capacity. The President and most of his cabinet, as well as many Senators and members, were present. Vice President Hamlin presided, and after a few appropriate words of introduction, presented Mr. Thompson to the audience. The prolonged and hearty cheering which greeted him as he rose, affected him almost to tears. It was some moments before he could control his emotion, or give volume enough to his voice to make it heard across the room.

Washington, the old Washington, has been fairly dazed of late by witnessing events "significant of the times"; it is beginning to understand that there are signs in these times which do not all fail, and events which mark the giant strides of progress in such a way that there can be no retracing them in the future. This event, the mere admission of the speaker to the place where he stood by the invitation of the national Representatives, was one of marked significance; and still more so, if possible, were the shouts of applause and cheers of approval breaking from that great multitude, as from one heart, and raining down from the gilded ceilings like glad omens to the doctrines of universal liberty and human rights. What a change from a few years past, and what a triumph!

Slowly and sullenly the dark clouds of barbarism are rolling away, and quick and bright the sunshine follows. Some of those long dwelling in darkness are sorely hurt and troubled by the light. It blinds and bewilders them: poor creatures, how they struggle and gasp, and stretch out their arms in vain endeavors to bring the cloud back again. Such a spectacle was witnessed in the Senate on Friday, when the resolution to amend the Constitution was before that body. Speeches had been made during the week by Senators Hale and Clark, of New Hampshire, and others, all bearing upon the great question of the amendment, and all in turn snarled, growled, yelped and whined at by Powell, Saulsbury, Davis, and McDougal. Friday, Charles Sumner spoke, and it was understood that the vote was to be taken before the Senate adjourned. Long before Mr. Sumner sat down, it was easy to see how the wrath of Powell, Davis & Co. was working, and the moment his last word was said, Powell was upon his feet, flushed, excited, angry. With all the vehemence of his portly body concentrated in his red face, and quivering, out-stretched hand, he proceeded to denounce the Senators who were so anxious to meddle with what did not belong to them; he sneered at Yankee patriotism as altogether mercenary, and multiplied taunts and invectives on Sumner's head, till his voice grew thick and hoarse, and his arms must have ached from the violence with which it cut the empty air. The honorable Senators, however, at whom he launched his thunderbolts, seemed to feel them as little as the air did his strokes. All were busy attending to little matters of their own, some writing letters, some looking over the piled-up papers on his desk, some with heads bent together, earnestly talking, some glancing over the columns of the newspapers, and not one with the attitude or countenance of a listener. Sumner now and then glanced up from his papers with a quiet smile, as much as to say, "Rave on if it please you; such words are powerless in this chamber now." And he did rave, denounce and protest till, finding he could not disturb the quiet indifference of the Senators, he dropped into his seat, and was succeeded by the mattered growlings of Saulsbury, who wanted to make compromises and peace-offerings; the piping yelps of little old Garrett Davis, who "considered that his niggers belonged to him the same as his horses did, and he wanted compensation for them," and the egotistic, whinings of McDougal, who, while glorifying himself, maintained his perpendicular with some difficulty by holding fast to the two desks between which he stood.

And so, with rage, and whine, and whimper the time wore on, and it was 5 o'clock before the vote was taken. But the Senators knew they could afford to be patient. When the yeas and nays were at last called, the resolution for the amendment passed by a vote of 37 to 6!

L.

April 19, 1864, page 4

Our Washington Letter
A Day in the Senate | Scenes on the Floor and in the Galleries | Passage of the Amendment Resolution

From Our Own Correspondent
Washington, April 9, 1864

" 'Twere worth whole years of peaceful life, / One glance at their array."

Friday, the 8th of April, was a proud day in the Senate, and a proud one for our country. It was the day on which the vote for the amendment of the Constitution was to be taken, and it was a pleasant sight to look down from the galleries upon the men who had the task in hand, and who were moving on steadily and unitedly to its consummation. The resolution has been referred to the Judiciary committee, by them thoroughly considered, and the demand of millions embodied in words approved by the committee, was now waiting the final action of the Senate before being sent to the House, and from thence to the Legislatures of the several States for their ratification.

Satisfaction, security, triumph, may be seen on almost every face in the Senate chamber today; not the mere triumph of man over man, the security based on numerical strength, or the soulless satisfaction of having gained a point simply for the defeat of an opposition. No; there is something better, nobler, grander in the faces of these men today; something that speaks of purpose based on principle, of deep and earnest thought, and self-reliant action for the right; there is a consciousness of responsibility appropriate to the occasion, and who shall blame them if they blend with this an air of confidence as they compare their position now with what it was in the long, dark, stormy days of southern rule and republican minority. They can speak now like freemen, and there is not a sneaking assassin at hand with knife or bludgeon to strike down the defenders of liberty. So Johnson and Howard and Hale and Clark and others have been speaking during the week that has passed, as so Sumner has been speaking today—speaking for humanity against the legalized tyranny of a slave aristocracy.

Is it to be wondered at that the feeble half dozen defenders of a dead faith, the few lingering relics of a once powerful class of graduates from the institution whose chief cornerstone is barbarism brutalized, should writhe under the truths they are forced to hear, should struggle as with a death agony against the mighty power that is crushing them between the ruins of their own bloody Molock? They do writhe and struggle in the impotence of their rage, and if the calm, confident giants only smile and bend to their task with still more resolute energy, can they be called merciless, unkind?

The world and the future will not call them so. Neither does the great, true heart of the present. With a warm, throbbing amen, in the name of humanity it bids them God speed, till these floors shall no longer be desecrated by the slaveholders' tread, or these walls echo back words that are libels alike on God and Man.

Such words Powell, maddened to desperation, is shouting in the ears of Senators, who hear as if they heard not, or only in the magnanimity of their approaching triumph, permit him to speak unchecked. In the same breath he boasts of what he calls "the staunch, true patriotism of the glorious Old Commonwealth of Kentucky," kills New England with a sneer, buries her with a grimace, accuses the Administration of unprecedented and unlimited corruption, tells us that this war is all for a brute race, who have not in them the elements of manhood, and that, so help him God, he will oppose now and forever every measure that would give them freedom. He raves till his face is like scarlet, and his tongue runs through all the degrees of abuse admissible in Congressional courtesy to find invectives bitter enough to vent his wrath against the Senator from Massachusetts. But sneers, taunts, mockery, and derision, are alike powerless from such a source now. His only attentive listeners are Saulsbury of Delaware who, with hands clenched under his coat tails, walks restlessly up and down his accustomed beat; Garret Davis of Kentucky who, with his little body in one chair, nurses his little feet on the cushions of another, and with a little smile on his little face, drinks in to the extent of his little capacity the wonderful words of his big brother Senator; and McDougal of California who should know better, but who sits open-mouthed to swallow all, that he may dole it out again in his maudlin way, diluted by the nauseous fumes and amber juices that scent his breath and stain his beard. These, after the speaker takes his seat, give back successively a characteristic echo of his words and sentiments.

But stay; there are other listeners, though not many now, in the galleries. A little while ago, when Sumner spoke, all these seats were full, but one by one, and dozens by dozens, the occupants have gone, all but the few scattered here and there, who are resolved to wait till dark, and after, if they must, to hear the vote. These, however, are waiting, rather than listening; for, in little groups, they are softly talking to each other; or, singly, smiling at the futile efforts of the slave-quartette below, to ward off as long as they may the blow that they know must come, and soon. But these are not all. Directly opposite us, and not far from the diplomatic gallery, is a long seat occupied by people who are evidently deeply interested witnesses of every word and act of the Senators upon the floor. They came early, were ushered into that seat by the door-keeper, and, unlike most gallery visitants, have kept their places quietly, and watched with intense and absorbing interest the proceedings of the day. They have attracted some friendly and some angry glances from below. I think Garret Davis would like to pierce them through and through with those little, stiletto-like eyes of his; and I know Saulsbury would be delighted to annihilate them with that terrible frown with which he clouds his brow when his "gentlemanly instincts" are disturbed. See how he scowls over his shoulder and compresses his lips in scorn. Do they see it, or know it, or care for it, those three men and three women in that distant seat? They are the best behaved people in the gallery today; they are handsomely and neatly dressed in black silks and broadcloths, and—their skins are almost black.

But now the pygmies have worried themselves quiet; and the giants are gathering up their strength. For the last hour they have been loitering about, apparently unconscious of the storm they had raised, or of the work yet to be done: now they come up from the corners where they had been gathered in little groups, from the side sofas where they had been stretching their limbs to rest, from anti rooms, from reading of newspapers and from writing at desks—they come, they are ready. Nearly all are standing now. The yeas and nays are called. They are no feeble, half-uttered, half-meant responses that come up and are recorded on that list of names which should be the roll of honor for the present age. There is a heart in every "aye" of the thirty-eight. The six short, sullen "noes" are as soulless as they are powerless.

The work is done, and the giants are men again, smiling and shaking hands amidst the hum and buzz of hearty congratulating voices. So we leave them.

L.

April 21, 1864, page 4

Our Washington Letter

The World After the Storm | In the House of Representatives | The Crowded Galleries | Temper of the Debate on Mr. Long's Expulsion | The Position of the Members | Portraits of Some of The Leaders in the Great Discussion

From Our Own Correspondent
Washington, April 14, 1864

The political correspondent of the *Advertiser and Tribune* will, doubtless, furnish its readers at an earlier moment than I can, the history and particulars of the past few days in the Hall of Representatives at the Capitol. I wrote you a few days since of a storm that was raging without those marble walls, of sleet and snow and driving rains, of flowers that bloomed and trees that budded in spite of all; and of the sun-break in the clouds lighting up the banners on the dome with glory in the midst of the storm. This warring of the elements without the Capitol was truly typical of the stormier times within. The winds have been blowing fiercely there, and the frozen rain of party strife has done all it could to pelt down and blight every effort that patriotism was making to match the budding bloom and promise of the spring. Now both storms are passed, and how looks the world? The sun is higher, the air warmer, and the breath of heaven purer; whole regiments of hyacinths, in true Union blue and gold have sprung up beside the green tents of the crocus pickets; the grass is starred with uniforms, and all the trees, the popular masses of the vegetable world, are tipped with crimson and tender green in token of the ever abiding principles of life and vigor, waiting but for the season to call them forth. Thank Heaven, the spring and summer come in spite of winter; and thank God the world progresses and patriotism lives in defiance of traitors.

The debate on the expulsion of Mr. Long of Ohio from the House, for expressing treasonable sentiments, has been one of exciting interest. Day after day and night after night not only the spacious galleries, but the floor of the great Hall have been crowded and packed almost to suffocation with eager, anxious listeners, while many hundreds have gone away, unable to get within seeing or hearing distance of the doors. As the sessions commence at noon, the crowd for favorite seats in the galleries would begin as early as eleven o'clock, and sometimes even earlier. By twelve, every inch of room in the five tiers of seats, extending around all sides of the great Hall, would be occupied; double lines of people would be standing against the wall, and pyramids of faces crowded the doors from the threshold upwards. The floor outside the seats of members was filled, generally with Senators and their friends. It was wonderful what order and decorum prevailed, considering the immense concourse and the excitement of the occasion; and what patient endurance sustained the interest that held them to their seats from 11 in the morning till 12 at night with scarcely one hour's intermission for refreshment or change of position.

That the occasion was one worthy of all the attention it called forth, the reports and speeches that have gone out to the world will show; but whether the world, that is the world of the United States, will approve of spending the time upon it or of the manner in which that time was spent, are questions of quite another sort. In as much as the Representatives saw fit to do as they did, it was well worth the time and pains of all who could go, to see and hear how the work they took upon themselves was done.

The discussion on both sides was characterized by far more of party feeling and party strife than was pleasant to hear; yet perhaps the nature of the case made it in a degree unavoidable. There were some noble individual exceptions, however;

some who did not bow the knee to that Baal, and some who were above the flimsy trickery of that Fourth-of-July, spread-eagle oratory, which so grates upon the ears and patience of people in these times when earnest thought and action are wanted instead of empty words.

The members of the two great political parties are separated from each other in the House, like sheep from goats, or eagles from crows, only the order from left to right is reversed. The Speaker's desk is at the south side of the Hall, and radiating from it like a spread fan are the ranges of seats for the members—the Democrats though greatly in the minority, occupy the position on the right, as they did in the days of Southern supremacy; and the Republicans are at the left of the aisle running from the Speaker's desk to the central door of entrance.

From this front seat in the gallery almost over the Speaker's head, we have a face view of every member on the floor, except, perhaps two or three who are so nearly under us that we only see the tops of their heads. Yonder on the right is S. S. Cox of Ohio, the Democratic member who has just spoken in defense of the treasonable sentiments of Mr. Long. He is a slender man, with thin black whiskers and beard, black hair, bald forehead, and physiognomy much resembling that of a fox, tapering to sharpness, and favorable for his propensity to make incessant interruptions when a Republican happens to be speaking, and his everlasting risings to "points of order." His speech has been pretty effectually neutralized by Thaddeus Stephens of Pennsylvania and he is quiet a little while for once.

Mr. Stevens sits in the fourth tier of seats on the left; he has a clean shaven face, and dark brown hair which some say has had another owner; he is looking pale from illness and the exhaustion of speaking. He is one of the most earnest and plain spoken men of his party; there is nothing of the spread-eagle or highfalutin about him; his words and manner of delivering them are sincere, earnest, and to the point. His features are large, clear-cut, and, in spite of a few crow tracks and many marks of severe thought, have at times a boyish expression, which makes him seem far younger than he is.

But turn again to the right. In the fifth tier of seats a tall, slender man has risen in his place to speak. He seems a well made-up man, square-shouldered, long-armed, clean-faced, and trim as an athlete, with not a single superfluous article of dress or ornament apparent about him. His dark frock coat fits him as if he had grown in it, and is buttoned close across his breast, leaving barely a suspicion of linen visible between the topmost button and the black necktie. Above this is the well-poised, erect head, crowned with its smoothly-brushed shining black hair. Look at him now, from the head downwards, as he steps out into the aisle; observing especially the sloping forehead, the soulless eyes, the wide, reptile-like mouth, the determined chin, and the expression of cold, brazen defiance over the whole face; look at the smoothness, the trimness, the polish, the matchless slipperiness of the whole outward man, and say if he does not deserve the title he has won for himself—King of the Copperheads. Yes, that is Fernando Wood of

Scene in the house. From *Harper's Weekly Magazine,* February 18, 1865.

New York. The copperheads, his namesakes, you know, do not jump, or spring, or writhe, or fling themselves about in unseemly and un-snake-like manner, but gracefully glide and slide and wind around in the most becoming and *peaceful* way; and so Fernando is gliding and sliding along the invisible line of neutrality, where patriotism and perjury meet, and asking in the most gentlemanly terms for compromise and peace between the two. Yes, he wants peace, and he hasn't a doubt in his heart but what Jefferson Davis wants peace too. It is very naughty of the Administration, he thinks, to send out men to murder a peaceful people; it ought rather to send Commissioners to Richmond to ask on what terms the Confederate government would accept of peace. As he goes on with his cowardly assertions and disgraceful propositions, you can see the fire kindling in a hundred eyes, and manly cheeks all around him are burning with shame. Does he see this? or if he does, will he care? Probably no. He has gone beyond manliness, beyond shame; they are meaningless words to him, as you will see when all this gathering indignation is poured out upon him, as it surely will be. He asserts boldly and confidently that there is no such thing as a War Democrat; and if you watch closely you can see the indignant denial trembling on many lips and flashing from many eyes. He will hear from this too, in time. But the one appointed to meet him first from the other side is Gen. Robert. E. Schenck of Ohio and he could not have fallen into better hands.

L.

April 22, 1864, page 4

Letter from the Capital

FERNANDO WOOD DISSECTED | THE COPPERHEAD FLAYED ALIVE | THE ELOQUENT AND PATRIOTIC SPEECH OF GEN. ROBERT E. SCHENCK

From Our Own Correspondent
Washington, April 15, 1864

As Mr. Fernando Wood, with a characteristic sidelong curve sways himself gracefully into his seat, there arises on the opposite side of the House a man of another presence and another manner. Short in stature, rather small than otherwise, but firmly and strongly made, with his fair, beardless, German features, soft, light hair, and complexion almost as delicate as a girl's, Robert C. Schenck stands before us. From this picture of him one might well doubt if he were the ablest man who could have been selected to cope with the wily adversary on the right. But the first tones of his clear, decisive voice, dispel at once all doubt in that direction. They strike like ringing steel. His eyes are like steel too, with the flash of a brigade of musketry in them. He is very quiet; he does not run ranting and screaming up and down the aisle, tossing his arms and pounding his neighbors' desks as some of the honorable members do in the hours of their delivery; he stands still in his place, and, having, in the first blow he dealt, seized his Copperhead majesty by the throat with a vise-like grip, he holds him there, slowly tearing from him his scaly hide, which crackles and gives way at every touch of the merciless flayer. For a while the creature writhes and turns uneasily in his position; two or three times he struggles to his feet with a feeble denial or protest upon his lips, but an impressive motion of his torturer's hand, an emphatic "not yet," from that quietly authoritative voice, forces him down again. Slowly and surely the work of dissection goes on.

At last the very vitals of the serpent are laid bare. We have come to the subject of the telegraphic correspondence between Mr. Wood, then Mayor of New York, and Robert Toombs of Georgia, in reference to the detention by the New York police, of arms intended for the use of rebels in that seceded State. When the assertion is made that he, as Mayor of the city, did telegraph that the police had committed the "outrage" of stopping arms intended for the seceded Georgians, and that he regretted he had no power to punish them for it, one last effort brings him to his feet again, and he cries out, "The gentleman states what is false." Mr. Schenck replies in tones which thrill through the galleries like an electric shock, "I have met rebels before, when they had something more than tongues to contend with, and I am not to be interrupted or put down here by the member from New York. As that gentleman has entertained the House by the reading of some precious extracts, I propose also to send something to the Clerk's desk to be read."

Now, like thunder, on the momentary death-like hush of the House, comes the Clerk's stentorian voice, reading, as proofs of Mr. Wood's complicity with traitors, the veritable dispatches that passed between Mr. Toombs and himself in January 1861. Word by word they drop like molten lead into the ears of the doomed hypocrite, who, with a little convulsive quiver, the last throe of expiring manhood, straightens himself back in his seat, puts on as much brazen indifference as the human countenance can assume when compelled to face the unanswerable proofs of cowardice, treachery, and falsehood in presence of such an audience, and without another struggle or the movement of a muscle, lets the flaying go on. He is powerless in the grasp of the hands that hold him, and nothing is left but to endure to the end. He knows there is not, even on his own side of the House, a single member who will venture a word or lift a finger in his behalf. So he sits in his ignominious isolation and listens, as perforce he must, to the black record of his own perjured life.

Mr. Schenck proceeds. Blacker and blacker the record grows, and more withering and indignant scorn is poured out upon the shameless traitorous coward, in the name of a loyal and patriotic people. The speaker tells us how he stood on the same platform with Mr. Wood in Union Square, in the city of New York, in April 1861, when that gentleman was addressing the assembled thousands there, and pledging himself that he was for the war and for the Union. Now he condemns the war, and says there can be no such thing as a war Democrat. "His present position is to crawl along on the border between patriotism and treachery, and try neutrality, which has never yet been attempted by any State or people that it has not proved their curse and ruin. He would purpose terms of peace, and that peace he would offer to those who scorn him. He would propose terms of peace to those who will extend him no hand of welcome at his coming. Still he will press upon his Southern friends his good offices, reluctant as they may be. I ask him what mode of peace is that, except to crawl prostrate to the feet of insurgents in arms and say to them, 'Do with us as you will; tear from the flag of our glorious Union half its gleaming stripes, blot out as many of those stars as you can reach and extinguish, only join us again and help to save the Democratic party, that we may hereafter, as heretofore, enjoy power and the offices together. For these we will so humble ourselves as none of God's creatures ever humbled themselves before."

"No," says Mr. Schenck in a burst of indignant eloquence which holds the listening galleries breathless, "We are in the midst of a war. Armies are confronting armies; bayonets are crossed with bayonets. The arguments now to be used, and the only arguments to be used are the incisive, cutting reasoning of the sword, the sharp pointed remark of the bayonet and the knock-down conclusion of the bursting bombshell. It is the midst of such fierce and practical debate as this that the gentleman from New York comes forward and proposes to yield to the arrogant and insolent demands of parricidal rebels. I declare that in my opinion the worst Tory of the Revolution was a patriot and a gentleman compared with a Copperhead of 1864."

When the quickly hushed applause has subsided, he proceeds to say that every man is a citizen soldier, members of the House no less so than others; and pertinently asks, "If a soldier in line of battle, instead of attending to his stern and given purpose, to the consideration how he shall best acquit himself in the deadly struggle before him, should turn to his comrades about him saying to one, 'we cannot beat the enemy,' to another, 'we had better lay down our arms,' to another 'our cause is wrong, we can never conquer,' and to another, 'let us demand of our commanding officer to stop shedding blood, and have a truce between the two armies.' If a soldier at such a time should talk thus in the ranks, what would you do with him? You would shoot him! And as a citizen soldier who undertakes to breed distraction in the country, who claims that we cannot put down this rebellion, who insists that the rebellion, in his view, is altogether right and justifiable, who would compromise, who would temporize, who would have his Government debased to the condition of begging peace from insurgents, is he less deserving of execution and punishment? Though we may not execute such a man on the appropriate gallows erected for criminals, yet, thank God, there is a gibbet of public opinion where we can hang him high as Homan, and hold him there, the scorn of all nations and of the world."

That is the benediction the eloquent Schenck leaves on Fernando's head, and all the thumps of the Speaker's hammer cannot stifle or suppress the applauding assent of the crowded galleries. The remainder of his speech is devoted to Mr. Long, whose case is under debate, and is clear, dispassionate and decisive. By the force and firmness with which he holds his subjects, and the quiet but resistless power with which he sways emotion and commands assent, he has aroused the malignant jealousies of some reckless spirits on the other side, who, though they cannot cope with him, will avenge themselves by misrepresentations and angry and vociferous denunciations. One is already on the floor, Daniel W. Voorhees of Indiana.
L.

April 23, 1864, page 4

Letter from the Capital

SKETCHES OF DEBATES IN THE LONG EXPULSION CASE IN THE HOUSE OF REPRESENTATIVES | MR. VOORHEES | MR. ORTH | MR. KERMAN | HENRY WINTER DAVIS | MR. FINCK | MR. WHALEY | MR. DUMONT

From Our Own Correspondent
Washington, April 16, 1864

Mr. Voorhees is a very ordinary looking man, and his looks do not, apparently, belie his intellect. He has, however, a great talent for barking, and it is probably on this account that he has been chosen as the mouthpiece of the circle that has been gathering about him while Mr. Schenck was speaking. He can rant and vociferate with tremendous power, making an astonishing amount of noise in a wonderfully short space of time. He chooses to misunderstand, misrepresent, and falsify nearly every word and sentiment the previous speaker uttered, and thereat works himself into such a paroxysm of rage that only now and then a word can be distinguished. We hear something about "withering, blasting infamy"; of an "insolvent party, bloated with unlawful power and steeped in the blood and tears of a nation"; of "satraps cracking whips at this side of the House"; of "defiance of damnable despotism," and of "blood running from the hills of New England to the mouth of the Columbia River—all over the Northern land." Verily his furious appeals to God and Heaven, his frenzied imprecations, his fierce denunciations, and reiterated threats of blood and thunder vengeance would be appalling if everybody in the House did not know that they were only so much "sound and fury, signifying nothing." It is a great relief to the ears of the galleries when the incoherent tempest of his disagreeable voice is stilled. It is gratifying, too, to have him, at the end, confronted by Mr. Schenck, and forced to acknowledge his misconstruction and assumed misapprehension of that gentleman's words. By this admission nearly all of his own speech goes for nothing; the pith is taken out of it, and his party evidently feels that a great deal of gas has been spent to very little purpose except to leave a bad odor about them.

Mr. Orth of Indiana here obtains the floor and commences a speech which he concludes at the adjourned session of the House, in the evening. During the delivery of this speech it is impossible to keep down the applause in the galleries, till the Speaker is forced by piteous appeals from the Democratic side to threaten their clearance, if they permit their approbation to become audible again. This speech is a most noble and telling one, patriotic to the core, and full of the most scathing and terrible rebukes for the Maryland traitor, Harris, that coarse, ill-favored man with the bald head, sitting in the third tier of seats on the right. No man but a traitor, lost to all sense of honor and of manhood, could sit in such as assembly as this and listen to such words of bitter scorn, contempt, and loathing as are poured out upon him here without stint or measure. It is a humiliating spectacle to see him sitting there—to think that a man can fall so low, and more humiliating still to know that members of the House calling themselves honorable, have voted to keep him there. Only once during Mr. Orth's remarks is he stung to speak. On being called a traitor, he exclaims.

"I say you are a liar; and you are a coward if you do not resent that." The answer he gets is:

"I can only say that the foul slabberings of a self-convicted, self-condemned sympathizer with treason fall harmless at my feet."

He will get used to the name the resolution passed on Saturday has fixed upon him before Mr. Orth is done with him, for now that the House has sanctioned his use of the word, he cannot bring it in too often, and the miserable old blasphemer must sit and hear it.

It is a pity that this speech of Mr. Orth should not be published in every newspaper throughout the whole country, so that everybody may know of what stuff traitors in the House are made, and how our true men deal with them.

Mr. Kerman of New York is next on the floor. He is a quiet, orderly, well-spoken, middle-aged gentleman, one who evidently would not for the world hurt a fellow creature's feelings, even though that creature were the foulest Copperhead that crawls. He does not agree with Mr. Harris of Maryland or with Mr. Fernando Wood of New York and he very politely declines voting to censure or expel either of them; it is a mere difference of opinion between members, that is all, and he hopes the matter will be passed over and all go on smoothly again.

After occupying just one hour in delivering himself of this opinion he very quietly takes his seat. The one who follows him from the other side is a man of another stamp.

Observe that small, wiry, boyish-looking man in the sixth tier of seats on the left, just behind Mr. Schenck. He is very plainly dressed; his straight reddish-brown sack coat hangs in loose, unbuttoned, schoolboy fashion about him; his features are small, sharp, and dry, and his close cropped, stubby hair, together with the light, bristling tuft on his upper lip, give him a peculiar terrier-like appearance about the head, which is perhaps heightened by an expression of earnestness that has settled into something like an habitual scowl around his eyes and on his forehead. He is all nerves and sinews; active, energetic, persevering and uncompromising. That is Henry Winter Davis of Maryland. He represents Maryland redeemed; and a truer, better, braver representative she could not have chosen. He is not a man to hold hand-and-glove fellowship with traitors under any guise. His keen eyes see through all their masks; his quick intellect grasps the very heart of their intentions, and his fearless judgment sets them at once in their true light before the world. As there is nothing superfluous, so there is nothing slippery about him. All the befogging sophisms, all irrelevant issues and flimsy tricks of oratory to avoid the point of the question under debate, are dispelled, brushed away like cobwebs by the first tones of his voice, the first motion of his hand. In five minutes he has the command of the House and the galleries, and throughout his entire hour sways them with emotion or holds them breathless at his will. Though it is night, and ten o'clock at that, the whole space behind and around the speaker is crowded with gray-headed Senators and other men of note privileged upon the floor, and the spacious galleries are still packed and piled to their utmost capacity. It is a night to be long remembered by the listening thousands, and a speech that should be read in every house where the news of this debate shall go.

How like grating discords upon the senses are the tones, the manner, and the matter of the man who next springs to his feet. Springs? yes, indeed, what else does he do besides spring, and jump and scream and tear around, up and down the aisle, pounding desks, throwing his handkerchief, doubling and undoubling himself, writhing, twisting, and vociferating? He is a perfect jumping-Jack, and after disgusting the audience with his antics for an hour, very much to the relief of all, sits down. He is Mr. Finck, and some part of the Buckeye State has the honor of being represented by him here.

Next follow a few sledge-hammer raps over the heads of traitors in the House, including Mr. Fernando Wood, by Kellian V. Whaley, a sturdy young giant from West Virginia, a man on the Democratic side too, one who knows what a War Democrat is, and who dares give the lie direct to the slippery ex-Mayor and all his sneaking crew. He is fresh from the guerrilla-hunted hills and vales of the Old Dominion, and with the impetuosity of inexperience, he pours out his honest indignation on the smooth-tongued traitors in the capitol who seek to shield, excuse and palliate the crimes of their murderous brethren in the mountains and in the army and the government of the infamous rebellion. His remarks are brief, but he crowds more into the five minutes he occupies than some others can get into an hour. He will vote for the retention of no traitors within these walls.

After this comes the speech of Mr. Dumont of Indiana. He is a plain, unpretending man, not much given to oratory, yet full of the right sort of sense, and apt in its application. His homely similes, dry strokes of wit, and odd illustrations, are highly relished, and hold the amused audience till after eleven, when the House adjourns.

L.

April 25, 1864, page 4

Letter from the Capital

The Debate on the Long Case | Speeches of Messrs. Eldridge, Spaulding, Smith, and Colfax, and Sketches of Messrs. Smith, Long and Colfax

From Our Own Correspondent
Washington, April 17, 1864

On Tuesday, the 12th, there was but one speaker on the floor of the House deserving special note, and that was the youthful hero from Kentucky, Green Clay Smith. Most of the afternoon was taken up by intemperate, partisan harangues, calculated more to embitter members against each other than to bring them to any friendly agreement upon the question under debate. Mr. Eldridge of Wisconsin, Messrs. Spaulding and Pendleton, of Ohio, and Mr. Myers, of Pennsylvania spoke. Fierce invective, misrepresentation of everything that could be brought to answer his purpose, and unscrupulous denunciation of the Republican party and the Administration, formed the staple of Mr. Eldridge's remarks. Indeed, throughout the entire discussion, misrepresentation was the chief weapon of defense used by Mr. Long's friends. Not one of them would endorse his sentiments. No, indeed; they all professed to disagree with him—thought him wrong in many respects—thought the expression of such opinions unreasonable, injudicious, even improper at this time; they would not for their lives have the world think they held any such; yet to protect him, to defend him from censure, they went all the rounds of all the political parties that have ever existed, and picked a phrase out of a speech here, a clause out of one there, took isolated and garbled extracts from everything within their reach, called them the expressed principles of the Republican party, and based Mr. Long's justification upon them. William Lloyd Garrison and Wendell Phillips were perfect Godsends to these men. Also in running their eyes over the House they would note what prominent member from the Republican side would chance to be absent, and forthwith drag up something that he had said, or that they would pretend he said, and go on to prove that Mr. Long stood upon the same ground. It was amusing and gratifying to see how quick they would be called to account when the quoted member returned, and very often obliged to eat their own words, or show by the unquoted context their willful determination to misrepresent and pervert the sentiments of others. When these subterfuges failed, or their barefaced dishonesty became too evident, the gentlemen of the defense would throw themselves upon their injured innocence, and cry out about partisan strife and the tyrannical despotism of the party in power.

So the discussion went on, interrupted every few moments by a running fire of questions, retorts, accusations, and recriminations. The main point seemed to be to show with what dexterity they could dodge the real question at issue. Everything, old and new, was raked up and brought forward to cover up the sin of the man whose whole corporosity, soul and body, were scarcely worth a tithe of the time and labor spent upon them. I think Mr. Long must have entertained some such convictions in regard to himself at the time, for he looked as though any hole into which he could have crawled and hid himself from both friends and foes would have been welcome. That even his professed friends, all but Fernando Wood, were ashamed of him, was but too evident. They would vote against his censure, of course, because he was on the Democratic side of the House; but every one repudiated him, all washed their hands clean of any participation in his views; he was a man who had done something they were ashamed of, but they would not have him punished, simply because such punishment would please the opposite party. The position was not a very enviable one, and Mr. Long, though a coarse, common appearing man, looked as though he felt it. He is rather a large-framed man, with large features, partially bald forehead, red whiskers and light hair. His face was a good deal flushed most of the time, yet he held up his head and braved out the indignation and repudiation with what indifference he could. The only time he seemed to manifest any emotion, except when making his defense on Thursday, was when the young Kentuckian, whose seat is near his own, just across the narrow aisle, was making his noble, manly appeal to the loyalty, patriotism and good sense of the people's representatives.

Green Clay Smith, is a young man, the youngest probably of any who spoke in this debate. He is a strongly built, well-framed man, with a dark, handsome face, small black mustache, and glossy black hair. He spoke with much earnestness, yet with few gestures, and with remarkable ease, grace, and self-possession. Being on the Democratic side, and denouncing as he did without stint the traitorous members of his own party, he was a sharp thorn in the tender flesh of such men as Cox, Voorhees and Co., who sought several times to embarrass and put him off

Part 2: 1864

the track, especially when he was showing up the corruption of that party in the times of Pierce and Buchanan, and charging upon them the responsibility of the war. But he was always ready for them, always courteous, gentlemanly, and always left them vanquished on their own ground. With a brave, bold hand he stripped the mask from those who in the name of Democracy had deliberately prepared the way for the rebellion, and then said, "'Look at the record gentlemen, and blush for the party you claim today to be the only salvation for the country.'"

He said further, "These gentlemen say that the abolitionists prolong this war, and if there had been no abolitionists there would have been no rebellion. Admit that. Then if there had been no slavery there would have been no abolitionists. If slavery is the cause of abolitionism, and abolitionism is the cause of the rebellion, than slavery is the cause of the rebellion. I say to you, Sir, I say to this House, I say to this country, that I believe as solemnly as that I am standing here today, that slavery is the cause of this war, and consequently I am for removing the cause."

This assertion, calm, deliberate, emphatic, coming as it did from the lips of a Representative from a slave State, brought down immense applause from the galleries. The applause elicited angry rebukes from the opposition on the floor, and at length the young champion of freedom earnestly requested his friends in the galleries to keep their feet still and their hands in their pockets till he could finish his speech. They tried hard to do so, but their very effort at suppression often became audible. His censures of Mr. Long, near whom he stood, were at once so severe in spirit, so courteous in manner, so deprecatory and impassioned in utterance that their effect was plainly visible on the recreant's face. Kentucky has reason to be proud of a son like this one; I fear she has not many in the national capitol now.

The debate on Tuesday was continued, with only about an hour's recess, till nearly 12 o'clock at night. The interest in the galleries was unabated to the last. Among the night speakers was Mr. Harrington of Indiana who screamed so that it was difficult to know what he was saying, except that two or three times his slang abuse of New England and of negro soldiers rung out pretty plainly, and every time brought down storms of hisses. Then there would be cries of order! from members, and threats to clear the galleries from the chair, and then Mr. Harrington's confusing screams again. Mr. Broomall of Pennsylvania made a very good speech during the evening, and offered an amendment to the pending resolution, substituting censure for expulsion. Mr. Winfield of New York made a speech in glorification of Gov. Seymour and that wing of the Democratic party. Mr. Grinnell, of Iowa, undertook a speech, but the constant interruptions made it more like a dialogue than anything else. Mr. Rollins of Missouri closed the evening session with a good, true Union speech, which was all the more appreciated that it came from the Democratic side of the House, and fully endorsed the doctrines of the Administration, that as slavery is the cause of the war, and in the way of re-establishing the Union on a secure basis, it must therefore be put out of the way, and destroyed, that Freedom may live.

The transactions of the closing day of this debate have been presented to your readers before this. The ranting tirade of Mr. Rogers of New Jersey was quite characteristic of the class of copperheads to which he belongs. The audience felt relieved when he got through to find that his head and limbs were still safely attached to his body in spite of the violent, spasmodic yerkings they had gone through with.

The discussion was closed by remarks from speaker Colfax, and Mr. Long. Mr. Colfax was constantly and persistently interrupted by members from the other side, so that when his hour expired he had scarcely half finished what he had to say in explanation of his course in calling for the expulsion of Mr. Long. They seemed determined that he should not speak, but he said enough to justify his act and to show that he felt no regrets for what he had done.

Mr. Colfax is a man of middle height, slender and rather spare in person. He has light brown whiskers and hair, small features, and a peculiarly pleasant and amiable expression of countenance. He is very quick and active in his movements; his speech is quick too, and earnest. For his affable manners, his genuine goodness of heart, and his purity as a man and a patriot, he is everywhere loved and honored. Even his political opponents, excepting one or two who tried to make political capital out of this movement in regard to Mr. Long, have invariably spoken of him in terms of the highest praise. They cannot regard him otherwise than with respect.

L.

April 26, 1864, page 4

Letter from the Capital

At The Union League Room | Lecture By Dr. Doane | Colonel Montgomery | Political Anecdotes | Story of a Union Refugee

Washington, April 21, 1864

As an offset to the blasphemous prayer of the Maryland traitor in Congress, and the traitorous action of the recreant members who keep him there, we had last night at the Union League Room a thrilling Union lecture and a detailed account of the escape of Union refugees from rebeldom. The lecture was by Dr. Doane, who made some strong points in regard to the pretensions and practices of the Democratic party as now existing. He enumerated towns in the State of New York which had given Seymour a majority, and said that wherever this was the case, a heavy vote had been cast against permitting soldiers to come home to vote, and all this while party leaders were crying out that Democrats had gone to the war, that Democrats filled the ranks of the Union army, and upon Democrats alone the salvation of the country depended. He told many humorous and illustrative stories, and kept the audience in an uproar of enthusiasm with his anecdotes, or breathless with his flight of impassioned eloquence.

He was followed by Col. Montgomery, formerly editor of the Vicksburg *Whig*, and who for his Union sentiments was imprisoned in that city when it was under rebel rules, and sentenced to be shot. The Colonel prefaced the narrative of his escape by many amusing and pointed remarks, all of which were made with such inimitable quaintness and originality of style and manner as to keep the whole assembly convulsed with laughter. He is a rather short, chubby sort of man, with round face, pleasant blue eyes, light brown whiskers and mustache, and heavy brown hair. While speaking he made no gestures, but stood quite still like a bashful schoolboy repeating his first "piece." His voice was a low monotone, yet distinctly audible in every part of the room, as the irrepressible peals of laughter following those quiet but incessant flashes of wit and comic drolleries of expression attested. It is impossible to reproduce such a speaker or his speech on paper, so I shall not attempt it, but merely state the points of one or two remarks and pass on to the story of his escape, which shall be given as nearly as possible in his own words.

Speaking of slavery, he said: "If I had a fester on the end of my finger, and the doctor told me it would spread up my arm and over my whole body and kill me unless the finger was amputated, (of course he would say 'amputated' for fear I should know what he meant if he said 'cut it off,') why I shouldn't want people telling me that it was a constitutional fester, and that it had just as good a right to be on that side of my finger as the nail had to be on the other; I should tell the doctor to cut it off and let the Constitution take care of itself; I think it would be able to much better with the fester out of the way."

He spoke in bitter terms of our whining, compromising peace-politicians, and said: "The Confederates have 600,000 men under arms, and *I know it and tell you it is so, as you will find in dead earnest soon,* and the only way to meet them is upon war principles. *You will have to fight or go down.*"

He said, "I have heard a good deal about the Democratic party, have heard of it all my life, belonged to it, belong to it yet—whenever I can find it. I used to think it was a party made by God and given down to man as a great blessing; but thinking of it now reminds me of a Sabbath School—can't say that it was a school that I attended, for the chances are that I didn't. But the teacher was to have an exhibition of his pupils; the minister was to come, and the parents and friends; and the minister was to ask questions from the catechism. The teacher had all the children numbered and arranged according to the questions—the first boy was to answer the first question, the second the next, and so on. The first question was, 'Who made you?' The second, 'For what did God make you?' The answer, 'For his own glory.' When all were in readiness, the minister knelt down to pray, and while at prayer the first boy, feeling himself sick, stole out quietly and unobserved and went home. After prayers the minister took the catechism and began: 'Who made you?' The reply came promptly from the second boy, who was first now, 'For his own glory!' The teacher felt scandalized, the minister and parents were amazed, when the boy, seeing some explanation necessary, bawled out: "The boy what God made has gone home with the belly-ache.' And that's the way with the Democratic party—it's gone home with—a pain—somewhere."

He said whenever he heard these peace croakers talking about the salvation of the country depending on the Democratic party, it put him in mind of a couplet from one of Dr. Watts' hymns: "Great God! on what a *rotten* thread / Hang everlasting things!"

"One year ago last November," said the little Colonel, "I was in jail in Vicksburg, condemned to be shot. I escaped one day; I ran home to my wife and little ones. It was about noon; a train would leave the city at three o'clock. I told my wife to pack up our trunks and we must go; she packed them and sent them to the depot by a negro, and then followed with our little girl and boy, while I went around outside the town, met the train going through a cut, jumped aboard and all went well till we got to Holly Springs. I must go to Memphis, 50 miles, and no railroad, and most of the way through rebel pickets. I must get a pass and a conveyance if I could. I went to the General's office; he was away, but his Adjutant was there and said it was of no use to ask for a pass; if I was Jefferson Davis' son and had my mother with me I could not be passed in that direction. I talked with him about other things; I asked him down to take a drink. He drank and I talked. I told him how many Adjutants I had known, and what smart men they were, and that I thought him the smartest of all, and was sure when his merits were known he would be at the head of all the Adjutants in the Confederacy. The General came at last, and the Adjutant begged him to grant a pass to this *very particular* friend of his, to take his wife and children to Memphis and *return*. I was particular about the return. He gave the pass, but it did not cover a conveyance, and there was none to be had. Then the telegraph brought news of my escape, and orders to have me sent back to be shot. The Adjutant had the order, and he told me to *git*. Do you know what *git* means? Well, I tell you, in such a case it means to—*git!* The Adjutant had endorsed me as his friend; he was afraid he had his foot in, so he wanted me to *git*, and I *did*. My wife made a bundle of what clothes the children must have. I put it on my back, took my little boy by the hand, she took the little girl, and we started on foot for Memphis. It was a day of scorching heat, the thermometer above 90, the burning sand six inches deep, my little ones both barefooted, my little boy with no hat, and my wife with only thin-soled slippers on, worth about 40 cents, but for which I paid $10 hard cash. There was no getting out of that burning sun, and as we went on, O, my God! the screams of those little children! the red, fiery streaks ran up their white ankles; every step was agony, and every breath. We dragged them on. Every moment we expected to hear the couriers behind, coming for me. My wife and little girl were before me, the little boy too young to keep up with them. At every rise of ground my wife would turn and look to see if a messenger were coming for me. One time, as she stood so my little boy reached her, his poor feet all red and blistered, his curls matted to his head with perspiration, with both hands clinging to her dress, and his dusty, tearful face lifted to hers, he cried out, 'O, mamma, can't you see our home now?'

"So we went on all one day. At night we stopped at an overseer's house, where we were permitted to stay. They were poor, but kind. A bed was made on the floor for us, but the agony the children suffered was so great they could not sleep, exhausted as they were. We bound their little feet in cloths and I sat by all night to keep them wet with cold water; then they could sleep. If in my stupor and exhaustion I chanced to forget myself, their shrieks quickly wakened me again. In the morning we had to start; there was no staying here. Those poor little feet, burnt all day and soaked all night, looked as if they had been par-boiled; yet blistered as they were, swollen till shapeless, and streaked with red and purple and blue, they must go into that burning sand again. O, my God! my God! those cries! will thine avenging angel gather up the tears that bedewed that fiery path, tears from those helpless little ones in their awful agony! (He covered his face with his hand an instant and then resumed.) But we dragged them on! I don't know how it happened that I did not notice when the little hand slipped from mine, but from whatever distraction of mind I was in, I was startled by a shriek that is ringing in my ears yet, and looking back I saw my little boy lying in the sand in the road behind me. He could not walk another step, and thought I had left him to die. I put my pack over on one shoulder and laid him across the other with his burning cheek to mine and his hot breath fanning my face. His mother and sister had gone on, and were sitting on the grass under a tree waiting for us. Little Freddy saw them and said:

'Papa, do mamma and sister see our home now?'

I said, 'yes.'

'Well,' said he, 'if Ponto sees them he'll know I'm coming, and he'll run past them, and I'll call him and get on his back and ride home and then you won't have to carry me, will you papa!' Ponto was a great dog we had at home.

I laid the child down on the grass beside his mother; she told me then that she could go no farther. There we were. Presently my wife saw a cloud of dust in the distance. I saw it too.

'It is the courier coming for you,' she said; 'he will take you from us, and what will become of you—what will become of us?'

I looked, and saw that the man was in a small buggy—just room enough for him and me—no provision for my family. My poor wife was on her knees—her face was white as marble and cold. She was trying to pray, but she only repeated over and over again, 'O my God! O my God!' not another word would come. I put my hand on her shoulder and said: My dear, there is but *one* man, and *no one man* takes me from you today!

The man in the buggy drove up. He stopped and looked at us. Said he, 'I see you are traveling?' No, sir, said I, traveling and I have quit. 'Well, you don't live hereabouts?' No. 'What is your name?' Montgomery. He looked at the feet of my little ones lying on the grass. "Have those children got the small pox?' No. 'The measles?' No. 'Well, what have they got?' My dear sir, they have got just as near nothing as it is possible for a human being to get. I found he was the rebel mail carrier. I showed him my pass and asked what he would charge to take my wife and children through the lines. He said $50 in gold. My wife and her mother had saved $50 in gold and 50 cents in silver, all of which I had, and it was all. I put my wife in the seat beside him, the little boy in her lap, the little girl at her feet, my bundle under the seat, gave the man the $50 in gold put the 50 cents in my pocket, and they drove off, I followed. When I came to a picket I showed my pass and asked about the buggy. The answer was always, 'Yes; the mail carrier with a woman and two children went by about an hour and a half ago, and reported a man coming with a pass covering the woman and children; all right.' I went on. At last I asked, how many more picket stations are there? 'Only one.' How far is it? 'Three miles.' That is the last? 'Yes.' I had on such boots as the slaves wear. I had paid $30 for them, and I made them earn every cent of the money in that three miles. I came in sight of the picket so soon that I was frightened. I thought of the telegraph wires; what might they not have told before this? Who knew but that man held my life in his hands? There was no help for it; I walked up to him as he sat on his horse and handed up my pass and asked about the buggy, yes, it had gone by an hour and a half ago. But why did the man not give me back my pass? Would he never be done reading it? Or, instead of giving it back, would he level his pistol and shoot me? There I stood, on the border of rebeldom; the United States was before me—the free, glorious United States and wife and little ones; and what was behind! O God! would the man never be done reading that little scrap of writing? That flag, our flag was before me, and freedom. My heart beat so loud I was afraid the man would hear it. I tried to stir. Was he reaching down his hand to shoot me? No; it was only to give back the pass as he said, 'all right,' and then I was a free man again—free, and in the United States and under the flag of stars! I was not long in getting to St. Louis with my family. We walked the streets of that city barefooted. There was a political meeting that night—a republican one. I happened in. The chances are that something was said. The next morning the copperhead paper stated that there was such a meeting and that it was entertained by the blatant ravings of a southern renegade. That meant me. Since then I have been in many of your northern cities and States, and without a pass.

Here is the difference, at the south you cannot turn round, cross the street, kiss your wife, or go to market without a pass; here, where Abraham Lincoln tyrannizes like a military despot, where he usurps all the people's rights and puts them in his pocket, every one can go where he pleases, like sheep without a shepherd. Jeff Davis takes better care of the liberties of his people.

Now I must say a word about that little wife of mine. I am going to take her home to die. (Here the tears almost choked his utterance, but he crushed them back and went on. Need I say that his simple touching narrative had already brought tears to many eyes, and that now there was scarcely a dry one in the crowded room.) Yes, I am going to take her home to die. The doctors have told us she cannot live long, and she wants to die and be buried among her own people. So we are going. The ladies of one of your northern cities have given her a beautiful silk flag—a flag with all the stripes and all the stars on it. We will take that with us, and if our old home is standing the flag shall float above it; if it is not standing then we will plant the flag upon its ruins, or over the place where it once was, and as we sit beneath its folds we will think with tears of gratitude of all the kindness of these free and happy northern people to the wandering homeless refugees."

He then most tenderly and eloquently eulogized the ladies of the North who are doing so much for the comfort of Union soldiers in the field, and closed by a tender and pathetic appeal and tribute to those present, and to all true loyal women. I could not do him justice by attempting to repeat that brief, thrilling and impressive exordium and benediction. Bowed heads and tearful eyes attested to the powers of those simply-spoken, heartfelt words.

When he sat down, a gentleman proposed to be one of 50 to refund the $50 paid to the rebel mail carrier. Another said, we will do better than that. Two men were appointed to stand at the door with hats and receive contributions as people passed out. In this way nearly $60 were collected, and besides this, I saw several gentlemen go to shake hands with him and slip a folded bank note into his hand, saying: "God bless you; I wish I had more to give you." I shook hands with him, too, and said God bless you and your wife and little ones. His eyes were swimming in tears, and scarcely able to speak, he said: "O, if my poor wife were here, this would be a proud day for her."

L.

May 3, 1864, page 4

Letter from Washington

SPRING TIME | SUNDAYS IN THE CAPITOL GROUNDS | LADIES' DRESSES | PROTECTIVE UNION LEAGUE | A RAINY DAY COSTUME

From Our Own Correspondent
Washington, April 26, 1864

Spring has come to us all at once, and gloriously. In a single day, as it were, the trees and shrubbery in parks and gardens have "covered themselves with glory." Peach trees are glowing rosy with blushes on awaking from their winter sleep, and finding that they had not so much as a leaf to cover them; plum and cherry trees have thrown on their white dressing gowns, preparatory to the perfect summer toilet May has in making for them; the ruddy maples, the graceful elms and stately plane trees are robing themselves in "Lincoln green"; the evergreens are losing their somber, funeral hue, and taking on the tenderer, brighter tints of newly awakened life; and the shadowy lindens, with all their trailing arms, are fast "gathering green/From draughts of balmy air."

The parks around the Capitol are beautiful now. The grass is full of violets and dandelions, and a thousand little star-eyed blossoms half hidden in its depths; the trimly kept flower-beds are gay with hyacinths and other early flowering plants and shrubs, and the trees are full of the tremulous and tender beauty of dropping blossoms and spring leaf-buds. The air is fragrant; it seems the very breath of life. Hundreds of people of all classes go there daily for the quiet, the freshness, the sweet enjoyment of nature; for it is Nature still, though under the tutelage of Madam Art.

Sunday is the universal holiday in Washington, especially when the winter storms are past. Not that people are irreligious here; oh, no. They have a great many handsome churches, which are usually filled on Sunday with very handsomely dressed people; but, having shown themselves to the Lord, and to the members of their respective congregations, they want to see and be seen of the world, to enjoy sunshine and fragrance and fresh air; so they promenade the avenue, or repair to the public parks where these delights abound. At the capitol grounds they usually have bands of music playing in the afternoon of Sundays, and then the scene is very gay. Last Sabbath being the first pleasant one of the season since the flowers have come out, it was almost like a fairy scene. Bright dresses, bright faces and bright uniforms abounded. All the seats under the trees were occupied by happy loungers or happier lovers; the broad granite aisles and gravel walks were filled with tireless promenaders; children frolicked about like brilliant butterflies, the music was sweet, the air was sweet, and gladness ruled the hour.

Washington ladies, as you will probably see by the papers, are making an effort at retrenchment in the way of dress, to prevent the ruinous importation of goods, which so enhances the price of gold and embarrasses the Government. It is very well that they have thought of it even at this late hour. All winter they have been dragging the price of the soldier's life along our pavements, till, weary with that disgusting process, they invented a system of pulleys to be worn under the dress, by which the skirt could be elevated at will, but, finding this too troublesome, they have recently resorted to hooking it up. Everyday ladies, I suppose they are ladies, may be seen on the avenue with heavy silk skirts richly trimmed, made from a quarter to a half yard too long for the wearer, and the surplus hooked up at each seam, giving a most ridiculous, baggy appearance to the costume; and the heavy, unwieldy mass over the swaying hoop adds anything but grace to the motions of the walker. It is very appropriate that such ladies would begin to think of curtailing.

However, I must say, that from what I have heard of the splendor of former seasons here, the extravagance of the past winter has been moderate in comparison. It has been sneeringly spoken of by some as due to the influx of Northern commonplace people, who did not understand the arts and elegances of dress as practiced by the aristocratic Southerners under Democratic rule. Be that as it may, there is room for improvement in simplicity and economy even now. They are going to organize a Ladies' Union League, to bind themselves for three years or during the war, not to buy or use imported goods where it is possible to substitute those of domestic manufacture. I think the gentlemen ought to be bound over to good behavior in this matter too. Their fine broadcloths and brandies certainly have some effect on importations.

Speaking of dress, I saw a nice thing on the street the other day in the way of protecting the *"woman* form divine" from the effects of a rainstorm. It was one of our rainiest of rainy days; I was going down 7th street and directly before me walked a lady whose unique costume drew all eyes after her. Men and women, regardless of the rain, turned and stopped to look at her. And yet there was nothing very singular about her, only so appropriate and so becoming did her dress seem that I imagined everybody was wondering as I was, why women had not thought of it before. It was simply a handsome black India rubber skirt, made short so as not to interfere with the free use of feet and limbs, which were encased in neatly-fitting boots, with tops reaching above the bottom of the skirt. A dark gray shawl was folded straight around her shoulders, a close black hat and veil covered head and face, and a small umbrella above protected them; while all the rain that came streaming down upon her skirt rolled off like drops from a duck's back, and

her ankles were untouched by dripping petticoats or draggled flounces. There was nothing outrageous or Bloomerish about this costume, nothing that could offend the most delicate genuine modesty, and nothing that prudery need elevate her nose at. I wonder why such a dress cannot be made the universal refuge for a rainy day?
L.

May 4, 1864, page 4

Letter from the Capital

RELEASED UNION PRISONERS AT BALTIMORE | THEIR STARVED AND SUFFERING CONDITION | APPEAL TO THE GOVERNMENT | AN ORIGINAL LETTER FROM A UNION PRISONER IN VIRGINIA

From Our Own Correspondent
Washington, April 27, 1864

I have just been listening to a description of the pitiable condition of the returned Union prisoners now in Baltimore. Miss Dix and many other benevolent people, of this city, have been to visit them, and give the most sickening and heart-rending accounts of the deplorable state to which these unhappy men have been reduced. Starvation and sickness have reduced to emaciation and idiocy men of once powerful frames and cultivated minds. When spoken to many of them can only reply by a vacant stare, or faintly muttered, unmeaning words. Their lank, dropping jaws, and sunken, hungry-looking eyes are pitiful beyond expression. Many have forgotten their own names, forgotten where they are from, or how long they have been in prison, and when questioned can only answer by a weary negative movement of the head, or the plaintive appeal, "Don't talk to us—we are hungry—we want meat." Poor fellows! they are crying and begging for meat, for strong, hearty food, they are so hungry; and their nurses dare not give it to them yet, but feed them like little babes.

One was asked what was his native State; he looked up wishfully, moved his lips, but could not speak. The questioner then began softly naming over the different States of the Union, watching carefully if any change of countenance might indicate where the poor sufferer's had been. State after State was mentioned; fainter and fainter grew the breath of the victim, and no change was visible on the dying face till Illinois was named; then there was a weary opening of the glazing eyes, a half-quenched ray of intelligence shot forth, followed by a tremulous flutter of breath upon the lips, and all was over; the martyr had gone to his reward.

Many of these unfortunate men are too far gone even to know that they are free. Hunger has been their ghastly companion so long that his gaunt visage and gnawing pains form the sum total of their knowledge and experience now. Eaten by hunger and disease from within, and preyed upon by vermin from without, dropping to pieces while yet alive with scurvy and emaciation, these hapless men present to our Government such an appeal, such a petition, as was never presented to it before. They join hands with the slaughtered heroes of Fort Pillow, and the butchered braves of Plymouth, and ask, in the name of God and of humanity, if such crimes are to be forever unavenged; if still in the nation's capitol are to be heard voices raised to excuse and palliate these monstrous wrongs; voices denouncing the Government that it does not get down on its knees to treat of peace with fiends; voices that pray Almighty God that the Union arms may never triumph over the black-hearted and bloody-handed rebellion, that is working all this war! We read in the Book of Life, "Vengeance is mine; I will repay, saith the Lord"; and listening to sounds in the air, and signs in the heavens and upon the earth, we may believe the thunderbolts as nearly ready. God send they may be swift and fatal.

Today a friend handed me the enclosed paper. It is, as you will see, a supplication in verse from one of our own Michigan man, confined in a Virginia prison. It is written with pencil upon half the cover of an old religious monthly, published in Richmond in July 1856, and is addressed to one of the members of Congress from our State. It came by way of a "flag of truce boat," is endorsed, "Prisoner's Letter," and bears the postmark, "Old Point Comfort, Va., Feb. 23." I wish you could give in your paper the title page of the monthly, just as it occurs, interspersed among those pleading pencil lines; that subject of the Rev. D. D.'s discourse, "Pious Solicitude for One's Own People," seems so appropriate, and yet comes in so like a reproach to the Government, which the poor prisoner, so long shut out from the world, evidently looked upon as culpably negligent in the matter of bringing about an exchange. Whether the writer of the verses is living or dead now, in prison or out of it, I do not know; but as he was a Michigan man he may have friends there who will welcome even these faint tidings of the captive.

L.

The following is the poem referred to above:

"The Prisoner's Refrain"
I wish that Stanton Edwin M., and General Halleck too,
Were in this place that they might see how prisoners live and
    do;
That they might feel the woes of want and live on prison fare;
That they might eat of prison bread and breathe the prison air;
That they upon the floor might lie in winter-time so cold;
Without a blanket, bed or fire, their garments thin and old;

No concourse with the world outside, no word from friends or
    home;
By pale disease and scanty food reduced to skin and bone;
No hopeful ray of liberty, no gleam of freedom's light,
To penetrate the prison gloom or cheer the dismal night.
Have we no friends in Northern home who pity our sad lot?
Or are all kindly feelings gone, and mercy's claims forgot?
Must we within these prison walls remain from day to day,
Until we by relentless death are called from earth away?
Where are our many brethren then, are they all dead and
    gone?
Are we of all a numerous race left on this earth alone?

Composed in prison No. 3, Danville, Va., by Wm. W. Wilson, a private of Co. I, 11 Michigan Infantry, Jan. 31st, 1864.

May 7, 1864, page 4

Letter from the Capital

A TRIP TO ALEXANDRIA | THE POTOMAC AND THE SCENES ALONG ITS BANKS | OLD PENITENTIARY GROUNDS—GEISBORO—MARYLAND HILLS—ENTRANCE TO ALEXANDRIA—THE CITY, ITS STREETS AND CITIZENS | RELIC OF THE F.F.V.'S | A CITY OF TENTS, ETC. | POOR OLD VIRGINIA

From Our Own Correspondent
Washington, April 28, 1864

Yesterday, April 27th, I made for the first time a slight incursion upon the sacred soil of the Old Dominion. Hearing that some of our Michigan regiments in whose ranks I had friends, might by possibility be lying over a day at Alexandria, I secured the company of a friend with a pass and went down to see. Alexandria lies six miles almost directly south from Washington, on the opposite side of the Potomac river. Street cars run from the center of the capital to the river some two miles distant, and thence steam ferry boats ply every hour between the two cities. The fare is 15 cents.

Part 2: 1864

The Potomac, where we take the boat, is considerably wider than the Detroit River at Detroit. The banks on either side are low and level, but at some distance back the ground rises in gradual slopes, forming the ridges that are known on their respective sides as the heights of Arlington, and of Georgetown. Our boat is the "Thomas Colyer," which we enter between files of soldiers who stand with arms ready for emergencies while passes are being examined. There are no wharves of any extent here, only two or three moderate sized platforms built out a little way over the water, and on the one where the ferry boat stops, is a little shanty capable of holding about half a dozen persons; this the "ladies' waiting room," and affords all the shelter to be had while waiting for the boat during storm or shine. At the narrow platform a little below, Government transports are taking on freight, government teams and government men are scattered along the uneven, sandy shore, and not far off, on eligible sites along the banks, are seated some of the government's grim dogs of war. They are dangerous looking animals, though so silent and innocent just now. They are not an unfrequent sight as we float down the broad Potomac; and cresting the distant ridges on either hand may be seen the walls of fortifications, the glistening tents of the soldiers, and the stately flagstaffs giving to the breeze the flag under which they fight.

The first point of interest which we pass on the immediate river bank, is the large handsome enclosure with its many extensive brick buildings, formerly the grounds and prisons used for Government criminals, the United States penitentiary. Since the war, criminals of this sort have been transferred to Albany, N.Y., for safe keeping, and the grounds and buildings devoted to the defense of the country on war principles. There are rows of mounted cannon, howitzers, and mortars, and cords of shining cannon balls and shells without the buildings, and from that we may judge something of what may be going on within. The clean, grassy banks are very pleasant to look at; the grounds occupy a point of land made by the junction of the East Branch with the Potomac.

Below the East Branch is another broad plateau used for Government purposes. This is Geisboro. There is one house here, a neat white cottage on a green knoll in the midst of a grove of trees. There are long ranges of sheds extending in every direction, and under the sheds and all about the fields, on the banks of the river, and even standing up to their knees in the river, are many hundreds and maybe thousands of government horses. They are gathered here and kept till wanted. A small wharf is here where boats discharge and receive freights, and near it a sort of gangway leading down to the water on which dead horses are tumbled, to be taken away by men whose business is to make money out of their carcasses. When too old or worn to be worth keeping, the poor animals are led to this bank and shot. Some fifty or more were lying on the gangway and piled above it, and one was led up and shot as we were passing.

Below this the low sandy hills of Maryland look barren and deserted enough; they might blow away like an ash heap, were it not for the little knots of stunted evergreens that seem to hold them down, something after the fashion of the knotted "comfortables" our mothers used to make. But the boat heads toward the Alexandria wharf, and all heads are turning with it.

Alexandria sits on the very margin of the river; she even has her feet dabbling in the water. Her whole river front is lined with wharves, and all along these and far out into the stream are crowded shipping craft of every sort and size. Many of these are vessels employed in the fisheries, but many more just now are doing special duty for Uncle Sam. The passage to the ferry wharf lies between a revenue cutter and a guard boat, both of which have handsome brass pieces pointing their muzzles at us in a friendly, admonitory manner. The guard boat has also a mounted mortar, about the size of a cast iron wash tub, holding up its ugly mouth, ready to belch forth destruction upon the country's enemies at a moment's warning. Alexandria secessionists have only to look at these modest hints, put their fingers on their lips, and play loyal.

One step on shore is enough to assure the stranger that, if not on sacred soil, he is at least on a very different soil from what cities in general are made of. If the reader can imagine a very filthy pig sty, laid out in narrow streets, and peopled by the dirtiest, most squalid-looking inhabitants he can conceive of, he will have some idea of the beauties and attractions of the present city of Alexandria. Here is where we begin to see the real evidences of the footprints of war. The city is almost entirely built of brick, and has been a center of much of the wealth and the refinement, such as it was, of this department of the Old Dominion; now it is little more than a thoroughfare for the army and the army trains of the Department of the Potomac. As our Michigan regiments had gone some three hours before we arrived, we gave an hour or two to wandering about the city, and then returned.

All the streets are still barricaded at the crossings, leaving barely a single wagon track in the center; and yards, door-steps, side-walks, gutters and streets, unswept and covered with rotting garbage and piles of rubbish, are filthy beyond description. Dirty looking men stand in knots at the corners, adding their tobacco salvia to the delights around them; and dirtier women gabble in the yards and on the front door-steps. One, of whom we asked a question, was sitting flat upon the ground, which was a level with her threshold, under a porch fronting on the principal street. She rose when spoken to. What the skirt she wore was made of, it was past the ingenuity of woman to discover, but the upper part of her body was covered by a garment made of coarse tow sacking, glazed with grease and dirt. She had a pale, haggard face, dark, bright eyes and black hair, worn *a la Meg Merioles,* or *a la Medusa*.

"Yes," said she in reply to a question; "there's been right smart o' soldiers along, and niggers in heaps: There is a chance o' *calvary* over the hill yonder yet, I reckon: Heaps o' calvaries went, but I reckon more's thar."

The cavalry was gone, however, as well as the "heaps of niggers." We passed the hotel where young Ellsworth was shot, and went to look at what was once the Young Ladies' Seminary. This must have been a beautiful place, with its handsome building and fine sloping lawn covered with stately trees. The building now looks like a forsaken barn, and the lawn is literally a barnyard. Union batteries were planted there in the early days of the war, and horses tied to those stately poplars stripped them of bark as high as their heads could reach, so that now nearly all are dead.

From the head of King Street where we stood there is a fine view of the fortress-crowned hills, the winding war path around their base, and the fairy-like city of tents on the green slope stretching downward towards the town. A regiment, I think they said the 48th New York Volunteers, being stationed under shelter of the hills, have planted their tents in streets, of which there are ten; and over the entrance to each is sprung a high and beautiful arch covered with evergreens. The evergreens are, however, changed to a rich dark brown now, and form a fine contrast as seen from the distance, with the clean streets and white tents beyond.

The railroad from Washington runs directly through the heart of Alexandria, parallel with the river. Soldiers on duty are at almost every turn and corner. Negroes are plenty, but I believe slavery is dead here. Our Michigan troops under Gen. Wilcox battered down the last slave pen, and struck the fetters from all captives found therein. With slavery the chivalry evidently went out, too; leaving only these wretched representatives who haunt their forsaken homes, and the men in blue who guard this as the great gateway through which the defenders of liberty go forth to the conflict.

Poor old Virginia, the once proud "Mother of President's!" That she had abundant cause for her pride of state, and wealth, and intellect, her history and her statistics show, that she has forfeited all by placing the bloody mark of the beast upon her own fair forehead, her present desolation but too well attests. The picture which Alexandria presents, sad and sickening as it is, is not, it is true, so much as the initial letter to the long chapter of Virginia's self-sought ruin and disgrace. But it is enough to show in a small way the consequences of slavery and secession, and if they have made such havoc along her borders, what must not the devastation be at her heart where the mighty contest she has invited there is going on! Let us hope men are now living who will write the history of the Old Dominion redeemed.

L.

May 9, 1864, page 4

Letter from the Capital

WASHINGTON LADIES | ORGANIZATION OF THE LADIES' NATIONAL COVENANT | ADOPTING THE PLEDGE | DISCUSSIONS AND DIFFERENCES OF OPINION | ENTHUSIASM OF THE RADICALS | AMUSING SCENES | THE PRESIDENT IN A PUZZLE | RADICALISM TRIUMPHANT | ACQUIESCENCE TO THE MAJORITY | THE LESSON LEARNED | WOMEN FOR THE TIMES | THE AUDIENCE PHOTOGRAPHED

From Our Own Correspondent
Washington, May 5, 1864

When correspondents writing from Washington speak of Washington ladies in connection with any popular public movement or organization, it should be understood that they are not natives of Washington, really and properly belonging here, but are representatives from all the States of the Union, who have been gathered here in one way and another; some as wives and daughters of Congressmen, some as literary students to see and learn, or as authoresses to collect material for future books; some as correspondents, some as Government employees, and many as wives of men in public life, officers of the army, and so forth. Society that is anything here is made up almost entirely of representative women. Therefore, when it goes out to the world that the ladies of Washington have originated the grand organization now called "The Ladies' National Covenant," for the suppression of extravagance in dress and to prevent the ruinous importation of foreign goods, it may as well be known that they are ladies who are stopping here only temporarily, and feel a pride in having a work like this commence at the nation's heart.

For some two weeks past the subject of forming an association for the above object had been talked of, and the talk finally culminated in a mass meeting in the lecture room of Dr. Sunderland's (Presbyterian) church on Monday afternoon, the 2d keep. As it was peculiarly a woman's meeting, and as notice had been given that an address would be had from the popular authoress, Mrs. Ann S. Stephens, it was of course supposed that ladies would preside and transact the business, and that the address would be delivered by the authoress herself. Many were, therefore, a little

Part 2: 1864

disappointed at finding a gentleman placed in the chair, or rather in the pulpit, to be the mouthpiece of the ladies on the floor. It was an awkward piece of business all around. The ladies who had thus far taken the lead, being too modest "to speak in meeting," could only make their plans and wishes known by beckoning down their president, giving him whispered instructions, and sending him back to the pulpit to repeat them aloud to the audience. This kept him running up and down about every other minute; a lively time he had of it all through, and it was most lucky that he happened to be one of the most accommodating gentlemen alive. He read the address of Mrs. Stevens, a very excellent one, indeed, and which has been ordered to be widely published through the country. After the address, the Constitution was read and adopted, and officers of the association nominated and accepted. Then came the subject of the pledge.

The leaders of the movement had the constitution, officers and pledge all prepared according to their ideas of what was required, and supposed they had but to be submitted to receive the approbation of all. With the constitution and officers all went smoothly; with the pledge it was different. This article was framed in the following language: "For three years, or for the war, we pledge ourselves to each other and the country to purchase no imported article of apparel not absolutely necessary; this pledge to take effect from the 4th of July next." The President of the meeting read the pledge deliberately and distinctly to the audience, and then called for a vote upon its adoption. A dozen or so of "ayes" came up very promptly from a certain quarter and a few scattering ones from other parts of the house, the majority not voting at all; when the "noes" were called there was but one voice replied. It was a very quiet but decided "no," and, as afterwards appeared, came from Massachusetts. The President, however, pronounced the vote unanimous on the adoption of the pledge, and remarked that the one dissenting "no" seemed to have more of mischief in it than serious earnest. This brought Massachusetts to her feet at once. In the same quiet and decisive voice she asserted that she was in serious earnest, and then asked why, if we desired to aid in saving the country, that aid should be withheld till the 4th of July next, thus giving ample time for reckless speculators and enemies of our government to complete the ruin already so surely begun? If our help is wanted, it is wanted *now*! We who are in earnest want to begin the work at once.

This sentiment was echoed by the hearty clapping of hands and murmurs of applause from those who had not voted for the pledge, and had been too timid to vote against it. Here their feelings had found a voice. Little Massachusetts went on to say that she also discovered in the pledge, as read, a loophole through which any one might crawl into all the foreign fabrics they might desire. That clause, "absolutely necessary," might be made to cover a broad range, according to the habits and tastes of the ladies adopting it. She would like to know what articles of wearing apparel absolutely necessary for women were *not* made in our own country? and if not already made, how long would it be till they were, if merchants could be forced to stop their importations? This again brought down the applause of the earnest ones; and now in reality the good work was begun in the right way. The originators of the pledge being called upon to explain why they desired to postpone action till the 4th of July, expressed through the President their fears that merchants who had imported largely might suffer. This called out a response from a lady of Kansas, who took up the words of Massachusetts, and said, if the country ever needs our help it is *now*, and not when help will be too late. The excellent address to which we have listened states that this action has already been deferred too long—then why defer it still longer? If the country is ruined the merchants and gold speculators will go down with it; if it is saved, they are saved too.

Then a murmur went up from all sides signifying that it was the will of the majority that the pledge should be for immediate action. An amendment was offered striking out the 4th of July clause, and the vote upon it was unanimous, the leaders acceding to the popular wish with a very good grace. But the real test was on the "absolutely necessary" phrase. Here Kansas came to the rescue again, and delivered a stirring little speech, full of pith and patriotism, referring to the hardships, privations, and self-denials of our soldiers in the field, and asking if their wives, mothers, and sisters could not, for their sakes, deny themselves for a time these luxuries of dress, that were draining the country of its gold, and thus embarrassing and endangering the Government? A hearty response showed that this was the popular sentiment of the meeting; that the majority of the women present had come with minds made up to subscribe to any sacrifice that judgment and patriotism might dictate, so they were assured it would be effectual, and not a vain show. They wanted no half way work in the matter, and now that they fairly understood what was before them, nothing but the total abstinence pledge would answer. Hereupon arose a confusion of tongues very like to what Babel must have been if women were present at that ancient mass meeting on the plain of Shinar. Every tongue in the room was in motion, each one talking to her neighbor or trying to speak so as to be heard above the general buzz and hum. This was just what was needed to bring them to an understanding of what they wanted and what they were doing. If each one could express her mind to somebody there would be no difficulty in getting at the right point in the right way; so the fullest liberty of speech was indulged in for the space of several minutes.

And here was the comical part of the scene; to watch the luckless President of the meeting, who felt himself between two fires, and could dodge neither. Now he was down among the halfway ladies, who instructed him to say that their desire was to compromise with certain ladies whose name and influence they could have by allowing the privilege of wearing such articles of apparel as were or seemed to them absolutely necessary to their station; then up he went into the pulpit, repeated his instructions, and came down among the radicals to listen to opinions, explain, and urge them to come to terms; then he would stand before them with the unfortunate pledge in his hand, and a puzzled expression of countenance laughable to see. At length Kansas moved to strike out the objectionable words, which motion was ably seconded by a voice from New York, well known and honored, and often heard in woman's behalf. The little speeches here made fully aroused the enthusiasm of the majority, and the motion to amend was carried, with only a few faint dissenting voices. Still it was evident that dissatisfaction existed in a quarter where it was very desirable to have harmony and hearty co-operation. Finally a reconsideration was moved and carried, and the pledge stood as before; but matters were no better. The majority would have the total abstinence pledge or none. They were not the compromising, temporizing sort of women. If they were to have an organization they must have it on a correct basis; they would join no other. Both the President and Dr. Sunderland, who was also present, looked as if they were at their wit's end, but never a moment ceased their efforts to bring about the object desired. The former proposed that there should be two pledges, which he thought a peculiar wording of the constitution would sanction. The radicals would not listen to that—"a house divided against itself" was not a safe one in these times—if the constitution admitted of such an interpretation they must amend it; and so they did at once, and threw themselves back upon the one pledge. On motion, and after some interesting discussion, the pledge was again amended as before, and by a vote so unanimous that all who did not vote for it, and they were few if any, were silent.

It should be mentioned that the halfway ladies held their position with much modesty and dignity, not talking loudly, making no speeches in defense of it, and expressing all their sentiments and wishes through the President. And they resigned themselves in the end to the popular will with becoming grace, and were among the first to give their names to the total abstinence pledge. Probably they had not been accustomed to take such practical views of matters as their more radical sisters had, and were not so well informed as to the desires and capabilities of the mass of their sex. They feared to ask too much, not remembering that woman's nature is one of sacrifice and self-denial, and so came short of their object by not asking enough. The result showed that their tender consideration for merchants, and for ladies who find it "absolutely necessary" to wear foreign fabrics, was not highly appreciated. They have probably learned a lesson which it will be well to remember; that the roots of patriotism have struck deep into the hearts of the people, and that they are ready, as their grandmothers of the Revolution were, to put aside every thing that stands in the way of the salvation of the Government.

On the other hand, the radical ladies, though lacking nothing of modesty and lady-like propriety, needed no second pair of lips to speak for them. They felt the full importance, the dignity, the grandeur of the occasion and the nobleness and whole-souled patriotism of their own hearts made them equal to it—aye, they even added luster to the cause by their uncompromising adherence to the true spirit of the movement. With courtesy and candor these representative women rose in their places and spoke what they believed and felt to be the wish and the will of the people; and the heartiness with which they were sustained proved that they were right.

The pledge as amended and adopted reads: "For three years or for the war, we pledge ourselves to each other, and the country, to purchase no imported article of apparel."

Altogether this meeting was one to be long remembered by all who were present. The Rev. Dr. Sunderland, who during the session, which lasted from one o'clock till six, made several spirited little speeches, was so well pleased with the object, the high patriotic tone and temper manifested and the gratifying result, that he sent for an artist and had the whole audience photographed, and intends adding to the picture the names of all who then signed the pledge, and have them framed together as an ornament for his study.

The association, if sustained and adhered to in the spirit in which it was organized, and in the true spirit of the pledge, cannot but have a favorable effect on the finances of the country. Organizing committees are appointed in every State, and it is to be earnestly hoped that the ladies of town and country throughout the Union will join heartily in the grand work of retrenchment and reform.

L.

May 11, 1864, page 4

Letter from the Capital

MORE ABOUT THE DRESS REFORM MOVEMENT | SHODDY REPRESENTATION AT THE CONVENTION | ONE OF THEM GIVES COUNTENANCE TO THE PROCEEDINGS | POSTSCRIPT | REPLY TO THE *NEW YORK TRIBUNE* | NAMES AND SPIRIT OF THE INAUGURATORS, AND OF THE TRUE LEADERS

Washington, May 4, 1864

The Shoddy family, several branches of which have been established in Washington, were not without their representatives at the convention for organizing the association known as "The Ladies' National Covenant." Whether these were natives "to the manor born," it would not probably be charitable in me to say. They had high pretensions of patriotism, however; were very anxious that the country should be saved; were sure it ought to be, and would be; but when asked to sign the pledge to help save it, one very politely replied:

"I thank you; I'm not prepared to give my name just yet. There is a heap of things I need, and I reckon right smart of 'em is imported. I'll wait awhile."

The 4th of July arrangement would have suited this lady exactly.

Another, whose portly form was enveloped in habiliments of the deepest woe, said in the most despairing tone as she lifted her heavy veil:

"I cannot sign such a pledge while I am in mourning, for this crape, you see, is all imported."

It was suggested to her that crape of very good quality was manufactured in this country.

"Ah, yes," she replied, with a deep-drawn sigh, "but the quality is nothing like this!"

"Where is our linen to come from?" triumphantly asked one no better informed than she should be.

"Linen is made in the United States, and if it were not, our grandmothers made it in their day, and we can learn the art if we cannot put up with cotton," was the quiet, reproving answer of New York.

"But our ribbons! I should like to know what we are to do for ribbons?" said a sharp-looking damsel with enough of the article about her to hang a regiment of rebels.

"Ribbons are made in this country, and very pretty ones, too!" replied a quick voice from the vicinity of Cape Cod.

One anxious housewife "wondered if such things as blankets were made in America; she couldn't sign no pledge to go without blankets for three years, that was the hull o' *that* story as far as she had anything to say!"

All these people would have reveled in the "absolutely necessary" clause; the idea of making a sacrifice of anything never once seemed to enter their miserable little souls. If they could have everything they wanted, and all the money necessary to buy it with, they would very gladly sign the total abstinence pledge, or anything else that might be asked of them! O yes; they wanted to do something to help save the country, but as for building up home industry, practicing self-denial in any way, or cutting short an inch of ribbon, such things did not come within the scope of their patriotism. All these were, of course, exceptions, and perhaps about all the exceptions there were, to the high-toned patriotism and intelligence of the ladies present. No; there was *one* more, an uneasy, vexatious piece of dry goods, vinegar-faced and sallow, who sat within hearing distance of my corner, and declared that she "wasn't going to give no such pledge to nobody; for whar was the French flowers to come from to put in her bonnet if she did? She would just like to know that!"

And the most ludicrous part of all was, that when the audience was being photographed, with the Rev. Dr. Sunderland in the foreground, this very piece was most anxious to have her face in the picture, and squeezed herself unasked into the crowd at the Doctor's elbow, where her sharp nose with the bunch of soiled pink flowers above it must make conspicuous show. She can at least have it to say that she gave countenance to the proceedings of that famous meeting!

It should have been noticed in a former article that no lady belonging to this association is prohibited from wearing or making use of imported goods she may happen to have on hand at the time of becoming a member. To show that she is a "covenanter" each member is to wear a badge, which is a black bee, with wings enameled according to nature, worn with a tricolor ribbon, a little in front of the left shoulder. This badge was designed by Mrs. Ann S. Stephens. It is understood that the bee is to be made of gutta-percha, and a little larger than life size.

In regard to the pledge as adopted, some, with no special gift to see through millstones, protest that they can discover in it, even now, a loophole quite as large as that which so alarmed the cautious little Massachusetts. It is asserted that as a lady only binds herself not to purchase imported articles, there is nothing to prevent her having others purchase them for her. This, however, is an aperture so small and so crooked that we should hope no true woman would so much as see it, and are very certain no one of that character would attempt to crawl out at it. Still, in other organizations of a like nature, there would be no harm in guarding against the temptation, since there are weak sisters in almost all communities.

Postscript:—Since the above was written, I have been shown the dispatch in the *New York Tribune,* of May 2d, where it is stated that misapprehension lent official influence to the force and truthfulness of the remarks made by Mrs. Elizabeth Cady Stanton, and that the influence was due to the supposition on the part of the audience that she was the wife of the Secretary of War. This is an entirely mistaken view of the matter. The lady's name was not known to the audience at all, till after the discussion on the amendment of the pledge was consummated by its enthusiastic adoption as amended; and even then only by the few who recognized her as one of the champions of woman's rights in the State of New York, or were near enough to hear her name when introduced to the President of the meeting amidst a buzzing like that of a beehive on a swarming day. It was not name or position that carried influence here, else why did not that first pledge receive the unanimous sanction of the assembly? See who were its authors and advocates: Mrs. Senator Lane of Indiana, Mrs. Ann S. Stephens of New York, Mrs. Senator Wilson of Massachusetts, Mrs. Loan of Missouri, Mrs. Pike of Maine, Mrs. Stephen A. Douglas of Washington, Mrs. Spalding of Ohio, Mrs. Woodbridge of Vermont, Mrs. Judge Hughes of Indiana, Mrs. Morris of the Navy, and others of like high standing and character, wives of Senators, Representatives and Judges, and one, Mrs. Stephens, an authoress of acknowledged ability and accustomed to control the minds of many. Yet they were powerless here, and so would the wife of the Secretary of War have been, or the wife of any officer, civil or military, standing on the same equivocal, or rather, uncertain ground occupied by these excellent ladies. No, not Queen Victoria, the Empress Eugenie, and the wife of the Secretary of War combined, could have forced that dilatory, compromising pledge upon the mass of earnest women who had come there prepared to give their names, and their souls with them, to a work of self denial and sacrifice. But for that one little "No" of

Massachusetts, the few, feeling that something ought to be done, as nothing better offered, would have given their names obediently to the easy-fitting compact, and perhaps would have felt conscience clear that their whole duty was performed; but the many would have had nothing to do with the temporizing business at all, and would probably have gone away silent, but not the less disappointed.

It was the right spirit that was wanting to make the sentiment of the meeting unanimous from the first. The right spirit spoke, and all felt it, when that quiet voice said "No; we will have immediate action, and we will have thorough work." And now, having begun to call names, it may as well be said aloud that this initiative voice belonged to Mrs. Barton, of Concord, Mass. Mrs. C. I. H. Nichols of Kansas, formerly of Vermont, very ably and eloquently sustained Mrs. Barton; and Mrs. E. C. Stanton of New York, gave to them both and to the cause, the sanction of her practical good sense. These are all women of thorough practical patriotism, accustomed to works as well as words, and therefore understood and took with them the heart of the multitude. It is to this fact and not to official position, that their influence is due. If men would lead men they must be up with the spirit of the times, and it is the same with women in these days.

The Advisory and Organizing State Committee for Michigan is as follows: Mrs. J. M. Howard, Mrs. Z. Chandler, both of Detroit; Mrs. F. W. Kellogg, of Grand Rapids, and Mrs. A. C. Baldwin, of Pontiac; all good appointments.

May 13, 1864, page 1

Letter from the Capital

UNION LEAGUE HALL | SPEECH OF HON. J. M. BROOMALL | HOW HE GETS OUT OF A RESPONSIBILITY | SPEECH OF A. M. SCOTT | PAYING TAXES FOR THE WAR OF 1812 | SCOURGING CONGRESS AND THE WALL STREET SWINDLERS | THE MOTHERS OF OTHER TIMES | SPEECH OF T. H. GIBBS OF TENNESSEE | HOW REBELS TREAT THEIR FRIENDS, ETC.

From Our Own Correspondent
Washington, May 5, 1864

The meetings at Union League Hall on Wednesday evenings are generally well attended and of the most enthusiastic and loyal character. Usually there are two or three speakers on hand, and the meeting is opened and closed with a patriotic song. Last week the principal address was by the Hon. John M. Broomall of Pennsylvania, a member of the House, and one who made one of the right sort of speeches in the Long expulsion case. He created a good deal of merriment by attempting to apologize for having been born in the same State with the old Public Functionary. He said Pennsylvania was very much ashamed of her first attempt to furnish a President, but that she had tried to atone for the disgrace she thus brought upon herself by making all her women so noble that none of them was found mean enough to be willing to perpetuate the race.

He stated his belief that the rebellion now cursing the country was by no means a rebellion of slaveholders alone, but of a great political party. It had been proved by the Democrats themselves that it was a rebellion of the Democratic party, for all who loved their country more than party had left that party; chief among them was Benjamin F. Butler.

He paid a just and deserved compliment to the ladies of the United States for what they had already done, but said there was still a greater work before them, and urged them to put on calicoes and homespun as their grandmothers and great grandmothers did in the earlier war trials of the country. While in the midst of this salutary advice the honorable gentleman, probably catching a glance of his own broadcloth, seemed struck with self-conviction, but showed himself as much of an expert in shifting responsibility as his father Adam before him. "The woman which thou gavest to be with me, she put these clothes upon me and I did wear them," was the substance of his justification! He said, "we men are just what our wives make us. I wear whatever my wife tells me to. If I have on broadcloth now it is her fault not mine." The meekness of Moses was nothing to this! Having cleared his own skirts in the summary fashion, he went back to slavery and the war, the Constitution, and the Copperheads. There, feeling conscience free, he was quite at home, doing general justice, to the great satisfaction of the audience.

After Mr. Broomall took his seat, Mr. A. H. Scott arose and said that somewhere about 50 years ago a little boy carried eggs and butter three miles to market, and sold the eggs for one cent a dozen and the butter for three cents a pound, and took the money home to his mother to lay up to help pay the taxes for the war of 1812. That same little boy had held the bag day after day for his father to fill with wheat which was sold at ten cents a bushel for the same purpose. And now in these times when the nation's life is trembling in the balance between political, moral and social ruin and financial bankruptcy, our ladies, bedizened in jewels and silks and laces, think it a sacrifice to lay the flimsiest of them aside and encourage home industry, which will furnish them with fabrics quite as good; and our Wall Street speculators and stock jobbers are wading in gold. "Why, Sir!" said he with a sudden burst of indignation, turning full upon Mr. Broomall who sat near him, "Why, Sir, you are one of the men most responsible to the nation for this thing! You, and other members of Congress with you! Why have you let these assassins bleed the nation to its last gasp before you could be made to move in the matter? The women may have their duties and responsibilities, Sir, but you have yours as well. Here you sit in your Congress halls and see the country's life blood pouring out; and those scoundrels fattening upon it—aye, worse; seething whole communities in corruption; and you clasp your hands and call upon the women to come to your rescue! Before God, sir, if I were in Congress, instead of passing gold bills, I would erect a gallows! and it should bear fruit, too! Gold is not a marketable article; these public swindlers have no right to tamper with its value. What do you do with men who tamper with metallic currency, with weights and measures? Why, that is misdemeanor, and you arrest, and fine, and imprison them. Yet here a poor man by hard labor earns his two dollars a day, and when the paper, endorsed by government, the representative of so much gold, is handed him, these atrocious scoundrels of Wall Street coolly tell him, 'Your Government pledges are worth only 30 cents on the dollar,' or even less; and the country submits; and what a government! to sit and hold its own throat passively to the knives of such villains! If I had the power, I would soon put an end to those damnable Wall Street operations!

"Ladies and gentlemen," continued Mr. Scott, "the little boy who carried his basket of eggs three miles, and sold them for a penny a dozen, and who carried butter to the same market and sold it for three cents a pound, the little boy who held the bag for his father to measure up wheat at ten cents a bushel, all to help pay taxes for the war of 1812, is living yet. He has lived to see the country that was poor then become a prosperous and a glorious one. His mother and sisters, and other women in those days of trial, wore homemade linsey and copperas-colored dresses. They went without shoes, or with very coarse ones, at home, and when they went to church carried their stockings and shoes in their hands till they were within sight of the meeting house, and when meeting was out took them off again as soon as they were out of sight of the house and crowd. Women of these days, though they abjure all foreign importations, will never know anything of such sacrifices as our mothers did. What the country does not already furnish, it soon will, when it finds that home industry is to be encouraged in preference to foreign."

His speech was received with the heartiest applause throughout, most especially the scoring he gave the dilatory Congress and the Wall Street swindlers.

Mr. Scott was followed by Col. T. H. Gibbs of Tennessee, who, by the humorous turn he gave to his remarks, kept the audience in an uproar of laughter nearly all the time he was speaking. He said when the Tennessee rebels asked him what we were going to do with the negroes when we got them all free, he told them they had better ask what we were going to do with *them;* that was a question in which they would find themselves somewhat interested by the time they lost all their slaves, and a Republican Government had hold of the necks of traitors. Such a reply made them look thoughtful. When he and his wife came away from Tennessee, as refugees, they left their home in possession of their three sons and two daughters.

The husbands of both daughters were in the rebel army. After a while the three sons were conscripted, and when the officers came to take them—behold! They were not there! Because these rebel chiefs could not find his boys, they turned his two daughters into the fields destitute, and set fire to the house and burned it, with everything in it. That was the way they treated the wives of soldiers who were fighting for them. He was not an abolitionist before the rebellion, but now he was ready to abolish everything this side of Heaven except the Government of the United States. People made a great fuss about the despotism of military authority, as if it wasn't necessary to have authority of some sort when civil authority failed! Talk of suspending the writ of *habeas corpus*! He would suspend the *habeas* and hang the *corpus!* If it hadn't been for that corrupted Democratic party headed by that pusillanimous old Public Functionary we need not have been in this fix. The poor old fool sold himself to the south when they hoisted him on the Cincinnati platform; he told them to do just what they liked only not to call their doings "Nullification." If they had got up this row and called it nullification, he would have known what it was; but when they called the thing secession, he didn't know what it was, and didn't know that there was any power in the Government to save its own life—rather thought there wasn't!

He said the loyal people of Tennessee know nothing but Abraham Lincoln and Andrew Johnson. [Tremendous cheering.] If we elect Abraham Lincoln President, and Andrew Johnson Vice-President, there will be an end to the rebellion soon. [Cheers.] All the rebels down there are fighting for now is to hold out till after election, when they hope somebody else will be President and they can give up and have it to say that they never submitted to Abraham Lincoln. He did not want them to have the chance to say that; and did not mean they should. He wanted to have Abraham Lincoln President of the *whole* United States; and if he was ever saved he believed it would be in consequence of his devotion to Abraham Lincoln.

Mr. Gibbs went to his seat amidst uproars of applause and shouts of "Go on," "Go on!" But, as the hour was late, it was concluded to adjourn, which the meeting did after a very spirited song, the words and music of which were composed by the singer, who accompanied himself on the guitar. The song was entitled, "That is the name I go by."

L.

May 14, 1864, page 4

Letter from the Capital

WASHINGTON | THE GLORY OF MAY | A PROFUSION OF FLOWERS | SPEECH FROM THE PRESIDENT | MUSIC | THE SAD UNDERTONE

From Our Own Correspondent
Washington, May 7th, 1864

"There was a sound of revelry by night in Belgium's capital" on the eve of Waterloo, and today there has been music and gaiety and revelry in Washington, almost within sight and hearing of the tramp of armies, the clash of arms and all the carnage and horrors of a more eventful field than that of Waterloo. Perhaps there is nothing wrong in all this. The world must go on; youth and health and happiness must make manifest their joy of life though thousands around them die to secure them that enjoyment. Washington has been very gay this Saturday, the 7th of May. From earliest dawn the streets and pleasure grounds have presented an almost carnival-like aspect from the abundance of brilliant flowers, the gay dresses, the crowds of people and the music; and even now, when the daylight has departed, the twilight deepened into the tender gloom of eve, and the young moon, blood-red, through the smoky haze trembles on the western horizon, there are sounds of "Wild waltz music, madly sweet,/Upon the night air borne."

Yet, beyond the two hours' music on the President's grounds this afternoon, and the consequent gathering there of some hundreds of people to enjoy the freshness of spring and the music together, there was nothing unusual going on, no public show or parade that would make the city gayer than any other days. It was nothing in fact but the fullness of spring as manifest in her abundant bloom, and the ready blending with it of human sympathy on the first thoroughly summer-like day of the season.

The morning dawned sultry as July. All the leaf buds seemed suddenly to have expanded into the perfection of June with their April spiciness and the dews of May yet fresh on them. The tulip beds were all ablaze, and the lilacs were a glory to behold. The lilacs! Yes, it was they that made this 7th of May the gala day it has been. It was the lilacs that arrayed themselves in robes of satin sheen, and stood all along beside the fences and in bustling groups in the parks, waving and tossing their purple plumes, and filling the sultry air with the delicious fragrance of their breathing. It was the lilacs, too, that made the marketers so gay in the early morning. I went down the avenue when ladies and gentlemen, and serving men and serving women, and little children, were all crowding the walks on their way home from market. They were like a walking flower garden to look at. Hands, arms, hats, and baskets were purple with lilac blooms. As I went nearer the market, fresher, and more plentiful and purple the lilacs grew. Tubs full of them lined the walks; they were gathered in heaps and in monstrous bouquets at corner stands; piles of potatoes were covered with them, and ham and lamb and roast wore wreaths and garlands of the royal hue. All who bought had lilacs with their purchases, and those who bought not were laden with lilacs all the same. For once there was universal freshness, sweetness, and beauty in the Washington market, even in the midst of all its filth; for, aside from the lilacs, it is filthy, a mere congregation of old tumble-down shanties in the midst of an uncleaned barn-yard. But this morning sweetness was supreme. The scene on the streets might have passed for the "procession of the flowers," granting that all flowers were lilacs. It lasted full half the day.

At four o'clock in the afternoon there was music at the President's grounds, in the rear of the White House, for the first time this season. The grass was green, the trees threw down their glimmering shadows, the fountains sent up their flashing sprays, and the inspiring music blent with all, drew together many hundreds, of all classes and ages. The Marine Band played. It was not such music as we had in the capitol grounds on Sabbath when "Robin Hood," "Blue Bonnets over the Border," and "Robert-of-Lincoln," rung blithely through the green branches above; yet it was very sweet, and much enjoyed by the gay throng promenading the walks, sitting on the grass, or chatting under the trees. The President was among them for awhile, shaking hands and talking. At length he drew quietly back to the south portico, near the steps of which he paused. Very soon the crowd began to press towards him. There was something like a smile on his face, as he watched them coming, as the thousands gathered about him and seemed waiting, he said:

"Ladies and gentlemen, you expect a speech from me. In place of that let us give three cheers for Gen. Grant, and all the armies under him."

Hats and handkerchiefs and voices went up, and cheer after cheer rung through the grove. Then everybody looked for the President to see what was coming next; but he was not to be seen. He had vanished when the tumult was at its height. The crowd went home, too, as the sun went down, all apparently happier for the music and the social two hours in those pleasant grounds.

The music that I hear tonight, the "wild waltz music," does not come from any hall or place where merry dancers meet. In front of my window, over the gravel roofs of two or three low houses between, are two windows opening into a room occupied apparently only by two gentlemen, who have a flute and violin between them, and almost every night while away the evening hours with such notes as are thrilling all the air around them now. And more than this; directly under my window, in the third story, counting downwards, is a piano, just now being touched by skillful hands, and accompanied by a voice that has held thousands under the spell of its enchantment in perhaps nearly every State in our Union—one of the noted Hutchinson family, now giving his lungs and fingers play to one of the spirited and patriotic tunes for which those sweet singers of the old Granite State have so long been famous.

Thus the day has been as it were a jubilee of flowers and music. But there is an undertone to all this song and joy; an undercurrent to all the sparkle of this brilliant surface. There are rumors of news from the front. There have been knots of men gathered at corners and at bulletin boards all day. There are eager, anxious faces everywhere; and hurried questionings and replies, and hopeful waiting for the news that a day or an hour may bring forth. Before these lines reach you the sequel to these reports will probably be known. Rumors promise favorably.

L.

May 17, 1864, page 4

Letter from the Capital

THE WOUNDED FROM THE BATTLE-FIELD | SCENES IN HOSPITAL | MICHIGAN SOLDIERS AT CAMPBELL HOSPITAL | SPIRIT OF THE MEN | OPINION OF COLORED TROOPS | GOOD CHEER OF THE WOUNDED

From Our Own Correspondent
Washington, May 12, 1864

I have been among our wounded soldiers today. It would be a great comfort to the wives, mothers, and sisters of these brave fellows to know how well they are cared for here. The worst of their experience after being wounded is during the long weary wagon rides over rough roads before they get here. Only the comparatively slightly wounded have as yet been brought this side of Alexandria; most of them are still at Fredericksburg, where nurses and all things necessary for their comfort are forwarded as fast as possible. Those brought here are met at the landing by crowds of good Samaritans who distribute among them coffee, lemonade and food of all kinds; then they are taken by ambulances to the different hospitals, where clean beds, clean clothes and kind attendants await them; their wounds are washed and dressed, they undergo a general cleaning process, and are put into clean new shirts and drawers, and lie down to rest, some of them for the first time in days or weeks.

You will have the news of our victories and of the price paid for them before this can reach you; but you have no telegraph stations at the hospitals, and if you had, even the lightning would be at fault to give expression to what is there to be seen and heard. Nothing short of the pen of inspiration, it seems to me, can do justice to such men as are lying upon those little cots today. As I looked at and listened to them, I thought if our Generals have still such men in their ranks the country has little to fear. There is no spirit among them but heroism of the truest and noblest kind.

In Campbell Hospital, the one I visited today, the wounds are comparatively slight; few, if any being of a dangerous nature; but even the slightest are ugly enough. Most of the shots are through the hand, arm or leg; some through the cheek, neck, shoulder or thigh. I was looking for our Michigan soldiers, but found few as yet brought to this hospital. The following, as far as I was able to ascertain, is a list of their names and the nature of their wounds: William Cooper, sen., Howell, Co. A, shot through right side of neck, rather severe; Geo. Thomas, St. Johns, Co. I, 27th Inf., flesh wound through the right cheek, not bad; S. B. Swain, Addison, 6th Cavalry, flesh cut from root of the left thumb by piece of shell, not bad; Patrick Moran, Ann Arbor, Co. II, 1st Infantry, shot through the right hand, lost one finger; John G. Klink, Detroit, Co. F, 24th Infantry, left hand, lost one finger; W. L. Tenbrook, Adrian, color bearer, 4th Infantry, shot through the ankle; Frederick Zeitz, 5th Infantry, knee; Henry H. Harris, Co. K, 4th Infantry, flesh wound in the thigh; Sergeant Albert Bigelow, Co. I, 24th, flesh wound in the thigh; Henry S. Marshall, Co. I, 27th, thumb amputated; Patrick Gorman, Co. B, 20th, wounded in the toe; Elisha Doane, Mendon, Co. A, 1st, shoulder and hand; Emmanuel Sharp, Co. G, 5th, ankle; Charles Sloffet, Co. G, 24th, flesh wound above the knee; Titus Goodell, Co. I, 4th, flesh wound above the knee; Francis Miller, Co. K, 24th, shoulder; John Lutz, Co. H, 27th, over left eye; Gilbert Salliatte, Co. I, 4th, cheek wound; J. B. Conkey, 4th, back.

Among the hundreds of these scarred and battered veterans I talked with, I heard but one murmur or complaint, and that was from the lips of the sturdy fellow from St. Johns above named, who said he "didn't think it was half fair to be popped over in the way he was without having a chance to shoot once! He was just getting into position when that ugly bit of lead came along, and spoilt his face, and his chance of returning the compliment." All the others could boast of how many hours or days they had been in action, how many rounds they had fired, and with what effect. They talk with flashing eyes and with eager motions of their wounded hands, as if they would fain be in the battling ranks again. Their enthusiasm for Gen. Grant is unbounded, and their confidence in his success entire.

In speaking of the colored troops, one who had been through some hard fought battles said he thought he had seen fighting before, but he never say anything like that when the negro regiments of Burnside's corps went in the with war-cry of "Fort Pillow and revenge!" "They made sure work of it," said he, "and encumber themselves with *no prisoners*. The bullet and the bayonet make quick end of all rebels within their reach." One officer who was in a regiment beside them in the fight, said he had heretofore objected to arming the negroes, but had changed his mind now. A large number of prisoners were taken by some of them, and it was soon found that all were shot. Some officers undertook to reprove them for cruelty, when the dusky warriors excused themselves by saying that the rebels got in the bushes and there was no other way to get them out. They were excused. On all hands are heard praises of their valor and intrepid daring.

Our boys now in hospital said they fought in the midst of thick woods and brush, and in many instances had to fire lying flat upon the ground, which was the reason of so many catching bullets in their hands and arms. They all have thrilling stories and adventures to relate, and are in such hearty good spirits that while listening to them it is not easy to realize that one is in a hospital with wounded mangled human beings on every side. Jokes and laughter are not unfrequent among them at their own and each other's expense.

Tomorrow I shall look up more of our Michigan heroes, and will report names and condition as fast as found.

The weather now is a constant succession of heavy thunder storms. We have had intense midsummer heat for a week or two past, but it is cooler now.
L.

May 19, 1864, page 4

Letter from Washington

From Our Own Correspondent
Washington, May 13, 1864

To relieve the anxiety of friends, I hasten to send you the few names and condition of Michigan sick and wounded whom I saw today. It is impossible to get full lists yet, or even to find, in a short time, many of our boys, scattered as they are among so many thousands:

CAMPBELL HOSPITAL
    R. C. Goyer, Flushing, Co. C, 16th Inf., foot crushed by wagon wheel.
    Albion Johnson, F, 16th, sick, not seriously.
    Charles Culver, Howell, I, 5th, left shoulder, badly.
    William Coon, Redford, I, 24th, cheek, slightly.
    David Frost, St. Johns, B, 8th, little finger of left hand shot off.

COLUMBIAN HOSPITAL
    Henry Rice, Detroit, I, 8th, flesh wound in left leg, slight.

Ira Abbott, Reading, C, 1st Mich. Sharpshooters, right side, slightly.
CARVER HOSPITAL
James P. Horen, Monroe, A, 24th, right arm off below the elbow.
David Phillips, Plymouth, II, 2d, head, not bad.
John T. Martin, Detroit, D, 2d, head, slight.
Christopher Mayhew, D, 24th, shot through wrist.

The above are all in cheerful spirits, many of them walking about where they please. The slightly wounded are to be furloughed and sent home as soon as possible, to make room for the hospital recruits coming up from the field.

Charles Culver, above named, had been in but a few hours when I saw him, and had not yet recovered from the exhaustion and pain of the long journey, and of having his wound probed and dressed. He was suffering much, but patiently.

One of the bravest, cheeriest boys I have seen, is James P. Horen, of Monroe. He says his pet, as he calls the stump of an arm he has left, has not given him much trouble yet; but he is a little troubled about writing, but found a comrade lucky enough to have a right hand sound, who wrote to his mother, and as soon as he gets up he will practice with his left, and make that do double duty. He is a son to be proud of.

All have thrilling stories to tell of that fearful time in the Wilderness when the rebels came so near, our boys could almost reach them with their guns, and yet could not see them for the thickness of the brush in which they themselves were lying. They had to load and fire while lying down, and when a hand was raised with the ramrod it was seen and became a target for the watchful foe. Hands and arms bear evidence that many went up in their country's defense when the vote was called there.

L.

May 23, 1864, page 4

Letters from Washington

Description of the Hospitals | Talking to the Boys

From Our Own Correspondent
Washington, May 16, 1864

The hospitals here are built much like your barracks at Hamtramck. On a broad plateau are erected long lines of low wooden buildings, all whitewashed, and most of them having covered ways leading from one to the other over the whole ground. To these, since so many wounded have come in, have been added rows of long,

Armory Square Hospital. From *The Photographic History of the Civil War,* 1911.

waterproof tents, with ranges of little beds down each side as in the houses. Each room or tent is called a ward, and these as well as the beds are all numbered or lettered; each ward has its ward master, with nurses under him. In the clerk's room at the headquarters of each hospital, are kept books with lists of names and descriptive lists of all patients admitted, with the number of the bed and ward assigned them. Thus, to find a friend known to be at a given hospital, a glance at the list will tell in what ward and even in what bed he lies. Douglas, Stanton, Judiciary Square, and Armory Square hospitals are within the city limits—almost in the heart of the city. Columbian, Carver, Mt. Pleasant, Harewood, and Campbell are along the northern boundary; Finley occupies Kendall Green on the east; Emory and Lincoln are in the direction of the Navy Yard, at the southeast, beyond Capitol Hill; and the Seminary Hospital, where most of the wounded officers are taken, is in Georgetown. Many wounded are at Alexandria hospitals, a few miles below, and many more, indeed all the severest cases, are still at Fredericksburg, whither corps of nurses and citizens have gone to give them needed help.

It may be thought from what has been said above, that these disabled men are eager to talk and garrulous of their exploits in the field, but it is not so. In general it is only by leading questions that they can be drawn and led to speak of their own part in the conflict they survived. It gives one a singular sensation to stand at the entrance of one of these hospital wards, and look down the long line of narrow beds on either side, each with a prostrate human form upon it, and to think that these are but a handful to the many thousands who have been shot down in defense of the Government. A handful! yes; there may be a hundred or more in this one ward; look through the open door at the other end, and the little corridor beyond, down another long aisle between the ranges of little beds, and know that there is still another and another beyond, all full; and branching off from these in every direction, ward after ward with their hundreds of pale and patient sufferers, and multiply these by many hundreds more, aye, even thousands in some of these sad receptacles of heroism, and yet we have but a faint idea of the greatness of the sacrifice our nation has placed on the altar of freedom.

Standing thus at the door, looking at those little white beds, each with its pale still burden upon it, you feel reluctant to disturb the sanctity of that silent suffering; but anxiety for a friend impels; you speak to the ward-master; now, if you observe, you will see many eyes turned upon you with a look that seems to ask: "Is it anyone inquiring for me?" It is touching to witness the quickly drooping eyes and expression of resignation on the mute lips when they hear a stranger's name asked for. The first time I was in an hospital, I was fearful of speaking to any one except from our own State, thinking it might be looked upon as an intrusion; but as I was passing down one of the wards, something in the eyes of a large-featured, bronzed complexioned man, drew me towards him. Hardly knowing what words came first, I said: "Well, you are among the brave men, I see; may I ask what State you are from?" You should have seen the light that came flashing into his eyes and kindling over his whole face, as he replied with a strong Scotch accent:

"I belong to no State; I have been fighting for your government and I would die for it; but, O, ma'am, before I say another word, I want to thank you for coming to speak to me! You are the first, except the nurse, since I came here, and that is two days. Some pass through and speak to nobody; some talk to others all around me, but none to me before. I thank you; it makes me almost well."

Poor man; it is doubtful if he ever sees Scotland or his three months bride again! He left his young wife and came over here to fight for our government; he is looking for a letter from her, and wants me to answer it for him when it comes. He has a dangerous wound through the shoulder, and some of the lungs were cut away in getting the ball out. The second time I saw him he had great difficulty in breathing, and there was a whitening line along his lips that told of terrible suffering; but he welcomed me with a smile, and talked cheerfully of making his home in America, "under the good government," he said.

Since then I have had such thanks from many others, and now can scarcely pass a cot without speaking to the occupant if he is awake.

One of them said: "You are looking for Michigan boys, I hear; we are all Uncle Sam's boys together; we have no State, till this war is ended right; it is our whole country we're fighting for, and we all like a cheerful word from our country's friends." Another said: "Don't be afraid of intruding by speaking to any of us poor wounded fellows; we are only vexed when people pass through with their long faces and never give us a word of cheer. Smiles and pleasant words give us new life."

However sad and wistful the expression on these faces may be, you have only to step towards them with a look on your own as if you would speak, to see the kindling eyes and the welcoming smile lighting up every feature as with sunshine. Then as you sit by their beds you will hear in a few sentences whole chapters of our nation's history; chapters which will glow with blood and flame, and which echo back the roar of the cannon, the sharp crack of the rifle and the rattling laden hail, all through your quiet sleeping hours—chapters that grow into volumes as you dwell upon them, and multiply the fleeting moments of rest into years of exciting life.

By these bedsides I have gathered incidents which I will give you as fast as I have time to get them into shape; little personal incidents which show what sort of men have been and still are fighting our country's battles.

L.

May 23, 1864, page 4

WOUNDED SOLDIERS—WRITING FOR THE BOYS—YOUTHFUL HEROISM—TALK WITH A WOUNDED REBEL—HE WANTS TO SEE UNCLE SAM—REBEL RATIONS

From Our Own Correspondent
Washington, May 17, 1864

In your issue of the 13th you give a list of "missing" from Michigan regiments, as taken from the *New York Herald*. Many of these are now in hospitals in this city. Most of them I have seen personally, and found them comfortably situated and doing well. The following are at the Campbell Hospital: Elisha Doane, co. A, 1st, wounded in shoulder and hand; Patrick Moran, Ann Arbor, co. H, 1st, right hand severely, one finger gone. Patrick said he had but one wish, and that was that he could be in St. Mary's Hospital, in Detroit; he had nothing to complain of here, to be sure, but St. Mary's was the place for him.

Wm. L. Tenbrook, Color-bearer of the 4th, in Campbell too—shot through the ankle. I had a pleasant talk with him about the terrible fight; he is in good spirits. James B. Conkey, K, 4th, was shot in the back. Titus Goodell, co. I, 4th, wounded above the knee, flesh wound. Emamuel Stamp, I, 5th, ankle.

Lieut. Sabine, of the 5th, is at Armory Square Hospital, slightly wounded in thigh; I spoke with him for some minutes. Several others are in different hospitals here; among them Patrick Courtney, Francis Raymond, Geo. E. Lovett, Geo. Williams, John Staley.

One of the sadly pleasant duties a visitor at the hospital may perform is that of writing home for the wounded boys. It seems most appropriate to call them boys, for a large majority of the hundreds I have seen are so young, many of them beardless boys, physically, but manly in all that makes a soldier. I sat beside one of them last Friday to take down the words he wished to send to his mother. With a brave, sweet smile upon his face, he said,

"Tell mother not to worry about me; I am doing well, and hope to be able to write to her in a few days myself." This is one of our Genesee boys, George Seymour, from Argentine. He was shot through both thighs, but says the most painful part of his experience was in riding 48 hours over corduroy roads in one of those four-horse army wagons to Fredericksburg. From thence it was 48 hours more in wagons to the boat at Aqua Creek. These long, rough wagon rides are fatal to many hundreds, but it is the only way they can be brought off.

Another instance of youthful bravery I witnessed on Saturday at Stanton Hospital. This is a Detroit boy, Jacob Baker, a little, black-eyed, auburn-haired fellow, who lies on a cot in the center of one of the wards with rows of wounded comrades on each side of him. He was born in Detroit, and is only seventeen years old. He welcomed me with a bright smile, and in answer to questions, said he was not half so bad as many others of the poor fellows. He said he got one of the boys to write to his father from the battlefield, but he did not know as the letter would get home. I thought it likely it would not, and so took the responsibility of

Hospital scene. From *The Photographic History of the Civil War*, 1911.

writing to him myself. The little hero thinks he would like to have kept with his regiment through the war, and seen the end of it. He is a member of co. F, in the brave 16th.

A few feet from the boy lies a wounded rebel, a young man from one of the North Carolina regiments. I had some talk with him, and among other things asked if he would go into the rebel ranks again if he were at home and free. He said, "there would be no choice; they take us by force; we have to fight." He said our troops came upon them by surprise and captured the whole brigade to which he belonged. They had thrown up breastworks and lay behind them when news came that their troops had chased the Yankees three miles; then, said he, most of our fellows went to sleep, and in less than 15 minutes your soldiers came around from behind where no one was looking for them, and charged right in upon us. They waked our fellows up in a hurry, but it was no use then; they took the whole brigade, and I don't know how many more. When asked how he liked Yankee treatment, he said he had nothing to complain of, they had taken good care of him. Reference was made to the cruel treatment of prisoners at Richmond. He said, "they had as good to eat, and as much, as we soldiers had; that is what we were told: our army has no such supplies as yours. You know we have not the whole possession of a single State now and where are our supplies to come from?" He says he came up under guard of colored soldiers: he had never seen any before and thought they were fine looking fellows; he didn't know as they could look and behave so well! He expects to be sent to prison as soon as he is well enough, but says he would like first-rate to look around Washington a little first. Looking up at me, he said: "This is where Uncle Sam lives, isn't it? I've heard so much about him."

Yes, I said; he lives here in Washington, and is a very fine, social, kind-hearted old gentleman. I think you would like to be acquainted with him.

"I reckon I'd like him well enough; anyhow I'd like to see him," was the reply. "Does he ever go down to the fight with the rest of 'em?"

He sends his boys down to do the fighting, and once in awhile goes down to look after them, said I.

"Well, Jeff. Davis was down amongst us when we were on the Peninsula; he passed along the line and they all cheered him, but I was asleep and didn't get to see him at all. I should like to see Uncle Sam." I told him I thought he would have a chance to see the old gentleman yet.

Our soldiers told me that the rebels they took had their haversacks filled with dry meal, and in some instances shelled corn, both of which they had to eat in a raw state, as Gen. Grant didn't give them time to do any cooking!

L.

May 27, 1864, page 4

Letter from Washington

MIDSUMMER IN MAY | VISITING THE WOUNDED SOLDIERS | SCENES IN THE HOSPITALS | UNWELCOME VISITANTS | LETTERS OF INTRODUCTION | STRANGERS IN THE CITY | OUR WOUNDED

From Our Own Correspondent
Washington, May 21, 1864

Strawberries in market and lamb and green peas on our table, with a sultry atmosphere, a burning sky, and all trees and vegetation in fullest leaf and bloom, crown the 21st of May in Washington with all the attributes of midsummer. The coolest places are most sought for now by comfort-lovers; they gather in little knots under the breezy shadows of trees in parks and pleasure grounds; they stretch themselves at the foot of old oaks crowning the grassy ridges that skirt the city boundaries, or hide within the dim recesses of brick-walled rooms, from which light and heat are banished together. It might naturally be thought that in a place and time like this there would be few seeking their own pleasurable comfort in this selfish way, but human nature in Washington is much the same as everywhere else, and has a large proportion of selfishness in its composition; so, despite the many thousands of wounded and suffering ones within and around the city boundaries, there is, to the outside looker-on, little perceptible deviation from the first great law of nature. Self-preservation and self-interest keep the world up to the level of the great draughts being made upon it by patriotism and progressive civilization. Even the suffering are happier from the consciousness that the world is not made wretched by their personal misfortunes. There is still enough of self-sacrifice and good Samaritanism to minister to their wants, and the cheerful life about them inspires fresh hope and courage in their own hearts.

It is something of a sacrifice of bodily comfort to start out in the middle of one of these sultry days when the thermometer is ranging between 90 and a 100 in the shade, and make one's way by street cars and footpaths to some of the distant hospitals with a basket on one arm and a satchel on the other, both filled with articles so much in demand among invalid soldiers—tobacco, oranges, lemons, and stationery; yet once within their whitewashed rooms and airy tents, weariness and the sultry heat are soon forgotten. The prostrate forms around, the shattered and mangled limbs visible, and the wishful, questioning eyes watching your progress and your words, are wonderful aids to self-forgetfulness. The cooling juices of the fruits, the welcome sight of the long wished for "Honey-dew" or "Mayflower," and the promise given of communication with home by means of proffered paper, pencil, and ready fingers have a magical influence on the listless and weary forms around. Lost limbs and splintered bones and ugly bullet wounds are for the time forgotten, and the stirring incidents of life in camp, the march, the charge, the rout, and the wild moments of victory are lived over again. It is worth many an hour's toil through heat and dust to witness the change a half hour's visit will make in the faces of occupants of these hospital wards.

Too few visitors understand what is wanted in such a place. I have seen ladies, and gentlemen too, as they entered a ward put on long funeral faces and march solemnly down the aisle, pausing now and then to make lugubrious comments to each other on the appearance or condition of patients on either side of them, but never giving one cheerful word or grateful look to express their gratitude, if they felt any, for the noble work these brave men have done. In some instances they pass along, only stopping occasionally, as if they had got into a museum, or show of some sort, which turned out not to be as pleasant as was anticipated, and they were anxious to see their money's worth and be off. I have watched the expressions of disappointment, changing to contempt, on the faces of the men as such people passed by, and felt to congratulate myself at having been furnished with such satisfactory letters of introduction from the Michigan Soldiers' Relief Association, as my basket and satchel contained. A plug of tobacco is a good entering wedge for conversation, where experience or assurance is lacking. A wounded soldier is well pleased with anything that brings pleasant faces near him, and especially with words of appreciation from those for whom he has given his blood.

Washington is overflowing with strangers just now, friends looking up the wounded and the lost. Scattered through the hospitals are wives, mothers, brothers, or sisters, comforting and caring for the suffering and dying. But there are hundreds, yes, thousands, who are dependent entirely on the kind offices of strangers and ward nurses. Our Michigan Association is doing all it can through volunteer agents, its regular ones being absent at Fredericksburg. I enclose a list of names of individuals visited by myself, which, if they had not already appeared, may give satisfaction to anxious friends.

L.

ARMORY SQUARE HOSPITAL, MAY 17

Albert Shaw, co. H, 17th, sick and sunstroke.
David Gibens, Coldwater, 5th cav., wounded in knee slightly.
Charles W. Carrick, co. E, 1st, flesh wound, both thighs.
Jacob Riley, Detroit, co. G, 16th, flesh wound, severe.
John Delamater, co. C, 26th, left arm amputated, doing well.

LINCOLN HOSPITAL, MAY 18
  Lieut. Col. John Pulford, 5th inf., body wound, severe.
  Lieut. Henry Dopson, co. C, 26th, flesh wound in body, severe.
  Thomas Fenton, co. A, 1st cav., hand, slightly.
  J. Taggart, co. G, 7th, sick, not seriously.
  H. Burch, co. K, 7th, finger, slightly.
  J. E. D. Cahill, Jackson, co. K, 8th, hand, severely.
  D. Gregory, co. F, 17th, sick, not seriously.
CAMPBELL HOSPITAL, MAY 19
  Sergt. Albert Hays, co. I, 3d, right arm badly wounded.
  R. Gibbons, co. B, 24th, arm, slight.
  J. F. Clegg, co. H, 24th, shoulder, slight.
  John Whitman (German) Detroit, co. A, 16th, both legs, badly.
  Thomas Hawkins, 2d Berdan's Sharpshooters, right arm, badly.
  Geo. Williams, co. B, 4th, right shoulder, slight.
DOUGLAS HOSPITAL, MAY 20—
  M. Broomfort, co. A, 27th, flesh wound, not dangerous.
  J. Munson, co. K, 1st cav., sick.
COLOMBIAN HOSPITAL, MAY 21—
  E. M. Halstead, co. D, 16th, sick, not bad.
  Alex. Hubbard, co. D, 16th, neck wound, slight.
  J. S. Chamberlin, co. D, 16th, shot through the right hand.
  N. Durbrow, co. D, 3d, left hand, slight.
  S. P. Barnhard, co. K, 3d, left arm, severe.
  H. H. Harvy, co. K, 3d, sick.
  R. H. Collinson, co. B, 24th, head, slightly.
  J. Chandler, co. D, 5th, toe, slightly.
  M. Sheffield, co. E, 3d, hit by shell, slightly.
CARVER HOSPITAL, MAY 21.
  John Livingston, co. A, 1st, Sharpshooters, right leg off below knee.
  W. H. Harrison, co. B, 4th, left leg off, very sick.

Many of the slightly wounded are being sent to Philadelphia, and many more are going home on furlough. As a general thing the wounded are doing remarkably well, and are in the best of spirits.

(Note—We have given in the above list only those whose hospital address has not already been published in the *Advertiser and Tribune.*—Ed)

June 4, 1864, page 4.

Letter from Washington

VISITS TO THE HOSPITALS | LISTS OF WOUNDED MICHIGAN SOLDIERS.

From Our Own Correspondent
Washington, D.C., May 29, 1864

Since our men in blue came back from the Wilderness to people the white-walled cities in and around the Federal Capitol, I have known little or nothing of life outside the narrow walls where they lie. One day's experience were it all written out would fill volumes of such history as ought to be known and read in the homes and neighborhoods these men have left. Never, till it is all known, can their sufferings and their sacrifices be half appreciated or understood by those dwelling in the peace and security these sufferings and sacrifices have purchased. But I have no intention of attempting the task of narrator now, a mightier hand than mine will be their chronicler, and write their lives and deeds for the ages yet to read on the pages of immortality.

During the past week I have made brief calls on some of my old patients at Campbell, Douglas, and Stanton Hospitals, but most of the time has been spent at the still larger and more distant one, Mt. Pleasant. At Campbell I was glad to find my Scotch hero so far improved in condition as to be able to sit bolstered up in bed. He was smoking a pipe, but quickly laid it aside, and told me with a pleased smile that he had the prospect of being transferred soon to New York, where he had friends, and where he thought he should get well faster; he wanted to go back to the army and help finish up the work so well begun. It would take a harder rap, he said, then he had yet had to destroy the constitution old Scotland gave him, and it would go hard, but he would be out and see the end of the fight yet. His features, whitened and sharpened by pain and loss of blood, looked as if it might yet be a hard struggle for life between him and the skeleton conqueror of all; but the fire in his eyes showed the indomitable will and something of the old constitution still there, and his desire may after all be realized, for, a day or two since, I heard that he had actually been sent to New York and, if the journey is not too much for him the famous Irish Brigade, to which he belonged, may see him in its ranks again.

I found in another ward a brave Canadian boy who had lived so near the Vermont border as to have imbibed something of the Green Mountain spirit of liberty. He said that when the war began, he felt as though he wanted to do something to help us, and so went over to Boston and enlisted in a Massachusetts regiment. He fought through several days of that eventful week of battles, and then, as he said, gave the best foot he had for the cause, and was brought off the field crippled for life. His right foot has been amputated. Opposite his bed was a Massachusetts boy who had also lost his right foot; a brother had come on from his far New England home to see and care for him, and it was pleasant to note that the young Canadian shared alike his kind, brotherly attentions. There were four or five on adjoining beds with amputated limbs, and one, with a shattered leg bandaged and hung in a sling, sat bolstered upright, his eyes turned back in his head, breathing his last with no one near him. I went to his side, but the ward-master said, "He is dying and won't know what you say; mortification has set in."

Death becomes fearfully familiar in places and times like these.

E. Olmstead of Ionia county, is at Douglas hospital, slowly sinking from internal hemorrhage of a shot wound through the right shoulder just above the breast. His brother was telegraphed to, and is with him now to see him through the last silent battle of life. Opposite him is J. W. Holcomb of Shiawassee, from the same regiment, the 5th who had his left arm very badly injured; but is doing well now, and healing fast. A little further up lies J. W. Hall, a printer from Adrian, I think, and a member of co. F, of the Michigan 4th; his left leg is off above the knee, but he is in good heart and spirits and rapidly recovering.

My little friend Jacob Baker, at the Stanton, is still flat on his back, and helpless from the very painful wound in his ankle. It has been and still is a matter of some doubt whether his foot can be saved from amputation, though every means possible are used by the physicians and nurses to that end. I went yesterday to carry him a letter, enclosed in one to me from his sister, Mrs. Weiber, of Detroit. For the first time since I have seen him, there was a misty look as of tears gathering in his eyes, but it was from gladness, the joy of hearing from home. He says he is well cared for, and has everything he needs for comfort, except his strength and the sound leg he had before the rebels shot him.

In this hospital, as well as in Douglas, Lincoln, and perhaps some others, are to be seen the "Sisters" with their white-winged bonnets, their straight black dresses, with keys, crosses and rosaries hanging from their girdles, gliding up and down between the long files of little beds, carrying medicines or cooling drinks to the sick and wounded men. There is one sister to a ward, and under her are men nurses, who dress the wounds and attend to the general wants of the patient.

Mt. Pleasant hospital is situated something more than half a mile beyond the terminus of the Fourteenth Street railroad, northwest of the city. It is an airy and delightful situation, with rolling ground, green banks and beautiful groves all around it. Mrs. Plumb, wife of Prof. Plumb, of the Ypsilanti Seminary, has been my constant companion in visits to this place during the past week. We have witnessed many sad scenes and much suffering, but all borne with a brave cheerfulness, a patient heroism of endurance, which often brings tears to the eyes of the beholder. Death is busy closing the eyes and sealing the lips of martyrs daily in every ward of that field of suffering. These men have been marching and fighting day and night, some of them, for weeks before they were wounded, and with scanty, ill-prepared and irregular food, and loss of sleep have become too much exhausted to bear up under the pain and loss of blood their terrible wounds have occasioned. For a while they seem to revive, and we hope that nature is still strong enough to bring them through, but in too many vitality has been tasked beyond the limit of its endurance, and when the reaction comes the enfeebled frame sinks quietly and silently to rest.

Our Michigan men at this hospital are mostly doing well, their wounds, though very severe in many cases, promising recovery through careful nursing. In one of the tent wards, I came across a wide-awake Jackson boy, Michael Barrett, of our famous Michigan 17th. He had his right hand shattered to some extent by ball and buck-shot. His description of the battle of Spottsylvania, on Thursday the 12th, was graphic and thrilling. Though but a boy, being under twenty, and uneducated, he gave a vivid picture of the desperate struggle for the United States flag carried by his regiment. "The rebels were determined to get it," he said, "and our boys were sworn to keep and protect it from insult. The enemy got in among us, and we had a hand-to-hand fight for it. Some of them captured the color-bearer, George Thompson, and ordered him to surrender the flag; but he refused to do it, saying he would die first—and they shot him dead on the spot with the colors in his grasp. I tell you we had a fight for them after that," continued he; "and Captain Logan got hold of them and cut the flag to pieces with his sword, so that if the rebs did get it they couldn't make much of it more than a handful of rags. We went into the fight with over four hundred men, and but thirty-five answered to the call when we came out. The regiment lost some thirty or forty in the Wilderness fight. Now the stragglers have come in, and they have gathered about 180 in all, but are put on detailed duties, instead of in the fighting ranks. I guess the rebs will remember the Michigan 17th at Spottsylvania!"

I found also a number of our 1st Michigan Sharpshooters, whose praises are in the mouths of all who know their deeds in battle. Indeed what regiments have we that are spoken of otherwise than in terms of the highest praise? I have heard of none. I recollect in one ward a wounded Lieutenant from some Eastern State say: "I hear you are looking for Michigan men, and they are men worth looking after. I was with them in Burnside's corps, and braver or more reliable soldiers I never saw from any State. We always felt sure that something would be done when the Michigan men were on hand, and they *were* on hand too, at the right time and place. There are none braver in the army, and you do well to care for them."

This testimony, unsought and unasked, was very grateful, and it is but a repetition of what I have heard in every hospital yet visited.

My mind is filled with incidents gathered in these daily rounds which it would give me pleasure to relate and your readers to hear, but I forbear now, and close with a list from which you will please select for publication such as have not already appeared in your paper. Most if not all the slightly wounded will probably be transferred or furloughed before this reaches you. Their places are all needed and more than filled by the many hundreds lately brought up from Fredericksburg.

MT. PLEASANT HOSPITAL MAY 23D TO 28TH.

J. N. McLenithan, A, 3d, left leg, gun shot wound, severe.
Serg't Millan Gleason, I, 27th, from Duplaine, sick, recovering.
Wm. Colestock, K, 16th, right leg amputated below knee, doing well.
J. Winman, F, 1st S. S., left hand, one finger off.
Sylvester Bates, E, 26th, heel, slight.
F. S. Lebaron, K, 20th, left arm off near shoulder.
Serg't Daniel Lyon, H, 16th, flesh wound, severe.
John Little, A, 5th, left arm severely.
E. Hoard, E, 3d, sick, not seriously.
Lester Westover, F, 27th, finger, slightly.
J. R. Brown, K, 27th, finger, slightly.
H. P. Gardner, F, 20th, knee, slightly.
S. Wilbur, K, 16th, side and arm severely.
J. Fitzgerald, Port Huron, I, 1st Mich. S. S., right arm, badly.
James Doolittle, Saginaw, K, 8th, left hand, severely.
E. Griswold, St. Johns, 27th, sick.
W. Raynor, Lansing, A, 20th, left shoulder badly shattered.
C. Lowring, Ottawa, I, 3d, flesh wound.
Seaton Spencer, Emmet, A, 1st Mich. S. S., sick, chronic diarrhea, transferred to Philadelphia.
E. C. Munger, Dundee, D, 7th, left arm, badly.
W. H. Wells, Coldwater, M, 5th cav., sick.
F. Bermore, Monroe, B, 17th, left hand, badly.
E. M. Evers, Kalamazoo, D, 17th, left thigh, severe.
Michael Barrett, Jackson, G, 17th, right hand, slight.
W. Willett, I, 1st Mich. S. S., left foot, slightly.
Henry Beighey, Hillsdale Co., D, 27th, right arm, badly.
J. W. Delong, Plainfield, B, 1st S. S., neck, not seriously.
Webster Tozer, Hillsdale Co., B, 1st S. S., right shoulder, badly.
James Miles, Detroit, C, 5th, left leg, slightly.
B. Overlock, Detroit, C, 5th, slight.
R. J. Compton, Grand Rapids, B, 3d, left arm, slightly.
J. P. Robart, Monroe, A, 4th, left arm off above elbow.

CARVER HOSPTAL, MAY 28.

J. Callahan, Breast, G, 17th, left arm off a shoulder, doing well.

Capt. Steinway, Ypsilanti, 1st, left arm, severely. The captain is to be transferred in a day or two to St. Mary's Hospital, Detroit.

Adjt. Raymond, Detroit, 1st, right heel, gone home on furlough.

STANTON HOSPITAL, MAY 28.

Corp. A. Bates, Tyrone, E, 26th, flesh wound in thigh.

Henry Walkensaw, Conovis, I, 20th, flesh wound, severe.

J. M. Stuart, Jackson, C, 8th, right side, severe.

June 7, 1864, page 4

Letter from Washington

Fighting with "Mit Sigel"

From Our Own Correspondent
Washington, June 2, 1864

In my hospital rounds, the other day, I came across the identical son of "Faderland" who "fights mit Sigel." He is a stoutly built, broad shouldered, able representative of the Teuton race. Seeing him in the uniform of the Invalid Corps, I said, you have not been in the late battles, have you?

"Yaas, I vos in heem," he replied; "I vos fight all I coot two, three, four day; shoost marsh, fight, marsh, fight all day, all night, no shleep, no eat, so mooch get sick, I no get shoot, never. Balls coom at me, hit me all over, troo mine coat mine cap many times, troo mine clothes pefo[]e, p[]int, all pout mine legs, mine arms; mine knapsack many holes in heem; mine canteen all shill out mit shoot of palls as go round spout mine pack; into mine poots, ant troo mine hair, ant into mine shacket palls coom; into mine pody, never! I fights hard to keel so many as I coot men who shall so weeked be to this Government."

Have you been in the Army of the Potomac all through the war? I asked.

"No, not all in heem; I fights mit Sigel first. Your Shenerals, till now, have all too mooch hoombug; not it is fight sh[]ost beginning, after all tree, four years hoombug. It was no hoombug in Sigel, when I figts mit heem! Sigel would show four Shenerals war as in old countries we have; but no, they will have the hoombug, the show, the what you call heem?—the strategy! They will harn nothing; they will hurt nopody so much as their own men, ant care shoost no more as a dog for heem, so as to get shtrap mit what you call teensel on him, to shine! Sigel got so mad as never could be mit so mooch hoombug. Now, he shoost care no more, but go under orders, and get beat, mit his hands tied on his pack. His men they have

give to other Sheneals who know not war, and the fight is lost. I have been transfer all apout, under Hooker, and more of others, ant last mit Hancock, under Grant. Now it has coom to war, I have been in heem many days, ant in all battels I tinks I fights mit Sigel!"
L.

June 20, 1864, page 1

Letter from Washington

A Visit to the Finley Hospital | Michigan Soldiers There, etc.

From Our Own Correspondent
Washington, June 14, 1864

Visits to Finley Hospital have so occupied my time during the past two weeks, that correspondence has been quite neglected. Justice to the men there lying, and to their friends at home, demands a few words of explanation of the condition and situation in which they are found.

Finley Hospital is one of the pleasantest located, and perhaps in most respects one of the best managed in the vicinity of Washington. Just beyond the extreme city limits to the north-east, the rising ground is broken into swelling wooded hills and grassy sweeps of valleys, over which extends what is known as the "Gales Farm," once the property of Mr. Gales of the well-known firm of Gales and Seaten, and, since his decease, owned by his widow, who rents to the Government for $4,000 per annum. The mansion once occupied by the Gales family is now the headquarters of the Surgeon in charge. It is shaded by beautiful groves of native trees, which are also scattered all about the low hills and mimic vales where the hospital wards are built. There is an extensive orchard of apple, peach, and other fruit trees on one of the slopes, and a handsome vegetable and flower garden in a sunny hollow. This garden with its great variety and profusion of luxuriant roses, is the delight of the convalescents who may walk in its pleasant paths, and enjoy the delicious perfumes.

The tents occupied by the sick and wounded are pitched in a green valley, beside the garden and at the foot of the orchard slope. They are sheltered by the hills, and by the stately oaks and deep-foliaged tulip trees. The wooden barrack-wards are mostly built on the crest of one of the ridges, rising above and nearly in front of the tented valley. From this ridge may be had one of the most beautiful landscape views the eye can rest upon. You stand facing south; Washington, with its spires, and domes, and towers, lies spread out in the broad, shallow vale before you, a mile or two away; Georgetown, scarcely visible through its green embowering woods, nestles along the slopes at the extreme right; at the left are the far-spreading suburbs of Capitol Hill, with that grandly beautiful Goddess-crowned temple of liberty in the foreground, and far beyond the gleaming sweep of the blue Potomac, around the green slopes of the fort-crowned heights of Arlington. The summer breezes here seem pure, healthful, and invigorating, even in the sultriest days.

Finley hospital contains something over 1,400 sick and wounded men from the Army of the Potomac. I have visited the place regularly for nearly two weeks, and yet the utmost diligence has not enabled me to go through all the wards as thoroughly as they should be visited. I have, however, reason to hope that my labors there in behalf of the Michigan Soldiers' Relief Association and of the Christian Commission, have not been in vain. I give here a list of our own men, whom I have personally visited, and whose wants I have had the pleasure of relieving through the means so freely supplied by the above-named Commission and Association. The visits made were from June 3d to June 12th, inclusive:

Edwin Perry, Williamston, C, 5th, left shoulder, severely, but doing well.

John Grant, Lake Superior, C, 27th, shot through left side of face, doing well.

Philander Allen, Casco, C, 5th, left arm off, healing fast.

Jacob Rhodes, Hillsdale, K, 27th, sick, transferred.

Corp. Ambrose Krake, A, 27th, left arm off, shot through lower part of body, lying very low.

Samuel Harper, Ceresco, A, 1st S. S., right arm off, doing well.

Aug. Lahser, Greenfield, I, 24th, shot through both legs, badly; amputation of one necessary.

Eugene Farnum, Pinckney, B, 26th, right leg, flesh wound, slight.

Thomas Tate, Jackson, E, 26th, thigh flesh wound, slight.

Fred L. Barker, Big Rapids, K, 3d, shoulder severely.

A. S. Shattuck, Lansing, G, 3d, right arm, doing well.

D. Buchor, Grass Lake, F, 17th, shoulder, doing well.

W. H. Edwards, Jackson, G, 16th, right leg, severe.

Ed. W. Flower, E, 8th, right leg off, doing well.

James Malley, Monroe County, left arm and side badly, improving.

Serg't. Homes Spencer, Chelsea, K, 20th, neck, severe, doing well, gone home on furlough.

Martin Lake, Rose, D, 3d, shot through thigh, arm, and right foot, severe.

W. B. Irwin, Lansing, 11, 26th, flesh wound in thigh, severe.

Robert Young, Olive, I, 27th, left arm off, doing well.

Geo. Seigmiller, East Saginaw, I, 27th, right arm off, doing well.

J. I. Christopher, musician of brigade band, sick.

W. Gleason, I, 20th, left hip, doing well.

E. Bennett, Ovid, 1st S. S., 27th, sick, erysipelas.

A. V. Haines, Grand Rapids, 2nd U. S. S. S., left leg, seriously.
Ira Green, Jonesville, A, 8th, left arm and side, severely.
Alex. Purdy, Dearborn, D, 24th, left arm, doing well.
Amos Hamley, Albion, 1st S. S., left shoulder, badly.
W. H. Armstrong, Litchfield, 7th cav., on hospital duty since October.
James Zufelt, Eaton, G, 27th, chronic diarrhea.
Geo. F. Hanna, Battle Creek, 7th cav., right arm slightly.
Charles Carroll, Grand Rapids, E, 3d, chronic diarrhea.
A. V. Cole, Lenawee County, G, 6th cav., left arm, badly.
A. Middlesworth, F, 8th, sick, exhausted by diarrhea and exposure.
Nelson Miller, Tuscola county, 1st S. S., 27th, sick, diarrhea.
Charles Hammond, Shiawassee, 1st S. S., 27th, sick, fever.
Antoine Gipp, L. S. C., 27th, shoulder and finger, slightly.
F. W. Oesterle, E, 7th, hip, nearly well.
C. Putnam, B, 8th, finger, slightly.
Andrew Blum, Detroit, A, 2d, sick, pneumonia.

At Campbell Hospital I found a young boy from Detroit, co. G, 27th, William McNesbit, who suffered great pain from a wound in his left hand, which was amputated soon after I first saw him. Every effort was made to cheer, encourage, and strengthen him, both by kind words and attentions and nourishing food; but his temperament was nervous and desponding, and in spite of all care he sunk away slowly and died on Saturday last.

Wesley L. White, of co. D, 8th, is at Campbell, with a dangerous wound in the thigh. Also, James Reynolds, Detroit, E, 27th, shot through the left shoulder, seriously.

At Wolfe Street Hospital, in Alexandria, I saw E. Tinklepaugh, of Gratiot County, who is wounded in the thigh, but doing well, and hoping soon to go home on furlough. Also, Isaac Evans, both of the 27th S. S., who has a serious wound in the thigh, and in much reduced from excessive bleeding.

If the friends of wounded soldiers could only know how much good a simple letter from home will do, they would write almost every day of their lives. The homesickness that grows so rapidly in these sad hospital wards, has no cure like letters from home. Write often, friends, and give the soldiers words of comfort and good cheer.

L.

July 9, 1864, page 4

Letter from Washington

A VISIT TO CARVER HOSPITAL | A WIFE AND MOTHER IN SEARCH OF A SON AND HUSBAND | LITTLE JOHNNY LIVINGSTON | DISAPPOINTMENT AND DESPAIR | CHANGES WROUGHT BY GRIEF

Washington, July 2, 1864

Going up Washington Avenue in the street cars a few days ago with a friend, our attention was drawn towards two persons beside us, who were inquiring the way to Carver Hospital. One was a young and pretty looking country woman, a little matronly in appearance, tidily dressed, and whose stout shoes, bare, brown hands and ruddy cheeks, indicated her innocence of city customs and city arts. The other was an old lady, apparently past her three-score and ten, yet plump, active and smiling, a dear motherly old woman, such as one feels instinctively drawn towards, to love and take comfort from. She carried a carpet bag, and the young woman had on her lap a large basket, through the crevices of which, came glimpses of oranges and russet apples.

As we were going to Carver, ourselves, to visit a favorite patient there, we willingly offered to escort the strangers, and learned on the way, that it was the son of the old lady, and husband of the young one, whom they were going to see. He was wounded at the battle of Coal Harbor; was brought to Washington a week ago, they said, and had written to them on Wednesday to come to him. This was Friday afternoon. I asked the nature of the wound, and my heart sunk within me when they said he had lost an arm and had been bleeding and suffering from chills, when the letter was written. Bleeding and chills three days ago! Those fatal chills; if those poor women had known even what my little experience had taught of their effect on wounded hospital patients, there would have been none of that hopeful looking forward to the meeting, which my sadder knowledge told me would never take place on earth. As we were going slowly up the hill leading to the broad platform over which Carver Hospital spreads its white barracks and tents and multiplied streets, they talked so confidently of seeing "John," and of repeating to him, as they gave him the russet apples from his own orchard, the sweet messages sent with them by the little ones at home, that I made one heart-sick effort to prepare them for the disappointment I felt must come.

"You are sure they did not say he was dangerously ill when they wrote?" I said.

"O no," said the young wife; "he was only very weak from bleeding, and had taken cold which brought on the chills, but they were not hard; and he will be so glad to see us, for we are come to take him home, you know. See; here is the letter they wrote; he is in Ward 67; can you tell us which it is?"

"Yes, there; that long tent with the figures 67 on the end; he was there when that letter was written."

"Come, mother," said she, eagerly taking the old lady's hand, "there is ward 67; there is where John is!"

They passed through the gate, and we turned across the street to one of the outside barracks where a dear, patient little fellow, one of our Michigan Sharpshooters, John Livingston of Barry county, was lying, and had been for weeks, with his right leg off below the knee, and his poor back covered with bed sores. Poor little Johnny! I touched his white forehead tenderly that night, for I knew that no mother's or sister's lips would ever press it again. Only a day or two before I had written again. [ ]I told him so. [ ] "O," said he, "I am sorry, [ ]would like to see father so much, I know he had a great deal to do, and no one to help him. Harvesting is just coming on, and he won't know how to leave. I shall get along, I think."

But he had symptoms of those terrible death chills even then. Three days afterwards, the morning paper chronicled his death and burial.

My friend and I left little Johnny's bedside, and went to look after those who we felt sure would need such comfort as we could give, strangers as we were. There was no need of our searching long to find them. The pitiful wailing screams and heartbroken sobs heard through the open door of the clerk's office, drew us towards them at once. The poor old mother seemed to have added the burden of forty years to her life within the last half hour. She sat on a bench, slowly moving her body back and forth, shaking as if with sudden palsy, and sobbing as only age, stricken helpless and hopeless, can sob. I sat down beside her, drew her head upon my shoulder, and let her cry and murmur to me of John, while my friend went to give such comfort as she could to the bereaved young wife and mother, who had flung herself across a chair at the other side of the room, and in the agony of her grief could only wring her hands and scream. The basket, with its golden oranges and russet apples, sat in a corner unheeded, and the sweet messages of the little ones at home, for papa, were frozen upon her lips. He had died the day the letter was written, and his body had been taken to the soldier's cemetery and buried out of sight of mother, wife, and little ones, forever.

It was long after dark before these poor women became reconciled enough to allow themselves to be led away from the place, and then it was only upon the promise that I would return with them in the morning, and go with them to the tent where John had died, that they might see the bed where he had lain, and talk with those who had been near him in his last hours. With the promise of this sad satisfaction for the morrow, we guided their trembling steps down the hill they had so lately gone up, so full of hope. As they were Pennsylvanians, we took them to the rooms of the Pennsylvania State Agency, where they were tenderly cared for without charge, and afterwards furnished with free tickets to their home in the valley of the Schuylkill.

The scene the next morning, awoke afresh the anguish of the night; but when it was all over, and all had been seen and said and heard, and the certainty that John was indeed gone, had time to fix itself in their minds, they settled down to something like calmness, and turned their sad, tear-stained faces homewards. But the change that had come over both, seemed like the work of years of sorrow.

Alas, how many hundreds, within the past two months, have come to this city with hopes as bright and hearts as happy, and gone away bowed with grief, and desolate-hearted. Such scenes are of almost hourly occurrence, and help to teach us the magnitude of the sacrifice our country is making.

L.

July 11, 1864, page 4

Letter from Washington

THE FOURTH AT WASHINGTON | APPEARANCE OF THE CITY | ADJOURNMENT OF CONGRESS | SCENE IN THE HOUSE | REVIEW OF THE INVALID CORPS | A COLORED PICNIC | HAPPY FOR ONCE

From Our Own Correspondent
Washington, July 4, 1864

After weeks of intense tropical heat, with only here and there a day breezy enough for breathing, the Fourth dawned cool, clear, airy and delightful as the most ambitious pleasure-seekers could desire. Should I say it dawned? No: I think some noisier word should be used to denote the manner of its coming: or rather, the noisiest combination of the noisiest words that pen of man or woman can devise. We had premonitions of its boisterous birth some days ago, and not even the intervention of the Sabbath could suppress the growing demonstration, for the fire-crackers and torpedoes which had peppered the sidewalks and pestered pedestrians all day, not only multiplied ten-fold as night came on, but grew into Roman candles and skyrockets, which lighted the pious home from their evening worship, and became as the stars of heaven for multitude and brightness, till the hour of midnight had passed, when was added to them the crack and clatter of all manner of firearms, the booming of cannon, and the uproarious clamor and joyful pealing of an hundred bells! Those who slept through the night of the third and the morning of the fourth in Washington, must have had steady nerves indeed.

As the sun came up the city was one blaze of banners. The Stars and Stripes were everywhere—floating from the Capitol, from the public buildings and principal hotels, and from many private residences; the street cars and their horses were decked with flags; parties of picnickers went "marching on" with bands and banners; children played with the magic colors upon the walks, and troops of veterans marshaled for review beneath their flashing folds.

The city is full of strangers. Thousands, perhaps, have come upon the saddest of errands, connected with the wounded, the dying and the dead that throng our city hospitals; but being here on such a day, they help inevitably to make up the apparent gaiety of the scenes in which they mingle.

It had been announced that both Houses of Congress would adjourn at noon today, and through the morning hours the crowd set in the direction of the Capitol. Supposing the occasion in connection with the day might bring forth something worth witnessing, I went with the crowd. In the Senate we were scarcely more than comfortably seated before the galleries were ordered to be cleared that the Senators might hold executive session, and with the throng we went over to the House. The dignity and majesty of these great bodies of national legislators are wonderfully lessened as one approaches them and becomes familiar with their ways. There are individual exceptions in both Houses where the above epithets may be applicable, but after listening time after time to the maudlin efforts of drunken Senators, and witnessing the senseless, blustering rowdyism of members as so frequently exhibited during the past session, one very readily comes to the conclusion that men are much alike after all, whether they be entitled to the distinction of Honorable before their names or not.

The House was in a turbulent mood today. Neither side would agree to what the other wanted, and spectators could not guess at what either party would have. Cries of "order!" resulted in most uproarious disorder. The Declaration of Independence was ordered to be read, and was finally worried through by the loud-voiced Clerk amidst continued interruptions by messages from the Senate and confusion among the members on the floor. The House indeed seemed like a great school of boys who have been overwearied by long confinement and hard lessons, and were impatient for their word of dismissal. It came at length in a brief, impressive speech from the Speaker, and then school was out.

Both Houses have been in session day and night for weeks past, and their impatience and irritability, to say nothing of their artifices for artificial strength, are scarcely to be wondered at.

In the afternoon there was a grand review of the troops belonging to the Invalid Corps. Some 12 or 14 regiments were on parade with bands and banners, and artillery accompaniments on the level plain between the President's grounds and the river. They made a very handsome show, and the artillery gave us a faint idea of the smoke and smell of battle, by wheeling into position and firing several rounds of imaginary balls at imaginary foes. The review passed off in fine style, and was witnessed by thousands of delighted spectators.

The Colored Sabbath Schools and their friends, meantime, were having a splendid picnic in the beautiful shaded park between the President's house and the War Department. When the review was over, I went around and took a look at them. It was really a sight worth going miles to see. There were several thousands of both sexes and of all shades and ages decked out in a brilliancy of coloring, dazzling to behold. A fine brass band of colored musicians, discoursed sweet music in one part of the grounds; there were groups of sable singers in another; tables loaded with refreshments were spread promiscuously under the trees, and general joy and gladness seemed to prevail. I stood for a moment near an old Aunt Chloe who, probably not having the requisite admission fee, contented herself with looking through the iron railing at the jubilee within.

"Well, Aunty," said I, "they seem to be having a happy time in there." "O, my God, I reckon dey is!" exclaimed she; "I reckon dey is *so!* A mighty good time, bress de Lor! Gov'ment done made de colored pop'lation happy dis time—'deed dey is! guvin' of 'em dis year woods paster for to 'spress derselves, and nobody to pester 'em! O, my God, I reckon dey is happy onst!"

Sunset put a period to their festivities; and with the twilight crowds of weary excursionists and pleasure seekers came thronging into the city from all directions. The day ended peacefully as it had begun, and now while I write, the Fourth of 1864 is being lighted to its midnight burial by streaming sky-rockets and parti-colored Roman candles, which are everywhere flashing across the blue, still, cloudless heaven.

L.

July 13, 1864, page 4

Letter from Washington

THE DEPARTMENT OF AGRICULTURE | PROSPECTS OF A NATIONAL AGRICULTURAL MUSEUM | WOOL SPINNERS—FLAX-COTTON AND OTHER FIBERS | COMMISSIONERS' CARE IN THE CHOICE OF SEEDS | NO MORE PATENT OFFICE FARMING

From Our Own Correspondent
Washington, July 9, 1864

In spite of the adjournment of Congress, and the hot weather, and the rains and rumors of raids, the resignation of Secretary Chase and consequent jolting of some of the wheels of government machinery, the staunch and "reliable" Department of Agriculture goes steadily on its course. Through the energy and untiring perseverance of the Commissioner, Hon. Isaac Newton, sufficient appropriations have been secured to enable the Department to enlarge its sphere of action considerably during the coming year. Several new rooms will be added to those already occupied in the Patent Office, and a better opportunity given for the display of specimen products and manufactures now on hand, besides allowing for a much larger collection in the future.

The design of the Commissioner, and one which he is already putting into execution, is, to have in connection with this Department a comprehensive Museum, including specimens of everything in any way related to agriculture, either for its benefit or injury. Beasts, birds, reptiles, and insects whose existence has any bearing on the farmer's interest, harmful or otherwise, will be here represented to life with such statistics and information as will enable him to guard against their depredations or avail himself of their ability to aid him. Professor Glover, the accomplished entomologist and botanist, will have this Museum under his immediate charge, and will add to it his splendid collection of *facsimile* fruits, of which I gave you a description last winter. A room is now being fitted up for his occupation, and the enthusiastic little Professor is up to his eyes in the preparation of specimens that are to adorn the shelves and cases now under the carpenter's hammer.

Added to the botanical, entomological, and pomological specimens, there is to be an extensive collection of samples of wool from all parts of the world, all arranged and labeled so that the effect of breed, culture, and climate may be seen and understood. Many beautiful parcels have already been received for this collection, and the Commissioner is taking measures through correspondents in other parts of the world to have it complete as soon as possible. The wool interests will thus be attended to in a way to show that if cotton is king he is in a fair way of being as unnecessary to civilization as some other kings the world may know of.

In connection with king cotton's waning dominions, mention should be made of the beautiful collection of fibers and samples of manufacture therefrom now in possession of the Department of Agriculture, and on exhibition there. Flax in all its shades and grades of texture and color may be seen, from the stalks as first pulled from the earth, to the finest, softest, whitest flax-cotton, as white, soft and fine as the southern aristocrat itself. Specimens of cloth are also shown, together with carpeting, calicoes, etc., of which the staple is flax-cotton. The colors of these samples are very bright and permanent, and the quality of the cloth seems excellent. There are parcels from Providence, R.I., from Oswego and Elmira, N.Y., from Pittsburg, Pa., and from Cincinnati, Ohio. The bleaching, it is found, is quicker, safer and better done in the raw material than in the web. Some wonderfully beautiful specimens prepared from China grass are also shown here; and something very like flax-cotton, though not so white, soft or fine, made from the fiber of the asclepias, or silk-pod milkweed so common in our Michigan fields; also snow-white paper pulp from the bark of the poplar, and many other vegetable curiosities, which, under the auspices of Mars, are fast developing into utilities.

Dr. J. A. Warder of Cincinnati is now in this department, and takes much pleasure in explaining the various processes of bringing out and perfecting the qualities of the fibrous family. Keeping special watch over all the interests of his department, the Commissioner is particularly vigilant in regard to the quantity of seeds required for general distribution. On coming into his office, when the new department was organized, he found on hand some thousands of dollars worth of useless seeds and cereals, which had been and were being widely distributed, and as widely execrated, as "Patent Office seeds." Old age and moths and mildew and ocean voyages in steaming heated ship-holds, had made these seeds utterly worthless, and Mr. Newton caused them all to be destroyed, and has since taken pains to procure and send only the best. He has the satisfaction of beginning to see the reward of his care in the growing credit of his department in this direction. The seeds he sends out are not "Patent Office" seeds.

The department is constantly receiving curiosities in the way of seeds, plants, bulbs, fibers, fruits and products of various kinds from all quarters and corners of the globe. With the appropriations now at command, with the energy, intelligence and perseverance of its officials, and a little time given for its organization and arrangement, a museum will soon grow up in this department worthy of the great interests it is designed to benefit.

L.

July 20, 1864, page 4

Washington During the Siege
Experiences of a Resident

From Our Own Correspondent
Washington, July 13, 1864

I write you today from the center of the besieged capital, not knowing how or when my letter may reach you. Communication with the rest of world by rail or telegraph, is, as Michigan doubtless knows before this date, entirely cut off. The Potomac, however, is still running, and, as far as we know, its connection with the Chesapeake and Atlantic coast is still unbroken. So there is hope that in the course of time the waves may wash this waif on its northward way.

After the adjournment of Congress and the "noise and confusion" consequent upon a proper observation of the Fourth were past, the old Federal city, having assured itself that between Christian and Sanitary Commissions and State Relief Associations its sick and wounded defenders would be decently cared for, quietly addressed itself to preparations for its usual summer siesta. Confident of Grant's ability to whittle, smoke, and burrow himself into Richmond, and devoutly believing that the rebels would kindly stay there to witness his *entrée* and grace his triumph, Washington stretched itself beside its slimy canal in the shadow of its unfinished monument, and said, "Now for a 'little more slumber, a little more folding of the hands to sleep,'" and was dreamily dozing off when startled by Maryland's cry of alarm and the smoke and flame of her burning dwellings. Hardly yet awake, she sprang to her feet barely in time to turn the key of her own door against the invader who already had his hand upon the latch. His coming was sudden, but still not altogether unprepared for.

This is the third day of our isolation from the civilized world, yet but for the lack of outside news, the addition of more stir among the inside military, and the distant roll of drums and roar of cannon around the borders, there is little to remind us that we are not one with the rest of the world as ever. Business seems progressing about the same as before, with the exception perhaps of a little rise in the prices of wares and goods. The workmen at the north front of the Patent Office still keep up their steady, monotonous pecking at the great marble blocks; laborers are quietly relaying and repairing street pavements; shop and tradespeople are going on with their business as usual; the tinsmith over the alley makes more noise than ever with the inevitable clattering hammer of his, and the dozens of rattle-brained children on the pavement rattle on, happily oblivious of the change.

It seems strange to be sitting here so quietly listening to the measured tread of armies and the ceaseless roll of their heavy trains through our streets. We know that "the front" now is no mythical or distant place far down the Rapidan, the Rappahannock, or the James; but, for the present at least, a reality terribly near, a dark horizon shutting us in, flashing with fire and streaming with blood. The neighing of the war horse in on our very ears—"the thunder of Captains and the noise of the shouting."

Yesterday and the day before there was considerable cannonading along our northern boundaries, only three or four miles from the city. Today we have but little; as yet there has been only skirmishing, and the throwing of shot and shell from the forts to prevent the rebels from concentrating in favorable positions. Surmises, conjectures, and rumors of every sort are in circulation, as to the number and object of the enemy, and as many differences of opinions probably, in regard to the result of this dashing venture. It will all very likely end in a little more than a great scare, some loss of life, the devastation of Maryland, the abstraction of millions of valuable property, and final escape of the daring raiders with it to Dixie. Even while I write, a rumor comes that they are across the Potomac again with their booty. Whether they will be intercepted or not remains to be seen.

Quite an engagement took place last evening, and it is said that the rebels have left some three or four hundred wounded on the field. They made Postmaster General Blair's house their headquarters, and did not burn it as they did the residences of known Union men. This fact is considered significant. It is reported that Sheridan will meet these plunderers on their way back to Richmond. Union people here will be terribly exasperated if they are allowed to escape.

L.

July 21, 1864, page 4

Letter from Washington

THE SIEGE RAISED | DEVELOPMENTS BY THE LATE EXCITEMENT | WEEDS IN UNCLE SAM'S GARDEN | DISLOYALTY IN DEPARTMENTS | THE SPIRIT MANIFEST | BRIGHT TINTS | AN INCIDENT OF THE SEVENTH STREET BATTLE

From Our Own Correspondent
Washington, July 15, 1864

The two days' siege of the capital is raised, cars are again running on the road that never was torn up, the valorous government clerks after enduring the hardships of war for several hours, returned yesterday, covered with dust and glory, to do duty at their desks and ledgers once more; secessionists, who in the moment of government alarm had become jubilant at the prospect of the fall of the capitol, and were shut in prison for safe keeping, are released and restored to favor—in short Washington is itself again, with all the symptoms of summer noontide somnolence creeping over its heart and brain.

The recent stir and excitement have had the effect to develop to a fuller extent than has heretofore been shown, the strong pro-slavery and Southern sympathetic elements existing here. People in distant States and cities have no knowledge of the prevalence and strength of these elements, or what inevitable, and it would seem irremediable, clogs they are upon the energies of the government.

The truth is, Uncle Sam's house, garden, and, for that matter, some of his large fields, too, have become weedy and foul beyond description. He has hesitated about pulling up the tares lest he might root up the wheat also; and now not only tares in the fields at large, but rank pigweeds, purslane, couch-grass and nettles, in his very conservatory and dooryard, claim his protection, and get it too, as it were in spite of himself and his most vigilant gardeners. It is easy to say, "pull them up and throw them to the dogs," but the doing of it is another thing. Still it does seem to some of us who stand peeping through the fence, that better use might be made of the rich ground occupied by those pompous pigweeds, sneaking couch-grass and purslane, and vindictive nettles.

It is a fact shamefully notorious here that there is scarcely one, indeed, I think it may be said with certainty, not one, of the government departments where the pro-slavery sentiment and the enemies of the Administration are not strongly represented. The representatives of rebeldom have secured appointments through the favor and influence of Copperhead Congressmen, or have bought them of tinctured or temporizing officials, and hold them probably because Government has more important matters to attend to than ferreting out "little foxes." Yet they are the very ones that are spoiling the grapes in the heart of the vineyard.

A case is publicly known and talked of where a woman employed in one of the departments, at a salary of $50 per month, had a brother in the Union army who was wounded and brought to one of the hospitals in the city, but whom she never visited or took the least notice of, though she went daily with a government pass to carry comforts and luxuries to a rebel uncle who was confined in prison in the Old Capitol. Many other instances of the same nature transpire everyday, and many of these lady employees of government have relatives and friends in the rebel army, with whom they are in constant correspondence, and to whom it is said portions of their salaries are often transmitted. Is not this a delicate and unselfish way of aiding and comforting traitors?

But the women are far from being alone in this business; indeed they would not be in it at all if men were what they ought to be; for if all heads of Departments and Bureaus were what they should be in times like these, no such traitoresses would find their way into them under such flimsy pretenses as they do, to plunder and betray. This last raid seemed for a while to promise certain success to the rebels; sympathizers here appeared confident of it, and were quite open and insolent in the avowal of their sentiments. In no way perhaps did they better manifest the true spirit of their principles than in their insolent behavior towards the colored population. Even little misses spread themselves across the pavement when one of that luckless race was seen coming, and signified that "nigger might take their place in the gutter again."

These things are humiliating to national pride, but they go to show that there is a great deal of human nature, with a strong cross of Southern blood in it, still to be found in this good city of Washington. What the President and his trusty advisers have to contend with in the manifestation of this mongrel nature among officials, civil and military, no pen need undertake to tell. Happy will it be for us if, in spite of all, the old ship of State is at last brought safely through the storm.

A woman living near the battleground north of the city, has a brother in the rebel army who took the opportunity of being near to make her a visit, hoping also to get much needed supplies of food and clothing; but she indignantly drove him from her house, and threatened to shoot him for a traitor, as he is, if he ever attempted to appeal to her or call her sister again. Union soldiers, though strangers, she fed and gave drink to with blessings and God speed, but the brother who had betrayed his country and sought its ruin, she cast from her as a wretch worthy only of the traitor's doom—the scorn and detestation of all loyal hearts.

L.

August 2, 1864, page 4

Summer at the Capital

From Our Own Correspondent
Washington, July 23, 1864

July is waning. Midsummer is past its prime. The morning splendors of this semi-tropical climate have lost their freshness. The sultry noontides are choked with dust, and there is no springtime spiciness or balm in the evening breezes. The moon, so late and so long a glory and brightness, impearling all the sapphire sky and flooding the earth with the abundance of her tender beauty, hangs now a great misshapen blotch, blood-red and angry in the midnight heavens. Still and dark the heavy foliaged trees brood over and blend themselves with their dusky shadows from which the fiery sun has long since burned out all the dewy coolness of early summer; dusky shadows that are but a mockery on the burning pavements at noon, and that cloud the dim night-walks with forbidding gloom. The tender green has faded from the far encircling hills; the river is low and creeps on as if a-weary of its downward way; dead along the margin of sun-dried pools the summer lilies are lying; parched with thirst that there is neither rain nor dew to quench, the altheas can scarce unfold their purple petals to the morn; all the June roses have fallen withered from the brow of noon; the sunsets charm us no more with their gorgeous cloud-pageantry of light and darkness, blending the dimness of earth with the glory of heaven; they are only appalling now from the ever-recurring lurid glare, the well-kept promise of a fiery morrow.

The season thus far has not been unlike a lovely woman, joyous in the flush and perfection of her beauty, blessed, and blessing all who look upon her. How doubtingly, how timidly, and with a show of maiden shyness did it first come forth! With the faint tints, and the dainty perfumes, the tremulous, tender hopes of dawning charms, and the sweet shamefacedness of girlish desire, it looked out from the April woods and up to the April skies. Heaven smiled, and the child came forth a goddess. The smile of heaven is the soul and crown of beauty always. And beauty that blesses, is, like virtue, its own exceeding great reward. A beautiful woman should be glad of her beauty and [ ] the world with it as our radiant, joyous spring and perfect summer did.

In this particular latitude, these two seasons mature rapidly and remain long at the zenith of their perfection. In no climate could there have been a more glorious summer than the one now passing has thus far been, and would still be, if showers might clear the sultry air and refresh the parched earth again. The abundant bloom and foliage, the long, bright, fervid days, the nights so welcome with their cooling airs and dazzling moonlight splendor, the balm, the glow, the glory, all have been perfect. But the torrid heats have scorched the verdure and withered the bloom. We are longing for rain, and, while yet July is with us, must write on dusty tablets, Midsummer is past its prime.

L.

August 3, 1864, page 4

Letters from Washington

Mr. Carpenter's Great Painting | The Figures Represented | Critics and their Criticisms | The Weather

From Our Own Correspondent
Washington, July 27, 1864

Aside from rumored raids and threatening demonstrations of the returning invaders, the great sensation of the city during the past few days has been Carpenter's picture of "The Emancipation Proclamation before the Cabinet." This fine historic painting, just completed at the White House, has been on exhibition at the East Room for a day or two before being shipped to New York, and as everybody was invited to go and see it, free of charge, of course everybody went.

The canvas on which this memorable cabinet council is represented, is something over fourteen feet long, and about nine feet high. The figures are life size, and are most accurate and life-like portraits. The President is the central figure, and sits facing the observer, at the end of a table, on which lies the Proclamation, grasped in his left hand. In front of the table, and looking towards the President, is Secretary Seward, of whom we have a full side view, with the sharply-lined profile of his peculiar face. His left hand, poised on the thumb and fore-finger, rests on the table. Opposite him and at the left of the President sits Secretary Welles, or, as he is often familiarly called, Old Neptune, with his grave face in its halo of silver beard and hair. Near him stand side by side, the late Caleb B. Smith, former Secretary of the Interior, and Hon. Montgomery Blair; at the end of the table opposite the President, and with arms folded upon it, sits Attorney General Bates, with a cautious and somewhat doubtful expression on a face surrounded by grizzly gray hairs. At the extreme right of the President sits Secretary Stanton, looking confident and approbative, while between the two, with arms folded complacently over his breast, stands Secretary Chase in the full glow and glory of his plump and portly manhood.

It was very amusing yesterday to stand quietly among the hundreds of comers and goers listening to the criticisms on this great work of art. The artist himself should have been there in some unrecognizable shape, and for aught I know, he was. I think some of the remarks would have done him good; some were certainly very

First reading of the Emancipation Proclamation.

appreciative, and others were more candid than flattering. One grave connoisseur who had struck a position directly in front of the painting, after squinting at it awhile first with one eye and then the other, poised his head widely on one side and remarked that "the legs of Mr. Lincoln's chair should have been made several inches higher than the others, as sitting on one of the same height made him look no taller than other men!"

Another would have had the President standing, "to show better!" One thought Mr. Chase made quite too much of a show, and seemed merely put in as an admiration point, standing there and saying, "look at and admire me, for I am the handsomest man in this crowd, and I challenge anybody to deny it." Some of the male critics were rather severe on this point, but the ladies "doted on Mr. Chase." They could not admire him enough; "his fine form," (a thin, whiskered face near me called him fat and coarse!) "his full, handsome face," the "sweet expression of his lips," "his noble brow," (the same whiskered face said he was bald headed!) One young lady declared "there is nothing so beautiful in the whole picture as Mr. C's plum-colored coat!" To her taste it was perfectly delicious, "so life-like and natural!"

Most of the interest of both sexes and all sizes of visitors seemed to center around the President and Mr. Chase; at least most of the expressed criticisms fell upon their heads. The others were scarcely noticed more than to ask "who are they?"

As a historical representation of one of the most memorable events of these memorable years, this painting with its striking likenesses and characteristic expression will be a national heirloom. It is to be finely engraved so that miniatures of it may be had.

A half day's rain has partially laid the dust which has been a great part of our breath of life for a month or more past. Vegetation has been parched and scorched, and crops and gardens are ruined by the long drouth. The sky is still sullen and the air sultry and stifling.

L.

August 16, 1864, page 4

Letter from Washington

The Capital as it is | Fine Arts | Improvements and Evidence of Prosperity | Visitors and their Views | Hospital Life | The Armies that have Gone

From Our Own Correspondent
Washington, August 8, 1864

Washington at this season is little more or less than one great hospital and workhouse combined. Idlers have left the city, except it may be a few tinseled military ones; and pleasure-seekers have turned their faces in other directions. There is little attraction for them in streets crowded with army trains, and squads, and straggling companies and serried ranks of war-worn soldiers; and still less satisfaction in the harassing anxieties about raiders and invaders from without, to say nothing of the merciless fleecings and skinnings they are constantly subjected to within; for a great share of the work done here in Washington is just fleecing and skimming, from Government employees down to the boot-blacks on the street corner. It is an art, a fine art, the only one, I believe, in which the capital claims to excel, and in which it can have no peer, and need fear no successful rival. The illustrious examples of Floyd, Thompson & Co. have not been in vain. Ambitious aspirants to share their fame seem to crowd all the departments of labor, especially the Government departments. Their mantles appear to have fallen piecemeal, and shreds and patches of greater or less extent have lighted on the shoulders of all who come within the charmed lines of the District.

But stop; this looks like slander, and we were talking of Washington in its present workhouse-hospital aspect. To an outsider the assertion made in the first sentence of this letter might carry the idea that dullness and desolation prevail. Yet the city was never fuller, never busier, and perhaps never more prosperous than now. Of its prosperity I judge mainly from the improvements going on. On almost every street new buildings are being put up for shops, stores, and residences: old broken sidewalks that have long disfigured some of the principal thoroughfares, are being relaid with beautiful flagstones; fences are springing up around and trees within the little triangular parks hitherto open to the commons at the avenue crossings; beds of steaming mortar, piles of brick and lumber, and perambulating paint pails and brushes indicate a general renewal and burnishing up of dilapidated domicils. Here gangs of workmen are laying broad and deep the foundations of a handsome church; only a day or two since the cornerstone of another on the same street was laid amidst imposing ceremonies with bands and banners and glittering regalia; yonder an aristocratic "brown stone front," is steadily rising to the light; here a row of less ambitious pretensions, and there a five story block receiving its roofing of slate. Thus Washington "lives and moves and has a being," still, in spite of the *hegira* of its winter fashionables, and the daily repeated rumors that Lee is peeping over Arlington Heights and Jeff. Davis has entered the canal with a heavy besieging force to attack the White House.

But the labor here is not all done by the hammer and trowel, the compass and square. The pen, if not "mightier," is at least plentier than all other implements. I wish I could give some idea of the number of hands daily gliding over blanks and parchment, red and blue lined foolscap, ledgers, registers, and the thousand and one devices for spreading ink through all the departments devoted to recording the doings of Uncle Sam's officials. Taking it for granted that his primary officials in the civil, military, and financial divisions are legion, as I truly think they are, with a secondary legion to officiate for them, and a tertiary legion to record the sayings and doings of all the three strata, and some approximation may be made to the number of pens in daily use; and, as every pen requires a hand, and every hand a body (and many of these bodies have families attached to them), it may be imagined that Washington is far from depopulated, even during the absence of the thousands who have taken their annual summer's flitting for health and pleasure. The workers have to stay, or, if they go out for a breathing time, substitutes take their places, and so the complicated Government machinery moves on.

The city, however, is not without visitors, even at this unwonted season. They throng the sidewalks and the street cars. They stand at the corners wistfully looking for the letter or figure that indicates the name of the street they have lighted upon. They glance into your face with anxious earnestness, and if they see an encouraging look thereon will very likely inquire the way to some one of the dozen hospitals about the city, or ask you how they shall find where a wounded son, brother, or husband is lying. They are no more curiosity hunters than they are pleasure seekers. To them the Smithsonian, with its massive walls and airy towers, and the world of wonders within, is only a "great brown house with steeple"; the Patent Office, in its pure and perfect Grecian loveliness, is only " a big white building"; and the Capitol, lifting its fair proportions and stainless dome above its green Arcadian groves and plashing fountains, is but a waymark to the low, white walled repositories of human suffering spread over the green plain beyond. Still they are, as one may readily see, able and educated people, and well capable of appreciating beauty when not blinded by sorrow.

Hospital life has developed the angel side of humanity as well in those who watch and wait as in those who suffer. In the fort, the foray, or the open field, have been shown no brighter examples of heroism and self-sacrifice, no more devoted patriotism, high courage and moral daring, combined with cheerful, hopeful endurance, than have been exhibited by the unnamed hundreds, aye, even thousands of attendants and quiet ministrants at hospital bedsides. Every State, every city, and nearly every town and county may find representatives here, and especially the army; for hundreds who can no longer endure the march and the charge are still doing efficient duty by their tender care of the sick and wounded. The past season has been one of terrible trial and most disheartening fatality. The broad fields around the Soldiers' Home, and the once fair domain of Arlington Heights, now all one vast cemetery, furrowed and ridged by the narrow beds of the sleeping brave, tell but too plainly of the armies that have gone away through the gates of suffering to that peace which man can neither make nor mar. They have left us the shining pages of their heroic lives, written over by the inspired hand of patriotism, sealed with their blood, and consecrated by their death. Shall the lessons they have given us be lost?

L.

August 24, 1864, page 4

Letter from Washington

WASHINGTON OUT OF DOORS | CROWDED STATE OF THE DWELLINGS | THE OLD ORDER OF THINGS—THE "COMMON HERD" | MISS FLORA'S SIGH | THE CITY AND THE PEOPLE BY MOONLIGHT | LIFE ON THE PAVEMENTS | CROAKERS AND THEIR CROAKINGS

From Our Own Correspondent
Washington, August 17, 1864

As soon as the sun goes down, all Washington turns itself out of doors. Porches, piazzas, porticos, doorsteps, and pavements are all alive, all swarming with the day-long cooped-up inhabitants of crowded back rooms, basements and attics. It is a pretty sight, and a pleasant relief to the day's heat and weariness to look at.

All the pleasanter, too, it is when one reflects how these people, for the most part, have spent the day.

Washington, in the first place, is not half large enough to accommodate decently the number of persons necessary, in times like these, to keep the wheels of government moving. Every house is like an overcrowded hive. On business streets, the front rooms are used for stores and shops; the upper ones most likely let to lodgers, or occupied by boarders, while the primary family of from five to ten or twelve compress themselves into one or two back rooms, and possibly a basement, where those not absent during the day honey and money-gathering, swelter through their household cares in an Eden-like simplicity of attire, till the five or six o'clock dinner hour arrives. Then the labors of the toilet begin, and soon after sunset culminate on the pavements in flowing draperies of lawn and lace, and other airy fabrics.

This is not alone on business streets; it is everywhere through the city, for everywhere the habitable houses are crowded almost to suffocation with boarders, or with lodgers who have clubbed together and taken rooms for the purpose of reducing the rent by division. It was thought by some that when Congress adjourned, rooms would almost go begging for occupants, and rents would be merely nominal. But the "some" who so thought were dreamers of a past age, who cannot seem to awaken to the knowledge that Washington has taken a step forward into the work-day world, and is not now the Rip Van Winkle it was when it dozed through Congressional sessions and slept soundly the rest of the year. It is alive with living people now, people who will keep it alive with work the year round, Congress or no Congress.

"Such a common herd!" sighs out a dilapidated Miss Flora, tenderly touching her haggard cheek with rouge and pearl; "alas, Washington is not what it was. Common faces, coarse hands, dresses chosen and made for economy rather than taste; no style, no refinement, no aristocracy; but then, with such a President, and such a crowd as have swarmed here after him, what better could be expected. The old order of things is so reversed I fear it will never be restored again, at least not in my day; heigho!"

Well, if the few Miss Floras we have seen are samples of the "old order of things," let us hope it will not be restored even though destiny deprive us of our honored President, and scatter the "crowd that swarmed here after him." This last, however, it will take a pretty broad and strong hand to do. It must be a hand that can compete with the energy and enterprise of free labor, that can resist progress, and re-clasp the broken fetters of slavery.

But let us come back to the Washington of tonight, and look at it as it comes forth to be looked at in its evening dress. All things are propitious. There was a delightful rain this afternoon, a real pouring down deluge of a storm, with sharp, blinding flashes cutting the sky in twain, and letting the loose thunder fall crashing in our midst, till all the air was made sweet and the pavements clean; then the sun looked out long enough to make a few dry remarks, and pulling a thunder cloud over his head, went quietly to sleep, while the full moon, now high in the East, pours down such a flood of silver light that his absence is scarcely noted, or, if noted, blessed. What a moonlight this is! Does such visit your northern latitudes tonight, I wonder? So full, so bright, so intense, yet soft and tender, as if the glory of heaven were shining on us through dissolving gates of pearl! The night comes on so perfect in its freshness and splendor that it seems rather the reflection than the shadow of day.

Now it is that one begins to see that the city is not deserted. The sidewalks are literally swarming with children, all in their airiest, gauziest dresses, with bright sashes, with bare arms and necks, and knots of ribbon on their shoulders, and tossing curls and merry laughter. They are like bevies of spring butterflies, and nothing else. One wonders where they have been kept through the day. It does not seem as though there was room in all these houses to hold them, to say nothing of the groups of older sisters and mamas clustering around all the doors, promenading up and down with sweethearts or brothers, and gathering in noisy coteries about favorite porches, where pleasant faces and voices attract, and where mirth and moonlight are brightest and merriest. But somehow they have all been stowed away somewhere, and have now come out upon the street to live.

Where there are no porches with seats for the purpose, chairs are brought out, and all are as much at home on the pavement as in the parlor; the ladies often knitting, sewing, crocheting, or reading by the light of gas in the window, chatting the while, and making the streets cheery with their gossip and gay dresses. Young girls, and older ones too, who have been bound all day to the copying desk, the counter, the needle, or other means of making a living, have put off their weary faces with their working dresses, and come out now with pleasant smiles and pretty muslin toilettes to be happy in the moonlight. Nursemaids of every hue and tint, in brilliant collars, bring out the infantry under their charge, to pass in grand review and dress parade before admiring mothers. Men, too, are mostly at leisure now for an hour or two of enjoyment, for Government clerks are free at 3 and 4 o'clock, and nearly all the stores and shops close early. At all events there is no lack of the masculine element among the moonlight gossipers and promenaders. They usually line the outside of the walk, making a sort of heavy fringe to the airy fabrics down the center and next to the walls. They loiter along with fair companions hanging on their arms, or sit smoking on dry goods boxes with legs crossed on the curb-railing higher than their heads. So vulgar, yet so happy.

A croaker now might come snuffling along, and tell us of filthy gutters steaming with rotten garbage at the very feet of these gay and smiling groups; of pools of stagnant green water before almost every door; of that literal River of Death, the slimy, loathsome canal winding its way through the heart of the city, wrapping "the Island" in its fatal coils, and tainting all the air with its putrid, poisonous breath; of the sickening streams and pools, and piles of pollution festering all around, and through that sink-hole of pestilence, swarming with human styes, and called the Central Market; of—well, yes; he might go on croaking till the moon went down, but he could never dim her pearly splendor, or cloud with care the smiling crowds rejoicing in her light. They have been prisoned all day in close and heated rooms; they must have space to breathe during one hour of the twenty-four—and breathe and be happy they will the moment the sun goes down and gives them the freedom of the pavement.

Pass the croakers by; this moonlight makes a glory of even their green pools and steaming gutters, and Washingtonians drink in the glory and the malaria together, and are content.

L.

September 19, 1864, page 1

Letter from Washington

The Material Our Armies are Made of | Brief Sketches of Two Michigan Boys | Their Record in Field and Hospital

Correspondence of the *Advertiser and Tribune*
Washington, September 5, 1864

We know a great deal, but not half as much as might and ought to be known of the valor and heroism of our Michigan boys at the front; of their wearying marches, sleepless nights, and days without food or rest; all borne with heroic cheerfulness and unwavering devotion to the cause in which they have enlisted, and much in general terms we hear and read of the long-suffering, patient martyrs to that devotion, who linger through weary weeks in hospital wards, and then either fold their hands in the last quiet sleep, or go out into the world dismembered, maimed for life. Now and then individual instances of bravery or endurance are brought forward, but not half often enough to show the people what material our armies are made of. Were the common soldiers better known and understood, I think there would be less grumbling, despondence, and want of confidence among the people at home. Their willingness and ability to endure are beyond all praise. Neither does "soldiering," in such a cause, "demoralize," harden, or blot out from their hearts all sweet home virtues, as some owlish apostles of total depravity would have us believe. The really depraved will, of course, be glad of freedom from restraint to betray their nature; but the truly noble and the manly will come out like gold from the refiner's fire.

I have been surprised at the large number of young, beardless boys who crowd the ranks and fill our hospitals; and not more surprised at the number, than at the uniform courage, patience, and cheerfulness with which they endure the dangers and fatigues of the field, and the untold sufferings which blanch their young faces in the weary months of their hospital life. Yesterday I sat by the bedside of one of these; a little fellow, who, with his pale, pitiful face, his cheek and chin as soft and smooth as a girl's, and his hands as slender, looks as though he should be by his mother's side, tenderly cared for and softly spoken to; his voice is gentle and boyish too, and listening you would wonder what there had ever been of the soldier about him, till you looked into his eyes. But look while he is speaking, and telling of the rapid marches, the surprise, the charge, the victory, and his eyes will betray the child nature yet strong within him, of such a soft and tender brown are they, and so sadly wistful in their expression. There is soldier's fire in them though, when he talks of war. He says: "Tomorrow, Tuesday, the 6th of September, I shall be eighteen years old; and Thursday, the 8th, it will be just four months since the rebel bullet went through my ankle."

Four months of soldiering in bed he has had; a still, stern, ceaseless struggle against death; for the great conqueror has seemingly had a hand upon him many times, and more than once I have left him fearing that the brave young heart would be stilled, and the slender hands folded in icy rest, before I could see him again. Still, in all these four months of agony, the first frown is yet to be seen upon his face, the first murmur to be heard from his lips. For two months he was unable to be even moved from his bed to have it made. The Doctor was trying to save his shattered limb from amputation; and he thinks now it is safe, though yet far from well. In anticipation of being able to get out of bed sometime, the little soldier has a pair of crutches hung upon the wall where he can see them, and enjoy in imagination the walks he shall have when he goes home on furlough, and that is to be "as soon as he is able."

He was wounded at Spottsylvania on Sunday, the 8th of May. The rebels who shot him were so near that he could almost touch them with his gun, he says; his party came upon them unexpectedly, when he fell. His comrades gathered him in a blanket, and ran with him from the field. After being carried from one regimental hospital to another, he was at length left in a tent at Belle Plain to be brought by transport to Washington. There he lay one night and a day soaking in a pool of water made by the pouring rains, and seeing the transports take on their suffering cargoes and steam away without him. The tents nearest the landing were emptied, re-filled and emptied again, and still his turn did not come. At last he discovered a pair of crutches; they were much too long for him, but he prevailed on some one to break them off, and then dragged himself out of the water and hobbled towards the boat, was picked up, carried on board, and has been lying on that little bed in Stanton hospital ever since. He is a native of Detroit. I think I have mentioned him before—in some letter last spring, perhaps. His name is Jacob Baker, and he is a member of our noble 16th, which had such a struggle to save its flag in that bloody Wilderness fight.

The Sister, a pretty-faced and sweet-voiced woman who has charge of the ward where little Jacob lies, said to me today; "He is the bravest, dearest boy I ever knew. See what he has suffered; and in all this time there has not been a complaint or murmur from his lips; not a fretful word has he spoken since he came here." That is his hospital record.

Another, perhaps, a little older, at least more mature and manlike in appearance, and of a hardier make, lies on another little bed in a tent about a mile away from the ward that holds Jacob and his wounded companions. This is a Detroit boy, too; Joseph E. McConnell, of the brave 24th. Taking his conduct and bearing since he has lain there as a sample of the material the 24th is made of, it may bear the palm for true, heroic endurance, and high, moral courage. He was wounded before Petersburg in June, and lay all day, with both legs broken, between the contending lines of battle, where neither friend or foe dared venture for his rescue, or make him prisoner. Under cover of darkness his companions found him, dragged his body upon a piece of tent cloth he had about him, and with his poor, broken legs dangling among brush and briers, ran with him to a safer distance, from whence on stretchers, in wagons and ambulances, he was carried many miles hither and thither from one hospital to another, and at last was sent up the Potomac and landed at Armory Square, where he has since lain, having left one leg to be buried in the sacred soil of Old Virginia, and bringing the other with him, shattered, broken, and mangled, to mend itself here as best it can.

All that has been said of Jacob in regard to heroic cheerfulness and patient, hopeful courage, is also true of Joseph. He says his limb was lost in a good cause, he has no regrets, unless it is that he could not have done more for his Government while it had so much need of help. Weeks have passed into months since I first saw him lying there, and still, though unable to move from that one position, or scarcely to stir the poor mangled leg in its bandaged box, there is always the pleasant smile on his face, the cheerful greeting, and the hopeful answer to enquiries; never a fretful or repining look or word.

Parents may be proud of having sent such sons to war, and will be proud to receive them back again, with all their scars of honor.

These boys are but samples of hundreds and thousands, both in hospital and field, who are giving away limbs and lives in defence of the fainthearted grumblers at home, who, because they have no confidence in themselves, seem to think also that the army is worthy of none. Ah, could the lost limbs and lives of our maimed and dead heroes be restored, there would be no need of a draft or even of a second call for 500,000 more to fill the broken ranks. Their first steps would be taken towards the front, and their first blows would sweep treason and traitors together from the land.

L.

September 28, 1864, page 1

From Washington

The City and the Weather | Ramblers Returning | Vacation Time and Vacation People | The Jungle and the Lions Roaring Therein | Living | Peaches and Milk | Fruits in Market | Freshness and Hope

From Our Own Correspondent
Washington, September 8, 1864

The city has been made gay with banners and bright with cheerful faces since the confirmation of the good news from Sherman's army. Everybody, that is, everybody with a loyal heart inside, seems full of good cheer, hopeful, and smiling. The weather has grown cool and comfortable now, too, so that it begins to be a pleasure to live and move and have a being in this latitude. Hundreds who have been away to escape the midsummer heats are gradually dropping back into their old places. We meet them on the streets and in business haunts, looking vigorous and fresh from the air of New England hills, or bronzed with prairie winds, or browned almost to contraband tint by the glowing suns of Kansas.

August is the general vacation month for Washingtonians. Government employees are allowed four weeks out of the fifty-two for a holiday, during which time their pay goes on, and they go where they please. They usually make it a point to have pleasure follow where business leads; that is, a majority of them being only temporary sojourners here, have homes, or lands, or property of some sort in distant nooks and corners, and so improve the vacation by a summer flight to the old nest, [ ] on without their services. It may be some of them feather their nests with pickings from the public goose. But let that pass. Many, also, go flitting away to the plains and mountains and forests, from pure necessity, for the breath of life. Pale-cheeked, stooping-shouldered, narrow-chested clerks, men and women too, bent over their desks here the year round, must straighten up and look the world in the face once in the time, or a double default might chance; they would soon be lost to the world, and it to them. Some go, too, for real pleasure, and more, still, because it is fashionable. But I notice that whatever motive takes them away, they all seem glad to be back again.

There probably never was a place more abused and berated by everybody for all sorts of faults than this same city of Washington: and perhaps never one deserved abusing and berating more; yet people are drawn here, and when once a foothold is obtained, however slight, seem held as if by a magnet; or if perchance they fly off in imagined disgust, they are pretty sure to come back at the first chance of a rebound, with a stronger attachment than ever.

There is a peculiarity about life in this heterogeneous mass of man and womankind that is terribly grating to some. Those who have played lion or lioness in their own little private bear gardens at home, and come into this great jungle, expecting to outroar everything here, soon find themselves awfully mistaken. After a few attempts, and filling their own and others' ears with something sounding very like a discordant bray, they suddenly drop to their own level and aim at nothing above braying afterwards. If they are real lions, though, the case is quite different. Then they can roar to their heart's content, and the public is very willing to hear them if they only roar loud enough. But after all, the noise, whether roaring or braying, sounds best and is best appreciated a good ways off, that is, it is much more musical to people at a distance than to us here in the jungle; still there are some whose voices are pleasant even here. And I think were they all out of their disguises our Washington world would be astonished to find how many of the royal leonine race it had been entertaining unawares. Stern necessities and circumstances as stern have brought numbers here, both men and women, whose talents should command, in a more genial employment, a better support than their fingers can wring from the precarious positions they get. Still they cling to the straws, and struggle on, and call it living.

Speaking of living, our living during the past six weeks has been one uninterrupted feast of peaches and milk. Nobody here is so antediluvian as to eat cream, but milk we do have, and very good milk too, considering the dry summer and the price of chalk; very excellent milk to come out of a superannuated, city milk wagon, and at only fifteen cents a quart. I said an uninterrupted feast—this relates to the luncheons and dinners which are alternate peaches, peaches and milk and milk and peaches, with a substantial substratum of sweet home-made bread and golden Pennsylvania butter. Talk about the "land where milk and honey flow," but give me the land where peaches grow.

Peaches and milk for six weeks past; peaches and milk present and prospective for six weeks more. Think of it! What are rivers of wine, or nectar and ambrosia, to the sweet, full stream, white and cool, that came down to us through all the burning days of August—the stream at which we have drank without stint or measure—its pearly surface blushing with the rosy flow from all the dropping orchards of the Maryland and Delaware vale! A twelve-weeks-long river of milk, cool and creamy, floating down to our lips day after day these luscious ruby-and-amber tinted fruits, full almost to bursting with this Southern summer's gathered sweetness! What was Moore's feast of roses in the vale of Cashmere compared to this? Long, rich, golden Carolinas we have for breakfast; bread, such delicious bread as this dear housekeeper of ours makes, with peaches for lunch; and peaches and milk, with etceteras, for supper; is not this living! Meat and its condiments go to the dogs, when such ambrosial diet floods our markets and blushes on our tables.

Fruit has been abundant in market all summer, but sold at what in other times would be considered high prices. Peaches, for all the enormous quantities brought in, have been held, on the average, to 25 to 30 cents the half peck, now and then falling to 20 and rising to 50. Apples are plenty at about the same rates; but they are very different fruit from our Michigan apples, smaller, poorer-flavored, and usually full of blemishes of some sort—scabby, or dry-rotted, or wormy, sometimes all together. Just now we are having some delicious, small, sweet, baking apples, which are brought to the table as a sort of foil or relief to the peaches; but with us, peaches like "ole Virginia" never tire.

The plentiful rains of late have freshened up the city as well as the country, washing the dust from faces and flowers, from parks and pavements, and giving the brightness of June roses to September hollyhocks and altheas.

The military firmament, too, seems growing brighter, and the political was never more radiant with hope since the bursting of the great Chicago water spout. The thing had an ugly look before it broke, and everybody seems relieved to find that after all there was little in it besides wind and water—and that little was smoke.

L.

October 4, 1864, page 2

Letter from Washington

EXPERIMENTS IN DYEING WITH COAL OIL AND SORGHUM | IMPROVEMENTS IN THE DEPARTMENT OF AGRICULTURE | ITS MUSEUM | UTILITY OF THE COLLECTION AND ARRANGEMENT | COME AND SEE IT | A COPPERHEAD AND A CHANGE OF SUBJECT | WHAT A SOLDIER SAYS

From Our Own Correspondent
Washington, September 12, 1864

Some very interesting experiments have lately been made by Dr. Henry Erol, Chemist of the Department of Agriculture, in testing the coloring matter in coal oil, and some sorghum seed. By combinations with different chemicals he finds that a great variety of colors can be produced from each of these substances, some of them very brilliant in tint, and delicate in shading down from the deepest to the palest. I have just been shown some beautiful specimens of silk and merino by him; small pieces, simply for trial. The prevailing colors were purple, red, and green. Of the red there is almost every shade known, from Solferino down to the daintiest peach-blow. There are different tints of purple also, and the beauty of them is that they are "fast colors," in the old-fogy-time meaning of that expression, before fast people came into date. These specimens had been tried with soap and boiled, but still held their own.

Several important changes have taken place in this department the past summer. The one first noticed by the visitor is the clearing away of the old partitions and hanging doors that used to obstruct the passage to the rooms, prevent a perfect ventilation, and shut off light from parts of the hall where it was most needed. The long halls are now clear of obstructions, from end to end of the building, some 300 feet one way and 400 the other. They have been cleaned and the walls whitewashed, so that now the twilight journey to the Commissioner's and Museum rooms has far less of sepulchral gloom than formerly.

The Museum rooms are fast assuming a character of interest, being provided with handsome showcases around the walls and through the center, which are daily receiving valuable acquisitions from all parts of the country. Prof. Glover, the naturalist and entomologist of the Department, is constantly employed in preparing and arranging the specimens as they are sent in, or procured by himself. Skins of rare, valuable, or destructive birds, animals, reptiles, and so forth, are almost daily received; and fibers, cereals, seeds, and insects are coming in and taking their places among the many beautiful specimens already on hand. The great beauty of this collection is its utility. All the articles are arranged in orders, families, and classes, and each labeled with name, nature, habits, and use; and the ultimate object is to make a perfect illustrated volume of natural history, which the visitor may study both with pleasure and profit. The appropriation made by Congress to this Department was of great service in aiding it to enlarge its area of usefulness; still it is cramped, and in less than a year will find itself in want of much larger rooms and greater facilities for carrying out its beneficent designs. The Commissioner is energetic in his efforts to show his appreciation of what has already been done, by making the best possible use of the money entrusted to him for the benefit of the farming interests of the whole country, and it is hoped that the class for whose advantage and instruction these labors are being performed, will instruct their representatives to see that the Department does not languish and find its efforts vain for want of means to complete what it has so well begun.

Everybody coming to Washington, especially everybody interested in farming, gardening, horticulture, and natural history, should visit these museum rooms, not only to see what they now contain, but to study the contents and design; to

Part 2: 1864

see not only how they can be benefited by the experience and labors of others, but also how they may add to that experience, for the benefit of others, the result of their own labors and skill. In this way a vast storeroom of knowledge is already being gathered, with bonafide illustrations from nature coming in from all parts of the world.

Among all the objects of beauty and interest here collected, very few indeed are for mere show or curiosity. The birds, insects, and reptiles bear their characters with them, all that have any, so that the visitor may see at a glance whether they live to harm or benefit mankind. Now and then we come across one that seems to have lost its character, or, rather, not to bear about itself the naturalists' endorsement for either good or evil. Of these, among the reptiles, is a venomous looking copperhead, which the Professor has not thought it necessary to name. It lies there, coiled in its slimy folds, with its sleek, slender neck and flattened head stretching out over its bloated body, and its wicked eyes intently watching for the next fated victim.

"It is lucky you have that fellow safely caged," said a visitor the other day.

"Why so?" was asked.

"Because, if he could get out he would be electioneering and voting for McClellan and Jeff. Davis with the rest of his tribe," was the reply.

And now, gliding by means of this slippery link to a paragraph on this subject to which it very naturally leads, let me quote a few words from a letter I received from a private soldier the other day; one who has served his three years time in the army, was shot through the shoulder while facing the foe, has spent several months in hospital, and will soon be on his way home, with a wound yet unhealed, and the effects of which he will feel through life. He is a Michigan boy, and a voter, and is going home to help the battle that is to crown Republican principles with victory. In reply to a letter sent to him he says:

"You say I must vote for Father Abraham: of course, I must vote for him! For he is the only man to be our next President. If any loyal man can vote for McClellan, standing as he does on the shameful pedestal where the Chicago Convention placed him, I think he must be dangerously affected with simplicity on the brain, or treason in the heart; perhaps both. It is said that McClellan affects to disagree with the peace platform on which they have set him; but, does any one suppose they did not know what would make an easy seat for him before they seated him? Does he think he will be able to deceive the people by this 'affecting,' and thus make them believe his party did not understand his sentiments before going to Chicago? I charge him to look out that he does not deceive himself. I believe him unworthy of the Presidency, nor do I think he will ever get it. Would to God I had the power of a Webster this fall, 'Little Mac,' (little enough he is, too) would be made to tremble, and his treasonable party should have no refuge this side of the grave."

That's the way soldiers talk. Let them go home and that is the language they will speak at the ballot box in November.

L.

October 18, 1864, page 3

Letter from Washington

Dr. Smith's Inquiry about the Weevil in Mullein, Referred to the Entomologist of the Department of Agriculture | Description of Wheat Insects | What the Department is Doing

Correspondence of the *Advertiser and Tribune*
Washington, September 27, 1864

In the *Tribune* of the 22d inst., I noticed an inquiry from Dr. I. S. Smith, of Grosse Point, as to whether the "wheat weevil does not breed in the mullein," and suggesting that weevils found in wheat-fields may come from mulleins left in the fence corners. There being no reply to the query in the paper, I took the liberty of referring to Professor Glover, entomologist and naturalist of the Department of Agriculture, for information on the subject. He says the question is altogether too indefinite for a direct reply. As there are three insects destructive to wheat, each of different nature and habits, and all indiscriminately called weevils, it would be necessary to know which of the three Dr. Smith found in the mullein.

The *Cureculio Sitophilus Granarius,* grain or wheat weevil, is a very minute insect, which deposits its egg singly on the ripe grain or seed, usually when housed. The larvae burrow into and feed upon the inside of the kernel; the puncture is generally so small as to be invisible to the naked eye. The pupa is found in the shell of the grain. These weevils infest cereals and grains, as corn, wheat, barley, etc., and are very destructive.

The *Cecidomyia Tritici,* or wheat midge, is a small orange-colored insect, with long, slender, pale yellow legs, transparent wings fringed with hairs, eyes black and prominent, face and feelers yellow, and antennae long and blackish. It deposits its eggs principally in June and July, two to fifteen to one grain; they hatch in about eight days. The larvae are orange yellow when young, and are found in the chaffy scales, preying upon the pollen of the flower and upon the juice of the grain when in the milky state. When mature, the body of the maggot shrinks within the outer skin; it then moults. Sometimes, however, the larvae descend to the ground, burrow into the earth, and remain there all winter. The pupa is formed in June without a cocoon, in the earth, and lasts a week or two, when the perfect insect appears and lays its eggs in wheat, barley rye, oats, and grass.

The *Cecidomyia Destructor*, or Hessian fly, have the antennae and thorax black; hind body tawny, more or less marked with black on each ring, and clothed with fine grayish hairs. The wings are blackish, except at the base, where they are tawny and very narrow, fringed with short hairs, and rounded at the tip; the legs are pale red or brownish, and the feet black. The eggs, which are cylindrical, and of a translucent pale red, are deposited in autumn or spring, to the number of twenty or thirty or more, in the longitudinal cavities or creases between the little ridges on the blade of the plant; in warm weather they hatch in four days, in colder weather they require twelve to fifteen days. The larvae are at first pale red; afterwards turn pale clouded with whitish spots, and through the transparent skins a greenish stripe may be seen. They crawl down the leaf, working their way between it and the main stalk till they come to a joint, where they remain and suck the sap, thus weakening and impoverishing the plant. They attain their full size in about five or six weeks. The pupa is found in the same place, in the hardened or dry skin of the larva, and is of a bright chestnut color, like flax seed. They may be found in wheat, barley, rye, and timothy.

Professor Glover says he never examined the mullein for the purpose, but that it is very probably a species of the *Cecidomyia*, may harbor and breed upon it, as they infest many kinds of plants, shrubs and trees. One species, the *C. Robinia*, may frequently be found on the leaves of the common locust, which they cause to curl or roll up. Other species have their favorite haunts on other vegetable productions, and it is not at all unlikely that some of them may choose the despised mullein; but your querist will observe that how-ever desirable it may be to clear the fields and fence corners of that vegetable pest, it does not follow that by so doing he will at all affect the ravages of the *Cecidomyia* or the weevil, in his wheat, unless it be proved that they resort only to that plant to hibernate and perpetuate their species.

If Dr. Smith's investigations in that line should be productive of any further results, the Department would be glad to be informed. It is seeking in every way through its officers, professors and correspondents, to gather in a fund of information on every subject in which the farmer is interested, from which the public at large, and farmers especially, may draw at any time. Every day letters are received from different parts of the country, giving the results of experiments made, or asking information, or bearing with them insects, with samples of their mischievous work, or accompanying packages of rare, curious or valuable vegetable or animal productions. All these things are carefully preserved, and, together with the beautiful models of fruits, and stuffed birds, and textile material and fabrics, are fast forming a very handsome cabinet.

By a circular issued from the Department, the friends of agriculture everywhere are invited to send in such things as may prove useful or interesting as samples of the vegetable or animal kingdoms. Skins of birds and animals may be sent by mail free of charge, if not weighing over two pounds. The skins should retain the head and feet, or they cannot be mounted; they may be rubbed on the inside with arsenic to prevent spoiling. Insects are sent in letters, or in vials imbedded in wood; little snakes come in bottles, and larger ones in perforated tin cans. Bird skins and skins of small animals, may be done up in two pound packages, or less, and come by mail. I think Michigan has birds which are not as yet represented in the collection here. A pair of whippoorwills would be very acceptable. Cannot Dr. Smith send some of his "mullein weevils" for examination?

The Commissioner is trying to make this a model Department, and the public only need to know what has already been done to be willing to sustain and aid him in every possible way.

L.

October 19, 1864, page 2

Our Washington Letter

Political Gathering at Armory Square | The Soldiers for Freedom | Capturing Rebel Battle-Flags | Dr. Tunnicliffe's Office.

From Our Own Correspondent
Washington, October 11, 1864.

One of the most interesting and enthusiastic demonstrations of the season took place at Armory Square Hospital last evening. It was a Union meeting got up by the invalid, wounded, and crippled soldiers, to express their approbation of the Republican platform and candidate for the coming Presidential election, and to test the feelings of hospital soldiers generally on the subject. An invitation was extended to the inmates of the several hospitals about the city to be present; and they came in long processions with transparencies and banners and bands of music. It was a sad, and yet a grand sight. Oh, the maimed and crippled heroes! What regiments of them, armless and legless, with slings and bandages, and crutches, this "cruel war" has given to our land! To see them gathered together thus by hundreds and thousands, one begins to realize something of the value of the sacrifice our people have so willingly offered up for the preservation of the government.

So general was the turnout at the meeting that after the immense hall of the armory building was crammed and packed to its utmost, there were still hundreds who could not get in, and a separate meeting was organized out of doors in the

Colors of the Second Michigan Infantry. From the Collection of the Clarke Historical Library.

bright moonlight, and speeches were made amidst the blazing of fire works and the cheering shouts of the multitude. There were speeches and music and cheers both within and without. Remarks of the most patriotic and soul-stirring were made by Brig. Gen. Terry and Col. A T. McReynolds of Michigan, by Capt. W. M. Edgar of the army, and by H. A. Pierce of California.

A preamble and set of thoroughly radical resolutions were adopted and passed without one dissenting voice, as embodying the sentiments of the assembled crowd. The whole scene and all the proceedings were of the most touching and inspiring nature. The sentiments expressed were those of men who know what war is, and what rebels are, and there was neither shrinking from the well-known horrors of one, nor toleration for the cowardly sympathy sought to be extended to the others by their northern allies. Depend upon it, intelligent, reading soldiers will vote right.

I was in the office of Dr. Tunnicliffe, our Military State Agent, the other day, and saw some of the trophies won by Michigan boys in the late battle in the Shenandoah Valley. His little room is completely draped by captured rebel battle-flags. Some of these are large and handsome, and made of rich, heavy silk; some are of common bunting, others of merino. One having inscribed upon it "Frayserviller," "Mechanicsville," and "Cold Harbor," was captured at Winchester, September 19, 1864, by H. M. Fox of co. M, 5th Michigan Cavalry.

Another was a brigade battle flag, of merino with heavy silk fringe, the Confederate red, white, and red, with blue field, and eleven stars in a circle.

This flag is attached to a stout hickory pole, and was captured at Winchester, also, by Gabriel Cole, Co. 1, 5th Michigan Cavalry, Sept. 19, 1864.

A large, handsome flag, made of heavy silk, has in its center a blue circle, in the center of which stands the figure of a woman with a decidedly yellow cast of countenance, holding up an apron full of flowers with one hand, and in the other a small green wreath. She is in the midst of what is intended as landscape scenery, and in the distance two or three "lean kine" may be seen with their noses to the ground, snuffing at the scant herbage. Below the circle is the motto, "A crown for the Brave," in large gilt letters. This flag is badly stained with blood, and bears a card inscribed, "Captured at Gettysburg, July 2d, 1893, by 66th New York Volunteers."

The flag belonging to the 35th North Carolina regiment has a red field, and is crossed from corner to corner by two bars, one white, the other blue. On one bar is the inscription, "May 20th, 1775"; on the other, May 20th, 1861. On the field were eleven stars, forming a cross.

Another banner is of red bunting, crossed with blue, and having thirteen white stars on the blue bands. This was captured at Chancellorsville, May 3d, 1863, by the 77th New York Volunteers.

A red, white, and red flag, with a blue field, has eleven stars in a circle with the motto, "Our Rights," in the center, and "Flat Rock Riflemen, Lunenburg county, Virginia," below.

But immediately over the Doctor's table against the wall, hangs the trophy around which the deepest interests cluster; it is "Stonewall" Jackson's brigade battle-flag. But it is not so much that name that gives it interest, as the number of battles through which it has been carried, each one marking the death doom of so many of our own brave soldiers. Look at the inscriptions, what tales of blood and butchery they tell! "Manassas, No. 1," "Kearnstown," "Winchester, No. 1," "Port Republic," "Manassas, No. 2," "Gettysburg," "Cold Harbor," Malvern Hill," "Cedar Run." This flag belonged to the 2d Virginia Infantry, and was captured at Winchester, by Massachusetts volunteers, Sept. 19, 1864. It is made of red bunting, crossed with blue, and has had thirteen stars on the blue bands, but many of them are partially or wholly shot away, and the whole flag is a mere mass of rags and tatters. Of the four divisions made by the bars, not one is left entire; all are hanging in shreds, grimed with battle-smoke and stained with blood.

These are some of the fruits of Sheridan's late triumphal march through the Valley of the Shenandoah. Does anybody believe the glorious soldiers who have written their names in light along the mountain walls of that now desolated vale, will endorse the Chicago India-rubber Platform, call this war a failure, renounce their rightful claim for pay, and accept instead the proffered insult of a treacherous "sympathy?" Soldiers around here do not talk that way just now—intelligent soldiers.

It may be added, in connection with the flags above described, that Dr. Tunnicliffe's office is the haven of resort for all Michigan soldiers who want assistance or advice. It is nearly always crowded, and they always find in him the ready, affable, and obliging friend. They have not a sorrow that he does not feel with them, nor a trouble that he will not help them out of, if it can be done by honorable means. The sympathy that he gives is that written out in deeds and words of real kindness.

Drafting is going on quietly in the district. President Lincoln has furnished for himself a representative for the army from each ward in the city.

L.

October 22, 1864, page 1

Letter from Washington

MOONLIGHT PHOTOGRAPHS AT THE CAPITOL

Correspondence of the *Advertiser and Tribune*
Washington, Sept. 18, 1864

We are having another succession of splendid moonlight nights. How Washington does enjoy—aye, revel in moonshine. The city is as beautiful as a dream on nights like these—a two-fold dream, partly a living, moving panorama, and partly still, white ideal beauty—thought embodied, petrified, glorified. I am speaking of Washington out of doors; doubtless it has enough of sin, and shame, and sorrow shut up within mercifully untransparent walls tonight. But with them neither we nor the moonlight have anything to do, so they come not within the field of vision where our dreams lies. Festus says: "Night hath had many bards,/She is so lovely." Never was she lovelier at any season, in any clime, than now and here. Come out and see. It is the night of the 17th of September. The atmosphere is like crystallized light—cool, clear and still. The moon, a day or two past her full, but large, of an intense and almost dazzling whiteness, floats some two hours high in an unfathomable depth of tender blue, over which not a film of vapor, or the faintest ripple of a cloud appears; and only now then a star glimmers tremulously through the flood of splendor that she, the empress of the hour, pours over earth and sky. Heaven and earth are baptized in glory, and whatever the children of heaven may do, the children of earth are bound to be partakers of the glorious baptism, for they come forth in crowds and plunge into the pearly waves in a perfect abandon of delight. Childhood forgets its sleep and runs riot in fairy rings and bewildering mazes of mirth on nights like this, and youth, and beauty, and love have found their element now. How enthusiastic they look, yet how humanly happy.

Hark! there is music. No, it is discord. Such a rub-a-dub-dub as that now coming up from the center of the great city, cannot be called music in the face of a night like this. Rub-a-dub-dub, bang, pop, whiz—and the drum, the cannon, Roman candles, and skyrockets have their effect, calling together, in a seething, mob-like mass, the drift and flood-wood from alleys, bye-lanes and pools of stagnant humanity, that no other influence could rouse to an appearance of life. Boot-blacks, news-boys, and toadies, the first two bought with a price, the latter volunteers, are bearing about transparencies and little colored paper lanterns on poles, now and then at the command of their leaders, shrieking out with their little cracked voices, three little yells for the little candidate on the little platform, sometimes calling him MacLittle and sometimes Little Mac—always at their work of supererogation, belittling what is already little enough, and as if littleness of any sort were a commendation in times like these.

We came out to see this marbleized dream of beauty, the Patent Office by moonlight; but the rabble have straggled down here from the City Hall; they spread themselves over the broad stone pavement, send their flaring rockets up into the pure, still heaven, and fill the air with sulphurous smoke, and the whole space of street and pavement with a motley, noisy crowd. This is no place for us. Come, I know of a dream we can look at undisturbed. The city is full of them if one only knows where to look. We might go to the East Capitol grounds, and stand there beside the marble Washington, and gaze up into the face of the star-crowned goddess on her cloud-like dome half way to heaven; or to the West Capitol grounds where flowers are blooming and fountains playing under foliage so dense that only here and there the silver rays fall through, and we can catch only passing gleams of the majestic and beautiful temple under whose very shadow we walk; or the broader Smithsonian grounds, where silvered gravel walks go winding their labyrinthine ways through 40 acres of bloom and verdure, so shaded and surrounded by trees, and so quiet withal, though in the heart of the great city, that we may fancy we have found the veritable lodge in the wilderness for which poor Cowper longed; or to the south front of the Treasury with its gleaming pillars and its fair command of wood and intervale and river view; or to the many lover-haunted parks gay with blooming shrubbery and gayer groups of youth and beauty; or we might—but no matter where we might go; there is one picture you must see tonight, if for no other purpose than to contrast it with the one just left, and to show the simplicity of security in which the Chief of our Government reposes.

Nearly a mile west of the noisy center where the rabble are bearing about those transparent lies on their lying transparencies, we find a large white three story house, flat-roofed, with deep projecting porch in front supported by four rows of plain round pillars, a conservatory bearing its glistening glass roof far out into the well-kept garden towards the west, and a long white carriage house extending wing-like through a basement court at the eastern end. In front of the house across the broad semicircular carriage drive, and to the east and west of it, are heavily wooded parks, rows and clusters of great forest maples, locust, ailanthus, poplar, sycamore, and linden trees, their somber foliage lighted up by the starlike blossoms of late syringas and altheas, and all silvered over by this dazzling moonlight splendor. No wild, untrodden forest was ever more silent than this spot at this hour. Not a human being is in sight except ourselves, our own little party of three; and not a sign of life unless it be the glimmering of the lamps around the pillared portico, and the bright gleam of gas light from two open upper windows. This is the White House of the nation, and those lighted windows belong to the President's own room. Whether he be there or not we cannot tell. There is not a sentinel in sight, not a whisper of noise aside from our own subdued breathing, and now and then, at intervals, the smooth, steady rumble of the street cars passing down the avenue.

This is one side of the picture; let us look on the other.

Passing around the end of the carriage-house towards the grounds in the rear, or to the south of the President's mansion, we come to a small whitewashed wooden gate, as common as that of any farmer's garden or door-yard; lifting the latch we enter upon a broad, clean, graveled walk, leading, in its semi-circular sweep, so near the house that we may almost touch the walls over the low iron palings surrounding it. The palings, the banisters of the winding, marble steps leading to the first floor portico, and parts of the wall itself, are overrun and covered from sight by wreathing vines. Inside the palings is a mimic forest of fragrant shrubs and flowers, and glistening, waxen-leaved magnolias. Outside, standing here at the apex of the circle, with our backs toward the house and our faces toward the south, we have on either hand the gently swelling knolls, and grassy sweeps of tiny vales and plains, all densely wooded, and dark with shadows below, as they are bright with silvery glory above. Directly before us is a broad open intervale, narrowing to a few rods' width just before it leaves the grounds, but widening again into acres and even miles, in the far, clear distance.

Look now, what a picture is here. First, and nearest to us, are large circular flower beds full of fragrance and bloom, then a fountain throwing up ten thousand jets of liquid diamond and molten silver; beyond that is the music stand where the scarlet-coated Marine Band weekly discourse sweet music to listening crowds, a common enough piece of carpentering it is, but glorified like everything else tonight, and, still more than by the moonlight, glorified by the banner of stars that floats above it in the clear bright air. Further on, the shadows of the great trees lie dark across the narrow neck leading to the broad plain beyond; look still further, beyond that plain, more than a mile away, and see that wide, flashing, darkening, brightening sweep of light rolling down along this side of the low, sullen Heights of Arlington. That is the Potomac. The far-off Heights lying against and blending with the sky, form a fitting background for so fair a scene.

Now, come around to this rising ground facing the east. Here let us be seated; there is a thicket of evergreens behind us; a great, spreading ailanthus holds it tufts of fernlike foliage above us; to the right spreads the plain and gleams of moonlit waves in the distance; at our left is the White House, intensely white wherever the rays fall upon it above the mass of foliage in which it stands imbedded; before us is the starry flag, the fountain of diamonds, and a forest of living quivering emeralds tipped with silver. The leaves of those old trees did quiver just now. A breath came fluttering up through them from somewhere; and see, it has found the flag, and one by one unfolds the rainbow tints and fans the pale stars into blazing. Another has found the fountain, and is tossing the light sprays about, and blowing its streaming, silvery hair far out among the sparkling grass and flowers. There is no other sign of life here besides ourselves. Does this seem like any part of the noisy, warring world we have been living in so long? Yet it is, and not only a part, but the very center. Is it not Festus again who says: "Earth's gleaming axle sleeps/While all around it moves," or something to that effect? And is it not so in the political world? The great center, the heart, the axle of the nature rests securely in the palm of Omnipotence, as undisturbed by as unconscious of the dust and pebbles thrown off by its far circumference.

Who sitting here could dream that the route we left but a half hour since were so near us? We are still in the midst of the city, but in a world within a world; we hear no sound of their frantic yells, and see not a gleam of their flaring rockets.

How the fountain flashes! Look at the flag! Look over the whole scene. Is it not all glorious? Is it not security—peace? There are no clashing arms about; we found no sentinel at the gates; yet what country farmhouse could be more secure? Tyrants have guards and sentinels around their castles, do they not? Yet who may not come in here as we have come? Away with those mockeries of lying words about tyrants and despotisms; they have no realities here.

The flag opens its glorious folds again. Our party, two of them, are singing the "Star-Spangled Banner." Still there is no motion but that of the flag and the fountain, and no sound but the echo of their own sweet voices. Now, rising for a benediction, they pour upon the crystal air the thrilling anthem, "My country, 'tis of thee!" And then we go as quietly as we came, seeing "By the moonlight/That 'tis most midnight,/And time we were home an hour and a half ago."

L.

November 17, 1864, page 4

Our Washington Letter

LIFE IN THE STREETS | AUTUMN SIGNS | PROGRESS | DESTRUCTIVE YANKEES | DISLOYAL MERCHANTS ARRESTED | SPIRIT OF THE SOLDIERS

From Our Own Correspondent
Washington, October 31, 1864

The streets of this city have presented an unusually animated appearance during the week past. The movements of military trains have been rapid and continuous, going and coming, loaded and empty, in almost endless lines, in every direction. This rumbling is hardly ever out of our ears night or day. The fine weather has tempted everybody out who was not absolutely tied within, and ladies have taken advantage of it to display their brilliant autumn toilettes. From three till five o'clock these pleasant afternoons, Pennsylvania Avenue, down the fashionable side, is gorgeous as a rainbow with its walking show of gay silks, taffetas and poplins, surmounted by bright ribbons, flowers and plumes, with here and there a dashing display of jockey-like scarlet cockades. These cockades, by the way, have been trying hard to win popularity during the past year, but seem as yet to have progressed no further on the road to public favor than to flaunt as guide-marks over a few heads whose brains run rather to show than sense. Bright colors, however, in plumes, ribbons, hats, and dresses generally, are very prevalent; and it is well enough in a climate like this that we may have something gay to brighten the downward way of the failing year, since the brilliant tints of Northern autumn forests are denied us. Trees have no second childhood here. The balmy and tender foliage of spring matures rapidly into the full, heavy luxuriance of summer, and the trees stand clothed with it till drenched by rains, scoured and worn by Saharas of dust, and blown and torn by winds, it fades, shrivels and falls. There is no romance of coloring in the autumn leaves, so we have it in fabrics for dress and ornament.

Another sort of life in the streets here, is that awakened by the steady and rapid march of a grander force than that of the armed legions who have made these pavements tremble to the tramp of freemen—grander, and yet but the sequence of their heroic advances for freedom, the force of progress, which is fast bringing Washington up to an equality with other towns of its age and facilities. An element is at work which will soon transform this sleepy old city into one of modern animation and enterprise. Indeed, the transformation is going on now as fast as possible. The "Northern hordes" have brought daylight with them. With emancipation came the dawn of civilization, which is rapidly growing into the light of noon-day. The humanity pouring in is waking up the old stagnant life that slumbered and vegetated here so long, forcing what it can to rise to a higher level, and overpowering the influence of that which cannot or will not rise.

That it goes hard with some to witness the progress of these innovations, is almost daily exemplified by the vexed and impatient exclamations one hears when any of these ancient relics are forced to encounter them. The street cars are great levelers of pride, and obliterators of the lines of exclusivism; yet so cheap and convenient are they that even pride and exclusivism are led to avail themselves of their privileges, though almost always under protest of frowning foreheads, daintily sneering lips, and a "touch-me-not" drawing aside of silken drapery. New lines of railroads are being run to accommodate the growing business in different sections of the city, and among the pavements torn up for the purpose is that on F Street. A lady toiling along the dilapidated sidewalk between Ninth and Tenth streets, cast vengeful glances at the gang of men working in the deep grading, and was heard to mutter; "O, these destructive Yankees! they are the ruin of the city!"

One other evidence of regeneration is the growing boldness and decision manifested in enforcing the laws against traitors and their treasonable acts. If treason were as strong and bold now as it was a year or two ago, and loyalty as doubtful and timid as it then was, there could hardly have been so many important arrests so quietly made and submitted to as have been within a week or so past. Several of the most prominent merchants of the city, and a number of proprietors of clothing and shoe stores, have been escorted to the Old Capitol, under guard, for selling goods contraband of law to smugglers and blockade runners. Their stores and shops, meanwhile, are all this time under the charge of armed guards, who stand beside the closed doors day and night, so that instead of the late brilliant display of dry-goods and draperies at doors and windows, we see only locked shutters and blue-coated sentinels with their ugly-looking arms. That the authorities might take one step further in the same direction, is devoutly wished by loyal people; those who happen to have greenbacks to spend would like to know that they go into loyal hands, and are suggesting that loyal Union merchants have some sign by which they may be known from the wolves in sheepskins so thickly sprinkled among them.

There was much excitement and great rejoicing on the streets a few days since in consequence of the parade of the guns and flags captured by Gen. Sheridan in his late victories in the Valley of the Shenandoah. It was a fine sight, and a cause for sincere congratulation that the muzzles of those cannon are turned, we may hope forever, from the breasts of the defenders of the Government.

The discovery of the monstrous frauds sought to be perpetrated on the New York soldiers, has roused the intended victims to the highest degree of indignation, if we may judge from the sentiments expressed by their representatives and brothers connected with the veteran reserve corps, and on duty at hospitals and other places about the city. All who can by any possibility go home, are going, as one of them said yesterday, "Not merely to give the lie to those infernal falsehoods and falsifiers, but to show them that soldiers are men, that they understand what the war is for, and who are the friends and who are the enemies of the Government."

"Yes," added another, "and it is not merely a majority that we want, but a majority so overwhelming—a mountain of Union votes so high that treachery, both North and South, shall be crushed out of existence, and no Copperhead shall so much as dare to wriggle his tail again!"

That is something of the spirit among voters on crutches; and a grand army of them will come up to the help of the Union, as fearlessly at the ballot-box as in the field.

L.

December 8, 1864, page 2

A Few Words of Explanation, and in Memory of the "Loved And Lost"

From Our Own Correspondent
Washington, December 2, 1864

My long silence through your paper will be accounted for when I state that I have recently been called home to Michigan by the sudden death of my beloved and honored father, one of the oldest and earliest settlers of that State. In mentioning his death I cannot but feel that something more than a passing line is due to the memory of one whose life and labors and interests were so closely identified with the growth and progress of the State he had chosen for his home. I hope, therefore to be pardoned for the following brief reference to his history in connection with the early settlement of Michigan.

As early as in 1823, before the first spadeful was lifted towards making the Erie Canal, when Michigan was hardly yet known as Territory, and when Detroit was nothing [line missing] town, John Bryan, then a young and ambitious mechanic, brought his wife and five little children from Western New York to a home in the wilderness. There was no such place as Ypsilanti or Ann Arbor in those days; indeed, no settlement of any kind west of Detroit, except some two or three log huts on the River Rouge near where Dearborn now is, and about the same number on the banks of the Huron about a half mile or so below the present town of Ypsilanti. These last were put up in the spring of that year by persons who had penetrated thus far into the wilds by means of the flat boat navigation of the river. When my father arrived in October, the boats had ceased running, but, nothing daunted, he hired ox teams, piled his goods and family into the great wagons, and, armed with axes, he and the teamsters set out from Detroit upon the Indian trail and cut their way through the unbroken forest to the banks of the Huron. It was there, in the succeeding February, that my second brother, *the first white child of Washtenaw County,* was born.

Having settled his family as comfortably as he could in their new log house home, my father returned on foot to Detroit to seek for work. He was fortunate enough to form the acquaintance of Mr. Robert Smart, a Scotchman of ability and means, and, I believe, uncle to the late David Smart of that city, and was soon furnished with employment as architect and master builder of the residences and blocks of stores than about being put up. But few of the old landmarks, his handiwork, are to be seen now. The old "Scotch Store" of Campbell & Linn, which was torn down a few years since, to make room for the Merrill Block, was one of them, and was quite a grand building in those early days. The "State House," now the Capitol School building, is another, and still bears traces of his skill, in the carved capitals surmounting its columns, all of which were prepared and carved by his own hands. But emigration soon began to pour rapidly into the country, and in the villages just springing up the mechanic found employment nearer home. Ypsilanti was called into existence, a bridge was wanted, and the first one that ever spanned the Huron was the work of his hands.

Of the hardships of those early years, of the months of privation, almost starvation, I will not attempt to speak. Detroit was the only market, and the only communication with that was through the almost bottomless swamps then separating it from the dry land of the interior of the State. My pen could not do justice to those sufferings of those venturesome pioneers, as I have heard them from the lips of my parents. But through poverty and privations they strove on, and the wilderness became fruitful fields, blossoming with peace and plenty. After eleven years of labor here, my father removed with his family to Constantine, St. Joseph County, then a region little known, and on the outskirts of civilization. There the pioneer life was lived over again—hardships, hard labor, and privations such as cannot be realized now, even in the new and far western States, so rapidly do the telegraph and the locomotive follow the settler's footsteps. For 30 years he has resided in that place, and has watched with pride the growth and prosperity of the mighty west to which his ax and strong arm opened the way in 1823. He lived to see his children, ten in number, grown to man and womanhood, all honoring him, and proud of his unsullied name and virtuous life. In a few more months they would have celebrated his "golden wedding," but were unexpectedly called to lay him down in his last quiet rest, and can now only give such comfort as loving children may to his life-long companion, their cherished mother, so suddenly bereft of the stay on which she had leaned so long. His many years of unceasing labor, both on his large farm and in his mechanical capacity, were crowned with reasonable success, but he has left his children no greater treasure than they possess in the memory of his pure name, his intelligence, his uncompromising honesty and temperance, and the gentler, social virtues which so endeared him to them in the happy home circle.

In so large a family it seems not a little remarkable that, until this occurred, there had not been a death in 24 years; and previous to that time there had not been one in 21 years. Those two were little children, and now our father, full of years and honor, is also gone. Of his 70 years, 41 have been spent in Michigan, and those who know him best may say without presumption, that no better man or purer patriot ever trod her soil or claimed a resting place within her bosom. Peace to thy honored dust, my Father.

L.

December 14, 1864, page 4

Letter from Washington

NIGHT ON THE TRAIN | NIAGARA

From Our Own Correspondent
Washington, December 5, 1864

We had a wild ride and some amusing incidents during our late trip through Canada on the Great Western railway. It was night and pitch dark when the train left Windsor; the very air seemed thick to blackness with rain which threatened to fall, but did not. The train was long and heavy, every car crowded, and two engines straining their iron nerves and puffing their fiery breath in the effort to keep it "up to time." Like a comet with two blazing streamers we sped away through the darkness, the lights of huddling villages and solitary Kanuck cabins whizzing past us like fireflies in the swampy lowlands.

For the first two or three hours there was the usual hum and buzz of preparation for the night's repose—strangers making friends with each other for the more social occupation of crowded seats, nervous ladies, fussy mammas, chattering girls, and crying babies, all hustling, bustling, nestling here and there, till at last, wearied out, heads are dropped on friendly shoulders, on softly encircling arms, on seat-backs, and against the jarring, rattling windows, and nothing is heard but the deep, sullen roar of the flying train. So we go till we are past Chatham and far into the heart of Her Majesty's Canadian wilderness, when suddenly a questioning shriek from our engine startles the sleepers and the echoes together, and calls out an answering scream from some kindred monster in the darkness before us. The train stops, drowsy eyes open and close again, and for a while all are content, thinking we are only "wooding and watering." A half hour passes, and a wondering restlessness begins to creep through and rouse the weary passengers; another half hour finds us still motionless, and now everybody is wide awake, and inquiry set on foot to ascertain the cause. A freight train just ahead of us has tumbled three of its heavily laden cars off the track, and here it stands, as unable to get out of our way as we are to pass by it. One might think all sleepy-heads would rejoice, and welcome this forced quiet for an unbroken excursion into the dreamy land of Nod. But it is not so; with silence and stillness comes wakefulness. It will probably be hours before we start again, and the great question is, how shall the time be passed?

On the rack above the seat in front of us was a mysterious looking box, towards which nods, and hints, and suggestions were aimed, till its owner, taking it down, produced from it a well-strung fiddle and bow. Then there was music and merriment, and crowding in from neighboring cars, till the fiddler's little stock of tunes was exhausted and the instrument returned to its case. Speakers were called for, but none volunteered. Presently a stentorian voice in another car started out on an old-fashioned Methodist hymn tune, and for half an hour or more kept the echoes and the passengers alive with the ringing cadences and soul-stirring sentiments of the Wesleys. Then, either his lungs, or his memory, or both, failed, and silence heavy as the darkness fell upon us. Some of the weariest tried to sleep, but a few restless spirits who courted no such gratification and would allow none to others, started upon a revival tour through the cars, shouting out snatches of songs, and calling on the singer and fiddler for music! more music! But the singer was dumb, and the fiddler would not hear. Fiddle! fiddle!! fiddle!!! was shrieked into his ears and from end to end of the car. It was useless, and finding their breath spent in vain in that direction, out they went into the midnight woods and set up such a chorus as would have astonished a native zoological orchestra. Little children, startled from their dreams, cried out, "Mamma, is the roosters crowing?" "Mamma, I hear Ponto barking." "O, mamma! is that the bears growling and coming to eat us?"

A band composed of wildcats, wolves, and hyenas would have made tame music compared to that which enlivened good Queen Vic's dominions during our detention there. But the track was at length cleared; we were allowed to proceed, after some four hours of waiting, and arrived at Suspension Bridge three hours behind the usual time.

A DAY AT THE FALLS

Niagara is an old theme, as thickly written over with sentiments and opinions as its rocks and bridges, and the walls of its towers and curiosity shops are with names. It has been described till words are wanting that have not already been worn threadbare in its service, and yet, ever fresh in that grandeur which no words can express, and unapproachable in that sublimity at which opinion and sentiment falter, it bids defiance to language, and is as strange to each new pilgrim's gaze as if no eye but God's had ever looked upon its far-sweeping emerald robes, its veil of mist and rainbow crown.

How the beauty, the grandeur and the thunder grow upon us as we gaze and listen! It takes hours for senses used to tamer scenes to comprehend the sublimity of this. Sight and hearing must be educated to an apprehension of the vastness of that mighty volume of beauty and of sound. At first we wonder where the splendor is, and where the thunder of its roar of which we have heard and read so much; but as we look and listen, appreciation grows, till the heavens seem pouring down an eternal tide of glory, and air and earth to be filled and thrilled and trembling at the majesty of some unseen power. Rejecting the proffered carriages of some dozen anxious hackmen, we wandered along the winding bluffs from the Bridge to the Falls, a distance of two miles, dipped our hands in the waters that flowed smoothly as a summer stream just before they went tumbling over the fearful precipice on the American side, to be dashed to foam on the rocks below; crossed the bridge to Goat Island, wandered through its muddy paths and wilderness of brush; stood upon Lima Island, and heard the roaring of the demons guarding the "Cave of Winds," climbed the airy tower around whose base the mad waves plunge and dash on the brink of the cataract; and looked far up where the river and horizon meet, to watch the waters as they seem leaping down to earth, and in the very abandon of joy, bounding over rocks and ledges till they fall into the arms of the river god forever calling them from below.

We visited the Canadian side too, from whence the most perfect view of the entire fall may be had. We were baptized by the mist, which was blown upon us like a shower of rain; and watched the brilliant flashing and fading arches spanning the stormy gulf beneath us.

But the day passed all too soon; the night train bore us southward; another sun lighted us down among the mountain peaks and palisades of the Hudson, and yet another shone upon us over the dome of the Capitol, and we were in Washington once more.

L.

December 15, 1864, page 4

Letter from Washington

MISTAKEN IDEAS IN REGARD TO HOSPITALS AND THEIR INMATES | THE WOUNDED AND SUFFERING STILL AMONG US | AN INCIDENT | CHRISTIAN COMMISSION AND MICHIGAN SOLDIERS | ARTICLES NEEDED IN HOSPITALS, AND HOW TO SEND THEM

From Our Own Correspondent
Washington, December 8, 1864

A little two-line paragraph to the effect that the hospitals in and around Washington were empty, has been going the rounds of the press for the past few weeks, and has been the cause of a great deal of mischief; or, rather, has prevented much good that might otherwise have been done. It is a mistake to think that hospitals so situated, in the midst of a war like that our nation is now waging, can by possibility be empty. Even though no great battles are being fought near us, skirmishing and picket firing are going on constantly, and little as these now familiar words may seem to signify, every act they represent costs the lives and limbs of men. It is only a few days since four hundred new patients were entered here at one hospital alone. They are all the time being brought in by scores and by hundreds, from "the front," and from the Shenandoah Valley, and other places where troops are stationed. The field hospitals send their sick and wounded in; and even if there were no fresh cases, what do the people suppose has become of the many, many thousands of suffering, mangled ones who filled these whitewashed halls through the summer months? Too many, alas, have been released from their suffering clay, as the low-ridged fields at the Soldiers' Home and at Arlington Heights may testify; many, too, have recovered and returned to the field again, and others still are transferred or have been taken home by friends, but hundreds, aye, even thousands, are yet lying on those little beds, some debilitated by lingering fevers, or chronic diseases, contracted through exposure and privation in the field, and very many even of those who were brought up from those terrible Wilderness battles, as well as from more recent actions, are still stretched on the narrow cots where they were laid in the early days of summer.

It must be remembered that bones are not formed in a day. Some of these men have limbs so shattered that the bones come out by bits and splinters, and are

Michigan State Relief Association ministering to wounded at White House, Virginia. From *The Photographic History of the Civil War*, 1911.

weeks, and even months, in working their way out so as to give nature a chance to make new ones; then time must be given for her slow process to be completed. Some have the bones of the arm or leg cut out entire for several inches in length, and must endure months of pain and patient waiting for the new bone or other substance to form, or for that slow decay to exhaust vitality, and set them at rest forever. It is not long since I saw a man in one of the wards at Stanton hospital lying with his swollen stump of a leg stretched out on a piece of board, and, on the stump, a lump of ice. I said I remembered seeing him in the same condition of a former visit. "Yes," he replied, "I have been lying here since early in June, with ice on that limb all the time, day and night, to keep the inflammation down."

These things are mentioned to put people in mind of the fact that though the hospitals may be *comparatively* empty, that is, not overcrowded with fresh thousands from bloody fields, there are still many hundreds requiring comforts, and delicacies, and kindly care. Under the impression that nothing more was needed, many good friends at home, and many associations, too, that have heretofore been foremost in the good work, have folded their hands and released their efforts, so that it is the hospital storehouses which are empty, and not the hospital beds.

I wanted some simple articles of clothing for a wounded soldier the other day, and having heard that our Michigan store-room and treasury were both empty, I went to the Christian Commission for them.

"Where is your soldier from?" asked the disbursing agent.

"From Michigan," I said.

"Well, now," replied he, after giving me what I asked for, "I wonder how it comes that we have more individual applications for relief for soldiers from Michigan than from any other State; and yet I think, (I will not be positive) but I think no other State has contributed so little, according to its wealth and population, to our Commission as Michigan. The calls upon us for relief for Michigan soldiers are almost incessant. Either the State does not care much for her men, or she sends her funds through other channels, and her agents and the friends of her solders here are so attentive and efficient that they furnish them all their own State supplies and call on us for more. We are glad they are well taken care of, and always willing to give of everything we have, but would like a little reciprocity in the matter, more particularly as many of our own stores are getting very low. Perhaps you can tell us how it is!"

I could not then, but have since placed in his hands the last year's report of the officers of the Michigan Soldiers' Relief Association, in which it is stated that the Sanitary Commission had absorbed most of the funds raised by the home societies and efforts, and which also makes due and grateful acknowledgments to the Christian Commission for its generous and serviceable co-operation, both in the hospitals and in the field. What the tenor of their report for the present year may be, I do not know, but am very certain, from my own experience, that our own soldiers are indebted to the Christian Commission for a majority of the comforts they have received through visitors and agents. I refer particularly to individual cases in Washington hospitals, and they may be counted by thousands.

The remarks made by the agent at the commission room led to some inquiries as to the principles of organization, the methods of working, the stores on hand, and the wants of the association. As I have already made the introduction to this subject so long, I will defer till another time all except an enumeration of the articles now most needed, and an urgent appeal to Michigan people to see to it that they are not needed long.

The agent informs me that among the edibles and delicacies most called for now, and very often lacking are apple jelly, apple butter, dried apples, boiled cider, cheese, and canned fruits and jellies of any sort. Elderberry wine is also much in demand, and is considered very beneficial in cases of jaundice and liver complaint. Among articles of clothing woolen socks, shirts, and drawers are very much needed. The shirts and drawers should be made large, and the socks too for that matter, so as to allow for the shrinking they undergo in the hands of inexperienced and careless washers. Woolen mittens are wanted too, any quantity of them; they should be made with one finger on the right hand, and the finger and thumb neatly laced with leather. Little girls, young ladies, and older ones too, can do the soldiers great service by making up some hundreds of housewives, and sending them on the Christian Commission, or to their State Relief Association, if they choose.

The housewives should be made small enough to be carried in the pocket without inconvenience, and should contain a darning needle, a few sewing needles, some thread, and half a dozen buttons, or more. The thread, black linen, may be wound on a small stick to roll up inside the housewife.

A great draft is made upon the stores of the Christian Commission for burial purposes. Old second-hand or half-worn sheets, shirts, and drawers will be very acceptable in such cases, and are quite as good as new ones for that use. Associations auxiliary to the Commission have been organized in different parts of Michigan, and to them I would say, in behalf of the soldiers, let not your hands be idle; and when your goods are ready for shipping, pack them in strong boxes, mark them plainly for the "Christian Commission Rooms, 300 H Street, Washington, D.C.," pay the express charges, and send them on. Of their distribution I will speak another time.

L.

December 19, 1864, page 4

Letter from Washington

WORK OF THE CHRISTIAN COMMISSION | THE STORE-ROOM AND ITS MANAGEMENT | DELEGATES AND THEIR DUTIES | THEIR SUMMER WORK AND LIVING | DISTRIBUTION OF STORES | WEARY NOT IN WELL DOING

From Our Own Correspondent
Washington, December 10, 1864

An erroneous idea has prevailed to some extent, that the hospital and field agents of the Christian Commission were chiefly engaged in distributing Bibles and other religious reading matter, and that when a wounded soldier asked for something to eat or wear, they usually handed him a Testament or tract, or some sectarian newspaper, accompanied with advice to seek the salvation of his soul first, and think of creature comforts afterwards. Whatever individual mistakes or abuses may have attended the early efforts of this organization, it has long since become an evident and established fact that its managers have taken a rational, common sense view of the work before them, and have devoted themselves as ardently to promote the bodily as the spiritual welfare to the men to whom they are sent.

The association has storerooms here in Washington, where provisions and goods are kept for distribution as they are wanted, in the field, on the battleground, or in the hospitals. There is a responsible superintendent, who has general charge of affairs, receives delegates, and so forth; and a disbursing agent, whose business it is to fill orders sent or brought in, and to give out of the stores such things as hospital visitors may find patients needing. Memoranda are kept of every article so given out, and to whom, and for whom they were given, and a book is kept in which all these items are regularly entered. The fruits, jellies, cheese, crackers, pickles, wines, shirts, drawers, socks, dressing-gowns, and numerous other bodily comforts there registered, go far to show their care for the material soldier.

The regular delegates consist of Christian gentlemen, both ministers and others, of every name and denomination, who all meet here as brethren, and are each assigned a field of labor, supplied with a haversack or satchel, filled with such materials as may be needed, and set to work. Some are sent among the armies in the field, some do severer duty on the battleground, and to others are assigned the

Office of the United States Christian Commission in Washington. From *The Photographic History of the Civil War,* 1911.

daily rounds of the hospitals. Any day you may chance to step into the storeroom, you may see from one to half a dozen of these hospital visitants, with big market baskets or satchels, sometimes both, and slips of paper or little note books on which are written the wants of the sick or wounded, their names, and wards, and the number of their beds. These lists are taken or copied by the disbursing agent, for posting in his book, the baskets and bags are filled, if not with the articles wanted, with things as near like as can be had, and the brethren hasten away to give what they have been promised or asked for.

The term of labor for each delegate is six weeks, when he returns home and another usually takes his place. Last summer their work was very severe, and many of them, particularly teachers and clergymen who were unused to such fatigue and exposure, became ill. I have seen ministers in that storeroom with coarse gray woolen shirts, their coats off and arms bare to the elbows, sorting out barrels and boxes of fruit, washing emptied cans, diving into pickle tubs, or packing their great baskets with delicacies and clothing to carry to a hospital some two miles away, and the thermometer at 90 or higher. They worked with a will in spite of debility and streaming perspiration, and seemed glad to do something for the brave men who had done so much for them. Doubtless they had their Testaments, and their tracts, and religious newspapers, too; indeed, I know they did, and have heard many a blessing upon them for such gifts, but their baskets and the agent's books showed that they cared for the body as well as the soul.

In the summer the brethren had a great tent pitched on a vacant lot opposite their store, and in it were some fifty beds, more or less, little, low, narrow ones like those in hospitals, and furnished with a hard mattress and quilt, and there, after the work of the day was done, and they had been served with what a housekeeper would call a "picked up" supper in the basement or cellar under the store, they would meet for rest and preparation for another day of toil. They had "family worship" there, I should judge from the regularity with which we used to hear their summer evening songs. They have a more comfortable place now, having built for themselves a long, low framed edifice, on the upper floor of which is their dormitory, and on the lower their kitchen and dining room. The Agent has his wife and family there, and housekeeping is conducted after a more civilized and Christian fashion.

It is probably well known that these delegates receive no pay for their services. They give their time and labor, and only have their actual living out of the funds of the association while in its employ.

As was hinted in my last letter, the labors of these men are not for the living only. The dying and dead claim their care, and for these friends at home should provide, as well as for those who are expected to live. Many who have been long confined by wounds or disease become so sensitive and tender over their whole bodies that they cannot wear the coarse, hairy, woolen shirts provided by the hospitals for patients; these need soft, homemade or store flannels. And when they

The Sanitary Commission a success. From *The Photographic History of the Civil War,* 1911.

die, as, alas, too many of them have, and many more must, decent under garments are wanted for their burial. Half-worn shirts, drawers, and socks are often called for, and too often none are on hand.

Another fact should be understood in this connection, and that is, that it is not to these delegates alone that the Commission stores are distributed. Any authorized agent or visitor belonging to local or State associations, or any responsible person desiring to carry comfort to the suffering, will be just as readily and cheerfully supplied. It is no sectarian or red tape affair, but a genuine United States Christian Commission, dispensing benefits as freely to all as it is in its power to do; and its power is limited only by the will of soldiers' friends at home. Michigan has drawn largely upon them in many ways for the benefit of her own men, and should not be behind in her contributions. Let her sustain her own State Association, and pour what funds and stores she chooses into the Sanitary's hands, still with all this, and all she can add to the Christian Commission, there is no fear of too much being done.

Remember that it is not merely once a month, once a week, or even once a day that the sick and wounded need the comforts your hands provide. They need them often more than once a day, and day after day for months, and sometimes for years. Picture to yourselves scores and hundreds of maimed, mutilated, and fever-stricken men, languishing for months far from home and the kindly care of friends; think

of the everlasting dry bread and apple sauce hospital diet, varied now and then by cold potatoes and tough meat, and ask yourselves if the few delicacies you can send them are too much for men who have done so much and sacrificed so much for you. Remember the soldiers in the field too, whose comforts are so few compared to those you enjoy; remember also that the Christian brethren are daily among them finding out and supplying as far as possible their wants, and do not let them go empty-handed. "Work while it is day," and "be not weary in well doing."
L.

December 24, 1864, page 4

Letter from Washington

Effort for the Increase of Clerks' Salaries | The Two Sides of the Question | Whales and Little Fishes | Lady Clerks, their Salaries and how they Live

From Our Own Correspondent
Washington, December 19, 1864

The combined effort being made by clerks in the different Government Departments for increase of salaries, has excited a good deal of remark one way and another, and been made the ground of several pitiful appeals through the newspapers for public sympathy. There are enough of them, Heaven knows, who both need and deserve not only the salaries but the sympathies in larger measures than has yet fallen to their lot. Like most other questions, however, this one of a demand for increased pay has two sides to it.

Many of these clerks with salaries of $1,600 and $2,000 a year, rent houses, crowd their own families into the smallest possible compass, and re-rent rooms or take boarders at prices which not only pay the original rent but supply the table, and in some cases meet most of the family expenses, leaving their own salaries almost if not quite untouched from year to year. Those who are fortunate enough to get houses with room to rent out in this way charge the most extortionate prices for them. They make themselves acquainted with the depths of their lodgers' purses and dip in accordingly. Yet of all clamors for more pay you will not hear one louder than from the mouths of these men. If salaries are increased, they of course will reap the largest benefits; for it is said by those experienced in Washington ways, that the moment salaries go up everything else goes up with them. Room-rent and board will advance in proportion to the ability of lodgers and boarders to pay.

So the rule will still hold good that "the strong prey upon the weak." Lucky house-holders will be reaping double profits, while the floating mass will have the satisfaction of paying out more as they receive more. Whales will probably never be done swallowing the little fishes, at least not while they are blessed with such excellent appetites; and it would be policy, perhaps, to starve the little fishes in order to spite the whales. The great question seems to be whether Uncle Sam can just now afford to feed them all up to the extent of the craving. This question, however, be it understood, never troubles the consciences of the whales. No, indeed; they could swallow all the funds in the Treasury, and Uncle Sam to boot, and then ask for more as innocently and with appeal as pitiful as they do now.

The above named salaries are those received by men employed as clerks in the War, Navy, Treasury, Interior, and other Government Departments. Ladies in these Departments, very many of them doing the same work as men, keeping books, briefing, recording, filing, engrossing, copying, or otherwise employed on letters, public documents, or general business, receive from $50 to $60 per month. How single ones without families manage to live here upon that sum is a mystery that it would take a sharp financier to cipher out. But numbers of them are widows with helpless families dependent upon them; and some have sick or crippled husbands besides; yet they live, month after month, with no other income, and cling to this crumb with a tenacity which shows, in spite of their murmurings, that it is better than they can have hope or expectation of in other employments. But such living as theirs is, few out of Washington can appreciate. The houses or rooms they occupy are usually far out in the suburbs of the town, where rent is cheap, and by long walks in all conditions of weather, they reach their places of employment at nine, leave at four, and devote the intermediate hours to the never-ending cares of housekeeping. Hired help on such a salary is out of the question. Some of them living in the outskirts of Georgetown, come four miles to their work, part of the way on the street cars, pay $25 a month for house rent, and support a family of five or six children on what remains of the $60, with wood at $12 and $16 a cord, and provisions at proportionate prices. There are ladies of culture and refinement, reduced by misfortunes, and performing the labor of first and second class clerks, for which men of fewer qualifications of intellect and education receive $1,400, $1,600 and $1,800 a year. Evidently woman's rights are not in the ascendancy in Washington.

Among young single ladies employed in the Departments, it is quite customary for two, and sometimes three, to club together, rent a room, and board themselves. This is by far the cheapest way of living, as the rent is divided between them; and they purchase only such marketing as they need, and make use of it all, so that nothing is lost, as through wasteful hands in kitchen help. Many also live simply, boarding themselves in the same way; but it is a dreary, unnatural state of existence for social human beings—worse even than Bachelor's Hall, I should imagine, from descriptions I have heard.

Petitions for increased salaries have been very generally circulated and signed, and have gone to the Capitol for the consideration of Senators and Members. If these prayers should not be answered, it is to be hoped, for the sake of woman-nature if not of human-nature, that the present high prices will have a downfall.
L.

3
1865

January 10, 1865, page 4

Our Washington Letter

The New Year | Calls and Calling | Prayers for the President | The Little Hills in his Path | Some Women and their Ways | Besieging the White House | Sorrows that will not be Assuaged | The Continual Dripping

Correspondence of the *Advertiser and Tribune*
Washington, January 2, 1865.

The old year went out in a snow storm, and the new one came in bright and vigorous, with keen north wind, and the sky full of sunshine. Already the streets are worn bare by ceaseless travel, but everywhere else, on roofs and sidewalks, on gardens, parks and commons, the ice and snow lie white and glare. Yesterday, boys and girls alike forgot that it was Sabbath, and only remembered that it was New Year's Day, that there was plenty of ice on the sloping streets and little ponds, and that there was use for the gifts of Santa Claus, the skates and sleds that had been idle all the week. Grown people generally attended church, while the girls and boys "a-sliding went."

Today, as on Monday last, all the Departments give holiday. All the heads of Department, from the President down, have receptions, and everybody goes calling to give the compliments and kind wishes of the season. It is the great day of the year at the White House. All the foreign Ministers and Government officials call to pay their respects to the President, and after them the populace generally. For two or three hours, the crowd around the door and area in front of the house is so great that no one can get near or in at the door except as they are moved along in the press of thronging hundreds, all anxious to see our Father Abraham, take him by the hand, and wish him a happy New Year. I cannot go, but send him a heart full of prayers and good wishes, the uppermost and most fervent of which is, that for the year to come he may be delivered from the tongues of women who go to him upon vain and foolish errands, and then abuse him because he will not promise to accomplish the impossibilities they require.

This may seem a little thing, and the wise and good and prayerful may roll their eyes in deprecation, wondering why weightier matters of liberty, law, and justice should be passed by, and only the mint and cummin be thought of in times like these. Do not I know that from every loyal pulpit in the land, yes, from every loyal heart, there go up continual prayers for the President's mental and spiritual good, beseechings that wisdom may be given him according to his need, that he may be endued plenteously with heavenly gifts, and be led to work out the will of the Lord in His own good time, and according to His own will and purpose? Yes; in our day things are the reverse of what they were in Bible times. The great words Freedom, Truth, Right, Humanity are uppermost in all hearts, and all lips are devoutly praying that President Lincoln may have faith to move mountains; but who ever thinks of the little hills that beset and block up his way to the mountains? of the miserable dripping, drizzling rains that pelt and blind and chill him every step he takes! Pray on, good people, good world, till the mountain tumbles into the sea and the hopes of humanity are realized; your prayers are needed for yourselves as much as for your Chief in office. Just now I happen to know he would be very grateful if my little prayer and wish were realized too. Teapot tempests are all the more annoying from their insignificant spitefulness.

The President is known to be kind and patient in receiving and listening to all applicants for favors; and is sometimes indulgent to a fault in granting what is asked for. How much men take advantage of this kindness is best known to themselves; they are not as likely to boast to the world of their success or ask it to whine with them over disappointments as women are; and if they want revenge they see it in some distant ballot box, and have only to nurse their wrath till that day of reckoning comes. With women it is different. There is no use in their nursing wrath—it would only be a waste of time; so when their anger is roused, out it comes at the tongue's end, fiery and bitter, and eager for instant vengeance. So many women, too, in these days, have their hearts wrung with sorrow, and want a scapegoat to bear the wrongs which have been the cause of it! And who can bear them better than the President? Who, they ask, is more responsible?

Mr. Lincoln is almost incessantly besieged by women having friends in southern prisons, or sons, brothers, husbands or nephews who through some misdemeanor have fallen into the hands of our own military authorities. They go to him begging for a release of the culprits, and insisting that he shall overrule Gen. Grant's arrangements and order at once that nothing further be done till every Union prisoner at the South shall be sent home.

"Why," said one the other day, "there is my poor cousin been suffering for eight months under arrest and tossed about from one place to another, and all for other people's fault. I have been to the President half a dozen times to have him interfere and get him released, and it's of no use; we might as well not have a President if we can't have justice done."

A little inquiry brought out the fact that the unfortunate cousin had been made drunk, deserted from his own regiment, sold himself to another, deserted again, and was caught. Some extenuating circumstances had prevented his being shot or hung, and because military authority still held him under restraint, the disconsolate woman must hang about the White House day after day; and when she found her importunity of no avail, must go and publish to the world a doleful tale of Presidential hard-heartedness and injustice toward injured innocence. For these women are not content to use the tongue alone; some of them have sharp pens as well, and dip them in gall when they write. They can rail in generalities, and so cover their own littleness with a fleeting notoriety. The world would be quite astonished if it only knew how many women there are more capable of managing the affairs of the nation, armies and all, than our Generals! Ah, if it did only know! But then it don't, and very likely never will; so it will have to get on with men as best it can.

One woman declares the President discourteous because he told her he had listened to her story five times, and had given her the same decisive answer every time; another thinks him unmannerly because he smiled in her face and declined adopting a plan she had devised for releasing the Andersonville prisoners; others yet aver that he should take the whole matter into his own hands, and send for the prisoners to be brought home, and have their cruel keepers killed without delay or mercy. They would do it in a minute if they had half the power he has! And so grievances and murmurs multiply, and the poor President must listen to them with what grace he can. They are all poured out to him. That is the worst of it—he has them all to listen to, and if it were once for each, even, he might not need that little wish; but it is untiring repetition, the teasing that will not be appeased, the drip, drip, dripping of the same old drops—it is from these that a prayer for deliverance for 1865 might call forth the Presidential Amen.

L.

February 1, 1865, page 4

Our Washington Letter

Depredations at the White House | The Scissors Discovered, and where the Responsibility Lies | A Day of Rejoicing

From Our Own Correspondent
Washington, January 17, 1865

It seems to have been customary in past days for visitors to the Executive mansion to desire to carry away some memento, probably for the purpose of proving their ability to disgrace, with the idea that they were distinguishing themselves. The

East Room and Green Room have been peculiarly favored by these genteel thieves. The edges of the carpets have been snipped off wherever they could be got at with scissors or knife, and so presented the appearance of having been nibbled at by a regiment of rats in pursuit of winter bedding. The heavy gilded fringes of the curtain-bands and tassels were clipped and borne away as relics, from time to time, till only ragged remnants remained, and finally the rich brocade of the curtains themselves began to disappear, bit by bit. Last fall from the drapery of one window in the Green Room silk enough had been abstracted to make a good sized apron; and matters at length came to such a pass that a watch was set to observe the visitors, and detect the scissors if possible.

These rooms, it may be known, are always open to the public, and hundreds of people visit and walk around in them every week; indeed, perhaps scarcely a day passes without its scores of curiosity-hunters coming to walk on Uncle Samuel's parlor carpet, and enjoy the satisfaction of seeing themselves in his big mirrors, and resting on his state chairs and sofas. All the clippings, snippings, and abstractions of upholstery had been charged to the luckless daughters of Eve, and imagination pictured them out in far away patchworks and pincushions; but observation proved that the stronger sex also had a hand in the work. At least a hand attached to an arm in a coat-sleeve was discovered in the act of unlawfully confiscating loyal property; and worse than all, the body owning the hand was a salaried clerk in one of the Government Departments! Not a young and giddy one, either, but a person of years and position, whom experience if not principle should have taught better. The moment the detection was made, information was sent to the head of his department who promptly notified him that his services were no longer needed. He proved himself a genuine son of Adam, though, for when charged with the deed he said, "The women who were with me, they tempted me and I did steal." So of course the guilt all came back to the right shoulders at last. Everybody thought it was the women who did it, and so it was!

The city today has been made joyful by the glorious news from Fort Fisher. It was impossible for Government clerks to keep at their desk; they must be out and among men to hear all that was to be heard, to listen to the inspiring bands, and the loud-mouthed music of the cannon firing their grand salutes.

The public buildings present a somewhat strange appearance with their long colonnades draped in heavy mourning, and the bright flags floating out gaily in the breeze above them. But yesterday the flags were at half mast, and idly drooping, while the white columns were being wreathed with black in memory of the honored Everett; today above these mournful badges the banners have multiplied to scores, shot up meteor-like to the tops of the highest flag-staffs, and are blazing out the people's gladness to the wintry skies. With Missouri and Tennessee disenthralled, Georgia as good as redeemed, and the door opening to let North Carolina out of her bondage, pro-slavery prayers have turned to groans, and secession faith is becoming dim.

L.

February 1, 1865, page 4

Additional Particulars

(Smithsonian Fire)

(Our special correspondent at Washington, under date of the 24th, gives the particulars in reference to the destruction of the Smithsonian, which are substantially the same as published above. That portion of the letter relative to Mr. Stanley's gallery of Aboriginal portraits will be found of interest to most of our readers.)

A few days ago a paper was handed me, a printed memorial to the State Legislature of Michigan praying for an appropriation to purchase these paintings for the University Gallery of Arts at Ann Arbor; and it was suggested that I should visit the collection for the purpose of giving some description of it through your columns. Prof. Henry offered the use of a catalogue, and any information I might desire in regard to the subject. To day I went over, and was in the gallery half an hour or more examining the wild, swarthy faces, looking down so life-like from the walls and the exquisite touches of forest and prairie scenery, of wigwam life and huntsman's perils. Prof. Henry expressed his high appreciation of the works as ethnological specimens of a race fast fading from existence, but said candidly that the Smithsonian could not purchase them, and that if the State would do so, it would doubtless be better both for the artist and for his collection. With the catalogue and the knowledge necessary to my object, I left the gallery, and had not been out of the building twenty minutes when the roof over that part fell crashing in, and the immense room, with all its contents, was one seething mass of flames.

Where or how the fire originated I have not yet heard; but it must have been burning between the ceiling and the roof above our heads, as we stood there so coolly considering the merits of the paintings, and the design of the Institution in which they were deposited. Alas, that we must say *were!* For they were, and are not. When I came out a black smoke covered the roof, and in a moment the red tongues of flame came lapping through; then roof and ceiling fell, and the holocaust was complete. Amid the ice and snow, and the thronging crowds, I dropped on my knees and wept. Poor artist! God strengthen thee in thy far-off home to bear these cruel tidings. The forest children have all gone to the sacrifice together. One winding-sheet, red as their own wild war-paint, enveloped them all. The offspring of years of love and labor are but a handful of blackened cinders now.

The public may understand something of the money value of this loss when it is known that there were in this gallery over 150 paintings averaging in size three feet by two and a half, and all mounted in rich gilt frames at the artist's own expense. They were portraits, painted from life, of 43 different Indian tribes, during a ten years' tour through the Southwestern Prairies, New Mexico, California, and Oregon. Few if any of them can ever be reproduced. The originals have vanished, and now also their shadows have gone after them. What a pity our State had not made the move and consummated the purchase in time to rescue them from this fate. I sincerely hope there may have been an insurance to at least partially cover the loss, and that Michigan, now the adopted home of the artist, may show him such appreciation as will in part compensate for the terrible calamity. From the roof where the flames first broke out they spread with fearful rapidity towards the eastern wing. Soon the whole main body of the structure above the first floor was one glowing furnace. The day has been bitter cold with a stinging north wind, and the ground is a glare with ice.

L.

February 2, 1865, page 4

Our Washington Letter

The Smithsonian Fire | The Stanley Gallery | Description of the Building | Smithson's Will | Its Interpretations and Interpreters | Aristocracy of Science

From Our Own Correspondent
Washington, January 26, 1865

I gave you on Tuesday evening a hurried account of the burning of the Smithsonian. The fire was then raging as I wrote, and nothing had been made public in regard to its origin. It seems to be now well understood that it originated from the pipe of a stove which had been put up temporarily for the benefit of workmen who were making repairs in the Indian picture gallery. The repairs were nearly concluded, and the pictures, which had been taken down for the purpose, had just been replaced upon the walls the day they were burned. I have learned that Mr. Stanley's collection was not insured, so that the whole is a total loss to him, and a loss also to the nation which no money can replace. The utmost sympathy for the artist is expressed by every one.

Our city papers here have some ludicrously erroneous stories in regard to my acting as agent for the purchase of this portrait gallery for Michigan. How they came by the knowledge they parade with so much assurance I know not. All the agency I have been conscious of is that mentioned in my letter of Tuesday. Had I known of the flames raging within twenty feet of where I stood when examining the portraits that day, I should have been proud to have rescued even one; and how much prouder, could I in any way have helped to awaken an interest in our State sufficient to have resulted in the purchase of the entire gallery. But it is too late now.

I have had the pleasure of seeing some very beautiful paintings by Mr. Stanley, and still his property, now in the care of a friend in one of the rooms of the Patent Office. Some of these are portraits, some fancy, and some landscape pieces. The landscapes are particularly fine. It is to be hoped that an appreciating public will in some way and measure remunerate him for his great loss.

The lower story of the Smithsonian building is fireproof; so that the Museum is left comparatively uninjured, while the entire upper portions of the main body are in ruins. The edifice is 449 feet in length, from east to west, and its depth is 160 feet. It was founded in 1846, and stands in the center of a handsome park containing some fifty acres laid out with winding ways, and shade trees and shrubbery. The material of the building is a lilac gray variety of freestone, and the style of architecture is of the twelfth century, usually known as Romanesque. It was an ornament among the public buildings of the capital, and its Museum halls and galleries of art and science were the daily resort of thousands during the Congressional season here.

It seems somewhat doubtful whether the Smithsonian, even if restored to its former proportions, will be appropriated to its former uses. The present Regents,

Study for a painting burned in the Smithsonian Fire. Tin-Tin Malikin by John Mix Stanley. Courtesy of the Founders Society of the Detroit Institute of Arts.

or a portion of them at least, do not seem inclined to favor the interpretation that others have given to the will of the founder of the institution. He, James L. Smithson, an Englishman, and natural son of the first Duke of Northumberland, and a niece of Charles the Proud, Duke of Somerset, himself unmarried and childless, died in Italy in 1828, bequeathing to the United States of America the sum of about $550,000, to be used in the founding of an institution at Washington, "for the increase and diffusion of knowledge among men." Different men interpret this last clause in different ways. The resident Regent and Secretary of the institution, regards the outlay of money in the erection of such a building as a perversion of the spirit of the bequest. He would have no splendid edifice, no museum or gallery of arts, or public library, or lecture room; nothing in short that would attract, amuse, or in that way instruct the masses of the people. Besides, he says, such an institution as this has been, is local, and does not meet the idea of the will in its broadest sense—"diffusion of knowledge amongst men." His idea seems to be that the money should be used simply for the encouragement of scientific, historic, ethnologic, and other explorations, experiments, and discoveries in all parts of the world, and that the only nucleus needed here at Washington is an office and publishing house to put the results of such experiments in print and scatter them to the world again. In a word he would not popularize learning, but would have an aristocracy of science, illuminated by sublime theories, and crusted about with impenetrable abstractions. He would not educate and refine through the medium of the senses, and thus lead the people up to an appreciation of science and art, but would wrap knowledge in papyrus, calf, and muslin, to be stowed away in catacombs of libraries whence they may be dug out like mummies for the astonishment of future ages.

Even the lecture room, most admirably constructed, and benevolently designed for "diffusion of knowledge" from the lips of men to whom the people might listen "without money and without price," has been considered a nuisance, because when its doors were opened, the "common herd" flocked in, and the secrets of science were profaned by being divulged to vulgar ears. So, all these long winter evenings those thirsting for a drip from the "Pierian Spring," have watched in vain for the signal lights upon the tall north tower. Not a twinkle of invitation have they seen; and thousands lacking the mental aliment they would have chosen, have gone to the play-houses and theater instead. These receptacles of "wealth, beauty and fashion," and everything else, are always attractive with brilliant lights, and warmth, and pleasure's all-seducing wiles. But Science turns down the gas in her empty halls, locks the doors, folds her hands and says: "I have published books; if you would have knowledge, read them."

Well, this long-deserted, disused lecture-room was fearfully lighted up on Tuesday last. As I looked at those flames, red and wrathful, surging through that magnificent chamber, thinking of all I had been listening to a short half-hour before upon its very threshold, I said to myself, the "annoyance" is being swept

away by a power and in a manner little dreamed of then, and the priests of the temple may dream in peace, knowing that no sacrilegious feet will invade that precinct more.
L.

February 4, 1865, page 4

Our Washington Letter

Winter Weather | Soldiers in the City | Sherman's Men | Scene in the Capitol | A Merited Rebuke

From Our Own Correspondent
Washington, January 28, 1865

We are having steady, stern, Northern winter weather. The ground is frozen and covered with ice; keen northwestern winds prevail, the Potomac is closed against navigation, and the natives here generally are coming to the conclusion that the inevitable Yankees have brought with them their climate as well as their customs. Thin walls, rattling doors and windows, and smoky chimneys are no great contributors to fireside comfort, with the thermometer at zero and below; but must be endured, because nobody supposes such a state of temperature can last. It certainly must moderate before night, says one; or before morning says another. One sees signs in the clouds and another in the air; but for weeks now, all signs have failed and the merciless cold has kept on. Still the windows rattle, the chimneys smoke, the doors grin, and the wind bloweth where no listing is; for is not summer coming by and by, and where will be the need of securing against cold then? So these shiftless Washingtonians go shivering in the wind and groaning at the price of fuel, while waiting for the warm days coming.

The city for the past few days has been full of soldiers, war-worn veterans from the army of the West. Portions of the 23d Army Corps are on their way to Fortress Monroe, and thence to some point not yet made public. They are the men who were detached from Sherman's army at Atlanta, and have been aiding Gen. Thomas in ridding Tennessee of Hood. As one of them expressed it today, they are "homesick to get back with their old General again." Their admiration of Sherman amounts to enthusiasm, and they are longing to be under his command once more.

The 103d Ohio Regiment, stopping for a day or two at the Soldier's Rest, near the Depot, have had the freedom of the city, and have been making the most of their time enjoying the genial warm, and novel sights in the public buildings. Their coats of blue are of course travel worn and soiled and stained with the dust of many hard fought battle fields. There are, even in this city, which owes so much to the valor and endurance of these men, individuals who see no farther than the soiled garment and withdraw themselves in manifest disgust from the wearer, unless indeed there be tinseled stripes and gilded bands to dazzle the eye.

One of these dainty creatures met with a merited rebuke yesterday. A party of soldiers from the above regiment were in the rotunda at the Capitol, and so absorbed in admiration of the paintings that they did not notice who their nearest neighbors were till a voice muttered something about "disgusting," and a lady exhibiting a fine display of dry goods and millinery, turned upon one of boys in blue and informed him that the coat he had on was very dirty.

"Well, madam," said he, "it is honorable dirt"; and, further provoked by the expression of contempt on her face, he added, "There is a great deal of dirt walking about this world with fine clothes on."

He then told her that the coat she scorned at had been through the siege of Knoxville; had done duty through all Gen. Sherman's campaign to Atlanta; had protected its wearer from the sleety autumn storms of Tennessee; had been his bed fellow by night and his companion by day through months of fighting and marching; had never once showed its back to the enemy; and, that, in short, he considered it a coat worthy to belong to the 103d Ohio, and it should stick to him till Uncle Sam could afford him a better one. The lady apologized handsomely before he was done with her, and has probably learned a lesson which may be of use to her hereafter.

L.

February 20, 1865, page 4

Letter from Washington

A New Chapter in the History of the Capitol | A Black Preacher in the House of Representatives | Public Sentiment Progressing

From Our Own Correspondent
Washington, Feb. 13, 1865

The day just past, the 12th of February, 1865, is the initial letter to a new chapter in our country's history; indeed, it might be called the introductory chapter itself to a new volume, so full of significance have been the simple yet grand events chronicled on its record. That the world moves can be no longer doubted, for what less than a revolution could have brought about what has now been witnessed by all Washington—the spectacle of a black man preaching against slavery from the Speaker's desk in the House of Representatives at the Capitol?

The announcement that the Rev. Dr. Garnett, of the Fifteenth Street colored church (Presbyterian), would preach in the House of Representatives, was made and accepted as quietly almost as any ordinary event. If there was some feeling among those in the District who have been forced by law to acknowledge the negro's claims to humanity, it has not been strong enough or bold enough to attempt to withstand public opinion, which has gone still further, and admitted his intellectual claims. The most that pride and prejudice could do was to stand aside, fold close their flimsy threadbare robes, and let the triumphant multitude pass on. And they did pass on—a strange multitude to crowd those marble portals, to throng the galleries and fill the seats of the lawgivers of the land!

Mr. Garnett, though born in slavery, is now an educated, well-read man, an earnest, pleasing speaker, and a fervent pleader for the rights of his oppressed and suffering people. Himself a negro of the darkest type, but well formed and with finer features than many an Anglo-Saxon has carried into the pulpit, he stood before his audience a fitting representative of the capability of his race. And such an audience in such a place was a novel and wonderful sight, even in these days of wonders. On the floor of the House were soldiers, officers, civil and military members of Congress, strangers, and citizens, with their wives and daughters, filling all the seats except those reserved for the members of the choir, (colored) some 15 in number; chairs and sofas from the ante-rooms were brought into the space outside the members' seats, and all occupied by colored and white as they came in. The galleries were thronged on all sides, the majority of the occupants being of the dusky race.

At 11 o'clock the preacher rose, the first black man who ever stood on that platform as a teacher and expounder of Bible truths. The hymn beginning, "All hail the power of Jesus' name," was given out and sung with spirit by the choir to a melodeon accompaniment. Then followed a solemn and impressive prayer, and after that a fearless and timely discourse, founded on the text from Matthew 23:4: "For they bind heavy burdens and grievous to be borne, and lay them on men's shoulders; but they themselves will not move them with one of their fingers." A sermon from such words it is not necessary to repeat; every one can understand what its import would be. It is enough to say that it was worthy of the occasion and of the times, and that more than once the eloquent earnestness of the speaker thrilled the vast audience with an intensity of feeling which only the sacredness of the day prevented from breaking into loud applause.

After an event like this the world may well ask: "what next?" All Washington was in a tumult last spring at the marvelous advance public opinion had made when it admitted George Thompson, the English Abolition lecturer, within the walls of the Capitol.

It was thought then that progress in that direction could go no further. Free speech did not dream of asking for more. Yet more has come, as inevitably as one wave follows another, and as irresistibly. So the day may not be far off when mind and soul, and not the color of his skin, shall mark the measure of a man.

It is good ground for hope for the negro's friends to find that when his chains are once off, physically and mentally, he is ready to keep step with the time as fast as a place is made for him to set his foot; and, once the gates of knowledge are open to him and he gets tools into his own hands, he will doubtless open up his own paths of progress. Passing events seem to indicate that he will soon have the opportunity to prove himself.

L.

February 21, 1865, page 4

Letter from Washington

A CHAPTER ON A DARK SUBJECT, WITH LIGHT BREAKING THROUGH

From Our Own Correspondent
Washington, Feb. 18, 1865

Since the abolition of slavery and the influx of the Northern independent element into the District, Washingtonians have had to rack their brains for devices to prove their superiority to the negro. So long as they held him under lock and key and lash they got along very well, calling him a brute and making a brute of him; but when emancipation swept those pretty little implements of tyranny out of their hands, the slave sprang to his feet, a man; and from that moment nothing has so tormented them as the fear that he will grow to be their equal, Heaven save the mark!

When through Yankee enterprise street railroads were introduced, not a colored face, save those colored at the toilet, was allowed to peep inside the cars, for fear the owners might fancy themselves equal to Mr. Puff-blow, or his wife or some pert Miss Topknot. Had it been possible, they would have been excluded from the street sidewalks, too, no doubt.

But the negro is patient. His life has been one of waiting. For a year or two he was content with the freedom to go where his legs would take him. Delivered of chains, slave pens, passes, and lashes, he trudged on, sometimes getting a ride on the car steps, but mostly indebted only to his own broad feet for the means of locomotion. Last year, however, his whilom masters consented to another concession in the way of establishing his humanity; graciously permitting him to have a set of cars for his exclusive use—exclusive so far as that he, being excluded from all others, might, if he could find room, ride in them. To indicate their pleasure in this, the devoted vehicles were duly labeled in great Roman capitals, "COLORED PERSONS CAN RIDE IN THIS CAR," and sent up and down the streets, staring contradictions to the popular faith in the black man's inability to read.

Somehow, by reading or "reckoning," colored people did discover the privilege granted them, and white people also soon discovered that if they would have a quiet ride with orderly, well-mannered companions, the "colored cars" afforded the opportunity. The consequences to the negro, though somewhat troublesome at present by crowding him out of the seats so definitely set aside for him, promise to open up to him the high mission of civilizer in general and teacher of good manners to all. For a proposition is before Congress, and has already passed the Senate, to admit him to all cars on all the city routes. When he once gets in, snobs, upstarts, Chivalry, F. F. V.'s, and other poor white trash step out, leaving sensible people to ride in peace and comfort.

An illustrative incident in this connection occurred on one of the Seventh street cars a few days ago. A lady(?) wonderfully got up in the way of flowers, feathers, silks, and jewelry, bustled in, displaced some two or three gentlemen to make room for her amplitude of crinoline, and after spreading and pluming to her satisfaction, looked up complacently to enjoy the effect in the countenances around her. Fancy her horror at discovering in the opposite corner a hoopless form, with a pair of black, ungloved hands, a melancholy black face, and sad eyes, seeming to reproach that wanton display of splendor. She turned her head to the right, and there sat another; to the left, another! then glancing at a pair of smiling faces of her own hue opposite, she started up, exclaiming: "What car is this? Conductor! Is this a *colored* car?"

Mr. Conductor was just stopping his train to take on another passenger of African descent, and before he could reply the silks flounced out of the other door with mutterings of unutterable indignation.

"Why could not she have known what car it was as well as these poor colored people?" asked an amused and puzzled stranger.

"Probably because they can read, and she cannot," was the quiet reply.

It is a curious fact that while the so-called colored cars are nearly always crowded with white people, the most accomplished man or woman suspected of a taint of blood darker than the standard Anglo-Saxon, is rigorously excluded from seats in the other cars. I know such a woman well brought up, of fine education and lady-like manners, who was forced to walk four miles through Washington mud and slush because an insolent conductor shut the door of his "white folks'" car against her, and there happened to be no "colored" ones on the track.

One of these same conductors struck a rough diamond the other day when trying to bully a person of color off the rear platform of his car.

"May I ask what State you are a native of?" said the emancipated chattel, with a bow and politeness irresistible.

"I am from North Carolina," was the answer.

"I thought so; plenty left there yet, though; and now may I ask your age?"

"Just past forty-five," replied the somewhat puzzled conductor.

"I thought *that too,*" said the freedman; "if you had been a little younger you would have been looking round for a colored substitute about these times!"

Conductor had business inside just then.

L.

March 1, 1865, page 4

Our Washington Letter

Washington's Birthday at the Capitol | Illuminations and Rejoicings

From Our Own Correspondent
Washington, Feb. 23, 1865

Yesterday was a grand gala day here. The birthday of Washington, crowned by the glorious news of the fall of Charleston and the re-occupation of Fort Sumter by loyal troops, fired the populace with a wilder enthusiasm than has been caused by any other event or combination of events since the war began. The day itself was glorious in brightness, and mild with breezes that had in them a touch of the warmth and softness of spring. With sunrise the starry flags went up from tower and spire and flag staff, all over the city, and the streets were soon thronged with the gay, rejoicing crowds.

At 12 o'clock the cannon of all the forts surrounding the city commenced the grand national concert, as ordered by the Secretary of War. For an hour the thunderous music rolled down upon us from the far-encircling heights, volley after volley, without an instant's ceasing, till the very earth trembled and the entire horizon was like a volcano with its wreaths and masses of smoke. The tops of the public buildings were covered with spectators viewing the scene. It was grand and inspiring, whichever way the eye might turn.

At night all the public buildings and many private residences, stores, banking edifices, etc., were brilliantly illuminated. The Capitol on its green terrace was ablaze with light from the basement to the top of its beautiful dome. The conservatory in the Congressional garden was lighted up and made a fine show.

The Patent-Office, Post-Office, Treasury, White House, Navy and War Department buildings were dazzling from foundation to roof, and most of them beautifully draped with flags. Fire works and bands of music added variety to the enjoyment. The office of the Secretary of State had on its front a large transparency surrounded with flags, which attracted all eyes in passing. On a white ground were these words: "Peace and Good Will to All Nations; But No Entangling Alliances, and No Foreign Interference."

A band of soldiers passing by, noticed, and stopped, and gave the sentiment three rousing cheers. Such exclamations as, "Good for Secretary Seward!" "Hurrah for the Monroe doctrine!" "That's the talk!" etc., were constantly heard among the crowd.

But, for the splendor of display of lights and banners, the War Department building bore off the palm. It was perfectly magnificent. The whole front was superbly draped and festooned with flags and ensigns, among which blazed thousands of lights, red, white and blue, in wreaths and clusters all over the walls, besides the almost countless numbers burning in the windows. Over the front porch was a large transparency bearing these words: "Sumter 1861. Union. Sumter 1865."

The pillars of the porch were wrapped and wreathed with American flags, and beneath it a band was stationed playing triumphant national airs.

The night was intensely dark, which added to the effects of the lights, and, notwithstanding the steady rain which commenced to fall about dusk, and continued all night, the streets, sidewalks and street cars were crowded and thronged to their utmost. It would have taken a heavier storm than nature could get up just now to cool the enthusiasm of such a day. Drizzling rain and splashing mud were scarcely thought of in the excess of joyful triumph which filled all hearts. I say all, for the secession minority are getting to be almost infinitesimal now in the devoted city.

Great preparations are being made for the second inauguration of President Lincoln. The iron mills of the gods seem steadily grinding to powder the hopes of traitors, and as the rail-splitter has proved an efficient power at the wheel, for the past four years, they are about reinstating him to finish up the business.

Rumors are afloat today of fighting near Richmond.

L.

March 4, 1865, page 4

Our Washington Correspondence

FEELING ABOUT THE FREEDMAN'S BUREAU BILL | GREAT ANNIVERSARY MEETING AT THE CAPITOL | THE REFUGEES | OLD SLAVE OWNERS

From Our Own Correspondent
Washington, Feb. 27, 1865

The friends of the colored race, as well as the interested individuals themselves, are rejoiced at the failure, for the present at least, of the bill for establishing a Freedman's Bureau, which has been before Congress. It is well known that there has been for some time past a swarm of hungry sharks gathering about the capitol, ready to seize upon every office that the creation of such a Bureau might necessitate, and, through the office, greedy to devour whatever of substance Government might design for the freedmen. Political hacks, disappointed office-seekers, soulless speculators, and others of that sort, have been praying with desperate energy, and waiting with open mouths, for the success of the measure. Never before, probably, were there known so many devoted admirers of the negro, never such crowds of disinterested, self-sacrificing philanthropists as have hung their hopes upon that bill. Their very souls wept out in longing to "take care of the poor blacks." Doubtless their care would have been very like that given by wolves to helpless sheep. It is said there is an effort being made to get the bill through yet in some other shape, but the friends of humanity pray that it may not be.

The colored people themselves have got a very able protest against any such measure, or the protection designed to be offered them through the creation of such a bureau. Last evening that protest was read before the anniversary meeting of the National Freedmen's Relief Association of New York. This meeting was held in the hall of the House of Representatives at the Capitol. The hall and galleries were packed to their utmost capacity, and by as strange as assemblage, probably, as ever met within those walls. Full one-third, perhaps more, were of the dusky race, and mingled promiscuously, just as they came in or could get seats, both on the floor and in the galleries, with Government officials, members of Congress, strangers, and citizens at large, of the most intelligent classes represented here. Chief Justice Chase presided; a prayer was offered by Rev. Dr. Garnett (colored), and several stirring addresses were delivered, the grandest and best of all by Theo. Tilton, of the *New York Independent.* I wish all the world could have heard that one speech. Many who were not there will perhaps read reports of it, but the words, to have their full meaning, want the soul of the man speaking through them in the fire and energy of action with which they were delivered.

Dr. Tompkins, Secretary of a similar Society in London, England, was also present, and very much encouraged the laborers in the cause here by assuring them of the hearty sympathy and co-operation of the working classes of England, and still more by stating that there were now on the way to this country goods and clothing to the amount of £600, to be distributed to the New York, Philadelphia and Washington Freedmen's Relief Associations. The central society at London has eleven auxiliaries at work collecting funds and clothing.

At the commencement of these anniversary exercises the choir of Dr. Garnett's Church sung the familiar hymn: "My country, 'tis of thee, / Sweet land of liberty."

Strange words to be sung by black lips under the very roof where Sumner fell from the blows of Southern slaveholders! And, stranger still, the evening was closed by the same lips singing the glorious John Brown Hallelujah hymn, the immense audience rising to their feet and joining in the chorus with an enthusiasm which made those frescoed walls and gilded ceilings ring as they never rung before. Is not the world, too, "Marching on"?

The suffering among the poor refugees from slavery has been and still is deplorable. Loyal people, individually and in associations, are doing what they can to give relief, but the utter destitution of these poor creatures, and the great number of them, added to the unusually severe and protracted cold weather, make it impossible that half their present wants can be supplied. It is wonderful to see with what uncomplaining patience their sufferings are borne. Scarcely ever is one seen on the street begging, and it is only by going to their miserable huts and shanties that their nakedness and starvation are found out. The men are mostly in government service or have been kept in rebeldom, and it is the old and decrepid, and the helpless women and children who suffer. It is estimated that there are some thirty or forty thousand of them in the District now. It is a heavy tax on loyal citizens here to care for them till they are able to care for themselves; but they are taking up the burden with a good will, to do the work bravely and well as they can.

The old citizens, especially those who have been slaveholders, are bitter and heartless toward all the colored race. Not a penny or a rag will they give to save them from death. "It is good enough for them," said a man who had been made rich by their labor; "they ought to suffer; they hadn't sense enough to know when they were well off, and now let them die. I wish every nigger in the United States could be starved to death, or frozen, either; I wouldn't care if it was both." That is a specimen of the love with which the master cherishes his slaves when he finds they are men.

L.

March 8, 1865, page 4

Letter from Washington

PROSPECTS FOR THE 4TH | CONGRESS AND SOME OF ITS MEMBERS | BEAUTY AND FASHION | BEAUTY AND THE BEAST

From Our Own Correspondent
Washington, March 2, 1865

Washington is full to overflowing now with strangers from all parts of the Union, come to witness the second inauguration of President Lincoln. Great preparations are being made for that ceremony, and for the succeeding ball which is to come off on Monday evening, the 6th inst. Crowd, confusion, jam, and jubilee seem to be the order of the day, not withstanding the rain is pouring in torrents, has been doing so for the past 24 hours, and gives fair promise, or foul, of holding on to the end of the week. The city is almost swamped in mud, secessionists are whispering about that Lee, with his army as body guard, is in the vicinity of Fairfax Court House, on his way up here to assist at the interesting ceremonies on Saturday, and altogether appearances indicate that the sources of enjoyment will be various—suited to the divers tastes of the mixed multitude here present.

Senators and Representatives are "sitting" industriously day and night, and the galleries of their respective Halls are crowded with strangers, thousands of them witnessing for the first time these august assemblies of the nation's lawgivers. With shame be it said, they too often witness scenes fitter to be enacted in the bar-room of a country tavern than in these national halls of legislation. The Senate has a few blots among its honorable names, a few who are a disgrace to the States they attempt to represent, and who almost daily shame their manhood and their position by efforts at speech-making when they are obliged to hold themselves balancing between two desks, one hand grasping each, in order to keep up the pretense of standing. More than once they have been stopped in their maudlin harangues, and forced to sit down like naughty boys. Delaware has the honor of paying $3,000 a year to one of these creatures; California sustains another, and Rhode Island may blush for a third. Luckily for the nation, the majority carry steadier heads on their shoulders; or, if accidents happen, are prudent enough to get leave of absence for a brief illness. However, all seem to have worked hard during the short session, and are doubtless exhilarated at the idea of being free so soon. I remember that last summer similar things happened at the close of the session.

The grand ball to come off on Monday evening will, it is said, be uncommonly brilliant with the blaze of beauty and fashion. One lady is having a dress made which costs $3,000, and that I suppose is a mere spark of the fashion part of the blaze. Rouge and enamel will do their share towards the beauty. It is sad and pitiful indeed to see to what an extent this practice of ruining the complexion is carried by some women of position who should set a better example. A preparation of chemical compounds called enamel is plastered over the face, neck, and arms of the aspirant for beauty, the cheeks are touched with rouge, carmine, or something of that sort and the eyebrows penciled and painted an intense black; at a distance, by gaslight, such faces have a doll-like appearance which some call beautiful, but undertake to talk to one of them, or have it talk to you, and there is a ghastly lack of expression reminding one only of some hideous mockery, or whited sepulcher. Crown a complexion like this with a shock of hair dressed *a-la-ramshorn,* topped off with a bramble bush in front, and a half peck of hair tied up in a bag hanging at the back, and some idea may be had of the extreme modern fine lady. Happily, all are not so. There is a great deal of country vigor and freshness and genuine worth and beauty at the capital now, and I doubt not these will predominate over art and artifice at the inauguration ball.

Something new in the way of street promenading has appeared on Pennsylvania avenue this winter. Instead of carrying lapdogs in their arms, ladies now have their little pets dressed in scarlet coats, trotting along in front of them, held by a string attached to their necks. Where the style originated I have not heard, but it was thought to be a "perfect success" till the diminutive brutes, not having the fear of the Secretary of State before their noses, ran into and formed "entangling alliances" with the hoops of ladies who were dogless, and who therefore considered this "interference of foreign powers" sufficient cause for a declaration of war. The question now is, whether hoops or dogs are to have exclusive right of way. The former, it is said, intend to stand out stiff for the Monroe doctrine, and trespassing puppies are warned of the consequences.

L.

March 10, 1865, page 4

Our Washington Letter
INAUGURATION DAY

From Our Own Correspondent
Washington, March 4, 1865

The grand ceremony of inaugurating President Lincoln for his second term is just past. The streets are still thronged with the brilliant pageant attendant on his course from the capitol steps where the oath of office was administered. He is going back to the White House, a second time made President by a freedom loving people. May the day as it now shines and smiles in the warmth and splendor of springtime glory be emblematic of the coming years of his administration.

A stormier beginning than this morning ushered in could scarcely be imagined. The rain which had been pouring incessantly for two days and nights, grew, towards daylight, to a perfect tempest with high winds and clattering hailstones, and torrents falling as if the ocean itself had been upset above the clouds and was plunging by the shortest way to earth again. The dawn came slowly, with cold, black, angry clouds shutting out every particle of sky, and streaming as though a second deluge had been asked for and they were doing their best to satisfy the demand. What a dawn it was for the thousands upon thousands who have gathered here from all parts of our still great country, thousands who never saw the Capital before, and probably never will again.

Hour after hour the day crept on, and still the heavens were black and the rain poured steadily. But, rain or shine, the President must be inaugurated, and, as best they could, the processions began to form to escort him to the capitol. The broad sidewalks meanwhile, for the whole length of Pennsylvania Avenue, covered with splashing mud as they were, were crowded and packed with human beings, and the surging tide was augmented by the constant streams of life pouring from every street and byway. Windows and doors were full from cellar to attic, and thousands of anxious eyes looked down from balconies and housetops. Flags were everywhere, but dripping and drooping. About the time the procession was to start from the White House, eleven o'clock, the rain ceased, streaks of light were seen along the western horizon, and gradually a breeze came up, lifting the clouds and the banners together, rolling the one out of sight, and letting upon the other the flashing sunshine of a spring noontide. Several fire companies from neighboring cities were here; regiments of infantry, cavalry, and artillery, each with banners and bands of music; part of a colored regiment, a large company of colored Odd Fellows

Part 3: 1865

in full regalia, citizens and others, took their places in the procession. The streets were kept clear by policemen, and made gay by some hundred or more of the Marshals of the day dashing up and down, with their brilliant sashes and Union rosettes flashing in the sunshine—for the sun did shine gloriously before they reached the capitol. The excited and gladdened crowd surged on toward the scene of the ceremonies, but not one-thousandth part of them could get even within seeing distance of the spot where the President stood to take his oath and read his inaugural. The mud was deep, and prancing horses splashed it upon each other and upon the people, but nobody seemed to care.

With all the bands playing inspiring airs, and the whole city like a rainbow with banners, the grand panorama is reversing itself, going back upon its track beneath a sky so pure, and an atmosphere so clear, that through its far transparent depths a star is seen brilliant at noonday, while the moon, white like a dove of peace, floats softly up above the grave of the buried storm. A stainless sky with sunlight, starlight and moonlight overhead, all at the same moment, and beneath them a pageant as emblematic of human freedom and equality as the broadest construction could require! Among other devices to show the tendency of the times there is a fanciful structure upon wheels called the Temple of Liberty; it

President Lincoln taking the oath at his second inauguration, March 4, 1865.
From *Harper's Weekly Magazine,* March 18, 1865.

is drawn by four horses decked with flags; banners float from its turrets, and its tent-like roof is of symbolic red, white and blue. Within this temple, as one of its pillars, stands a black man. He is at the rear end of the edifice, but the tallest man in it, and the only one standing.

The new-made President sits in an open carriage drawn by four gray horses. He is on the back seat with his little son beside him; his head is uncovered, but he seems not to see the thronging multitudes who wave flags and handkerchiefs and cheer him as he passes. Two other gentlemen occupy the seat facing him, and the carriage is surrounded, preceded and followed by the military under command of the Marshals of the day. Tonight he holds a levee at the White House, and everybody will be there to shake his hand in congratulation. So the Inauguration day passes in peace, and Lee has not yet made his appearance.

L.

March 14, 1865, page 2

Letter from Washington

"Doing" the Capital, and the Consequences Thereof | The Clerks and their Resignation | The Ball | Fashions | Spring

From Our Own Correspondent
Washington, March 8, 1865

The skies that rolled off their storms so gloriously on Inauguration morn, have given us four successive days and nights of sunshine and moonlight splendor, and are now pouring down their torrents of spring rains again. The thousands of strangers, still here, have had time to look about them and see the city and listen to the growling of the lions thereof. They have stirred up to unusual animation the weird-looking pale-faced messengers who haunt the halls and corridors of public buildings; have astonished plodding professors and heads of departments by their unique queries and refreshing criticisms; have exhausted all the superlatives of admiration and the platitudes of advice and suggestion, and are now gradually dropping off in a beatific state of mind, conscious of having "done" the Capital to some purpose. It does these dusty old spiders of government officials good to have this annual invasion from the outside world of action, letting in a breeze of fresh air to their dim basements and attics and the snugly carpeted corners where they drone away existence over public documents. They might else forget that there is a world beyond the walls that enclose them.

Then, as every State in the Union is represented in the Department here, what a world of visiting can be done in connection with sightseeing. Everybody's friends come to see them, if not every winter, at least on inauguration occasions, and so manage to kill whole flocks of birds with one stone. Hence the delight in coming to Washington, and in receiving the comers, are, in a degree, mutual.

It is somewhat amusing to notice how quietly the Department clerks are going on upon their old salaries, in spite of their last fall and winter protestations that they could not live, that they must resign and break the government's heart and their own if they could not have more pay. The shabby coats they wore when their agony was at its height, have retired into dark closets and corners, perhaps to reappear with an additional rent or two at the next winter's campaign, and Uncle Sam has not now to blush for the ragged elbows tauntingly flaunted in his face by the naughty boys who protested that they were so compelled to bring him to shame. No better dressed people are to be seen at receptions, levees, balls, or on the avenue promenade than these same troublesome boys and their families. Yet last winter, to listen to their petitions and pitiful prayers, one would think they were at the point of starvation, and had absolutely "nothing to wear." Clerks receiving $1,800 and $2,000 per annum assumed a defiant attitude, and bullied Congressmen with threats to resign and leave the government wheels and pulleys without hands to manage them if their demands were not acceded to; heads were shaken ominously and hints of a general "strike" dropped here and there; but Congress went steadily on its way to adjournment, threats and strikes were forgotten, and the *resigned* clerks have nestled down into their old salaries as quietly as kittens in baskets of warm cotton, and as comfortably.

And why should they not be? For the most part their rents are paid and tables supplied by letting rooms to lodgers and boarders; or, if not lucky enough to get a house, they go up to attics and homeopathic rations, and so shine in purple and fine linen when they come down among the crowds of common life. There are, as I have said before, individual instances where larger salaries are needed and deserved. The wrong was in fixing them so low at first, for now it seems that an advance cannot be made in one grade without all others follow, and so as soon as the big fish found out that the little ones were getting fatter, they would open their greedy mouths and gulp down all the advance without mercy.

The great Inauguration ball passed off with all the splendor appropriate to the occasion. The display of flags and fine dresses gave credit to the taste for bright colors and rich material. The prevailing fashion of dressing the hair with curls and flowers gave a flowing, flowering appearance to that vast assembly of ladies. Ringlets are greatly in demand for head ornaments nowadays; they are worn in great clustering bunches tied to the back of the head and facetiously called waterfalls. Really they are a marked improvement on the bagged hair so lately in vogue, hanging at the nape of the neck.

Signs of Spring are fast coming upon us. These deluges of rain have taken the frost from the earth, and already buds are beginning to swell, and grass to sprout. Washington will soon be in its glory of greenness and bloom.

L.

March 25, 1865, page 4

Letter from Washington

Lights and Shadows of Things Celestial and Terrestrial

From Our Own Correspondent
Washington, March 20, 1865

Nothing in the way of celestial scenery as viewed from an earthly standpoint can be more splendid than we Washingtonians hourly by day and by night may turn our wondering eyes upon. The terrific storms of wind and rain that have dashed and blown about here at intervals for two or three weeks past, seem to have indicated a sort of "spring cleaning session" with Dame Nature, and the results, now that the fit has worked itself off, are as satisfactory as the merciless splashing were disagreeable. What an illimitable depth and purity now in the tender blue transparent atmosphere through which the sun floats, a golden haired Apollo, smiling love and life into the bosom of the coy, upglaring earth. If Italian skies can excel thee, I should like to know in what that excellence consists. The splendor here is not like the cold, hard, steely splendor of our northern skies; nor is it like that I have seen from the rolling uplands of Kentucky, low-bent as the brows of Kentucky girls, and seeming so strangely near in its voluptuous softness that one might well doubt whether he breathed most of earth or heaven. Here the distance up to the eternal arch of blue seems infinite, immeasurable (as no doubt Heaven really is, in a practical point of view, a good ways from Washington), yet the foundation garnished with all manner of precious stones are plainly visible, as also are the sapphire tint and amethystine glow about the jasper walls and gates of pearl. During these still, bright days the depth and clearness of the atmosphere is remarkable, and every breath seems an inspiration of new life and vigor (provided, always, that the dust is in a semi-liquid state, as left by a recent rain).

The sunsets here are most magnificent. No foreign skies I am sure could surpass them in variety and gorgeousness of coloring. And the grandeur of it is that the whole heavens partake of the sunset glow and glory. It is not merely a bright spot in the West, with many-colored clouds hanging over and grouped around it, but East, West, North, South, and zenith and earth together grow radiant in the ever-varying splendor. I have seen clouds like rainbows lying all about the North and East after the sun was out of sight, and a light in the zenith as if Aurora had stolen a march on time and gone up to take a peep at the sleeping Phoeus.

The starlights and moonlights, too, are it seems to me, all that could be desired in the way of painting, poetry or romancing; yet artists, both with pen and pencil, go wandering off to foreign lands and skylark among brigands and *lazzaroni*, wickedly ignorant, or willfully ignoring the diamond-lighted roof covering their own birth place. They are of the zealous Christians who can find nothing to do at home, but spend their money and their prayers in unavailing sailing and sighing for conquests in foreign lands.

This last comparison, if it has no other merit, luckily brings me back to earth and earthly matters again. The foreign mission fever prevailed here to quite an extent this winter, and took off large sums which humanity would have retained to relieve the distress of the thousands suffering and perishing in our very midst. The wretchedness of these poor refugees, both black and white, is past description. I was glad to notice in your paper such flattering reports of the success of the Freedmen's Fair lately held in that city. If all the friends of humanity who are able to do, combine their efforts, and do all they can in all ways, they can scarcely meet the demands for help that come up to them from every quarter. There are about a dozen relief associations in this city, the members of which meet regularly to make up clothing, and many ladies, and gentlemen too, give nearly all their time to the work of looking up and giving such comforts as they can to the worst sufferers. Government is also doing what it can to supply fuel and blankets, and yet the half is not done that mercy calls for.

I was in a wretched hovel not long ago, one of some fifty or more sheds and shanties clustered together in a low muddy locality; it was the home of a father, mother, and four little children. In a space not over ten feet square, and with a flat and leaky roof so low that a tall man would have to stoop under it, they sat and slept and had their being, such a being as it was, or is, for they are there yet. For this miserable shelter they pay five dollars a month, which the father earns by chopping wood for Government somewhere in Virginia, where he stays, only coming home once or twice a month to see if all are living, and to pay his rent. The one bed is a mere pile of rags, drenched through with every shower; a little, broken stove in one corner holds the fire when fuel can be found to put in it; and in a broken chair beside it, when I was there, sat the mother, sick with consumption, and holding on her knees a two-year-old baby. Both were clad in rags. Of the three little boys, two were barefooted, and the third had an old boot on one foot and a man's shoe on the other. He was doing the housework—washing some cracked dishes in an old tin basin. The little glimmer of coals in the stove and two small sticks of wood in the corner were the only signs of comfort there. Ice and snow were without, and cold and hunger within.

This is a faint picture of the helplessness and suffering of one family among some thirty or forty thousand pleading in their silent patient manner for relief. What are the well-fed heathens, contentedly worshipping their harmless gods, to these poor pitiful faces with their hungry eyes looking in at our very doors?

I seem to have wandered somewhat from the celestial views with which I set out; and yet the little picture just drawn is a part of the scenery which suggested the first sentence. It is only that since framing the first words the night has deepened and lent its shadows to the thoughts as they crept on. The diamond-lighted roof is over the great city now, and the far purple depths of the empyrean seem not more hushed and still than these streets and avenues so lately thronged and noisy with the rushing tide of life. From my window as I look out, there is no sound to tell of joy or sorrow, and no sign of life save here and there a twinkling lamp. What miracles are wrought by night and sleep. Only they or death could have struck this Babel so dumb, so still. And what a Heaven of glory is that above; so near, and yet, alas, so far! One blessed thought, however, brightens and shortens the distance. The angel world is all between, and as near the lowly hovel as the palace of the rich and proud.

L.

March 31, 1865, page 4

Letter from Washington

March Days | Coquetry and Its Consequences | Washington as it Was | Haunting Spirits | Spring Perfumes | Magnolia Blooms

From Our Own Correspondent
Washington, March 29, 1865

The wind is on its high key at the Capital nowadays. March seems to be in a great bluster to get out of the way of April, who was last week coquetting about him with sunny smiles, soft airs and warm-dropping tears. She even brought bouquets of crocuses, snow drops, jonquils, and tender grasses all scented with balsam buds and maple blossoms, and held them under his nose while she fanned him with south winds steadily for seven days together, and so nearly succeeded in ruining his reputation that he now has as much as ever he can do to make up lost time, save his credit and go out of the world in respectable March style. Yesterday he completely shook off his enchantress, put on airs of his own and went about the streets peculiar to no one but himself. What a day it was of scowling skies, lightning and thunder, and tornadoes of wind and torrents of rain. Roots went kiting through the air; steeples were inverted; hacks turned their wheels upward; horses stood on their heads and went through other unusual acrobatic performances; trees became antic and took to waltzing down the streets with flag staffs and telegraph poles in honor of the great Blusterer, while milk wagons incontinently upset themselves and poured their frothy libations at his feet. And a sadder sacrifice than this he had, for one man was killed outright, and several severely injured by falling trees, signs and timbers. It was a fearful day, and has been succeeded by one nearly as bad, with high winds, dashes of rain, spittings of snow, and cold as January.

Situated as Washington is, in a sort of basin made by the low surrounding hills, or heights, as they are called, one would hardly think that it could be so subject as it is to these terrific gales, but as the heights are not high enough to keep off the winds, they only serve to ruffle them into greater fury, and they come rushing down upon us like maddened wild beasts after their prey. The heavy forests which grew along these hills before the war began, were probably some protection, but they are all cut away now, and the heights bear bristling forts and stately flag staffs instead.

This immense basin, now holding a densely populated city some four by six miles in extent, was, 64 years ago, as thickly covered with trees and shrub-oak bushes as it is now with houses. At the time the Capital was established here in 1801, Pennsylvania Avenue for the whole distance from the Capitol to the President's house was a deep morass covered with elder bushes, and was not even cut through the width intended till the ensuing winter. Snipe-shooting was common then where the heart of the city now is. The valley was called Conococheague by the Indians, that being the name of a little stream which Anglicized is Roaring Brook, a tributary of the Potomac. Writers of those early days here give gloomy accounts of the prospect as they looked out over swamp and thicket, and tried to recognize the streets and avenues, portrayed on the paper plan. Not one was visible, and the few country roads around were muddy and unimproved.

But there is no need of going back to those early writers to prove that all Washington was once a swamp. There are little haunting sprites about here yet that go up and down the streets, through all the long summer evenings, flashing their tiny lanterns into dim alleys and by-ways, flitting silently above the gay avenue promenaders, darting into cellars one moment, and up among the branches of unfamiliar trees the next, in their ever restless search for the mossy bogs and alder thickets of the olden time. Sometimes there will be whole flocks of swarms of these fireflies, with their pale yellow-green lights clustering about some favorite spot, and again only here and there a solitary one, like a wandering spirit seeking rest, and finding none. I fancy they are searching for their old haunts, the morasses hidden under the pavement of Pennsylvania avenue.

The native vegetation also, remnants of which are still lingering even in the well-kept public grounds, show the former marshy nature of the soil. In Lafayette

Square in front of the President's house, and in most of the parks about the city may be found specimens of water-loving plants struggling to maintain an existence among the cultivated flora, and tufts of wild garlic are everywhere thickly interspersed among the grasses. In early spring it is a very common thing to see groups of children sporting about these parks with their hands and mouths full of wild onion or garlic tops, which they gather from among the grass to browse upon, so mingling their pungent perfumes with the spicy fragrance of althea buds, magnolias and sweet jasmines.

Speaking of magnolias, a gentleman of this city has one of the grandifloras now a perfect marvel of beauty, standing robed and crowned with magnificent blossoms to the number of a thousand or more. It is a wonder and a glory to look upon, and a splendor which all the storms of March cannot dim.

L.

April 1, 1865, page 4

Letter from Washington

THE PRESIDENT'S HOUSE AS IT WAS AND IS

From Our Own Correspondent
Washington, March 25, 1865

The White House now so beautifully situated in the midst of blooming parks and embowering groves, is thus described by the wife of President John Adams, who took possession of it in the fall of 1800.

"The house is upon a grand and superb scale, requiring about thirty servants to attend and keep the apartments in proper order, and perform the ordinary business of the house and tables—an establishment very well proportioned to the President's salary. The lighting of the apartments from the kitchen to parlors to chambers, is a tax indeed, and the fires we are obliged to keep to secure us from daily agues is another very cheering comfort. To assist us in the great castle, and render less attendance necessary, bells are wholly wanting, not a single one being hung through the whole house, and promises are all you can obtain. This is so great an inconvenience that I do not know what to do or how to do. The ladies from Georgetown and the city have many of them visited me. Yesterday I returned fifteen visits. But such a place as Georgetown appears! Why, our Milton is beautiful. But no comparisons; if they put me up bells and let me have wood enough to keep fires, I design *to be pleased*. But surrounded with forests, can you believe that wood is not to be had, because people cannot be found to cut and cart it. We have indeed come into a *new country*.

The house is made habitable, but there is not a single apartment finished, and all inside, except the plastering, has been done since B came. We have not the *least fence, yard or convenience without,* and the great unfinished audience-room I make a drying room of, to hang up the clothes in."

This thrifty Yankee housewife then concludes her somewhat satirical letter by the assertion that, "If the twelve years in which this place has been considered as the future seat of government had been improved, as they would have been in New England, very many of the present inconveniences would have been removed. It is a beautiful spot, capable of any improvement, and the more I view it the more delighted I am with it."

A visit to the grounds now, on some genial day in the budding springtime, or when in the full glory of their summer foliage and bloom, will convince any one that the judgment of the accomplished lady above quoted was correct. Now that the years have improved it, it is a "beautiful spot" indeed.

The foundation of the house was laid on the 13th of October, 1792, and the whole building is one hundred and seventy feet front by eighty-six deep. It contains two lofty stories of rooms above the basement, and the roof is surrounded by a balustrade.

The roof is so old and often out of repair that as long ago as 1860, the Commissioner of Public Buildings called the attention of Congress to its condition, and stated, that owing to the copper not having been properly put on at first, it is now constantly needing expenditures of money to keep the building in habitable condition. So it will be seen that Uncle Sam, with all his other family troubles, has a leaky roof over his head, and like many common mortals, often has the mortification of looking up at disfigured ceilings. It is to be hoped that when his rebellious children come to order again, they will reward his forbearance and integrity by uniting to build him a house worthy of the head of so great and rich a family.

L.

April 8, 1865, page 4

Letter from Washington

THE OCCUPATION OF PETERSBURG AND RICHMOND | HOW THE NEWS WAS RECEIVED

From Our Own Correspondent
Washington, April 3, 1865

We thought the loyal inhabitants of the Capital were crazy with joy on the 31st of January, when the vote on the constitutional amendment was taken; and again on February 22d, when they celebrated, with processions and illuminations, the fall of Charleston and the birth of Washington; and yet again on the 4th of March, when President Lincoln was a second time consecrated to the great work of leading a mighty nation on to a glorious destiny. On all these occasions the rejoicings have been enthusiastic, but today has exceeded them all in the perfect abandon of excitement with which the dispatches from our noble army have been received. People seem almost to have gone mad with joy.

It is said that when Secretary Stanton received the telegram informing him that our troops occupied Petersburg, and that Weitzel was taking his colored soldiers into Richmond by the front door, he read it through, and then went out before the people waiting to hear the news, exclaiming, "Praise God, from whom all blessings flow!" which the crowd at once took up to the tune of Old Hundred, and sung the Doxology to the end, then added the "Star Spangled Banner," and finished up with Yankee Doodle and deafening cheers.

In the Patent Office building the wildest excitement prevailed. Commissioners, heads of bureaus, chiefs, and their clerks, messengers, and all, rushed from their rooms and went up and down the long halls and corridors, shouting, cheering, wringing each other's hands, embracing and congratulating each other. The news spread from floor to floor, and the long arched halls and galleries rang and echoed with cheers and exclamations of joy. But this was not enough; they could not be bounded by walls. The Secretary of the Interior promptly dismissed all hands and ordered the building closed for the day. In a few moments several hundreds had gathered about the portico of the south front; flags were displayed, and men tried to make speeches, but the excitement was too great; the efforts resulted only in vociferous cheering, and then they formed in procession with a flag at their head and marched off to the War Department.

At that point the crowd was immense. Speeches were made, cheers given, cannon fired, and all possible demonstrations of delight indulged in. All the Government departments were closed, and the principal merchants and men of business on the avenue followed their example, and instead of a card, hung the Star Spangled Banner over their doors to tell the people why they were "not at home." Business was out of the question except for a few demi-semi-secessionists, who, with victory and the downfall of gold staring them in the face, and their high-priced cottons weighing heavily on their purses, were frantically pushing their goods in the way of passersby, piling them out on the sidewalks, all placarded with invitations and temptations. "Yard wide cottons reduced from 75 to 25 cents!" said one. "*Oweing* to the decline in gold we are *seling* cheap!" said another, the orthography probably affected by the panic. But little heed paid the multitude to anything but the popular excitement.

Flags were up everywhere, and bands of music; and impromptu processions were got up, marching here and there to pay their respects to Secretaries and Senators; bells rung out the joy from their brazen throats for an hour or more, and cannon from the far-encircling forts rolled their white wreaths around the horizon and shouted victory and freedom across the broad valley where the city lies.

But among all this gladness there are none who rejoice with deeper or more heartfelt thankfulness than the colored race, thousands of whom now among us have children, husbands, brothers and other near and dear relatives in the fields and slave-pens and bloody trenches of the South. One poor old woman had her seven sons taken from her by the chivalry, and thrust under the crumbling fabric of the Confederacy, to help stay it from falling. Whether they will be crushed in the ruin, God only knows; but the faithful old heart is now trembling with hope. Another had her husband and all her children taken, and she alone escaped with life and three helpless grand-children. She was on the street today, and telling the little boy she led that she "Reckoned Massa Lincoln would set daddy free now, and the Lor' would send him right up to Washington."

The streets were everywhere crowded with happy-looking black faces. They mingled in every crowd, listening to all the speeches and the news, and cheering with the rest. In some places they formed an assembly of themselves and had speeches of their own; they read the telegrams on the bulletin boards, bought extras of the newsboys, and ran with the glad tidings to families and friends.

The sad cost of all this rejoicing, the price of life and blood and suffering, we know not yet. Particulars have not yet reached here as I write, but you will doubtless have them by telegraph before this reaches you.

L.

April 15, 1865, page 1

Letter from Washington

The People's Jubilee | General Rejoicings | McClellan Worshippers in Obscurity | The *Intelligencer* in a Dilemma | What it Says and how it Feels | Colored Quarrels

From Our Own Correspondent
Washington, April 11, 1865

There is no use in trying to multiply words expressing the joy of the people over the great event of the week—Lee's Surrender. The tumult of excitements so intense, so rapidly succeeding each other during the past ten days, has almost bewildered our senses. Yesterday all nature seemed to sympathize with the demonstrations by which men were trying to give vent to their feelings. With the dawn of day began the roar of cannon, the ringing of bells, and the down-pouring of rain, the flash and glow of starry banners floating, streaming, wreathing everywhere. The trees, shrubs, and flowers, which for days past have been on tip-toe for a "burst," could hold in no longer, but shook out their colors and filled the air with fragrance and spicy odors. The rains have opened the leaf and blossom buds, as the good tidings of great joy have opened the hearts of the people, and beauty and incense, rejoicing and thanksgiving fill the land.

The rain was almost a steady pour the whole day through, but did not in the least dampen the loyal ardor, or prevent its enthusiastic expression. The streets were full; bands and batteries playing and firing salutes as they went; steam fire engines decked with flags and screaming desperately; soldiers, sailors and citizens singing "Rally round the Flag" and Yankee Doodle. Twice during the day the President was called out by the crowds thronging around the White House, anxious to see him, hear him speak, and to congratulate him on the grand consummation. Both times he made a few remarks and was loudly cheered, but declined making speeches till he should be better prepared. Several buildings were illuminated last evening, but to-night more general demonstrations are to be made by processions and speeches.

It is noticeable that where McClellan flags were hung out last summer and fall, no Union flag or other sign of joy has been seen. The thunders of victory make harsh music in the ears of the chivalry and their obsequious sympathizers. They are struck-dumb and seen to have vanished into dark corners, with the owls and bats, whose foreboding tones they have been so long imitating. They will doubtless crawl out again, however, when the effect of the shock is over a little, and they have time to think what policy it will be best to take up next.

Their semi-organ, the *Intelligencer*, is seriously exercised as to just what ground it ought to take in the emergency. The fence where it has been sitting so long is becoming more shaky and uncomfortable every day; but as yet the astride position is maintained with wonderful skill and ingenuity. The truth is the thing has amazing long legs, with no great weight of heart or head above them to make it top-heavy, and so plants a foot on either side and proceeds to befog itself and readers by means of wordy mysticisms into the belief that there is no fence at all in the way, and that it is marching right along to the tune of the Union as it is to be. It begins an article full of patriotic fever and exultation, and presently slides off into the old whimpering fears about "irritating" Southern pride, and begs that the North will "observe a decorous silence" in regard to everything that might have that effect. It would even throw all the wrongs that slavery has wrought, and all the responsibilities for them, over on the well backed shoulders of that poor old scapegoat England, and maintains its own innocence and integrity by saying:

"*If slavery has been our curse, as many upright men believe,* then it has been a common curse, inflicted by the mother country, and is not to be especially visited upon the South by the 'bolts of human thunder.'"

Then if it be right to mete out punishment to evil doers, somebody should go over and flog that wicked old grandmother instead of correcting the naughty child who hugged the nurse to her bosom, and would destroy her own wise and beneficent mother and all the family besides, to say nothing of the prospects of humanity at large, rather than give it up, and even keeps it in her own lap. Because she had the plague, why should she try to infect the whole human race with it.

The question, however, is settled for her now. The mudsills and mechanics have carried away the key to the slave pen, have knocked the walls down and the bottom out, so that men now can be men if they will. On this subject the *Intelligencer* puts his Southern boot down flatly, and says: "It is only the over-zealous among men, who esteem the blacks as the equals of the white race. The most that statesmanship proclaims for the black man, is that he shall be protected in his natural rights, to earn his bread as he pleases, to be defended by the laws, and to be amenable to the laws. The rest is all philanthropy and sentiment."

There is a sneer for you! One worthy of the source from whence it comes. What a text for men of progress in these times; for the humanitarians of the day! But let the black man answer it—and he will. He will work out the intellectual problem better than anybody can do it for him; and quicker than many are willing to believe.

But this self-selected prompter of a nation's conscience pleads pitifully again for the "removal of all cases of irritation," and cites as one the guarding of rebel prisoners by colored soldiers; as if anything in human form could be too black to typify the treachery and barbarity exercised towards the helpless brave men from our ranks, who have fallen into their hands, and who have perished by tens of thousands in their horrid prisons, or been starved into idiocy and sent home to die. Kid gloved handling and beds of down are not what these men earned. Our black soldiers have given them soldier treatment, which is all they ought to expect from either black or white.

Washington saw the spectacle a day or two ago, of a good-sized regiment of captured traitors handsomely escorted through her streets by sable guards, and much good it did loyal people to see it too; neither did the delivered Johnnies seem sensible of any unpleasant "irritations." Why should they? having been cared for by black men all their lives. A soldier is a better soldier whatever his skin may be stained with, provided it is not treason.

L.

April 21, 1865, page 4

Letter from Washington

OUR MURDERED PRESIDENT | THE CITY IN MOURNING | INCIDENTS | PAROLED REBELS | HOW THEY REWARD THE HAND THAT SPARED THEM | THE SPIRIT THAT PROMPTED THE MURDER

From Our Own Correspondent
Washington, April 15, 1865

Every tongue is dumb and every pen paralyzed with the great woe that has so suddenly come upon the nation. The city is like a widow in the first desolation of her grief today. The revulsion is so sudden from the delirium of joy which had made the past two weeks one gala-day of delight, that men scarcely know how to act or what to do. They meet upon the streets, wring each other's hands, and in broken sentences try to express their horror of the awful tragedy last night enacted in our midst. Old and young are weeping, and the whole city is shrouded in mourning. All places of business are closed, public buildings and private dwellings are alike draped in black, and the mourners literally go about the streets. All the church bells are tolling solemnly.

The murdered President, his frantic wife and child, the venerable and almost dying Secretary of State stabbed in his bed, one son butchered in his defense, and another bearing ghastly marks of the assassin's knife, all together form a combination of horrors so appalling that it is impossible for the mind to grasp or words to measure them.

You will have had all the particulars as far as known, before this reaches you. As yet, so sudden has been the shock, we cannot realize that the man to whom the nation has looked up to with such faith and trust, is gone from us past recall. The noisy newsboys in the streets are shouting the particulars of the murder, and in spite of what we know of the awful truth, we hold our breath in listening for some word of hope, some contradiction which we long for and yet know too well can never come.

One poor old colored woman among the crowd gathered about the house from which the President's corpse was taken to be carried to the White House, wringing her hands and crying, said: "O, they have killed him—the best friend we ever had." "Yes; but there is one satisfaction left—they cannot kill God," said a gentleman standing near.

Part 3: 1865

The city, for the past day or two, has been full of prisoners and paroled rebels. A number of officers of high rank from the rebel army, Ewell among them, were, only yesterday, feted and feasted at Willard's, and it is said the dinner given them was at the Government's expense. There were some 25 or 30 of them. And the reward the Government gets is murder, and the most cold-blooded, cowardly assassination. There are hundreds, perhaps thousands of secessionists here who are full of secret joy at this awful deed. Not many dare show it boldly as yet, but would rejoice to have a chance to do so with safety. The paroled rebels themselves are no better friends of the Union now than when fighting the ranks under Gen. Lee. They are only vipers which our too generous Government has taken to its bosom and warmed into life that they may sting it again.

Only a day or two ago a large number of these paroled villains were furnished with Government transportation down the river, that they might go to their own homes in peace. While waiting at the wharf they indulged in expressions of bitter hatred against this Government, and talked secession as rabidly as if they had been in Richmond instead of the District of Columbia. One of them being asked if he had not taken the oath, replied: "Well, they prescribed something for me up there, and I put my name to it, they may call it the oath or what they like; but what the devil do I care about it?"

These are the "erring brethren," over whom there has been so much clerical and editorial nonsense preached and written of late. What are oaths to traitors?

President Lincoln's funeral procession in Washington City.
From *Harper's Weekly Magazine,* May 6, 1865.

who have violated the most solemn obligations human and divine, that men ever knew! What is a traitor's oath good for? He is a perjured wretch at best. No pledge or obligation could be more solemn than all these men once willingly gave, and cheerfully placed themselves under to sustain the Government they are now trying to destroy. Yet they violated them purposely, and why should they be trusted again.

I do hope our loyal papers will have done with this nonsensical magnanimity, their silly similes and twaddle, and remember that justice has claims as well as mercy. Men are not insects of an hour, capable of stinging but once in a lifetime. In dealing with them principles are at stake, and not merely one individual's present pain. The blow their cowardly treachery has dealt us now will be felt by the whole nation, as no calamity has been felt before. Will rosewater philanthropists pray that the fiends may be spared, in hopes that they may not strike again? Yet those who did the deed are only fools; the spirit that prompted them is the spirit of the rebellion. Shall we pity and pardon and caress it still?

Thank God, the nation is not dead, though they have taken from us its greatest and best man, our beloved President.

L.

May 9, 1865, page 4.

Our Washington Letter

The City in Mourning | A Shock that Does Not Pass Away.

From Our Own Correspondent
Washington, May 2, 1865

The past two weeks have crept on slowly and with such a leaden weight that the experience of years seems to have been crowded into them—an experience of such horror that few if any would wish to live to pass through it again. The appalling gloom which fell with the fatal bolt that took from us the great heart we loved to lean upon, is too heavy to pass so soon away. That great, pure, loving heart is still and cold, and the form that held it has gone from us forever even before we can arouse ourselves from the terrible shock to believe that it is really so. The stroke came, the stunning, paralyzing horror, the days of silence when earth and heaven were shrouded with black, and men were dumb, and only the brazen bells in mid air dared to speak of the nameless deed; then a pale, beloved face turned heavenward in mute appealing, was gazed down upon by hundreds of thousands of tearful eyes, and then came the grand and mournful pageant with death marches and shrouded banners and tolling bells and minute guns. Now all are gone but the memory and the gloom. Mourning drapery still darkens all the streets, and sad faces are met at every turn.

Spring has been trying to smile, but it seems like an effort without heart in it. The sky is cold and steely blue, and the white sun glitters like ice through the chill atmosphere. Trees and plants are in beautiful bloom nevertheless, but their brightness of beauty seems only mockery beside all these mourning badges and drooping, crepe-wreathed banners.

The Departments were opened again a day or two after the funeral, but more than a week passed before men could compose themselves to their old routine of desk labor. They would gather in little whispering groups here and there, and in the midst of every group was a corpse and a murderer. It was the same on the streets, in the stores, in the parlors—everywhere; even at our tables, in our closets, and in our dreams those haunting shapes were seen. Weary of the ever-present horror we wandered off toward the hills hoping to find breathing and thinking space beyond the black-draped houses and sad-faced groups about them. But sentinels were posted along the green hills; a cordon of bayonets deep and strong surrounded the city and spread far out along the Virginia and Maryland valleys; armed and vigilant pickets were everywhere, and side by side with each one walked the victim and his cruel murderer. And there hour by hour and day by day they walked till the one was taken and the other avenged. There was no passing beyond such a line as that.

In the beautiful parks everywhere about the city, nature is smiling over her resurrection from the long, cold winter burial. Trees are in full foliage, and shrubs and plants brilliant with the freshness of spring bloom. We have been looking through tears so long, however, that their dimness yet seems to cloud all things; and even if we wished, we could not escape from the black memorials that on all hands remind us of the nation's loss. From the green and fragrant Capitol grounds we look up at the long white marble colonnades, festooned with sable drapery, even to the feet of the statue of America crowning the dome. Glancing up the long avenue towards the White House, we see the same sad emblems every foot of the way, only varied here and there by flags, bordered with black and drooping at half mast.

But the saddest sight of all is from the park immediately in front of the Presidential mansion. The White House, so lately the resort of the gay and brilliant throngs of levees and reception days, has now hanging about it the gloom and loneliness of the sepulcher. All the columns of the great portico are shrouded in black from the roof to the ground, and from end to end of the broad front are looped the emblems of mourning for its late beloved and honored occupant. She who bears his now immortal name is a stricken and desolate mourner within. A silence like that of death seems to have settled on all around. It is true the street cars, and long trains of Government wagons, and cavalrymen, and squads of soldiery, fill

John Wilkes Booth. From *Harper's Weekly Magazine*, April 29, 1865.

the avenue with their incessant clattering, but with all this the stillness that has dropped like a pall over the great mansion seems undisturbed.

Across the street from this park, and facing it on the east, is the residence of the Sewards. It is a plain, four story house of red brick, and all across the front are stretched the black arches of mourning, while armed guards pace steadily to and fro, guarding the precious lives within. There are soldiers all about the premises, and no horseman or vehicle of any kind is permitted to pass that square by day or night. Around the corner, and a little farther to the north, is the handsome mansion of Hon. Samuel Hooper, the temporary home of President Johnson, also closely guarded, and bearing the emblems of the nation's sorrow. On the other hand, almost hidden in their stately groves, are the War and Navy Departments, heavily shrouded, and with mourning flags at half mast.

Since the murderer Booth met his fate, the horror that so oppressed the city has somewhat passed away, but it will be long before the gloom and sadness leave us.
L.

May 11, 1865, page 4

Our Washington Letter

EFFECTS OF THE PROCLAMATION OF MAY 2D | POSITION OF SYMPATHIZERS DEFINED | TREASON IN CRINOLINE | AN INSTANCE OF LOYALTY | PUBLIC OPINION TO EXPRESS ITSELF

From Our Own Correspondent
Washington, May 6, 1865

Have you, in your cool Northwestern towns, men who, through all these past four years of the nation's struggle for life, have laughed at its calamities and mocked when its anguish was heaviest; who have been dumb when its arms met with success, and quick to censure when reverses came; who threw out no banners or symbols of joy when the land was ablaze with the splendor of our victories, but who hung about them the mockeries of woe at the shock which marked the culmination of the crimes they had so long encouraged? If you have, then you have also men whose lips turned white with apprehension and terror as they read President Johnson's proclamation of Tuesday, and 2d of May. There are far too many of such here in Washington, and not only men but women, who understand the awful import of the "evidence" referred to in that proclamation. Their hypocritical crapes and draperies of black cambric but heighten the pallor of their conscious faces. Their defiance is at an end now. They would sink into oblivion if they could, rather than to court the notoriety of which they were so ambitious less than one brief month ago. They feel as if on the brink of a fearful chasm, with the ground crumbling under their feet, and the avenger of blood close upon them.

There is a definiteness about the situation of these sympathizers now quite unlike anything they have experienced since the war began. The arch fiend of the rebellion stands before the world in his true light at last, branded all over with infamy, and his satellites have so far identified their interests with his that they cannot escape their share of the ignominious fame to which outraged humanity has consigned him. They must feel and know this, and they do. However they may rally when the first shock of this awful revelation is over, they can only stand dumb with terror now, or shrink, if they may, from the sight and knowledge of man and of God.

There are houses in this city where all was life and gaiety up to the moment when the rebel chief was made an outlaw with his hands stained by the nation's life blood and a price set upon his head; since then the silence and darkness of guilt are within and around them. But they are marked. Those to whom are entrusted the destinies of the nation are learning that *eternal* and not *occasional* vigilance is the price of liberty, and the dangers surrounding them are making them Argus-eyed and Briarius-armed. The events of the times are aiding our new President to teach the people and their rulers the true definition and application of the word treason; and among other things concerning it they have learned that it is not distinguished by either sex or dress; and that loyalty consists in principles and deeds, not in birth or color.

Secessionists, traitors in crinoline, have swept the streets with defiant airs and openly scorned "the low-born rabble who swarmed here after"—but no, I will not insult the blameless and beloved dead by repeating the taunting words they flung at him in their insolent pride. His is the exaltation now, and theirs the guilty abasement before a once despised people now risen in the simple majesty of right and demanding retribution "to the end that justice be done." Steadily and surely the avenging Nemesis is tracking the traitors, and whether the bloody footmarks are made by boot and spur or by dainty slippers it is all the same. O these guilty, guilty women who in their mad and thoughtless pride have urged their husbands and sons into the commission of the blackest crimes; who have spurned a lover's suit unless his hands were stained with loyal blood; who have opened their doors to welcome murderers to the protection of their homes, and have given to highway robbers and assassins the sanction of their presence and their smiles, thus basely prostituting all the most sacred offices of social life, home affections, love and hospitality, to the end that wickedness might triumph. What punishment can atone for the wrongs they have done, and the still greater ones they had the will to do, against their sex and against humanity? They have a fearful responsibility for the aid they have given in plotting, planning and pushing on the rebellion.

That there are loyal women here, however, let me prove by relating a little incident. The day before our President's death a young girl, who had been at school in Baltimore, came home for a vacation, bringing with her two young lady friends of that city, who were to spend the spring holidays here. In the morning, while they were dressing, the news of the murder reached them. They began to dance and sing, and expressed their joy in such terms as to shock a little daughter of the family who heard them, and she ran to her mother. The lady called on her guests, and learning from them what their sentiments were, she bade them put on their bonnets, pack their trunks, and leave her house at once. Rain was falling heavily, but no delay was allowed, not even to send for a carriage; the trunks were dragged down stairs, shoved out upon the sidewalk, and the Misses Baltimoreans after them, where, in the rain and with the door closed and locked behind them they had liberty to indulge in such transports as they might fancy best suited to the occasion.

A great many individual instances of a like nature with the above have occurred here since the memorable 14th of April, and so rapidly has public opinion grown in strength and confidence, especially since the Proclamation of the 2d inst. was issued, that I think it may now be truly said that loyalty is in the ascendant. It is so confident, at least, that a great mass meeting is to be held on Tuesday the 9th, to give expression to the sense of the District, and to determine on the course to be pursued towards the traitors in our midst who have given countenance and sympathy to the perpetrators of the horrid crimes against the nation's life. Long suppressed indignation is finding its way to action, and it is expected that something more than soft words will be the result.

Washington for her purification just wants the laying on of Ben. Butler's hands after the manner they were applied to New Orleans. Her moral and physical condition would be greatly improved thereby.

L.

May 29, 1865, page 1

Letter from Washington

REVIEW OF THE ARMIES MARCHING HOME

Washington, May 24, 1865

For two days past Washington has done nothing but watch our national heroes marching home. The display, though embracing but comparatively a small portion of the entire army of the Union, has been a very grand one indeed. The manner of the review was not such as would permit of military evolutions by the troops; it was simply a street parade, and as such only limited numbers of the immense masses passing by could be seen from any one point. The best view was from the head of Pennsylvania Avenue, where it bends to the north past the Treasury building. Standing there and looking towards the Capitol, the scene was a most grand and imposing one. As far as the eye could reach on either hand, the sidewalks were densely crowded with spectators, and every window and balcony and even the roofs and the trees along the way were full. As brigade after brigade swept up the noble avenue with their war-worn flags and inspiring music, they were welcomed with cheers and songs, the waving of flags and handkerchiefs, and now and then a showering of bouquets and wreaths of evergreens and beautiful flowers. Many of the Generals had their horses' necks wreathed with garlands, the gifts of grateful hands along the way.

Grand review in Washington—Sheridan's passing through Pennsylvania Avenue, May 23, 1865. From *Harper's Weekly Magazine,* June 10, 1865.

    The children of the public schools dressed in uniform white, with black sashes, assembled at the Capitol and greeted the troops with songs and flowers. Everywhere, through all the grand pageant, blended with the symbols of rejoicing were to be seen also the emblems of mourning for the dead President—he who so longed to see this day, and was caught up out of our sight before it came. All the National flags about the city were at half-mast and heavily draped with black, and every ensign, banner and battle-flag in the passing regiments had crape upon it, while mourning badges were worn by all the officers and very many of the soldiers.

    Immense temporary pavilions built in front of the White House and occupying all the broad pavements on either side of the avenue, were handsomely decorated, and filled by Government dignitaries and officials, from the President down, together with Foreign Ministers, attaches, etc., and here also was stationed Lieut. Gen. Grant, before whom these two grand armies passed in review. Standing back of these, almost hidden by the dense foliage of the great trees around it, the White House with its tall pillars still shrouded in black, was desolate and silent as a tomb. It was as if life and death, joy and sorrow had met, and hope had crowned them together with victory and peace and the bloom of spring.

    The entire of yesterday was occupied with the passage of Sheridan's cavalry and the 9th, 5th, and 2d Army Corps, together with artillery and engineer corps. Sheridan of course was not here, as he has gone to crush out the one head of the hydra yet alive, in Texas; but his gallant troopers, under command of our own brave Custer, were wildly cheered as they swept up the avenue. Indeed, all were cheered, as they well deserved to be; but, oh, how poor, how empty does all this pageantry and cheering seem, compared with what we owe to these bronzed and war-torn veterans. Shouts and songs and fading flowers seem almost like mockery when offered to such men who have accomplished a work so grand, and yet what else had these gratified crowds to offer?

Sherman's magnificent army passed through the city today. It was worth a lifetime of common events to witness a sight like this. If your Northern doughfaces and copperheads could but look in the iron faces of these men, as they come up in their mighty strength, they would easily understand why chivalry begged for peace and then took to its heels, in petticoats, at their approach. Grinding between the upper and nether millstone wouldn't have been a circumstance to the pulverizing all secession would have got, if it had not crumbled in pieces and scattered just as it did. No one can look at troops like these without feeling sure that an enemy's country, through which they have once marched, must be pretty thoroughly conquered. They are not the men to march without a purpose, and certainly not the ones to leave till that purpose is accomplished.

There were some particulars about this army, and some little incidents, which I will try to gather up this afternoon, and give you in my next.

L.

May 31, 1865, page 4

Letters from Washington

THE GRAND REVIEW | AN ENGLISHMAN'S OPINION | CITIZEN SOLDIERS | SOUTH CAROLINA'S PUNISHMENT | SHERMAN'S MEN | GRANT'S IRISH BRIGADE | SERENADE TO GOV. CRAPO AND SENATOR CHANDLER | MICHIGAN'S RECORD, ETC.

From Our Own Correspondent
Washington, May 27, 1865

For twelve hours, from 9 till 3 o'clock on Tuesday, and the same on Wednesday, we stood at the head of Pennsylvania Avenue and watched the moving masses of men crowned with glittering steel as they came pouring around and down the slopes of Capitol Hill and went rolling on like a mighty river past the stand where the great review took place. It was, without doubt, the grandest military pageant ever witnessed upon the American continent. I overheard an Englishman speaking of it, and he said, "I have witnessed military reviews in England and France, and other parts of Europe, but never saw anything that could equal this. I only wish John Bull at home could see what we see here today." There was an emphasis in the tone that gave a peculiar force to the words; coming from English lips, too, it seemed to mean something, especially when it was added, "And to think that this is not more than one-third of the Union army! and the grandeur of it all is that these men are citizens."

Yes; there is where foreigners see the grandeur, if we do not. These are all citizens who know the value of their country and their Government; they saw the danger menacing both, they made heroes of themselves, they have averted the danger, have given a progressive interpretation to the old Constitution, and are now quietly disbanding to go home and be citizens again. The heroes made by Kings and Emperors are not to be compared with these.

I remember in the early part of the war there was a great anxiety on the part of many as to what should be done with the soldiers after the war was over. But even the most anxious need have no uneasiness on that score; the soldiers will take care of themselves just as well as they did before the war, and better too, many of them. I have talked with hundreds of them, and the universal expression is one of joy at the prospect of going home—home to their families, their farms, and their workshops. Home is the first word they speak in connection with their discharge from service. Our soldiers don't know what "demoralization" means. They had something dearer than life to fight for; they fought, and won, and are now going home to enjoy the peaceful fruits of their victory.

Some of Sherman's men who had fallen out of the ranks from weariness yesterday, came and stood beside us and told us of the hollowness of the Confederate shell through which they had been marching. They said that if ever there was a thoroughly whipped and conquered people it was the Southern rebels; and, said one, "South Carolina is, as it deserves to be, the most completely humbled and desolated spot in all rebeldom. We had no friends there, and we made the country support us. I think it will be some time before that State will want to set up for herself against the Union again!"

It is impossible to describe the feeling of these men towards their commander. They speak of Sherman as a beloved and indulgent father. "There's no place this side of Tophet," said one, "that Sherman's boys wouldn't take if he asked them to; and I reckon they'd go clean that out if he said so!"

The troops came up the broad avenue in splendid marching order, 26 abreast, each corps of infantry followed by its artillery, the shining brass pieces and wicked steel rifled guns, each drawn by eight stout horses, and their accompanying caissons the same. These cannon, which have been talking thunder to the rebels so long, looked peaceful and innocent enough now, and many of them were wreathed with evergreens and garlands of flowers.

One peculiarity of Sherman's army was the great numbers of heavily packed mules between the divisions, and the long train of loaded army wagons, and the promiscuous masses following in the rear. Most of those leading or riding the mules were contrabands of all ages, from little boys to old men; one black woman was among them. But what created great amusement among the thousands of spectators were the roosters perched on tops of the mule-packs and seeming to enjoy the display as much as anybody. They looked around with great apparent satisfaction on the laughing, clapping, shouting crowd, and every now and then answered the cheers by flapping their wings and crowing triumphantly as they "went marching on." They evidently understood that there was victory to be celebrated and that they were expected to do their part; and they did it. In one instance there was a beautiful white goat, a pet of some good soldier boy, standing on one of the mule-packs eating from a pannier as contentedly as if born to ride horseback and live on rations.

No colored troops were on review either day, except the few with Sherman's army who were attached to the Pioneer corps and armed with picks and shovels. The black soldiers are still in the field, in the army of the James, or at the West and Southwest.

The Irish Brigade, under Grant, the first day made a fine appearance, every soldier in it having a sprig of green box in his cap. Looking over and down the long columns, the effect was very pleasing. The green flag of Erin was carried beside the national colors, and the tattered battle flags give token of the hard service they had seen.

The weather for the grand review could not have been finer. For a week or more past there had been a constant succession of thunderstorms, day and night; so that when it did clear off the atmosphere was pure and fresh and cool. Both days were perfectly delightful, with clear blue skies, bright sunshine, and sweet invigorating airs.

Hundreds of Michigan people have been here to witness the spectacle. It was chronicled on Monday that Gov. Crapo and staff, Senator Chandler, and others were in town, and on the evening of that day they were serenaded by the band of the Michigan Cavalry Brigade. The Governor was called out and made a patriotic speech. Senator Chandler also spoke, and the band were handsomely entertained at the Governor's rooms.

This cavalry brigade, comprising the 6th, 7th, 1st, and 5th Michigan cavalry, was commanded by Col. Peter Stagg, of Trenton, Mich. He was a Colonel day before yesterday, but is a Brigadier General now, having been promoted since the review.

It was amusing yesterday to hear the little boys as they ran up and down among the crowds on the side-walks, crying "Photographs of Jeff. Davis trying to escape in his wife's clothes."

Here, if ever, from the scene in the avenue on one hand, to the pictured masquerade on the other, the oft talked-of "step from the sublime to the ridiculous" was a visible, tangible reality.

But the splendid pageant of the day passed on, and as the sun went down the armies of the Union spread their tents on the hills and along the valleys, around about the capital they have guarded so long and so well. The city, with its 70,000 visitors, seemed as quiet as ordinarily, save the serenading bands, with their pleasant music at the hotels, where their Generals were quartered.

Today the boys in blue have taken the city by storm. They are everywhere, seeing the sights and making the most of Washington while the opportunity lasts.
L.

June 21, 1865, page 4

Letter from Washington

GOING TO CAMP | THE FIRST MICHIGAN ENGINEERS AND MECHANICS | THE HOSPITAL TENT | DINING IN CAMP | HOW THE BOYS LIVE | IN GOD'S COUNTRY AGAIN

From Our Own Correspondent
Washington, June 13, 1865

"Come with us to the woods and see how the soldiers live in camp."

The opportunity I had been wishing for so many months came to me at last in the above invitation, which, though more than half begged for, was accepted with all due gratitude, both felt and expressed. To get into the woods for one day, those deep green fragrant woods, whose waving skirts just sweep the far horizon that bounds this dusty and crowded and sultry city, to breathe once in a year the freshness of forest leaves and wild flowers, would be a thousand times worth all it cost in strategic hints as to the probable result of an invitation; to "see how the soldiers live in camp" was a consideration against which no other, consistent with duty and possibility, could weigh. So the opportunity, so rare for me, and so highly prized, was secured and improved.

Our carriage was an old army ambulance drawn by two sleek-coated, long-eared *rabbits,* which as if fully conscious of their importance as members of Sherman's army, spread themselves as far apart as the wide latitude of harness would allow, and with high-stepping paces whirled us up the grand avenue so lately honored by the tread of our returning braves. There were five of us, four ladies and a Captain, the latter a happy captive to one of the former; and there were baskets and boxes, and bundles, all well crammed with things for the soldiers in camp. There were oranges, lemons, strawberries, canned chicken, etc., etc., for those who might be sick; and letter-paper, stamped envelopes, handkerchiefs, shirts, and other goods for all who should need them.

Two miles or less from the city our road plunged into delicious depths of blossoming woodlands, covering all the hills and valleys on either hand, and then ran winding along within sight and sound of a miniature river flashing through the trees, and rippling with music over its rocky way. Who could have believed that such a wilderness of verdure lay so near the heart of the great, dusty metropolis we have just left? There is not a human habitation in sight, birds are singing all about, and the rocky banks, glowing rosy with abundant bloom of the mountain laurel, echo back only the rattling of our wheels, and the exclamations of delight that follow our wondering eyes. We dash through the little river, pass the old stone grist-mill on its bank, and wind away around and up the hills till the signal flag of the 1st Michigan Engineers greets our sight.

The ground where this splendid regiment, one of the largest in the army, is encamped, is high and rolling, being broken into pleasantly wooded hills and valleys, and well supplied with springs of clear, cold water. All about among the trees on the green slopes were stretched the little shelter tents of the soldiers; in the narrow streets between the tents little curling eddies of pale blue smoke showed where the camp-fires were smoldering. It was a very pleasant and romantic certainly, to look at.

Our first call was at the regimental hospital. This was a brown, war-stained tent, large enough to hold five narrow beds and leave standing room in the middle for the Doctor, whose canvas house was pitched close beside it. The five beds were all full, not with wounded, but with those sick from fever, pneumonia and exhaustion. How grateful to these men were the fragrance and taste of the fruits their thoughtful visitors brought—especially the strawberries. The Doctor need not have told them how much better to men were these little gifts than all his medicines—their eyes told that plainly.

At the Doctor's tent we were quite unexpectedly treated to an excellent dinner, improvised by his cook, and set out upon a board neatly covered with a newspaper tablecloth. See what a dinner it was for such a place; hot boiled potatoes, cold sliced ham, bread and butter, sardines, canned peaches, tea, and the trimmings, most delicious camp-made doughnuts, and a boiled fruit pudding with sauce—altogether such a dinner as seldom gladdens the eyes or the palates of Washington boardinghouse victims. It was all man's handiwork, too, for excepting the visitors, there was not a woman about the camp, and as we ate and gave thanks, the gratified cook at the tent door unbagging the smoking pudding under the shade of an oak sapling, enlightened us on the mysteries of camp cooking, and of his experiences as to the merits of hartshorn compared with soda as a general "lightner" of dough. He greatly preferred the hartshorn.

After dinner several hours were spent in distributing paper and envelopes among the men in the tents of the different companies. Here was where we saw something of the realities of camp life as it is outside the officers' quarters. Some of them had a blanket spread on their little beds of green poles, and some had not; many lay sound asleep on the ground, taking hours of uninterrupted rest for the first time in many months. Here and there over a fire would be hanging a camp kettle with the inevitable pork and beans bubbling into preparation for supper-time; "chunks" of salt meat were lying around in the leaves at tent-corners, laid up on chips at bed-heads, or hung like nondescript fruit from the tree branches overhead. Towards evening the blackened coffee pots were set over the little smoky fires, frying-pans were put in requisition, and after the well-done slices of pork were taken out, hard-tack and crackers were fried brown in the gravy, and served as a relish to the stewed beans. The "boys" took their suppers on battered tin plates, and ate sitting on the ground at their tent doors, or leaning against friendly stumps and tree trunks in the neighborhood.

It seemed like a hard way of living, after all that they have been through, and now that they were resting in sight of the luxurious city whose bulwark of defence they and their brave comrades in arms have been for so long. But they took it cheerfully and said:

"Beans and hard-tack are about played out; we shall be home soon, and thinking of that is both sauce and seasoning—we can eat anything between now and then."

The sultry weather and the sudden relaxation from the excitements of the march were having their effect, and every now and then we came across one drooping with symptoms of fever. But they cheered up at the sight of visitors, and said: "Thank God, boys, we have got back to civilized life again! This begins to look as if we were in God's country once more, don't it?"

Most of them are probably at home, or on their way before this; for my letter has been delayed some ten days by serious illness, the seeds of which may have been developed by that exciting and delightful day's soldiering in camp.

L.

June 21, 1865. supplement page 2

Our Washington Letter

The Capital and its Contents | Loyalists at the Eleventh Hour | Devotion to the Government | Disturbed Districts | Deference to Southern Sensitiveness | Beatitudes of Conservatism

Washington, June 17, 1865

Washington is a seething, steaming, groaning maelstrom of used-up humanity just now. Numerous as the soldiers are, turning the very atmosphere blue by their presence, I think even they are outnumbered by anxious politicians, whose new-born patriotism prompts them to rush in deputations and delegations to throw themselves at the feet of the new President. They come burdened with advice and groaning to be delivered that the country may be saved. The suffering country of course is all their care. Pity for her that some of them had not awakened to their duty a little sooner. If these late protestations of loyalty had been as energetically made against the incipient rebellion of five years ago it could never have put forward even the pretensions of success it did. Many of these who come forward now begging [for] reconstruction on terms easy for the Southern people to swallow, are men of wealth and position, who managed to keep out of the rebel ranks, and out of the way of making themselves notorious in any manner till they should see which way the scale turned. When rebellion was found to be at its last gasp, they came up Simon-pure patriots on the other side, and, are now praying for magnanimity towards a betrayed and desolated people. "Better late than never," says our good President by his acts; and straightway helps clear the path for the torn feet of the willfully and wickedly "erring sisters."

The crowding for office seems almost as great about the Presidential doors as if a new administration had come in. If by chance a change in any department seems probable, it is smelled afar off, and most victims come by scores, prompted by the most unselfish motives to offer themselves for the service of their country. After all the complaints of small salaries, these Government employees cling to their places with a self-sacrificing spirit wonderful to see; and if ousted from one they plunge after another with a desperation so blind that even though it be occupied by their dearest friend they could not see him. Truly, Government little knows with what zeal it is served.

The new Secretary of the Interior has been disturbing a good many of the old spiders who have been spinning their gold and silver webs through successive administrations in the richly carpeted rooms and in dim and unknown nooks and corners of the Patent Office. Men who where content to eat crumbs from Buchanan's table, saw nothing debasing in making a pretense of loyalty to secure crumbs from his lamented successor, and so many have quietly dozed on in snug offices, well satisfied with the plump quails and dropping manna, and little concerned about equivalents returned, either in thanks or otherwise. Some of these cozy old fogies have been startled from their blissful dreams, and now, spider-like, are looking about for a chance to devour some weak brother whose coveted nest they may possess.

It is amusing, yet vexatious and humiliating to note the timid, truckling spirit of political office holders of the District. Though it is more then four years since this devoted territory was absolved from the curse of slavery and annexed to the civilized portion of the United States, the governing functionaries have a truly Southern horror of such words as abolitionism, radicalism, progress, etc., and if by chance a man suspected of a taint of either of these principles looks towards a vacant chair or office, they fly to protests and petitions to the effect that such an appointment could not prove acceptable to the sensitive and still unreconciled masses crowding the capital. If slavery is dead, its spirit is not; and it is an tenacious of its old haunts as was ever ghost or goblin under the tutelage of mediumship. Generations must pass before even the whites can free themselves from the vassalage in which that spirit bound and still holds them. What, then, can be expected of the blacks, upon whom the curse fell double—a physical as well as a mental bondage? That cunning old fence-rider, the *Intelligencer,* put on its thinking-cap and spectacles the other day, and speculated itself into the most blissful beatitudes in regard to the troublesome question of negro suffrage. The pith of its argument in the self-complacent settlement of the subject was, "There is no earthly reason to presume (unless he is egged on to it incessantly,) that the free negro now expects the right of suffrage. He will be content to earn a support under the protection of laws which have hitherto ignored him."

That little parenthesis has a world of meaning in it—more by considerable than the whole column of well-chosen dictionary words outside of it—a world of meaning, involving warning, caution, adjuration, and pleading for the abolitionist not to be "incessantly egging the negro on," to an assumption of the manhood that has been so solemnly promised him; and deprecation, penitence and humble abasement towards the forlorn chivalry, as much as to say, "We meekly kiss your feet, and will prevent the negroes being egged on to an equality with you if such prevention be possible."

What a pity Washington could not have a newspaper endowed with soul, mind, and heart, and with stamina enough to enable it to stand erect in the path of progress, and march steadily on with events, guiding if not leading, these semi-chaotic elements of political life to the truest and noblest interpretation of the times in which we live. But there is hope for the nation so long as the country sustains such papers, even if the Capital does not.

With these thousands of political wire-workers and visitors, and the tens of thousands of soldiers wandering seemingly at will, the city is crowded almost to suffocation, and the weather is gloomy with low-hung clouds, and sultry and oppressive almost beyond endurance.

L.

June 29, 1865, page 4

Letter from Washington

WEATHER AND MARKETS | HEALTH OF THE CITY | FIREFLIES AND NIGHT-LIFE | QUIET COMING | THE GREAT TRIAL | PASSING REBELS | COLORED PEOPLE AND THE FOURTH

From Our Own Correspondent
Washington, June 23, 1865

June has in a measure cleared up her clouded brow, and instead of lowering misty days and deluges of rain, we are now having glimpses of blue skies and gleams of summer sunshine. There has been no extremely hot weather yet, though the damp and sultry atmosphere which has prevailed thus far through the present month has been very oppressive and trying. Vegetation is most rank and luxuriant, and the markets are filled with everything in that line that the season affords. The early small fruits are also very abundant, but the prices still hold remarkably high, owing probably to the unusual number of consumers now in the city. Cherries and currants though now nearly past their prime are held at 15 cents a quart, and dewberries, or, as they are called here, blackberries, though they have been plenty for a week or more, keep up to 25 cents. I think our old-fashioned Northern blackberries, as big as your thumb and as luscious as nectar, are unknown in this region. The fruit that goes by that name here is comparatively small and seedy, but in quality is very acceptable in the absence of better. Tomatoes are selling at 75 cents a dozen, and are rather exclusive as yet.

As the sun gets higher and hotter, all who find a summer flitting practical are thinking about and preparing for it. Washington must naturally be a remarkable healthy place, since in the midst of such fearful disadvantages it still preserves the character for salubrity it has and is justly entitled to. Almost any city subjected to the tests by which this has been tried during the years of the war, would have become a very hotbed of pestilence; but here with its overcrowded population, its filthy streets, reeking gutters green with slime, its dirty market places and the foul canal winding through its midst, rank with poison enough to infect a whole community, it goes on the even tenor of its way through heat and cold alike, as sound in general health as other places are under the most favorable circumstances. The war population of Washington has been a great drawback upon its cleanliness. The presence of armies and army trains is not very conducive to neatness and order, especially in a community not greatly given to enforcing these principles in the quietest times. The great number of hospitals also in and around the city, and all crowded with disease, would, it might be thought, spread contagion; but health seems quite as secure in their vicinity as elsewhere.

The moist warm weather we have had has been very prolific of lightning bugs. As the sun goes down the air is full of them; all the shade trees and shrubbery along the streets are alive and sparkling with them, while the sidewalks and doorsteps and porches below are quite as brilliant with the airily dressed children who come out to enjoy the evening coolness. Twilight is the signal for these human hives to swarm. As the shadows lengthen towards nightfall, doors and windows that have been closed tight as prisons all day, are flung open, and the gay and gauzy troops come forth to sport with the cool breezes and the fireflies. People don't pretend to live in the daytime here; they only pant and swelter and manage to retain a hold on their breath till night comes, and then, under these soft skies with their starlit and moonlit splendor, life becomes a luxury.

The city is much quieter than it was a few weeks ago. The armies which encircled us round about and thronged the streets and public buildings almost to suffocation, have been rapidly and silently vanishing away. The hospitals are being emptied, and the soldiers' aid societies are settling up with their agents and sending them home.

The interest in the great conspiracy trial seems to revive somewhat, as the arguments for defence make their appearance in the papers. Hitherto there has been very little excitement, locally, considering the crime and the number of the accused. This was probably in a great measure owing to the distance from the city to the arsenal building, where the court is held, and the difficulty of curiosity hunters getting in when there. A ride of two miles in the street cars, and a walk of nearly another mile through heat and dust, or mud, as the case may be, will take them to the place; if provided with proper passes they may go in, and take their chances of ever coming out alive from the small, thronged and crowded room, where Judges, counsel, prisoners, witnesses, and spectators, men, women, and children, are jammed and sweltering together. Hundreds do go there daily, and have all through, but the majority only out of curiosity to see what the prisoners are like, and come away again. Still, except as we see it in the papers, there is less on the subject than might be supposed; very likely because the public mind has settled down confidently on the probable result, and is content to wait.

A day or two since a company of paroled rebels passed down Seventh Street, on their way to Dixie. They had all their army equipments except their guns, but as they wore the Confederate gray they soon attracted the little street boys, who gathered about and ran after them, shouting, "There go the rebs!' "How are you, graybacks?" "Chivalry's gone up!" "How's old lady Jeff?" etc., etc. But the conquered took it all in good nature, and marched on smiling, as much as to say, "Even such words are softer than Union bullets."

The colored people of the District are making preparations for a grand celebration of the Fourth of July. They are to have the use of the beautiful grounds south of the White House for the purpose, and have secured the services of some of the most eloquent men of the nation to speak on the occasion. The District colored people deserve great credit for the stand they have taken in regard to their race, and for the good example they have set in showing what progress can be made in the way of education and general intelligence. They are proving themselves worthy of the privileges conferred on them by the Emancipation Proclamation.

L.

July 14, 1865, page 3

Letter from Washington

THE FOURTH | CELEBRATION OF THE COLORED PEOPLE | SENTENCE OF THE CONSPIRATORS | WEATHER AND HEALTH

From Our Own Correspondent
Washington, July 6, 1865

As far as the city at large was concerned the Fourth for 1865 passed very quietly. It was proper enough, too, for the energies and capacities of its population, both for joy and sorrow, seem to have been exhausted by the great events of the past few months. The extremes of excitement, so great and so intense, are followed by a reaction which it is difficult for any ordinary event to disturb. In the city proper, the day seemed more like a Sabbath than a holiday. The stores and public buildings were closed, and general quiet prevailed, except that the street cars were crowded, and hacks and omnibuses in brisk demand. People went out of the city to celebrate. Family and neighborhood picnics were among the groves, on the hills, and in the valleys and beside the springs, about all the circumference of the capital for miles away. The river boats were full of gay excursionists, and the green banks and the islands gave back the echo of their rejoicings.

The city, I said, did not celebrate: but its adopted citizens did, and I was there to see. The colored people honored the day in a most becoming manner. Their exercises were got up under the auspices of the Lincoln (colored) National Monument Association, and were of the most interesting and creditable character. The extensive and beautiful grounds south of the President's house were entirely given up to them, and never perhaps was the same space made better use of or more thoroughly enjoyed. The children, several hundreds in number, were marshalled by their Sabbath school organizations, and with their teachers and friends marched in procession bearing appropriate badges and banners. They were accompanied by a fine band, and made a beautiful appearance, most of the little girls being dressed in white with pink or blue sashes, and everywhere among the boys were to be seen rosettes and streamers of the national red, white, and blue.

The speakers' stand was erected in a beautiful grove, and was festooned with flags interspersed with the banners of the different schools. In front was a fine portrait of their Emancipator, beneath which were his words, "With malice toward none, / With charity for all."

There were several speeches made during the day, the grandest and most eloquent of all being by a colored speaker, Prof. Wm. Howard Day, of Massachusetts. Mr. Day is a graduate of Oberlin, a man of fine mind, well cultivated by reading and by extensive travel in England and Europe. I doubt if the oration he gave could be excelled by any that were pronounced in the United States on that day. The only one I ever heard approach it in strength and elegance of expression was Theodore Tilton at the capital last winter. Senator Wilson, of Massachusetts, also made a striking speech, which was received with shouts of applause. Side by side among the colored speakers and preachers on the stand were many distinguished civil and military men, several of them accompanied by ladies. I noticed Gov. Haln of Louisiana, Secretary Harlan, Rev. W. H. Channing, Rev. Mr. Nadal, Gen. Gregory, Gen. Harris, Dr. Elder, and others; while many of our best citizens, ladies as well as gentlemen, mingled freely with the audience, and listened with deep interest to the exercises.

Thousands of the gaily dressed and happy throng, unable to get near the stand, amused themselves in various parts of the shady grove. Tables with refreshments were spread under the trees, lemonade and ice water were abundant, as well as other elements for a genuine hearty Fourth of July celebration. The whole affair was handsomely got up and carried through, to the credit and satisfaction of all.

The day itself was glorious in all respects—the sky cloudless, and the gleaming splendors of the sun tempered by winds cooled and freshened by the recent rains. In the evening there was a very brilliant display of fireworks, at government expense, on the same grounds. At 10 o'clock, the immense crowd collected to witness then quietly dispersed, and long before midnight the Federal city was asleep. So ended the Fourth of July, 1865.

Yesterday, the Judges fixed the sentences of the conspirators, and tomorrow they pay the penalty of their terrible crime. There is little sympathy expressed for them—none, I believe, except among the Catholics, who are said to be besieging the President to give them more time to prepare for their awful end. Doubtless there are many who, if they dared, would not only speak their sympathy, but reach forth their hands to give aid and comfort, but this swift-coming vengeance strikes terror to their hearts, and keeps them hushed and dumb.

The crowds of reporters here from all parts of the country to witness the execution, will soon give full particulars to the public.

Summer heat has now commenced in earnest. The very air seems ablaze and quivering with its intensity. It is not the best atmosphere to recover lost health in, and to my inability to regain the strength prostrated by severe illness, you will please charge my late delinquency as correspondent. I hope now to mend my ways in both respects.

L.

July 15, 1865, page 3

Letter from Washington

MUSIC AT THE PRESIDENT'S

From Our Own Correspondent
Washington, July 8, 1865

Twice every week during warm weather, Washington gives itself a three hours' play-spell, puts on its holiday clothes, goes into its pleasant parks, walks on the grass, sits under the trees and admires and criticizes itself—listening meantime, to the music of horns and pipes and cymbals, and the plashing of cooling fountains. It is very pleasant, if for no other reason than that it gives human nature a semi-weekly right to bid defiance to the flinty-faced orders to "keep off the grass," which at other times meet one at every turn, and thrust trespassing feet back upon gravel walks and glistening flag-stones.

Twice a week, Wednesdays and Saturdays, from five to eight P.M., Washingtonians, high and low, male and female, old and young, may walk upon the grass, sit upon it, lie upon it, roll upon it, in short consider themselves literally turned out to grass to enjoy it according to the dictates of their own fancies, with no fierce police or surly watchman to molest or make them afraid. This is a most beneficent provision of the Government, for the Government it is that provides the grassy parks, the trees that shade them, the music, and for that matter, a majority of the people who enjoy them all. The Department clerks, of whom there are many hundreds, both men and women, have great delight in these semi-weekly refreshings from the presence of nature. From their close, crowded, and often badly ventilated rooms, and the monotony of rustling papers and scratching pens, the change is very grateful. But it is not for them alone. Everybody goes "to the music," and wife and children too. On Wednesdays it is at the Capitol gardens; on Saturday at the President's.

It is Saturday evening, fresh, breezy, and fragrant since the morning shower. On all other days of the week, the Departments retain their clerks till 4 o'clock; Saturdays they are set at liberty at three. They have now had time to rest and dine, and dress for "the music." Let us follow the crowd up the avenue and see what we shall see, and hear what we shall hear. From the Seventh street crossing, where we strike the avenue, we might take the cars, but they are already full to overflowing; so let us join the well-dressed throng on the sidewalk—the fashionable side—nearly all of whom are facing the same way, towards the west. The sun, still an hour above the horizon, seems dissolving in a sea of orange-colored glory just over the spot towards which all feet are tending, the grove, whose topmost branches we can see all a-flutter with excitement a full half mile away.

The modes of entrance and exit to and from the President's grounds are, so to speak, rather at loose ends as yet. The mode proper is around by the avenue bend to the front of the White House, and so past it on the east side to the rear; very proper people, conservatives, select, and elect, go that way. Radicals, progressionists, short-cut people, and the masses generally, make a bee line from the south end of the Treasury building, scramble over sand heaps, gravel heaps, rocks and lumber piles, squeeze through a narrow wooden gate, twist around in a cramped turnstile, and lift their eyes to find themselves under the spreading skirts of the wood which, a little farther on, with its music, its fountains and it fairies, becomes acadia itself. We are going in this way, excusing irregularities as we go, in consideration of the harmony that is to come out of all this confusion of matter when the delvers in sand, and the hewers of wood, and workers in stone, shall have finished their labors.

Within the gate a winding graveled walk leads us to the rear of the White House, whose glistening walls we can almost touch over the low iron palings surrounding it and protecting those narrow borders of shrubs and flowers. From the pillared portico above the basement the ground is reached by two winding flights of stone steps, the bannisters of which from top to bottom are solid masses of honeysuckles and roses, generations old, yet fresh and sweet as if born of this morning's summer shower. These steps lead directly into the open grounds, and back and forth, from one to the other, by day and by night an armed sentinel is pacing. Just here we have the finest view of what we have come to see—the park and its population.

We stand facing the south. A few rods over the green sward and flower beds in front of us springs the fountain, throwing high the silvery jets which fall with a cooling sound into the broad brimming basin. Beyond the fountain is an elevated circular stand, capable of holding 50 persons or more, furnished with seats and sheltered by an awning. The seats are occupied by the famous Marine Band in their scarlet uniforms—all scarlet and gold from the caps on their heads to their very shoe-ties. A brilliant, blazing circle it is; and the music they make is as brilliant as the color they wear. To right and left of the music stand the ground rises into swelling, rounded knolls, thickly covered with grass and shaded with a great variety of forest trees. The grass, however, cannot be seen now for the people lying, sitting and standing upon it. They are for numbers like the multitudes who came up by the sea of Galilee through the coasts of Decapolis, but gayer in dress and spirits.

Washington ladies deserve credit for their independence in the matter of fashions, if for nothing else. They are not mere copyists of the milliner's *modiste* or of each other. Individual taste goes farther than an edict from Paris, or any display by a self elect leader (or would-be leader) of the town. Hence the great charm of the show before us now—variety. No one seems to have patterned after another; neither as a whole do they appear to have been made up and turned out as attempted facsimiles of the last Parisian models. There are many very elegant toilettes among those of the more pretentious class; but the most charming and appropriate of all are the light, airy muslins, white, and rose color, and blue, and the thousand delicate neutral tints that suggest, but do not challenge, admiration. The exhibition as it strikes our eyes at the little distance, is like a vast garden of gay and beautiful flowers swarming with butterflies as gay and beautiful.

The children cluster around the fountain. Men and boys lie at full length on the grass, or sit listening to the music and watching the gay processions of promenaders, the ladies and their attendant cavaliers, as they go slowly winding in and out among the standing crowds and the shady groves. From the center of the music stand a small flagstaff runs up, and from its top the flag of the Union, the whole Union, is flying. We only wish the eyes that so lately looked upon it from those upper windows were looking on it now. But that was not to be. Strangers are in the White House today. We see two or three faces at a distant window, but none are familiar. The President, over-worn by his oppressive duties, lies on a sick bed, and the great house is like sepulchral marble in its white and solemn silence.

But the world must go on. The music strikes up inspiringly. That is the Nightingale Polka, or some such misnomer of a tune—as if nightingales ever did "polk!" It pleases the people, however. See, the little girls are wearing it out in their airy motions beside the fountain; older ones, envious of the freedom which propriety forbids them to imitate, smile approval of the application; and stately dames and sedate mamas, betray the spirit that is in them, by keeping time with stealthy motions of the foot and hand.

The sun went down an hour ago or more; the long, sweet twilight is slowly fading out of the purple and golden west, as the nightingale song trills to its close. Suddenly the notes of a double-quickstep march are struck; loungers spring to their feet, ladies draw their shawls closer about them, husbands and lovers secure their charges by the elbow, and all faces are turned gate-ward. A moment more and no sound is heard, but the murmur of many voices, and the trampling of hurrying feet over the grass and along the walks. The musicians, like a flock of scarlet tanagers, suddenly dispersed, are scattered here and there among the multitude; the gates are passed, darkness settles over the drooping flag, the hushed fountain and the lonely sentinel. So ends the "music at the Presidents."

L.

July 18, 1865, page 4

Letter from Washington

Our Daily Food | The Conspirators and their Doom | Women Traitors | Miss Harris | Ford's Theatre

From Our Own Correspondent
Washington, July 13, 1865

Tragedies, great and small, civic, political, domestic, and individual, are the order of the times at the nation's capital. Rebellions, conspiracies, murders, homicides, and their kindred vices, form the daily food of the press, and without their accustomed morning feast of horrors from the reporter's pen, Washingtonians would hardly know how to exist, sensation correspondents would be driven to extremities, and the social world would really seem to be going back to its old-time peace and proprieties.

The trial of the conspirators is over, and with all the awful array of evidence against them, each has been assigned to the doom awarded by their judges; now coppery and disaffected politicians and secessionists are combining with the Catholic friends of the condemned to array public opinion against a judgment which all true patriots must pronounce just. The plea of sex is used with much force in regard to Mrs. Surratt; but while we acknowledge that it is an awful thing to hang a woman, we must remember that it is a still more awful thing for a woman to be so wicked as to deserve hanging. But no executions of this sort, though multiplied by thousands, can atone for the wrongs these Southern women are guilty of in connection with the rebellion. All through they have been the bitterest, the most defiant, unreasoning and dangerous enemies the Government has had to contend with. They have been defiant because they have not felt themselves amenable to the laws, and the same cause has made them unreasoning and dangerous. They have incited and inspired men to act like demons; they have been smugglers, blockade-runners, spies, and informers against the Government that protected and held their lives and persons sacred. Washington has been full of them, and they are not all gone or all converted yet. While the Government suffered they rejoiced; while the world mourned for our martyred President, they mocked, and laughed and danced, and sent congratulations to each other. One has suffered, and a thousand hands are thrown up in holy terror at what they choose to call an outrage on the sex. They forget that it was the crime and not the woman that judgment was passed upon. It was the guilty soul and the flesh it made its willing tool, and not the sex, that suffered.

Only a year ago a boat was captured, carrying contraband goods to Richmond. Among these was a trunk containing an elegant dressing gown, richly embroidered slippers, and smoking cap, and other valuable articles, labeled, "Presented to President Jefferson Davis by his lady friends in Washington." There were also finely wrought handkerchiefs, and such other useful adjuncts of the toilet as a lady in a blockaded city might require, affectionately consigned to Mrs. President Davis. But these harmless offerings of affection were not all. Letters in cypher were found conveying important information to the rebel chiefs, and, being de ciphered, the names of the loving "lady friends in Washington" were brought to light. Nothing, however, was done towards punishing or even exposing these she traitors, partly, probably, because they were "old women," and partly because heavier work was on hand, and a mightier power tasking the Government's energies, while no real harm resulted, as the dispatches never reached their destination. This is but one instance of the sex's treachery in the Capital, and a very mild one in comparison to thousands that might have been told. If then the fearful crime that shrouded the nation in sorrow was incited and inspired by one of these, who shall challenge the hand of justice lifted to mete out its punishment? The helpless and desolate daughter excites the pity of all, while execrations follow the cowardly and guilty son.

The trial of Miss Harris now progressing creates some excitement in a certain way, and is a godsend to newspapers pending the anticipated arraignment of Jeff. Davis and his co-laborers at their country's altar. In regard to the former, Miss H., it seems to be nearly a foregone conclusion that she will be acquitted on the ground of insanity. Her history and her conduct since she has been in prison here have won for her many friends and much sympathy.

There continue to be occasional rows among scattering companies and squads of the soldiers yet lingering about the city; and now and then an outrage or a murder, in most of which the helpless blacks are the chief sufferers.

In regard to the opening of Ford's Theatre as a theater, there is an intense under current of feeling here, which would inevitably break out in open violence if the profanation should be attempted. While his advertisement was in the papers that it would be opened on Monday evening last, there were mutterings low and deep in many quarters, suggestive surmises, compressed lips, and eyes that said more than tongues dared. The lovers of peace and order breathed free again when it was announced to be closed. It is safer, for the present at least, to keep the guard with their crossed bayonets at the door. Tragedies follow each other fast enough in fearful reality without desecrating our Martyr's death scene by mockeries, and so courting dangers which common prudence in deference to public opinion may avoid.

L.

July 27, 1865, page 4

Letter from Washington

PLUCKING THE PUBLIC GOOSE

From Our Own Correspondent
Washington, July 22, 1865

"Picking geese" is a very homely, barnyard transaction as ordinarily performed, and the above expression has a coarse, uncouth sound; nevertheless, the act it represents is one of the fine arts as practiced at the Capital. As an illustration take the following, which, though not quite as successful as under other circumstances it might have been, shows something of the refinement to which the art is carried, and exhibits the serene assurance with which the editorial fraternity from their cool heights of impudence swoop down upon the coveted prey.

The Department of Agriculture, since the establishment of its beautiful and useful Museum, has become quite conspicuous among the national lions, and so much sought after by the sight-seeing public that the report of its merits at last got to the ears of one of our enterprising *Dailies,* whose editor at once conceived the idea of patronizing the new pet and causing it to roar a little for his own benefit. He straightway visited the Museum, examined into and praised its system and its object; said the public did not half understand its usefulness; and after expressing an earnest desire that his paper should be the special medium for promoting that understanding, begged that items for publication might be sent him, whenever any new object of interest was added to the collection. His own time was too much occupied by editorial duties to permit him to write out these items, but as he wished to make his a "live paper," and the organ of this very useful department, he would be under the greatest obligations, if the above information could be furnished to him, and would even pay for it if necessary.

Pay, of course, was not considered necessary by those whose business it was, under cover of their salaries, to forward in all legitimate ways the interests of the department, and so, from time to time, the paragraphs or material for them were supplied as the work progressed, and additions worthy of public notice were made. Not content with this, however, the enterprising editor employed two of his own correspondents to scour the ground, and press into service things both new and old, that his columns might be filled, or rather that his meditated grab at the unsuspecting goose he was so fondly petting might be productive of the anticipated "feathers." At length, when his hired item-hunters became an annoyance, so that the Department would almost have paid them to stay away, lo! and behold, a bill is sent in wherein every line and paragraph is charged at the highest advertising rates, so much per square, and amounting in all to the nice little sum of *one hundred and fifty-five dollars!* This was very modestly presented at headquarters and payment demanded. It was a government affair, and of course government would not be niggardly in rewarding those who had labored to build up its interests. The Commissioner, who knew nothing of the nature of their "labors," set about investigating, and being informed of the facts protested that he "couldn't see it in that light." It wasn't a part of the business of his Department to edit a paper and then pay for the privilege of doing so out of Government funds.

This shameless charge was presented a second time for collection, and again sent back under a protest that will probably convince the ambitious editor of the futility of making another grab in that direction. Very likely he will soon discover, as others quite as badly baffled as he have already done, that the present head of the Department is made of material too stubborn and uncompromising for practical purposes—such purposes as would favor his sharp practices. Integrity in that sort of Government Officials is at a discount among those who, being in a position to do so with impunity, consider it the first law of nature to feather well their own nests from the pluckings of the public goose.

L.

August 1, 1865, page 4

Letter from Washington

END OF THE HARRIS MURDER, AND WHAT COMES OF IT

From Our Own Correspondent
Washington, July 13, 1865

The Mary Harris farce is over at last, and the silly victim of misplaced confidence has gone home with the jury's compassionate verdict of "Not Guilty" ringing in her ears, and the consciousness of murder with its guilt of premeditation and preparation stamped and burnt upon her inmost soul. That consciousness no jury's verdict can relieve her from. It will follow her like a haunting presence to her grave. The pretence of insanity everybody knows was a mere pretence and nothing more. Her counsel were far nearer crazed than ever she was, and acted it out in their insane conduct and maudlin huggings and kissings on the closing day of the trial. The whole scene was disgraceful in a court of justice, however well it might have suited a private courting scene. It was very evident that the amative letters read were not without their effect on both Judge and counsel, and made them eager to atone for the shortcomings of the murdered lover. The fainting was about on a par with the insanity. As the latter did not prevent due deliberation and steady aim in the shooting, so the former did not hinder the proper time for the judicial kisses, and giving her somewhat mature but tenderhearted counsel such a hugging as has made him a standing object of envy to his younger legal brethren. One man, swinging his hands in an extacy, or rather we should say, in a "paroxysm" of insanity, declared if he had a million of dollars he would marry the girl at once and make her a Princess! Another, still farther beside himself, hoped that if he ever had a daughter she might come to as high honors as Mary Harris had, to be thought so much of by the Judge and the lawyers! Could moral insanity be beyond that?

The poor misguided girl came to Washington, so she says, to vindicate her honor; and now having committed a deliberate murder, and made an expose of her own and her lover's private life, such as any woman of sense with even a moderate

Miss Mary Harris. From *Harper's Weekly Magazine,* March 4, 1865.

share of modesty would have shrunk from, aye, would have died rather than make, she goes home stripped of everything that makes pure and dear and blessed the life of woman. She has made her name most unfortunately notorious, and has won an empty acquittal based upon a false pretence: that is all.

"But the example!" says Miss Olintha Wintergreen; "Mama says the example Miss Harris set is just right; just what the young men needed; they are so heartless, courting one and marrying another just as they fancy. Mama says this will make them careful."

Yes, I know; Miss Olintha's mama attended the trial all through, and held daily tea-table consultations at her boarding house with some dozen other mamas in presence of their anxious daughters, regarding the fickleness of mankind in general, and the necessity of establishing a precedent for their guidance in the path of duty; said duty being of course to make prompt proposals of marriage and cast their happiness at the feet of the first pretty girl they may chance to look at. Mrs. Wintergreen is a very shrewd mama as the fashionable world goes, but for all that she still has Miss Olintha and her three or four younger daughters on her hands; the younger ones crowding up to womanhood so fast that mama and Miss Olintha have been at their wits' end for expedients to wring a proposal from any one of the three beaux who alternately take Miss O. to the theater or excursions, or who drop in of an evening for a game of whist in the boarding house parlor. Since the verdict Mrs. W. begins to see her way clearer, her comments on it in presence of Miss Olintha have not been lost, and that estimable and severely virtuous young lady may now be seen looking pistols at her tardy beaux, two of whom she is sure she can prove an "engagement" with—one having squeezed her hand while helping her out of a hack two years ago, and the other having sighed and looked at her tenderly when they were witnessing a love scene at Grover's theater last winter. Pop goes the pistol, will be the tune for young ladies to play and young gentlemen to dance to nowadays. I don't suppose many of the latter will covet the pleasure of lying in poor Burroughs' grave, but then think of their pretty paroxysmally insane murderess walking straight over their dead bodies into the loving arms of judge, jury, and lawyers, to be petted and kissed and called angelic! Well, there are silly uncultivated natures that would rejoice in such notoriety, and for them Miss Harris' example has its charms. Their general lack of nerve and courage, however, will be a pretty good safeguard for the fickle admirers. Much as they might enjoy the closing farce, there are few who have stamina enough to go through the tragedy which must precede it.

Miss Olintha, for instance, would be as harmless as a statue of putty as far as the shooting is concerned; and on the other hand quite as impossible in regard to the tender finale. She looks pistols, though, and it is said that the two lovers against whom she has designs are about resigning their clerkships and joining the Mexican emigration scheme. They prefer warfare on a large scale, and where both sides may have part in the fight.

But it is not single men alone who walk the streets with fear and trembling, and turn pale at the crack of a whip or the dog-killer's pistol. A Dutchman expressing his opinion on the verdict the other day said:

"Who shall be any more safe? I had once courted Katrina one leetle while, den I courts anodder more as she, but not likes her so well and goes back and marries Katrina. Now I must be shot as I hat no married the one I coorts most. It is bad business."

A "big policeman," too, is trembling in his shoes for the same reason, only that he had gone further and promised marriage to one woman, but finding her ill-tempered, gave her up and married another. He hears that she has threatened to shoot him for breach of promise, though she has been married and is now a widow with three children. She isn't a bit afraid or too good to do it, he says, and she can prove both the promise and the breaking of it.

And so the example goes. Mrs. Wintergreen says it was needed, and that it will serve to keep men straighter hereafter; while the big policeman declares that the verdict will make women crookeder and more perverse than ever, and the puzzled Dutchman shakes his head and says "It is bad business."

L.

August 4, 1865, page 1

Letter from Washington

ENTOMOLOGICAL CONVENTION AT PARIS | MR. GLOVER TO GO AS REPRESENTATIVE OF THE DEPARTMENT OF AGRICULTURE | THE OBJECTS OF HIS MISSION IN EUROPE AND ENGLAND | HIS ABILITY AS ENTOMOLOGIST | AGRICULTURAL READING IN DEMAND | LIMITED ISSUE OF THE DEPARTMENT REPORTS

From Our Own Correspondent
Washington, July 31, 1865

Commissioner Newton, of the Department of Agriculture, is doing a good thing for the country in sending Mr. Glover, the naturalist and entomologist, to represent that department at the great Entomological Convention, to be held in Paris, France, during the month of August. It is expected that all the first entomologists of the old country will be there convened, and hold such an exhibition as has never before been known, of all insects and subjects of entomological study. The objects of this novel convention are to call together naturalist from all parts of the world, especially of Europe, to exhibit insects and their productions, or drawings of the same, to compare notes and observations, and to discuss the methods of destroying those known to be injurious to agriculture.

Mr. Glover takes with him one hundred and sixty-five plates of his own engraving and coloring, each plate 8 1/4 by 12 inches, and averaging from 15 to 25 insects a plate, representing in all, one or more of nearly every family known in this country. In connection with these he has original notes descriptive of their nature and habits, which will be compared with the observations of foreign naturalists in order to elicit all that can be known in regard to them and the best means employed for the destruction of those known to be injurious. For this object alone the Commissioner would deserve the thanks of the entire agricultural community; but Mr. Glover has other important missions to the Old World in connection with the interests of the Department, and the objects for which it is laboring. He will visit the Jardines des Plantes, and note the results of experiments made by the Society of Acclimatization, and will also institute a system of exchange between entomological and agricultural associations there and the United States Department of Agriculture, so that the latter may reap the benefits of the large experience and superior facilities of the former at the earliest possible moment. From France he will go to England, visit the zoological gardens in London, and make arrangements for obtaining specimens of the true types of domestic fowls of foreign breeds for the Museum of the Department; and also for securing such other exchanges as may be desirable between the British and American Agricultural Associations. The entire object of Mr. Glover's trip is to advance the interest of agriculture in this country; and the mission could not be trusted to better hands. His devotion to the cause is only equaled by his enthusiasm in the one branch which he makes his specialty—entomology.

Few men on this continent have devoted more time, study and hard labor to the science of practical entomology than Mr. Glover. His aim is not to dazzle and bewilder by a parade of scientific terms, but to teach in ordinary phraseology, as far as may be, the application of the science to every day use among farmers, gardeners and horticulturists. The work he has in course of preparation will, when finished, be one of extraordinary simplicity in expression, profound in research, and eminently practical in application. It is understood to be his desire that the Government should purchase the material for this work and publish it for general distribution through the Department of Agriculture. Could this be done it would be worth more than gold to the farmers throughout the country.

If there is one subject more than another that needs now to be kept before legislators, lawgivers, and indeed all men of influence in a public capacity, it is the necessity of supplying the agricultural population with the instruction so much needed and coveted by them just at this time. This period of transition from war to peace is one of peculiar interest to agriculture, and few unacquainted with the facts can imagine the intense desire of our returning farmer-soldiers for that general and comprehensive sort of information which is embodied in public documents, such as reports of exploring and scientific expeditions, giving a knowledge of the extent, capacity, and condition of the newer regions of our country; and the monthly and annual reports of the Department of Agriculture containing concise, fresh, and most desirable information as to the development and progress of that great science upon which all other national interests are based. It seems a very short-sighted economy, or policy, or whatever it was, that limited the number of annual reports of the above department to 10,000 for distribution by the Commissioner through the mail, and by personal application for the same. In 1862 the number allowed him was 20,000, for the report of 1863 it was cut down one half by order of Congress. It is true that members of Congress have a large number, 150,000, for themselves and their constituents, but thousands of these never get beyond the committee rooms at the Capitol where they are locked up for the year round, while the Commissioner is daily besieged by hundreds of applicants whom he is unable to supply. It is safe to say that were the number allowed him quadrupled it would still be insufficient for the demand. And this demand during the past year has increased beyond precedent. Scores of orders by mail are unfilled, and many hundreds of soldiers returning from the war to their farms, hungry for such just such knowledge as these volumes could give them, have been turned away from the Commissioner's door saddened and disappointed. They wanted the book to begin their farm life again, but it is not to be had, unless by chance they may stir up some sleepy representative to remembrance of their claims during the coming winter.

Farmers must learn to take their interests into their own hands more than they have yet done, if they would have their rights respected by the men elected to legislate for them. The tons of public documents yearly piled away under the dome of the Capitol, should be delivered to the rightful owners, the constituents of the representatives who receive them in trust from Government, and who too often make only a partial distribution or none at all. The constituents at home should learn their rights and demand that they be respected.

L.

August 4, 1865, page 4

Letter from Washington
THE CITY AT MIDSUMMER | CHANGES AND THEIR CAUSES | DEPARTMENT OF AGRICULTURE AND EXPERIMENTS AND DOINGS THEREIN

From Our Own Correspondent
Washington, July 29, 1865

Earth, air and sky are ablaze with midsummer heat. All who can leave are going north, east, west, anywhere for change from the scorching winds and blinding dust. Still Washington is by no means empty. All kinds of business are apparently as brisk as at any season; streets and street cars are full; grading and paving are going on; stores are crowded with customers, the avenue and the parks at the fashionable hour with promenaders; a great deal of building is being done, both of public and private structures, and house rents and board are as high as ever.

The several Departments, meanwhile, are pushing on the labors and interests of each, and showing their ability to survive and progress, in spite of an involuntary suspension of labor on the part of individuals who have hitherto assumed to be indispensable to the existence of Government. The new Secretary of the Interior, discreet and quiet in his dealings, has very wisely compassed the resignation and dismissal of several whose chief employment for years has been to draw large salaries, eat, drink, and feather their nests at Government expense. The arts and artifices to which these creatures resort in order to perpetuate their official existence, would be ludicrous and excite laughter, did they not savor so strongly of fraud and corruption as to inspire contempt. It is well perhaps that the public are not aware of all the causes for these quiet removals and apparent voluntary resignations. If they were, human nature would seem to have put on a blacker shade of depravity than the most ultra Calvinist ever invested it with yet; and it is lucky for the deposed parties if they have sense enough to "Fold up their tents like the Arabs, / And quietly steal away," instead of fighting for other positions, and so stirring up investigations, and provoking an exposure of stealings of a less creditable nature. Witness the case of the late Superintendent of the Census Reports. When dislodged from a position he had long abused, his excessive conceit inspired him to claim as a right that he should be placed in the chair of the Commissioner of Agriculture. He pulled innumerable wires, bought over agricultural journals to do the dirty drudgery for him, caused petitions to be written, beset Senators to use their influence in his behalf, and in short left no effort untried to effect his purpose. The last desperate blast, however, from his own trumpet has been met by a counter blast which has already partially unmasked him, and threatens to complete a revelation by no means creditable to the integrity of a Government official. He is one of the many who have fawned to all above them in power, and fondly flattered their souls and their friends that their continuance in office was essential to the regularity of the solar system. Secretary Harlan, however, had a different opinion, acted upon it, and the result is that the earth still moves in its orbit, and the sun would never have missed the lost Pleiad in its daily round if the *Journal of Commerce* and other kindred tools had held their tongues.

The Department of Agriculture, in the meantime, retains its honored head, and is still progressing in its labors for the benefit of the farming community at large. Considerable attention has been given to experiments with silkworms this summer. A number have been raised in boxes in the Museum, and fed on the Maclura or Osage orange leaves instead of the *morus multicaulis*. This trial has proved very successful, and shows that strong, fine and even silk can be produced from the Osage orange, which is much easier of cultivation, cheaper, and more abundant in the west and northwest than the *multicalusis*. The worms throve well upon it, and the cocoons reeled off silk of a superior quality, samples of which are now on exhibition.

Some experiments have also been made with the new Chinese *ailanthus* silkworm, but the facilities have not been such as to give a favorable impression of its practicability here. The silk produced is of a much coarser texture than the others, and cannot be reeled off the cocoons, but has to be carded and spun like cotton or wool. A great many of the eggs of these worms were sent to different parts of the country for trial last spring, soon after they were received from France, and it is probable that when the reports of the experimenters come in they may show that better facilities have been productive of better success. The insect is very hardy, and eats ravenously of the *ailanthus,* from which its silk is made. The Commissioner has just received from China a sample of the silk spun and reeled, and also branches of the fetid and fragrant *ailanthus* and prickly ash and oak on which the native silk worms of the Celestial Empire feed.

Some very choice samples of sorghum seed of superior quality to any heretofore brought to this country have also been received by the Department. They are however only samples for exhibition, but the Commissioner, convinced of the necessity of having fresh importations of pure seed, has ordered a large quantity of the same, which he expects will be on hand in time for distribution next winter. The specimens received are of the red, black, mixed, and sugar sorghums, and are in heads composed of short panicles densely packed with seed, somewhat resembling the large bobs of the sumacs with which all are familiar. They excite much admiration among those interested in sorghum sweets.

The demands made on the Department for seed during the past winter and spring have been enormous—the result of the satisfaction experienced by recipients of the same during the three preceding years. This universal expression of satisfaction has been very gratifying, and will stimulate the Chief of the Department of still greater efforts, if possible, to merit in future the confidence he has so well deserved in the past. His thorough practical knowledge of what the everyday farmer needs is the true secret of his success; and his foresight and energy in supplying those needs form the ground of his popularity among the masses who are looking to this Department for help. With the appreciation of such to encourage him, he can well afford to let disappointed politicians growl, and to listen with a smile to the scoffs and jeers of Eastern speculators in stale seeds, who have not money enough in all their coffers to buy his patronage or corrupt his integrity.

L.

August 10, 1865, page 4

Letter from Washington

THE WORLD OF CLERKDOM | FACTS AND PHOTOGRAPHS

From Our Own Correspondent

Washington, August 3, 1865

The Government clerks take a new lease of life with the incoming of the present month. Heretofore their working hours have been from nine till four; now they are dismissed at three, and to note the eagerness with which they grasp at that one hour of freedom, one would think they were galley slaves the balance of the twenty-four. And they will be just as eager next winter in besetting Congress for an increase of salaries, as if the hour had been added to, instead of taken from their labors. Three hours a day at $3,000 a year would suit many of them better than the present arrangement, and then they would feel as if they were conferring a great favor on the Government by serving it at that rate.

What a strangely compounded world this world of clerkdom is. It requires a great variety of talent, and many busy hands and brains to keep the complicated machinery of Government in working order, and at work, and it needs not to be wondered at that among the many thousands of employed, some of the least creditable traits of human nature should be developed. It would rather be a matter of astonishment, if generally known, that so many whose names were once familiar in the world as artists, poets, editors, clergymen, statesmen, men of wealth and talent and of public note in various ways, were here quietly, and to some it may seem ingloriously devoting themselves to the duties of Government clerks. In one way or another they have dropped out of their old spheres, or been supplanted by a more vigorous and progressive generation, and dropped into snug, carpeted rooms, stifling with dust and a dead atmosphere, where they pursue the endless round of desk labor, sinking name, fame, ambition for worldly honors, and, in time, individuality itself in the not too highly honored title and occupation given above. For making mummies and machines of men there is no process equal to this if it is only persevered in long enough. There are specimens here so antiquated, so sallow and withered and dried from their long seclusion and burial among wrappings of papyrus and moldy relics of past ages that it would require little stretch of the imagination to fancy them recently exhumed mummy factions from Egyptian catacombs. They are written all over with hieroglyphics, which being interpreted read, "fossilized Government clerks." In place of the scent of Egyptian myrrh and other embalming spices, one may detect about them the aroma of sour ink bottles, gum elastic bands, mucilage, and Spaulding's glue.

New comers or novices are often restive and impatient during their initiatory years; some endowed with an excess of vigor and nerve break through before the fossilizing process is complete and go back to the world again; some yielding to the force of the rotation principle are pushed back to let new ones in, and so there is more or less of the world's breath freshening the sepulchers where so much of manhood is sacrificed; but with many the quiet routine of one decade after another is all sufficient for existence. Perhaps also the security of the salary and the regularity of the monthly pay day have something to do with inspiring this seemingly worldly content. This surmise gathers strength from the fact that a majority of this latter class are men who have failed in their singlehanded struggles with fortune, men who are no longer young and so prefer a certain competence, even at a sacrifice, rather than trust their age to the doubtful results of independent effort. As they are only machines for performing a certain sort of labor, political principles seldom come in their way, and they glide along in their respective grooves from one administration to another till they become as much a part of the Government property as the offices and buildings they occupy.

There is another sort who buy place and power by promises and otherwise, and then grow rich and endow their friends out of the perquisites. They are sharp, shrewd, cunning, talented villains, with smiling faces, soft words and kissing proclivities. They are too often successful for times and seasons, but are very likely to get their deserts sooner or later when it happens, as it sometimes does miraculously, that an honest man is in power above them.

Let me give you a photograph or two representative of the classes daily going in and out of these monstrous human hives, the great Department buildings, where money is made instead of honey, and Uncle Sam and his money bag is the great King Bee that all others are swarming after.

Here is a man who was a boy in General Washington's time, who remembers sitting on his knee when he was President of the United States, and who has seen every President inaugurated from that day to this. His family were of the genuine, original F. F. V.'s—none of your secession shams. He has been a spoke in the wheel for grinding out patents so long that there is scarcely enough of him left to make a shadow. Gentle and genial in the social circle, to look at him with his silk white locks and soft, colorless, beardless face, one might easily fancy how he looked as a boy sitting on our first President's knee; he is only a child now, and yet so much a part of this wonderful machinery that one is led to wonder if his existence is coeval with it, or if there will be a pause or a jar in its working when he drops out.

Contrasts are sometimes pleasant. Let us have one. It is not many years since the sitter for this picture was known not only in literary circles east and west, but was an aspirant for oratorical and political honors, some of which I believe he won, and wore in Michigan. Can those who knew Louis Fitzpatrick Tasistro there fancy him deliberately settling down as an integral part of the government machinery? Here he is, plump and pulpy, clean shaven and careful of exertion, leisurely examining claims or affidavits or some such thing in the Pension Bureau, while waiting for the months to roll round with their welcome rolls of greenbacks. Can so much flesh and blood become fossil?

Not far from him is an ex-editor, reformer, newspaper correspondent, etc., etc., from the far West, who is struggling against the ossification slowly creeping over him; who protests he will never become the machine he is already half converted into; who still has moments of longing for his old independence, his consequence, his influence; and yet cannot bring himself to let go the poor half plucked bird in his hand for the two full feathered and cheery ones tempting him from the western bush. The spell is upon him, and strengthening. Last year he despised himself for staying; now he feels a sort of tender half acknowledged pity, mingled with a very little shame; next year he will be fully convinced that Government could not get on without him, and so, rather than throw the mighty wheels off their balance, he will complete the self-immolation and let the Juggernaut pass over him. Thus the Government will retain a good clerk, and the world will lose a man. However, the balance scales would probably hang about the same, relatively, were the subject reversed. Either one might lose, and neither one might gain.

This man represents a class whose name is legion.

There are many easy going nonentities who are just as well here as anywhere, and would be just as well anywhere as here; they fill the chairs, help do the work, and the world knows and cares as little about them as they do about it.

The most pitiful cases of all are young men, poor, who accept positions, aye, even beg them, for the sake of the salary and the advantages it and the position may give them for attending lectures and getting an education to fit themselves for other professions. If they are conscientious a weary time they have of it between two stools, on neither of which they can sit with comfort or profit.

But resolute wills work wonders, and as good once came out of Nazareth, so manhood may spring from a Government-clerkship. At all events the pale-faced, worn looking fellows deserve their reward if it is only in name.

L.

August 14, 1865, page 4

Letter from Washington

The Armies of the Departments | How Washington is Fed | Government Patronage Illustrated

From Our Own Correspondent
Washington, August 8, 1865

A late report of some official of the Treasury Department states that there are on file over 15,000 applications for clerkships in that Department alone, and that about 2,000 are already employed there as clerks and copyists. What an army, taking applicants and employes together. Then consider that the War Department counts even more than that in all its branches of Quartermasters, Paymasters, etc. which, add to the Navy Department, the Interior, and the Department of Agriculture, all as populous as it is possible to be with their enormous capacities for accommodating the outside pressure by improvising work or the semblance of work where none in reality exists; and then consider that the majority of these many thousands, both workers and hangers on, are lodgers and boarders, always demanding room and consuming food, but producing neither, and it will not be wondered at that rents are high and the price of bread and beef at the top of the scales.

Washington, it is well known by those who have seen it within the last four years, is situated in the midst of a country rich enough naturally, but long ago worn threadbare by slave labor, and devastated of late by marching and encamping of armies, so that a comparatively small portion of its supplies come from farms or gardens in the vicinity. Then it is entirely isolated from the rest of the world, at least from the cultivated and civilized portion of it, except the slender line of connection its one railroad makes with Baltimore, or as vessels may find their way down the Potomac and Chesapeake and up the Atlantic coast. Pennsylvania is the great storehouse or dairy on which it draws for butter and cheese, and many fruits and vegetables, but for every turnip and pound of butter double toll must be paid at the gates of Baltimore. The transshipment costs time and money, and the consumers here must pay for it. The best potatoes come by shipping from Maine. Maryland and Delaware pour down their peaches and melons upon us, and these just now, from their great abundance, come within reach of limited purses. Luscious luxuries they are, with a perfection of coloring and a plumitude of sweetness undreamed of by peaches and melons under Northern skies. Till October wanes the markets will glow and blush with them.

As the armies are gradually fading away from the capital and its vicinity it is probable that cultivation, under a better system than formerly, will renew the wasted farms, and in time not only contribute to the support of the city by their products, but furnish labor for some of these 15,000 hungry, idle applicants for Government favor. The great question, though, in a majority of cases, is whether it is really the labor that they are after. An incident, which occurred here in the reign of the Old P. F., may illustrate this query, and the same incident, varied slightly by circumstance, sex or name, may find its parallel a hundred times a year in any reign.

A young gentleman, of gay and festive proclivities, wished to spend the winter in Washington; that is to say, he wanted to dance and have Uncle Sam pay the fiddler. He had sold his vote at the fall election to a Senator, who promised to use his influence with the powers that were. The Senator demanded of the Secretary of State that a clerkship should be given his constituent. The Departments were overhauled to find a vacancy. One after another all protested that they were full; there was no more work, no help wanted. Disgusted at last, the Hon. Secretary said to a certain official:

"Make work, then, and give this man an appointment."

So the work was made, or at least the appointment was, and the treasury was minus one hundred dollars a month during the next year. The winter dance to that tune was so agreeable that it was prolonged through spring, summer and fall, much to the edification of the young man and his admirers, whom he had plenty of time to entertain.

Such things will always be where Government patronage is, and only go to show that all applicants for place are not seeking labor.

L.

August 25, 1865, page 4

Letter from Washington

Colored Photographs

From Our Own Correspondent
Washington, August 19, 1865

Passing through a quarter of the city thickly populated with contrabands, the juvenile portion of whom were swarming outside the huts, I heard a chorus of them singing a new version of the old song called "Uncle Sam's Farm." Led by two bright little girls they made the walls of their old shanties ring with the chorus: "Come along, come along, don't be a fool, / Uncle Sam is rich enough to send us all to school."

That very thing Uncle Sam has been trying his best to do ever since he took the shackles off their limbs in 1861, at least for those in his own peculiar district. But thus far it seems the city authorities have been too much for him. In one way and another they have evaded the laws he has made, refusing even to let the funds raised from taxing the property of colored people go to support schools for their own children. There are many wealthy colored people here, who of course pay taxes and all their money thus paid has gone to the white schools exclusively. Last year a more stringent law was made obliging the city Fathers to "set apart from the school fund such a proportionate part thereof as the colored children between the ages of six and seventeen years bears to the whole thereof." It was confidently believed there could be no dodging this; but what is there that Washington politicians cannot dodge? It was of the school fund only that they were required to set apart for the colored schools, so they cunningly arranged to have no school fund at all. The white schools, this year are sustained by increased real estate and other taxes, so that colored people are forced to pay for an educational system in which their own children can have no share. Yet if the black men who pay their taxes ask that they and their children be recognized as citizens, legally and politically, these same city Fathers coolly tell them to go to work and educate themselves and let the world see whether they are worthy to be called men or not, before more privileges are granted them. And saying so, the aforesaid Fathers fold their hands under their coattails and complacently thank the Lord that they are free of any further responsibility in the matter.

What steps Uncle Sam will next take in behalf of his swarthy boys and girls is a matter of much interest. It is to be hoped that he will soon give them a chance to sing,

> Now chivalry and slavery have given up the ghost,
> Obedience to the high demand of Freedom's mighty host,
> Our mental night has passed away since Yankee spirits rule,
> And Uncle Sam looks on and smiles to see us all at school.

HOW THEY LEARN

Many of these colored children of the poorer class pursue knowledge under difficulties that would totally discourage the majority of whites. I have seen little boys sitting on doorsteps with a bit of slate and pencil and scraps of printed paper before them, learning to write by copying off the letters. Black, ragged, uncared-for little fellows they seemed, but evidently they cared for the learning and meant to have it. Very likely their fathers were at the same time paying taxes to educate their little white neighbors in schoolhouses and seminaries. One handsome-featured mulatto boy I saw studying his First Reader on top of a load of rubbish he was carting out of town. A colored waiter at an eating-house, where I have often been, always has a book open on a shelf where he can glance at it in passing, or study over some sentence in every moment's leisure. A nurse girl carries a leaf or two of an old primer in her bosom, and when drawing the baby in its little carriage, spells out the words which she gets any of the street children who can to pronounce for her. Servant girls and grown women too, often have a book or two in the kitchen table drawer; and may be sometimes let the meat burn or the tea-water boil away in consequence. A man, black as Egypt, among half a dozen other hod-carriers in the yard under my window, after filling his hod with brick, and while waiting for the others, took something like an old spelling-book out of his woolen shirt-bosom, but had scarcely opened it when he was ordered to fall into line. Slipping the book back and shouldering his hod, he marched on, singing with a ludicrous mixture of waggishness and pathos: "If I had died when I was begun / I wouldn't had this race to run."

REASON ENOUGH

Mrs. Airy Stocracy got into one of the street cars the other day. It was as much as her crinoline was worth, she knew, to risk the company and the crushing, but there was no help for it, a storm was coming, and like a resolute tug boat in she sailed, pulling and struggling through the silken and muslin billows on either hand. About the center of the car a gentleman rose and she subsided into his place. Soon the aisle was full of standing passengers, and Mrs. Airy happening to cast up her eyes saw, oh horror, close before her, touching her sacred skirts, Southern miscegenation illustrated. It had on calico too, clean and tidy, but without hoops, a Shaker sunbonnet, and a little basket on its arm. The lady drew in her drapery as much as possible, and as soon as she could command strength and breath, brought her parasol to bear against the calico and exclaimed:

"Why are you in here? Go out on the platform, where you belong!"

Everybody of course looked around, but as everybody knew that car-laws on that road had ceased to distinguish between shades of color, nothing was said. Mrs. Airy's heart was fired. Giving a vigorous dig with the parasol she cried out:

"Go along, I tell you! Why don't you go out on the platform where you belong?"

Missy Genation, holding on by the strap, listening to the rain, and evidently aware of the rights of her situation, turned a pair of large, quiet, brown eyes upon her adversary and simply said:

" 'Cause I don't want to."

There were too many smiling faces around to suit Mrs. Airy after that. The car couldn't hold her, even to the next crossing. Out she got in the rain and went on her way, a wetter and perhaps a wiser woman.

L.

September 6, 1865, page 4

Letter from Washington
Photographs a Little Colored

From Our Own Correspondent
Washington, September 1, 1865

Last week I mentioned the little adventure of Mrs. Airy Stocracy with Missy Genation in the streetcar; well, unexpectedly it turns out that, to speak in phrase polite, thereby depends a narrative. These times are fruitful of strange events in domestic as well as in political life. The old order of things has been so reversed, and the plans and practices of old time Washingtonians so utterly subverted that, as Mrs. Airy said at the house where she stopped to dry her dripping garments: "There would be no telling the difference between niggers and white folks if it wasn't for their color!"

Poor woman, she was too angry to weigh or measure words just then—too angry to think what she said at all. She felt that she had been crowded out of the car by a "nigger"; the bit of silk and lace patchwork miscalled a bonnet that lay on the top of her head was ruined; her waterfall had gone to try titles with its namesake in the gutter; the drenched folds of her gauzy blue dress had imparted plentifully of their heavenly dyes to the limp and mud-bespattered crinoline beneath, and altogether, considering that she was a woman, and human at that, there seemed cause enough for temper, and excuse for any little incongruities of speech.

But in truth there was something more than anger, more than a fall of water or a lost waterfall troubling her at that moment. Those quiet brown eyes looking down so steadily into her own in the car had aroused a sleeping demon within which struck its fiery fangs into her heart. So there was pain as well as anger at the bottom of these petulant and passionate demonstrations; but pride kept the pain out of sight and let the wrath vent itself on the "nigger" as a race, and the inconvenience of rainstorms in general. While she is smoothing her ruffled plumes and temper, let us take a glance at the antecedents of this little episode in her life, and see whence the origin of the demon with his fiery fangs.

Among the many worn out farms surrounding Washington perhaps none were more utterly threadbare, or bare of all the qualities that give land the title of farm, than the old Cartwryght estates of some six or seven years ago. Indeed, the barrenness of the fields dated back some generations, and the owners thereof in despair of being able any longer to draw funds from them through tobacco leaves and "truck patches," turned their attention to the raising and selling of live stock. Not your Northern four-legged cattle which would require heavy crops of grass and grain and much care to prepare them for market, but a peculiar race of yellow-skinned bipeds capable of fattening on clay banks and abuse, and yielding larger returns on shorter time than the most popular and prolific Durhams ever imported. The Cartwryghts were very aristocratic people, as all Virginians are, descendants of some offshoot of the old English nobility in those times when said nobility was so corrupt that it could boast of more offshoots than a barnyard can of mushrooms on a foggy morning. They confessed to no relation with any of the plebeian race who spelled their name with an "i" instead of a "y." There was a grocer in Georgetown who had "Cadwallader Cartwright" on his sign, and the very sight of it so scandalized the Singleton Fairfax Cartwryghts that always in coming through that city to Washington they went around two squares to avoid looking at it. What was still more humiliating, the "Cadwallader tribe" as Mrs. Singleton F. Cartwryght called them when she deigned to speak of them, claimed to be heirs to a goodly portion of the old estate, in which by some means they had been supplanted by the Singleton branch some two or three generations ago. But they were quiet claimants, having litigated all their spare cash away many years since, and being now content to live by the comfortable income of their stock in trade.

The two tribes were as much distinguished by their Christian names as by their "i" and "y." They were never without a Cadwallader on the one side, or a Singleton on the other. There was another distinction also; the former owning no slaves, but depending on their own hands and wits, and what help they needed, or could afford; while the latter had so many human chattels that they were obliged to take a certain number of them to the Alexandria or Baltimore slave pens every year to keep from being eaten alive by them; or, rather, to procure means whereby themselves might eat and live. The lands were worn out, as I said, by endless cropping, and for lack of brains to renew them the proprietors turned their attention to the stock business.

The present Mrs. Cartwryght, the lady we left drying her dripping gauzes, was one of the Fairfax Tayloe family, also one of the aforesaid offshoots of nobility. They were not in the slightest degree related to any of the vulgar Taylors; they repudiated the "or" as stoutly as Cartwryght's did the "i," and based their claims of blood and birth and chivalric descent firmly on that terminal "e." There were Taylors everywhere, but the Tayloes, at least the Virginia Tayloes could run their line back to the identical individual who brought the name over the ocean sometime in the eighteenth century; and it was known positively that he was the son of a certain lord who, to save a fuss in the family, bestowed upon him the original name of Tayloe, together with possessions of land in the new world, provided he kept the Atlantic ocean always between himself and the place of his birth. As no doubt he did. The Tayloes multiplied in the land, and so consumed the fruits thereof that in Mrs. Cartwryght's girlhood the main object in life of the female portion of the family was to make a good match, to marry somebody with plenty of land and niggers. This she did when she married Mr. Singleton Cartwryght, and she considered that when she gave him herself and interpolated the aristocratic Fairfax into his name, she returned a full equivalent for all the "worldly goods" with which by promise he endowed her. And perhaps she was right. Her pretensions to beauty are said to have been of a high order in her young days, but of the beauty itself one could not say so much at present, and yet she is by no means an old woman. Old, indeed? with that costly lace topknot, and that airy dress, and that splendid waterfall that was before it fell into the water! No, truly, she is not an old woman—not 40, even, judging from her face, but her age is no consequence now. It is enough to know that there are plenty of people here, or were here before so many of them fled southward at the beginning of the war, who well remember her as one of the gayest at balls and routs, and one whose pretty and petty efforts at political intrigue gave as much amusement to sharper intellects as they did to her own. She had her carriage in those days, and her men servants and maid servants; and she adorned herself with sumptuous raiment, and armlets, and earrings, and head tiras wonderful to behold. She was one among the many who scoffed at the idea of permitting our late beloved President to enter the White House; who waited with trembling hope to hear of his murder in Baltimore; who "would have given half the niggers on the place" to have been near enough to kill him on the day of his inauguration; and one of the heartless and infamous clique, calling themselves ladies, but deserving any other name, who attended Mrs. Lincoln's first reception with the design of "putting her down," as it was genteelly termed: in other words, of crushing her by their own mighty superiority, the splendor of their appointments and the bold audacity of their mocking homage.

I wonder if any who were not there to see ever thought what a cruel ordeal that first reception was to our President and his wife. Not only among bitter, prejudiced, unreasoning, scoffing enemies were they, but strangers to the place, the tactics, the etiquette; inexperienced in the so-called courtly ways of the sycophants who had been used to thronging the Presidential mansion, they stood there through the hours of that trying night, receiving the doubtful congratulations of the timid and fearful few, and the sneering obeisance and mocking deference of the many. Fresh as they were from their plain country home life, they were not too dull to see and feel it all; at the same time they lacked the ready tact and confidence of the worldly-hardened to hide from the keen eyes watching them the effect of all they saw and felt. One after another the haughty dames trailed their elegant silks in front of the new Lady of the White House bowed themselves, with their faces to the ground, before her, and passed on, to gather in coteries around the room, where they might watch that rigid little figure now flushing painfully, and now marble white with the cruel consciousness of all that was expressed by the pitiless eyes around her. Conspicuous among those eyes were the black, merciless ones of Mrs. Singleton Cartwryght. The lowest, most servile obeisance made that night was hers; and hers were the half audible expressions of mocking admiration of the manner in which Mrs. President held her bouquet or handled her fan.

Again, poor woman; she was very angry then, and with greater cause than now, for she had lost something of more value than a waterfall, and she had been nursing her anger the whole summer through; so it might be expected that, being a woman, and human as I said, she would take a little womanly revenge when she came face to face with those whom she considered the authors of her misfortunes. It will be remembered that the act of Congress abolishing slavery in the District of Columbia received the President's signature and went into effect the spring before this reception took place; that is to say the 16th of April, 1861.

But I am getting ahead of my story, and having already made my letter too long, will go back in my next and try to get a little more at the heart of the matter.
L.

September 13, 1865, page 4

Letter from Washington

PHOTOGRAPHS A LITTLE COLORED (CONTINUED)

From Our Own Correspondent
Washington, September 8, 1865

An error inadvertently made in my last letter should be corrected. The law abolishing slavery in the District of Columbia was signed April 16, 1862, and not 1861.

Going back some 18 or 20 years to the time of Mrs. Cartwryght's bridal days, we find the honeymoon that rose with such brilliant promise over those broad estates gradually passing into the shadow of that black eclipse that more or less darkens every Southern household. Though vain, fond of dress and wealth, and the power it gives, the young bride, then perhaps not more than eighteen, had also a very creditable share of womanly affection for her husband. As a Southerner, raised among slaves, she could not have been quite ignorant of some of the worst features of that ugly shadow which she saw slowly coming up to her threshold, and which threatened to assume tangible substance and form, and seat itself permanently at her own fireside. She may have had some indefinite idea that it had crept around other doorsteps, sat at other firesides, and darkened the joy of other hearts; but as for its ever coming a-nigh herself, it had not occurred to her that such a thing could be possible. A husband with "plenty of land and heaps of niggers" was what she bargained for in her matrimonial adventure, and what she secured; but not all.

Mr. Singleton Cartwryght had, like his father before him, come in possession of a tract of land which, as the saying was in that neighborhood, "was of no 'count *but* to raise niggers on," and finding it exceedingly good for that, he raised them accordingly. There was a fine market for that sort of stock in Washington in those days, there being a brisk competition between the buyers in that city and in Baltimore for the Southern trade. Alexandria, six miles down on the Potomac, was the great depot to which all the slaves picked up by Legrees in the District and the region round about were gathered, and where they were exposed for sale to the highest bidder. Our Michigan soldiers who were here during the first year of the war, under Major General, then Colonel, O. B. Wilcox, could tell the story of the breaking up of that Alexandria slave market, the throwing open of the gates, and battering down of the walls thereof; and many a man and woman now living in comfort here will clasp their dusky hands in gratitude for the deed then done. Many of them can tell of tears shed and agonies endured within these walls, of the brutal examinations by those traffickers in human flesh, of the sale to Southern masters, and the subsequent escape with freedom under the flag by the light of whose stars "Sherman marched down to the sea."

There was a man in Baltimore, old Joe Slaughter, who had grown as rich as he was grey in the trade, and as his avarice grew by what it fed on, the Baltimore trade could not satisfy him, so sending a son, Jim Slaughter, to Washington, he opened a branch of the stock business here; thus playing into each other's hands, the father and son soon grew as famous in the eyes of the Southern traders as they were infamous in the eyes of God and humanity. Jim Slaughter, in pursuit of his calling, made frequent trips through the country round about to bespeak the refusal of any likely niggers, of either sex, that might be coming into market. Of course he was no stranger on the Singleton Cartwryght plantation. The money that paid for Mrs. Cartwryght's new furniture, from cellar to garret, of the old mansion, came through his hands in consideration of certain yellow girls and boys to him delivered, and by him exposed and sold from the blocks at the Alexandria slave pen. Moreover, Mrs. Cartwryght's dainty appetite was often appeased by the delicate flesh of little yellow babies, mostly of the feminine gender, for the males were less in demand till of a more mature age; and moreover, still, Mrs. Cartwryght disported in the splendid appointments of her toilet a variety of tawny orange and black tints drawn from the same source, and could say with truth that "in the nigger she lived and moved and had her being." Not that the pretty yellow girl babies were literally baked or boiled and set forth upon her table garnished with mint and parsley with apples in their crisped mouths after the manner of nursling pigs, any more than their reputed but innocent black papas and their dusky mammas and mature brothers were hung about her neck and shoulders for pearls and rubies and ermines and velvets; but the price of them was there and that was all the same. She saw no spot of blood on any article of her costly wardrobe, and heard no wail of anguish in the musical jingle of her jewelry; such sweet music as it was to ears that had been longing for it so many years! So in the early part of her honeymoon she feasted, and adorned her house and her fair person, and made herself the admired of all beholders. But the shadow was coming.

Among the cabins in the negro quarters was one conspicuous for its size, the neatness of everything within and around it, and the number of children usually playing about the doorstep or sleeping in the grass beside it. Old 'Meriky, short for America, lived in this cabin. She was the oldest slave on the place, and mother, grandmother, and great-grandmother to nearly all the others. She was black as an Ethiop, and had several daughters of the same hue who had long been married to men of their own color, some belonging to the estate and some owned by neighboring farmers; married, that is in such a way as slaves were (thank God, we can say *were*) permitted to marry; and they also had daughters who were mothers. Tracing these generations down from their supposed ancestors, a theoretic student in anthropology might be puzzled to account for the paling hues and varying features of each successive race. To practical experimenters, however, like the Cartwryghts, fathers and brothers and sons, there was no mystery whatever, but what to them was of far higher consideration, a very perceptible and acceptable profit. Whether the previous Mrs. Cartwryghts were happily oblivious to this progression of the races, or whether they philosophically shut their eyes and their lips and took it all as destiny, or whether there were jealousies, and strifes, and latter reproaches on account thereof, we cannot know, and it matters not now. The present lady of the manor was young and high-tempered and exacting. She loved her husband well enough to be exceedingly jealous if occasion offered; which it very soon did.

Old 'Meriky's cabin was a sort of nursery where all the little ones of the place were kept to be out of the way of their mothers while they were at work. The old slave was too decrepit for labor, but she could take care of the cabin, and see that the little woolly heads did not get seriously singed when their owners coiled up in the ashes of the chimney corner to sleep. She was a faithful creature, and, as she expressed it: "The little nigs took to her mightily."

L.

(To be continued)

September 15, 1865, page 4

Letter from Washington

PHOTOGRAPHS A LITTLE COLORED (CONTINUED)

From Our Own Correspondent

One day, a year or so after her marriage, Mrs. Cartwryght took it into her head to go down unannounced to old 'Meriky's cabin; that is, she went without speaking of it to any one beforehand, so that none of the house hands dropped in before her to say that "Missis is coming." Very unexpectedly to herself, she met Mr. Singleton C. coming out of the door; and the surprise was as patent in his face as in hers. He partly turned to go back, then as quickly changed his mind, and walked rapidly away, calling to one of the slaves in the garden, and pretending to have been in search of some missing implement. Mrs. Cartwryght went in. There was an old box-cradle standing in the corner; over this 'Meriky carelessly dropped an apron as she saw her mistress enter; but the witness within was not to be choked down in that way; it kicked and bellowed fiercely, and so drew to itself the very attention the apron might have been intended to avert. "What are you smothering this little wretch for, 'Meriky? Hush your mouth now," said the mistress, tossing the apron to one side, and discovering a pair of little yellow heels vigorously thumping the naked end-board of the box, a pair of little yellow fists straining frantically hither and thither, and a mouth opened so wide in its indignant protest at the sudden stoppage of breath, that the eyes were quite closed, and even the nose seemed to have vanished in the yawning chasm. In a moment, however, the little quivering limbs were still, the mouth shut tightly, and two great brown eyes staring wonderingly up into her own. There was no mistaking where the expression in those eyes came from; she had seen the same a hundred times before in one pair of eyes; she saw it in the pair that had looked into hers with questioning surprise and alarm as she came in at that door! How the angry blood tingled in her cheeks and then left them white and cold with the jealous rage that was creeping up from her heart. There was no *wool* on that little tell-tale head either, but thin silky wings of black hair so like—well, she was not going to make herself ridiculous before an old slave; it had taken but a glance to tell her all, and from that glance she turned carelessly to old 'Meriky and asked which of the women on the place that child belonged to.

"It 'longs to none on 'em on de place, Missus; its Martha's baby, dat young 'un is."

"Martha? where is she?"

"Marse Singleton hired her out two year ago; down to Fredericksburg I reckon," she added, answering a question of "where," that she felt was on her mistress' lips.

Very anxiously indeed after that day did Mrs. Cartwryght long for a sight of Jim Slaughter. She had heard that there was a nursery in New Orleans where little yellow girls who promised to be pretty were taken and kept till they were old enough for market, and that the original buyers and sellers of this sort of stock made large profits thereon. That the baby in the old box cradle promised to be pretty she readily enough acknowledged to herself, whatever she might have said to another, with her heart so full of bitterness as it was. She said nothing definitely to her husband for awhile, only complained that old 'Meriky had too many children to take care of, and as cold weather was coming on it would be best to dispose of some; besides she needed a new set of furs herself; her ermines had been worn two

Part 3: 1865 305

winters and were quite out of date. Is it strange that her husband knew what she meant as plainly as if she had said it in so many words? It seemed to her that Jim Slaughter would never come. She did not know that her husband had taken pains to see him in Washington and give him such information as would obviate the necessity of his going out to the plantation to make his usual inquiries.

The months passed on, and Mrs. Cartwryght received a handsome set of rubies for a Christmas gift, while the little brown-eyed baby still kicked its heels and grew fat with gnawing corn dodgers on old 'Meriky's cabin floor. Suddenly Mrs. Cartwryght be-thought herself of a dear friend living in Fredericksburg, one whom she had not seen for years, and whom she felt it an imperative duty to visit at once. If any objections were made they availed nothing, for to Fredericksburg she went, and while there accomplished the object of her trip—she saw Martha. If there had been bitterness in her heart before, there was anger now, fierce and flaming. Martha was no common "nigger wench" whom the outraged mistress could look down upon and put beneath her feet as a mere animal, and never think of again except as a source of profit to the owner. Such a creature would never have kindled a spark of jealously in Mrs. Cartwryght's heart, because she would have known that no spark of love could have been kindled in her husband's heart by such a creature. But Martha, with her slender form, her pale oval face, her small and tender mouth, soft eyes and shining jetty ringlets, was quite another thing. She was a slave, hired out as a slave, and dressed in coarse slave clothing, but there was no disguising or denying the fact that there was something about her that might suggest love to a man of even less sensual temperament than Singleton Cartwryght. Martha had been sewing girl at the old mansion during Mr. Singleton's bachelor days when there was no white woman on the place; and when that gentleman made up his mind to put Miss Fairfax Tayloe at the head of his household, he very prudently hired out his little creole mistress as nurse-girl and seamstress at what he considered a safe distance from home, and in a place where he felt sure his wife had neither friend nor acquaintance living. He counted without his hostess, however, as we have seen. The baby he was obliged to bring home or have Martha lose her place, as it was in the way of her other duties. Some men would probably have set the young mother up in a home of her own, and so divided their attentions between the primary and secondary formations of social life, keeping each independent of the other. But, as Mr. Singleton said to himself, where would have been the profits? Martha was a slave and Mrs. Cartwryght was not. The one must be supported, the other must help do it. Love had evidently not gone beyond the practicalities in Mr. Singleton's case; but one thing it seems he had promised Martha, and that was that the baby should not be sold, at least not to be taken South, and he apparently had either affection enough for her, or interest enough in the baby to enable him to keep the promise.

Mrs. Cartwryght returned from her Fredericksburg trip, and straightway there was a fuss in the family. Angry accusations, and bitter words and tears and threats spiced the next year or two of her life, but as the only visible effect seemed to be to drive her husband still more and more from home, and to longer absences on unknown business, unknown to her at least, she grew weary of it at last. The skeleton was fairly and surely in her house, and she saw that an attempt to drive it out would only result in driving from her also all that was most desirable in her estimation—the full and free enjoyment of the property she married when she accepted her husband's name. She gave up the struggle when it had worried and worn out of her the little saving leaven of love she had brought to her new home. O, how many thousands of her wronged and wronging Southern sisters have done the same; only many of them have perhaps more of love to lose, and so the struggle is longer, and the anguish more terrible than hers. Who will wonder that women leading such lives exhibit little innate delicacy or true refinement of character? The great wonder of the age is that they cling with such tenacity to a system which has reduced their social life to a lower level than even Mormonism has yet dragged its victims. Lower in reality it is, and more unprincipled at heart, whatever fictitious sanctity time and custom and commercial interests may have thrown over and around it; a godless, heartless, corrupt, degrading system, which has been debauching men and perverting women's natures till it inevitably resulted in the great national catastrophe of civil war. But in spite of all that women have suffered from slavery they are the last to be willing to give it up. They have become accustomed to the brutalities connected with it, and as it favors their false notions in regard to the degrading nature of labor, they would cherish it as the basis of an aristocracy their life-long education has taught them to venerate. Even in her moments of greatest anguish Mrs. Cartwryght could never have been convinced that slavery by means of the laws to which its victims are subject was the sole cause of what she suffered as far as Martha was concerned. And had Martha gone before her and told her the horrible story, and true as horrible, of threats and beatings and brutal violence by which she had been dragged between her master and his wife, it would have made no difference in the wife's estimate of slavery. The "niggers" she must have about her to scold and beat and brutalize as evidences of her gentility. It was not the system she was angry with on her return from Fredericksburg; her thoughts never went beyond the helpless victim who had been forced by the laws of the system to wrong her. From that day to this she has only been enduring accumulated wrongs from the same prolific source; and yet she would accept the risk of them all over again if slavery could be restored to its old status in the District of Columbia, and she be able once more to put her foot on a few necks which so vexatiously to her escaped from its pressure some time about the middle of an eventful spring month in 1862. I said she was full of a fierce and flaming wrath when she returned home from her Fredericksburg trip; she did not think it possible for human anguish or anger to exceed that day's experience; on that ever memorable 16th of April, however—but this is anticipating. All heights, physical and mental, are reached by degrees; let us go up this Vesuvius with Mrs.

Cartwryght herself, clambering over the crusted lava of the irruptions of other times, till we stand with her on the verge of the crater where so many hopes and aspirations were engulfed.

(To be Continued)

September 18, 1865, page 4

Letter from Washington

PHOTOGRAPHS A LITTLE COLORED (CONTINUED)

From Our Own Correspondent

Mr. Singleton Cartwryght was several years older than his wife, and aside from his extensive livestock speculations, took a great interest in the politics of the times and especially of his native State. He had an intense admiration for the dash and bravado of the Mississippi fire-eaters, and wished exceedingly that some of their spirit could be infused into the staid old dignitaries of the Old Dominion. This feeling grew upon him as he saw the issue approaching for the great national contest between freedom and slavery. He wished the F. F. V.'s had more fire and less fossil about them; not that he had a doubt as to the result of the contest if it should come; chivalry could never yield to the mudsills, of course; but he wanted Virginia as the old mother of Presidents to take secession to her venerable arms and heart and become mother also to the twin abortion of the times, the pre-doomed abomination of the ages, Rebellion and the Southern Confederacy. All honor to the grand old State; she folded her arms over the sacred relics and memories hidden in her bosom, and protested against the shameless prostitution which her degenerate sons would drag her. She would not be the mother, and if she came in afterwards as godmother at the birth and bloody christening of the unholy thing, it was through fraud and force and guile. Now that the awful horror has breathed out its sanguinary life, and lies a ghostly corpse in her arms, she sits in sackcloth and ashes and calls upon her recreant sons to take it from her and bury it out of her sight forever.

Poor old Virginia! May she yet rise redeemed, stronger, purer, and nobler than ever in the palmiest days of her glorious youth; but if she does, she will owe none of her strength, purity, or nobility to Mr. Singleton Cartwryght's efforts. His tastes and inclinations never ran in the way of making either himself or any one else purer or better. But he was a fiery politician, anxious to have the chivalry of Virginia shine before the world and take the lead in forming the new empire that was to be founded, with slavery for its chief cornerstone. So for several years before the war he was much from home, often among the sharp schemers at the Capitol, and often at Richmond.

Mrs. Cartwryght, meantime, was left pretty much to follow the devices and desires of her own heart. That organ suffered somewhat for years from the rankling poison she took in from the eyes of Martha's baby, and what was worse, the added years gave it added cause for suffering, if its owner had weakly allowed it to be affected thereby. When a second baby opened its accusing eyes to hers, she stifled her feelings with a consideration more effectual than old 'Meriky's apron in the case of the first. She said to herself, "It's nothing but a nigger, and what's the use? the more we have the richer we are, and I should be a fool after marrying so much property not to take the good of it." And so, after her way, she set about taking the good of it. She had no children of her own, which was a pity, for then she might have been a better woman—more merciful to those who needed mercy at her hands. She made the adornment of her person, visitings, and entertainments, the chief joys of her life. The winters she sported away amidst the gayeties of a certain class in Washington, and the summers she usually fluttered away at springs and watering places.

In regard to Martha's children, whatever indifference the mistress might feel or feign towards the second one, a sturdy, flat-nosed, crinkle-haired little imp, several shades darker than his sister, but with the same eyes, however she might ignore his presence or toss him out of the path like a troublesome puppy, she was always conscious of a very different feeling towards the first one. Jealousy, spite, anger, revenge, whatever that feeling was, the little girl was sure to suffer from it whenever opportunity offered. A blow upon the head, or a sharp cut across the neck with the little red rawhide, which Mrs. Cartwryght always had within reach, were the tenderest marks of affection the child ever received from her. In consequence, it very soon became a shy, frightened little thing, scared and hiding itself behind old 'Meriky, or in dark corners, whenever it caught sight of its mistress' shadow, or heard the rustling of her garments. This conduct seemed the more to provoke the rage it sought to avoid, for if the child was not at once called out to receive a box on the ear, the same was bestowed with compound interest at the first chance that offered thereafter. It is not to be wondered at, therefore, that little Betty grew up to be not so bright in intellect as might have been expected, considering her high connexions; in fact, before she was twelve years old she received the title of stupid Betty, and so she is called to this day.

It was a burning shame, old 'Meriky said, to have a child so bright and pert as dat young 'un was when it was first fotched to her cabin made a fool by jes' hevin' de sense knocked square out'n its head for nothin' but its father's badness. De Lor' knowed de chile couldn't help itself more'n Martha could, poor gal! She jest wished Marse Singleton would only stay at home long enough to see how things was gwine on. But goodness, we'se nothin' but niggers, an' what's the use?

She ended her reasoning, you see, with the same argument that the mistress did hers—"only niggers, and what's the use?"

But if the father could shut his eyes to this cruel injustice, was it likely that the mother would, and be patient under it, if she knew it? If she knew it? you ask. And did she not? Aye; every stroke of that cruel rawhide, and every blow of that crueler hand she knew and felt, and mourned the blighted intellect of her child, though she had never visited her old home since the mistress came, and never seen the little Betty since she was taken, a scarcely weaned baby, from her arms. These poor colored people, though they may never be able to read a word or write a letter in their whole lives, have yet a more perfect mail and telegraph system that ever Uncle Sam could devise or Morse invent. The invisible lines run from heart to heart, and from lip to ear, as far as acquaintance and sympathy extend. It is well that they are invisible too, or the Legrees, Slaughters, Cartwryghts, etc., would have had them down in the dust long since, and ground to powder beneath their iron heels.

Yes, Martha knew very well how it was going with little Betty, and she was young and foolish enough to think that it would not be so if she could only see her mistress long enough to tell her something that was near killing her with the keeping. If her mistress only knew! But then she was forbidden under awful penalties to go near that mistress, and so the years wore on till she heard of the sickness and brain fever which threatened to terminate her child's life. How she ever got to old 'Meriky's cabin no one inquired, but there one dark, stormy night she was, half famished and with torn garments and bleeding feet. With little Tom hugged to her bosom she sat upon the blanket spread upon the floor which was poor Betty's bed, and with tearless eyes and steady voice told old 'Meriky that she had come to tell her mistress how innocent she was of any intent to wrong her, that as a slave she had been subject to her master's will against her own, and to beg to be forgiven and taken home where she might have protection and be with her children as the other women on the place were.

"Lor bress ye, you's jes' better say nuffin 'bout de facs; 'taint de likes o' her to lister to yer no how. She hates de chile fur what she sees in its eyes, and she aint gwine to bleve no story you tell dat's 'ginst wat she's got her mind made up to; now you may take my word for dat, an' it's de 'vice o' ole experience," said 'Meriky.

"But she blames me, I know," said Martha "and I cant bear that; and if I lived here where she could know—O, 'Meriky, I'm sure if I lived here things wouldn't be so."

" 'Taint de *place whar yer live* as makes any difference, gal; *it's de color o' yer skin, de race ye 'longs to*. Dere's heaps of gals, some on 'em bright as you, lived in dese berry cabins, an' been done worse by dan you is. 'Deed was they! an' der husban's tied up an' give a hundred *good* ef a mouf was opened 'bout de goins on, else toted oft to de slav pen, an' sold out de way. An' de chillun went to. O Lor', chile, ye dont know niffin yit; but it'll come, an' ye can't help it *sure's you're born a nigger.* Ole 'sperience teached dem doctrines to me long ago."

That was all the consolation Martha could get from Old 'Meriky; but she had come up from Fredericksburg for a purpose, and meant to accomplish it or know why she failed. She knew her master was not at home, and believed her mistress would listen to and pity her. Poor foolish girl!

Soon after breakfast time, Martha went to the house and ushered herself at once into her mistress' presence. She was so changed from what Mrs. Cartwryght had first seen her, that she was not recognized till she began her story by saying that she ran away from Fredericksburg, but only for a day or two, just to see Betty before she died, and to say, "O, Mistress, Mistress, it wasn't my fault, indeed it wasn't, about Betty nor little Tom; for I loved Ben Allen and wanted to marry him, but Marster Singleton—O, Mistress, I can't say it to you—I thought I could—O, let me come home to live where you can know—where I can—where—where Marster—"

She sprang to her feet as the keen, cutting strokes of the rawhide fell quick and fast across her shoulders and over her face, for she had thrown herself upon her knees and covered her eyes with her hands in her shame and confusion, and had not seen the gathering wrath in Mrs. Cartwryght's face, nor the hand trembling with rage as it grasped the ever ready implement to execute her vengeance.

"Master, indeed! I'll Master you! Come here to my very face with your impudence and your lies, will you?" cried the mistress, emphasizing every word with a blow, which Martha, standing in stupid amazement, as if sense and feeling had forsaken her together, took as quietly as if only a snow flake or a feather had touched her. "Yes, I'll Master you! I'll teach you to come to *me* with your impudent lies about my own husband! How dare you, you dirty huzzy? Don't you dare to call this your home, never. Come home, indeed; where you think you could have your master at your elbow

"No; not that! O, Mistress—"

"Hush your mouth, and be off out of my sight. Don't you dare to open your lying lips to me again, and don't you never dare to call this your home—out, away with you!"

And so Martha's experiment was over. She went back to Fredericksburg, but her sorrows wore upon her so that in a short time her employers sent word to Mr. Cartwryght that she was getting to be a "no count nigger," and they could not keep her any longer. Either her master's passion had worn itself out, or it faded away with the fading beauty of its object, or he was too much engrossed in politics to care more for her than any other, and when she begged him to hire her out in Georgetown, he did so, though he knew that Ben. Allen was there. Indeed, he seemed not in the least displeased to know that it was Ben's master who wanted to hire her, and that it was through Ben.'s recommendation that she got the place. The reader must understand, however, that it was from no feeling of delicacy or

Part 3: 1865

compunctions of conscience that he did not take her home. He could never accuse himself of wronging his wife by anything that occurred in regard to Martha. She was "only a nigger," you know; and if it came to that, and a man was obliged to be more nice than wise in such matters, how many women servants, or slaves, rather, do you suppose would be left on the plantation?

No; whatever might have been Mr. Cartwryght's reason for removing Martha from home before he brought his young wife there, he was actuated by very different motives in keeping her away after that stolen visit of hers from Fredericksburg. Mrs. Cartwryght had affectionately told him the whole story, her own version of it amplifying on the shameless conduct of the huzzy who wanted to come and set herself down under her, Mrs. Singleton Fairfax Cartwryght's aristocratic nose; and she, the said Mrs. Cartwryght didn't doubt that he, Mr. Singleton, would have been quite delighted with such an addition to his family; but she gave him fair warning that if he brought her there or permitted her to come, "he might very soon consider himself as good as a thousand dollars out of pocket, and with a dead nigger on his hands."

When he told her that she set a higher value on Martha than he did, for he never thought her worth a thousand dollars, she replied,

"Of course not, as she is looking now, a haggard, worn out, no 'count nigger; but let her run with Ben awhile, and how long do you reckon before Jim Slaughter would offer you a thousand dollars for her for the New Orleans market?"

There spoke a woman with a woman's knowledge of her sex, and of man's nature as well, and, also, with an unwomanly shamelessness and a refinement of cruelty such as no other system of social life under God's blue heaven but that of Southern slavery could have engendered. Poor Martha, in her agony at this woman's feet had revealed an object of legitimate love; that love indulged would bring happiness, restore beauty and make marketable what was otherwise comparatively worthless.

So, to keep the peace, and that Mrs. Cartwryght's heart might not be further fired or irritated, a compromise was made. Martha was to "run with Ben," as Mrs. Cartwryght elegantly expressed it; she was to have the two children as near her as she could get places for them, and the understanding between master and mistress was that when, by Jim Slaughter's opinion, Martha would bring the highest price on the auction block, he was to take her to Alexandria, and the proceeds of the sale were to go to Mrs. Cartwryght's purse for her own exclusive use. Then the fiend that had made them unhappy so long was to be at an end, and, like the fabled couples in fairy tales, they were to live happy ever after.

(To be continued)

September 22, 1865, page 4

Letter from Washington

Photographs a Little Colored (Continued)

From Our Own Correspondent

Little Betty was about ten years old when she lay on old 'Meriky's cabin floor sick with the brain fever. She did not die, but on her recovery, though no kindlier treated by her mistress, grew a healthier and stouter girl. There was little improvement in her intellect, however; she was shy and silent, seldom speaking unless when spoken to, and always using the fewest possible words in answering questions. But she was good-tempered, and trusty, and fond of little children. Stupid Betty, they all called her.

It was nearly two years after Martha went to Georgetown before Ben Allen could persuade her to forget the past and become his wife. She was sick and worn and haggard with the experiences of that bitter past; but after a little time she yielded to the love that had been kept for her through all; and when she was married a place was found very near her for Betty as a nurse girl, and soon after Tom was wanted as an errand boy in the same family. Tom had not a delicate organization like his sister's to suffer from. He was a stout, well-grown boy for his years, with a head that would bear any amount of knocking without being the worse for it, and supple, active limbs that were generally used to good purpose in taking him out of harm's way. In this last peculiarity he proved himself a true Cartwryght, and in this activity, combined with his frank and fearless honesty, lay his great merit as an errand boy.

Thus they were all out of Mrs. Cartwryght's path at last, and that estimable and long-suffering lady was waiting with commendable patience for the day when the price of Martha's flesh and blood, enhanced by her restored beauty, should gladden her own purse and minister to the rejuvenating of her own fading charms. It was not in the programme that Martha should be informed of her impending fate, or that she should know why Jim Slaughter's ugly face was to be seen moving up and down High Street at intervals of four to six months; but here the invisible telegraph lines had been in operation also, and it was very likely the news had some effect on Martha's health and spirits, if it did not also cause the long delay in her marriage. But long familiarity with danger deadens out fear of it; and besides, why should slaves deny themselves a day of fleeting happiness because the morrow may snatch it from their grasp forever? This was Ben's reasoning, and to it Martha yielded at last.

"At last!" thought Mrs. Cartwryght, with a great sigh of relief when she heard of it; "the good-for-nothing, contrary piece; and I'm to be cheated out of my furs this winter just to gratify a spiteful whim of hers, the wretch!"

Mrs. Cartwryght, it will be observed, dealt largely in furs. They were her weakness, if she had one. She loved furs; to use her own words, she had a passion for them, she adored them, or rather herself in them. But she was, in regard to them, like a coquette with lovers. She was always longing for a new set, never long content with the one she had. What were furs, when the freshness and novelty of them were worn out? Nothing, certainly, that Mrs. Cartwryght should take any pride in them. Moreover, the coming winter was the first of the new Administration, and although she heartily despised the Black Republican President and his wife, she did not intend that on their account the gay world at the Capital should be deprived of the light of her countenance and the splendor of her raiment. She and her friends would show the Northern rabble gathered within and about the White House what aristocracy meant. But she must have dress to do it with, and especially furs. Now these furs she knew could not be had unless Martha's sale should put the price thereof into her hands; for, if the truth must be told, cash on the Cartwryght estate was not just then as plentiful as it was wont to be. In fact, things in general were in rather a dilapidated condition, owing the master's long absences on his political missions; hence his worthy lady's anxiety.

That spring and summer of 1861 was rather a busy time for Virginia politicians of the Cartwryght stamp. In truth they had been hard at work and spending money freely since the November election trying to coax and urge and drive the old State up to the seceding point. By fraud and force it was at length accomplished, and then the tremendous up-rising of the Northern people made the recreants turn pale and strain every nerve lest they should be overwhelmed by the coming waves of indignation. Singleton Cartwryght was at Richmond adding what fuel he could to the flames of war, and now and then writing comforting letters to his wife—comforting to himself at least, in that they were full of promises of unimaginable glory for the dawning Confederacy, and of visions of titles and grandeur for the genuine "y" Cartwryghts in the future Imperial Court to be established at Washington. These pleasing visions very naturally inspired Mrs. Cartwryght with a desire to practice a few Imperial airs and graces before hand, which she did in the Blue Room and Green Room, greatly to her own satisfaction, notwithstanding the lack of the coveted furs.

Before the winter was past she was Mrs. General Cartwryght, for her husband had obtained that rank in the rebel army, and she was confidently looking forward to the time when the plain "Mrs." would be dropped altogether, and she would be received at court as Lady Fairfax Cartwryght. But in the meantime troubles were thickening and clouds darkening. The Federal troops were surrounding Washington, throwing up their forts and planting their guns on every hill. The flag she was trying to teach herself to hate was floating before her eyes whichever way she turned. Looking from her own door she could see those blazing stars, almost like the stars of heaven for number, shining over all the hills and brightening all the valleys. And worse and worse, a fort was built upon her own farm, and the negroes from her own fields helped to build it! It was very well known by the Federal authorities where the husband was, but she, being a woman, was allowed to remain in her home. Then she could get no letters from her husband, and was by no means sure that of any of hers ever reached him. Still she tried to solace herself with her present title, and with the hopes of that higher and prouder one in the brighter future.

As the spring advanced another calamity threatened to demolish her fairest prospects. A few crazy Radicals in Congress persisted in dragging before that body the subject of the abolition of slavery in the District of Columbia. Now Mrs. Cartwryght did not attend the debates in the Capitol that season; furthermore she did not "take the papers" very extensively, and so her sources of information were rather limited and her ideas on that subject somewhat indistinct. She did not believe that Congress could do such a thing as free slaves anywhere, and if they did, of course it would only be for a little while, till the glorious Confederacy should be established, when all such crazy notions would be set aside and niggers would be slaves forever. She saw Jim Slaughter early in April and asked his opinion, which was to the effect that the Radicals never were so weak in their lives as they were in that present Congress, and that accounted for the immense amount of noise they were making. He didn't believe the measure would pass, never; and couldn't amount to anything if it did. He admitted that a parcel of Federals had somewhat disturbed his slave-pen arrangements at Alexandria, but the Confederates would soon bring another Bull Run about their ears and make matters all right there. He had no fears.

Mr. Slaughter, it will be seen, was not fully posted in regard to the popular feeling on the subject of slavery, either in Congress or out of it. But then he had been South all winter, among the Tigers of Louisiana and the Fire eaters of Mississippi, and being thoroughly imbued with their chivalric spirit, had a very poor opinion of Northern principles, and Northern courage. The Yankees might talk, he said; thus comforting Mrs. Cartwryght to the best of his ability. She, poor woman, took in what consolation she could, but still she trembled when she thought of Martha and her children, for she had resolved, so she now told Mr. Slaughter, that, as things had gone so badly in the General's absence, she would sell the three, Martha, Betty, and Tom, together.

"The *three?*" exclaimed Mr. Slaughter. "Why, you don't keep track of your own stock! There are *four* now. She's got one of the peartest little things I ever laid eyes on, worth his weight in gold, nigh about; mighty bright he is. Ben's as good as white, you know. I don't reckon she's out yit, but before the month's gone, Madam, I'll put a right smart sum into your hands, for I know jest who wan's the lot."

"But if the abolitionists *should* free all the niggers in the District," began Mrs. Cartwryght.

"Don't pester yourself with that nonsense," interrupted Mr. Slaughter with a consequential flourish, as he turned to go; "don't pester yourself; there's no such thing coming to pass in our day and gineration. I reckon I know the strength of the Democratic party as well as the next man. I dropped in at the Capitol on my way over here, and heard Cox and Vallandigham give the nigger-worshippers a few sharp raps. Val's one of our big guns, and as he goes so goes the party, and so goes the day. We hold a strong hand, and in another month Lincoln wont dare to say his soul's his own. Take my word for that, Mrs. Cartwryght."

She took his word, and made herself as easy as she could, under the circumstances. She had little chance to know what was being done at the Capitol either for or against human liberty, and, of course, feared far more than she knew, but, as the sequel proved, not more than she had cause for. On the 11th of April she went into the city, and heard with consternation before she left it, that in both Houses of Congress the Abolitionists had carried the vote; the bill for the emancipation of slaves in the District of Columbia had passed the House that day and only waited for the President's signature to become a law. She felt like a lost woman. There was a compensation, she heard, of $300 to be given to the owners of slaves thus freed; but what was that miserable sum to Martha's real value? Besides, it was only *loyal* owners who could claim even that, and she had a very poor record to show for loyalty. There was but one way left for her—she must get Martha and her children out of the District before the President's name was given to that bill, for on them was her whole dependence now. Old 'Meriky was still at home, it was true, and two or three young children, and an old woman who acted as housekeeper; nearly all the available slaves on the place had been sold to supply General Cartwryght's needs, or rather to aid him in helping Virginia out of the Union; the few who had been left to take charge of the farm were for the time impressed into the Federal service, so that in fact the four chattels in Georgetown were about all that Mrs. Cartwryght could count upon. How long could she count upon these? was a question which kept sleep from her eyes and slumber from her eyelids through all that anxious night. Would Jim Slaughter fail her now? She knew he was gone to Baltimore, but would he not hear of this and return in time to save her property?

But she would not wait for him; it might be too late. So in the stillness and darkness of night she formed her plans, and early the next day proceeded to put them into execution. Going to the city, she hired a handsome hack and drove at once to the house where Martha was living. Seeing a child at the door, she sent it in to tell her a lady was waiting to see her. The trim little figure that came down the walk with its small oval face, a trifle pale from recent illness, but beaming with a beauty ripened in the atmosphere of love, proved that Mrs. Cartwryght's idea of the effect of happiness was correct, but also sent a thrill of anxiety through the heart lest the prize should escape her at last. Martha looked up with wondering eyes as if questioning who might be doing her this honor. Mrs. Cartwryght hastened to array her face in its pleasantest smile, and say,

"I heard you had been sick, Martha, and reckoned a ride over to the old place would do you good. It's still and quiet there now, and rather lonesome since the General, your master, is gone so much, so I thought I'd drive round and take you and the children out to make us a good visit. You can be spared, I reckon?"

How ashy Martha's face grew, but she replied with a steady voice:

"Thank you, Mistress; I'll go in and ask."

"And come right soon, Martha, don't keep me waiting long with this hack at four dollars an hour."

(To be concluded in our next)

September 23, 1865, page 4

Letter from Washington

Photographs a Little Colored (Concluded)

From Our Own Correspondent

As Martha went up the steps, the lady of the house came out upon the porch. Martha said a few words to her, to which she replied aloud: "O, certainly, certainly;" and then came down and stood by the carriage, talking pleasantly of the weather, of Martha's fine baby, and of what a treat it would be for them to all go to the old home once more. Mrs. Cartwryght was all smiles and graciousness at first, but she was not in a mood for gossiping just then; she was mentally counting the minutes and summing up the dollars that were at stake.

"It takes the girl a long time to get ready," she said at last; then turning to the child she had before spoken to, she added, "Go in and tell her not to mind her clothes; we can send and get them again."

The child went in; ten, fifteen, twenty minutes more, and no Martha! The lady could not understand it, she would go in and see. Mrs. Cartwryght could not tell how many ages she sat there in that agony of suspense, before the lady came out again, and quietly told her that no Martha was to be found about the house! She was gone—no one knew how or where. But the baby was there; would Mrs. Cartwryght have that?

No; Mrs. Cartwryght was not in a temper for taking charge of a nursing baby then; at least not while there were older ones to look after. She ordered the hack to be driven at once to the house where Betty and Tom had been hired. By some strange coincidence they had also disappeared within the last hour or so, and no amount of searching and calling could bring them to light. Mrs. Cartwryght threw herself back on the seat in despair. It was almost night, and Saturday night too, there was nothing for it but to go home and wait for Monday. And what a waiting it was for the unhappy woman! What if President Lincoln's first exercise on that coming Monday morning should be to write his name on that fatal paper? Why was not her husband, the General, there to see to his property? Where was Jim Slaughter? How could he have been so blind as not to know what those hateful Yankee Abolitionists were about? If he were only there he could work on Sunday as well as any other day; that is, he could watch around that corner in High street, and secure Martha when she came for her baby, which she would be sure to do; or he might get the police to help him and waylay Betty and Tom.

The police! That was a lucky thought, Mrs. Cartwryght said to herself. Yes; she would be in town early, before business hours on Monday, and what she could not do the police might do for her; and it was more than likely that Jim Slaughter would be down in the early train from Baltimore—all of them together. Well, with plans and dreams of what might be done, she solaced herself till Monday morning. There were plenty of police in both Washington and Georgetown in those days, who wanted no better employment than "running down skulking niggers," and the species is not entirely extinct yet, judging from incidents constantly occurring under the present municipal arrangements of this city. Mrs. Cartwryght had no difficulty in getting help, but not satisfied with putting them on the track of the fugitives, she determined upon one more desperate effort of her own. With another hack, a cheaper one this time, she drove again to the house which had been Martha's home. A policeman was ready to step through the back gate, down the area into the basement, where a plump little baby was sleeping. In a few minutes more the baby was in Mrs. Cartwryght's carriage, and sending in word that Martha could have her child by coming home for it, the lady drove off in triumph.

Home! Did this woman remember that terrible day when Martha lay in shame and agony at her feet, begging to be taken to that home, begging for her Mistress' protection against the wrongs and outrages of a licentious master? Did she remember the cruel wrongs with which she had answered those pleadings, the bitter, heartless words with which she had driven the poor girl from her presence, forbidding her even to open her lips to her or to call that place her home again? It was not likely that she troubled herself with any reflections of the sort during those exciting, anxious hours. She had something else to think of, with that hungry, crying baby on her hands, and the prospect of losing chattels of so much value, almost her sole dependence now, by a single word which she felt sure was just trembling on the point of Mr. Lincoln's pen.

She kept the baby, and waited in most unspeakable anxiety for comforting news from the police. All day Monday, all night, and through the weary Tuesday following, those faithful and energetic gentlemen haunted High Street, and all other suspected streets and quarters, both in Georgetown and Washington, and still Martha, Betty, and Tom were invisible. For the thousandth time Mrs. Cartwryght wondered what had become of Jim Slaughter, that he was not there to help her in her extremity. She might have spared her wonder and anxiety, if she had known that, having been caught in attempting to run an opposition to Uncle Sam's mail arrangements through the Federal lines into Dixie, her distinguished friend was at that time luxuriating in the Old Capitol at the Government expense. But she did not know it, and so [ ] of the infant Ben Allen till endurance ceased to be a virtue, and the police informed her that their labors were in vain. As the child was gone there was no inducement for Martha to show herself, and they should give up the search.

It was Tuesday night, and Martha was still her property. Would there be another day of grace? Was not Providence interfering in her behalf, in withholding that dreaded signature? She would change her tactics; take the baby back to its basement home, and so entice her refractory property into the arms of the police, who should be kept in waiting one day more. The baby was taken back, and all night the police listened to its frantic screams for the mother who did not come. The little Ben evidently understood what his rights were, and was determined not to resign them without a struggle vigorous in proportion to the value he set upon them. What was bread and milk, though taken from a silver spoon, that he should be content therewith? and what were cakes and sweetmeats, though tinctured with the costliest spices, that he should deign to feed thereon? But he ate, nevertheless, as Martha knew he would, enough to keep him from starving, and spent his time in snatches of sleep between vehement outpourings of angry cries, refusing to be comforted because of the mother who did not come.

Mrs. Cartwryght's anguish and suspense during those terrible days, it is useless to try to paint. But the climax came at last. The name, beloved and honored of the world, was traced with careful hand at the bottom of that document; the Capital was free, and human slavery on this continent was virtually dead. For did not Vallandigham, the great oracle of a great political party, standing in his place on the floor of the Hall of Representatives, on that memorable 11th of April, 1862, declare in this wise: "I am opposed to any bill for abolishing slavery in the District of Columbia, for do we not know that this bill is brought forward as the beginning of a grand scheme of emancipation, and there is no calculation where that scheme is to end!" He foresaw that it would end slavery, and hence his opposition, and hence his vote stands, with the thirty-eight others, recorded in that infamous minority who would have seen the nation sink in blood rather than that a fetter of slavery should be loosed. But the blow was struck, the beginning was made, and from that day to this slavery has been reeling to its fall, rending the nation and shaking the earth with its dying agonies.

So Mrs. Cartwryght's suspense was ended at last. In her great anxiety for Martha and her children she forgot that her slaves at home were also subject to the new law, or she might have had them run out of the District, and so saved or sold them for her benefit. Old 'Meriky afterwards said she was "en a perfect trimble for a week, fearin' the Missis mought member herself and 'hev 'em all toted off; she jes' held her bret all day and prayed to de good Lord all night, an' praise to Goodness dey was all free together at last."

Yes; the mistress was free as well as her slaves. How she managed to live through the years of the war was a matter of business in which few interfered, and little or nothing was heard of her till peace was settled, and the "General" returned. He came home a miserable wreck of a man, penniless and broken in health. His whole estate was wrecked and ruined too. The forests were gone, the fences burned, and over all the fields had been the bristling forts and the broad camping grounds of the Armies in Blue. Uncle Sam had taken possession without so much as by your leave.

It was understood that the Cadwallader Cartwrights of Georgetown have been very kind to their aristocratic cousins, and that the latter have condescended to receive pecuniary favors at their hands. The Cadwalladers have suffered too, by the war, but honorably. One son was killed and another severely wounded in the fight for freedom and humanity. The old gentleman and another son have driven a thriving business with the grocery, however, and the prospect is that they will soon take possession of a goodly portion of the old Cartwryght estate. Mrs. Singleton Fairfax in the meantime is making the most of the remains of her old wardrobe. She is just as aristocratic as ever, and in order to be in the fashion with her Southern sisters, she intends, as soon as she can command a decent suit of mourning, to go through the ceremony of asking President Johnson to pardon her husband. Nor that she thinks he has done anything wrong, or anything but what he would do again, and ought to if a chance offered; but then, it is the fashion to be pardoned through the intercession of the gentler sex, and ladies in deep mourning, with their faces whitened with enamel, and dark shadows painted under their eyes, do look *so* interesting! Yes, she could forego furs forever if she only had a handsome suit of the heaviest mourning. It is possible that some of the sympathizing ladies of this city who have so freely subscribed to relieve the wants of Mrs. Jeff. Davis will take Mrs. Cartwryght's case in hand next. It is surmised by some that magnificent waterfall of hers is, or was before it went into the gutter, a secondhand affair, and that the reason it kept its place no better was because there was not enough of the original material on her head to fasten it to properly. But the unfortunates are ever the objects of slander.

Mr. Cox of Ohio, in his remarks before Congress on the 11th of April, 1862, said: "Whether the national capital may be called the paradise of free negroes or not, the people of the North do not want to pay for the curse of making black communities among themselves." If he was in Washington on the 16th day of the same month, did he not find himself in reality in a "paradise of free negroes?" If ever there was joy upon earth it was among the ransomed slaves of this District of Columbia on that day. And nowhere was there deeper, purer, tenderer joy than in Martha's heart when she clasped her baby to her bosom, and Ben Allen held them together in his strong arms and called them his own—his own forever.

The Allens have been keeping house now for two years. Betty and Tom live at home, but have both repudiated the Cartwryght name, having, as Tom says, "an abomination in their hearts, 'specially for all mean rebels." Betty is a well grown girl, with strangely beautiful, but mournful eyes, and an absent dreary way with her, as if she were living in another world, and only breathing in this. She retains her old habits of silence, and when spoken to makes the briefest possible replies. When Mrs. Cartwryght met her in the cars, the other day, it was the first time she had seen her since she was sent to Georgetown, several years ago. Observing at first only the little brown hand holding by the strap, she was convinced that there was a "nigger" in her presence, and gave her a vigorous thrust with her parasol to drive her out, for, as the lady is often heard to say, if there is one thing more offensive than another to a Fairfax Cartwryght, it is a "nigger." She cannot endure them about her, and especially in the cars. She had forgotten that they were allowed inside the F Street cars, but will be careful not to patronize that line again. She wondered why the "nigger" did not go out when ordered, and so gave her another push, and exclaimed, "why don't you go out on the platform, where you belong?" Then those strange, sad, wondering eyes looked down into hers very like the ones that had looked up into them from that old box cradle so many years ago. How the old thoughts came rushing back—the jealousy, the rage, her own suffering, and then the cruel vengeance she had wreaked out upon that helpless child, the blows that had fixed that look in her eyes and made her a child for all time—alas, it is little wonder that she went out into the storm herself, scarcely hearing poor Betty's simple answer, " 'Cause I don't want to."

L.

September 27, 1865, page 4

Letter from Washington

THE PARIS EXPOSITION OF INSECTS | EXTRACTS FROM PROF. GLOVER'S LETTER TO THE DEPARTMENT OF AGRICULTURE

From Our Own Correspondent
Washington, September 19, 1865

The Department of Agriculture is in receipt of an interesting letter from Prof. Glover, the entomologist, who has been sent to attend the exposition of entomology in Paris. I make the following extracts for your columns. He reached Liverpool on the 15th of August and went thence by rail to London. He says: "During the day's passage through England I found the only subject of conversation amongst the farmers was the

CATTLE DISEASE

now raging in that country. There are conflicting opinions on the subject of its origin. The foreign cattle dealers insist that the disease is not imported from Russia or elsewhere, but that it is brought on by the cow keepers and milk men of the large towns, whilst the farmers of England are as positive that it is an imported disease, and that it spreads from cattle shipped from the continent to supply the beef market. This last opinion appears to be the most probable, as there are so many authenticated cases of imported cattle being in a diseased state when landed in England. It would therefore be well to warn the farmers of the United States not to import any stock at present for breeding purposes; and it may be as well to observe also that sheep are said to be capable of carrying and disseminating the disease among cattle if they have been kept in the same field, although they themselves are not liable to be attacked by the "Rinderpest," as the Germans term it. Should any animals be imported to America now, they ought to be quarantined till it is certain they are in perfectly good health and will not spread the disease.

"Long and loud are the complaints of Brother John about this cattle sickness. Without beef an Englishman is much like a steamship at sea without boiler and engine. John Bull and roast beef have been inseparable companions so long, I do not see how the one could exist without the other. I will, on my return to England, make all the inquiries I can about this disease and communicate my information to the Department. From what I have already learned it seems to me in many respects similar to the cattle complaint prevalent in Florida and Georgia several years ago. * * * It has been stated that in one particular instance the cattle fed in a field where there were two springs of water, one impregnated with carbonic acid and the other with iron and they were not attacked by the disease, although it was very destructive all about the neighborhood. Iron alone in the water, it is said by some, is an antidote to the disease. These, however, are mere newspaper items, and I give them for what they are worth.

PASSPORTS IN EUROPE

"For the benefit of the American traveling public I must mention that the authorities at Dieppe demanded my passport and would not let me pass without showing it, although I was informed in Washington that it was unnecessary for an American citizen to show, or even carry a passport when in Europe—that if they took one it was a mere matter of form; not a necessity. Mr. L., who was with me, a naturalized American citizen, was also treated in the same manner; we two alone, being selected out of a whole packet load of passengers. Accordingly we had to get our trunks from the crowded baggage wagon, open them to the gaze of an admiring but not sympathizing mob of spectators, and go through the ceremonies of having them examined in a small dark room by an official who was no doubt just as wise before looking at them as he was after the farce of reading the description of our personal appearance, height, age, teeth, etc. etc., and comparing our official written photographs with our own humble selves in 'propri persona.' When speaking of these occurrences at Mr. Bigelow's office (Mr. B. being out of town,) an attaché informed me that such things occur very seldom, but that all American citizens ought to be provided with passports when traveling in Europe, as they are liable to be stopped and examined whenever an officer feels particularly interested in any individual of peculiarly prepossessing appearance, as no doubt he did in my case. Englishmen, dogs and horses, however, require no pass in France.

"THE EXPOSITION

of useful and injurious insects in the Industrial Palace is not as large or as general as I expected to find it, although for a first attempt it is highly creditable to the managers. The exposition is held in a very large glass-roofed hall. Beginning our tour of inspection, on the left hand, arranged on long tables we find a variety of books and pamphlets on insects injurious to crops, on bee culture, silk worms, etc. Then come specimens of the *Pyrethrum roseum* and *P. 'reigidium'* growing in pots, and all the various powders and preparations made from these plants, and which are sold by our druggists as 'Persian insect powder,' 'Lyons powders,' etc. *Pyrethrum reigilium* I did not recognize, and shall endeavor to procure seeds in order to try it in our Department gardens, to prove if it is such a certain death to insects as the venders of the powder profess it to be. The dust or powdered particles of the flower is blown upon insects by means of variously constructed bellows and other machines, samples of which form a part of this exhibition. Fly paper for poisoning flies, instruments for the destruction of insects, such as circular stiff brushes for brushing bark lice, etc., from branches of fruit trees, and scrapers for the bark are also exhibited. We then come to some very large specimens of wood injured by larvae of

WOOD AND BARK-EATING INSECTS,

such as *hylesinus, scolytus,* and *cassus;* also branches and leaves eaten by the tortrix and other leaf-eating insects. Mr. B. Gehin exhibits notes on insects and 22 small glass covered boxes containing specimens of the root, wood and leaf attacked, with the insect causing the injury. Mr. Macquerye has a very fine collection of 13 large glass covered cases containing European destructive insects, and a short description of injury, etc., written legibly on one side. This plan is most excellent, and should be adopted in every State agricultural collection; it would disseminate the knowledge of agricultural entomology better than any other plan I can think of, and at the same time cost very little money. Mr. Dillon shows six cases of insects, leaves, etc., much upon the same plan. We then come to more large specimens of wood from the Museum of Natural History, injured by insects, and also specimens of grain, skins and vegetables in the same state. Large galls, or wellings produced by the *Myoxylus mali,* or *'puceron lanigere,'* on the apple wood; nests of various wood-eating ants, such as *Formica fusca,* and others; nests of caterpillars, cocoons of *'Lapryrus ciecae,'* or pine saw-fly, and larvae of the *galleria cerealella,* or hive wax-moth. Large pillars of wood, registers or documents of Rochelle, eaten and destroyed by the *Termes lucifugum,* a species of white ant, also here exhibited, are very interesting, as showing the destructive powers of these small and apparently insignificant insects.

AN AMERICAN LOBSTER

"At the end of the hall are exhibited specimens of edible crabs, lobsters, etc., amongst which a mammoth specimen of our American lobster figures conspicuously; but why these crustacrae are put among the real insects I cannot imagine, and must own that to me they appear somewhat out of place in a purely entomological collection.

BEE HIVES

of wood and straw, covers for hives, with all the apparatus for making straw hives, fill up the rest of the space at the end of the hall. The best hive in the exhibition is a wooden one made by M. E. Thierry Meig, having parallel square frames on which the bees form their comb, fitting on a ledge inside; these frames, with comb and honey, can be withdrawn at will without disturbing the hive; but as I have seen many in the United States upon the same plan, I need not here describe it more fully; all I can say in regard to this department is, that I was very much disappointed with the display of hives, and should there be another entomological and agricultural exhibition here, I think our American bee culturists would do well to send over some of their best patent hives to show what Yankee ingenuity can accomplish.

"The right-hand side of the hall is also filled up with more hives, feeding troughs, fumigators, gauze wire face protectors or helmets, leather gauntlets, scrapers, a species of puff ball '*Lyooperdon,*' (the smoke of which is used to stupefy the bees when the honey is being taken out,) sweetmeats, bonbons, gingerbread, hydromel and various other solid and liquid preparations from honey, liquid wax for painting, wax candles, Italian and common bees in glass hives, and all such things as belongs to the culture of bees in general.

THE SILK INTEREST

"The entire of the room is mostly devoted to silk culture. Here may be seen specimens of eggs, worms, cocoons, moths, and silk of all varieties. The ailanthus silk worm is here in all the different stages of its existence, depositing its eggs, feeding as caterpillars on leaves of the ailanthus, spinning its cocoon amongst the foliage, or fluttering by hundreds in the moth state in large gauze-covered boxes. * * * Amongst the crowd of strange moths I was much pleased to recognize two old American acquaintances I have often met in the woods and fields of Maryland— namely *Attacas Coeropia* and *a. Polyphemus;* and I must do them the justice to say that they appeared as well, and perhaps will in the end prove quite as useful, as any of their foreign, and therefore more highly prized brethren. On another table was exhibited a nest of processionary caterpillars from Madagascar. * * *

"Some of the common silk worms, preserved in alcohol or some other preparation, were of the most gigantic size—perhaps being swollen by the liquid. A very large case containing cocoons of common silk worms, injured by the silk worm disease, is most interesting. This case is exhibited by Eugene Brocke & Son, and is labeled 'price 5,000 fr.!!' Some of the cocoons measure at least two inches in length, and many are as large as a good sized pigeon's egg.

"Whilst on the subject of the ailanthus silk-worm, I ought to have noticed that there is a large specimen of the wood of this much abused and not fragrant tree in the Exposition, to which a label is attached with an inscription giving its tenacity and density in comparison with elm and oak, and which, if correct, may turn the tide of popular favor, and raise the reputation of the present much despised ailanthus. The results of experiments on three sorts of wood show that the ailanthus ranks No. 1 in tenacity, and No. 2 in density; the elm No. 2 in tenacity, and No. 3 in density; the oak No. 3 in tenacity, and No. 1 in density. It is also stated that the ailanthus is very good for fuel.

"THE IDEA OF SUCH AN EXPOSITION

As this was excellent, and had it been carried out more fully would have been invaluable to the farmer as a means of identifying *all* his insect loss. To be really useful, however, such an exhibition ought to be *permanent to some public building and free to the public.* It should likewise be duplicated for various States and climates, and form a perfect object library of reference for farmers desiring information on the subject of entomology as connected with agriculture. In our country there would be no occasion to have a large, general and expensive collection of insects of all sorts, but merely a selection of such as are really injurious or beneficial, and with references to the valuable works of Drs. Harris and Fitch.
* * * * * * *

"In my next letter I hope to give you some information about the garden of acclimation, and furnish more notes on insects. I send you 'Galignani's Messenger' and 'Cosmos,' in both of which you will find notices of the Exposition. The French article is very flattering to our Department, but is somewhat incorrect in some particulars, which cannot be helped, as I have to convey information to them in my wretched French or in English to those who do not understand our language fully."

I will keep you informed on such topics of interest to the public as may be hereafter received from Mr. Glover.

L.

September 28, 1865, page 4

Letter from Washington
THE CAPITAL ENTOMOLOGICALLY CONSIDERED

From Our Own Correspondent
Washington, September 22, 1865

It was Mrs. Partington, I think, who was so disgusted at the idea of the "Diet of Worms." It will be well for her and other squeamishly inclined old ladies not to visit Washington just now. Worms, or caterpillars, are holding high carnival here during this month, and are assisted in their festivities by multitudes of creadae, grasshoppers, and others of the grylidae, whose saltatorial performances are apparently highly enjoyed by the ministerial Soothsayers or Mantes, and their solemn cousins, the Phasmidae or Walkingsticks.

Caterpillars, silver-gray, black, brown, yellow, and indeed nearly every variety known among the Lepidoptera, are disporting themselves at the Capital in advance of the gay season, more especially appropriated by the genus homo. They run races on the pavement, attach themselves to floating crinoline, take liberties with every style of ankle, or hang from the tree branches, dangling by their silken threads in the sunshine to the terror and disgust of nervous ladies, who are obliged to pass under them. They drop in velvety coils among costly flowers and laces, surmounting expansive and expensive waterfalls, stretch themselves lazily out to feed, and finding that leaves and flowers of verdigris green and Prussian blue, are not to their taste, go wriggling down the dangerous descent among meshes and folds of loosely hung laces towards recesses sacred from entomological research; or slip into silken folds, where they lie in wait to be sat upon and crushed, to the horror of the wearer and the ruin of the raiment. The silver-grays are particularly destructive to the foliage of poplar, sycamore and other shade trees that line the streets, stripping from them every vestige of green so that many of them stand as bare of foliage as in midwinter.

The grasshoppers seem to be very generally turning their attention to the pursuits of civilized life. They may be seen with their sorrowful faces and inquisitive antennae exploring every department of the household, from the pantry shelves and kitchen mantelpiece to the parlor what-not and the mysteries of bedroom drapery. They sit in the windows of an evening, after the manner of pretty young ladies across the way, and tune their chirping taborets in blissful unconsciousness of the jarring discords; they climb up the library folios and puzzle their comical heads with the wonders of science, or plunge among cradle treasures to study that mystic phase of human existence. Some of them have taken to theology, attend church, and sit demurely attentive on the brethren's shoulders and the sisters' bonnets. I saw one last Sabbath perched on the petals of a yellow muslin rose just above an immense waterfall all glittering with crystal drops and spangles. At first he seemed all attention to the discourse, but finding in its exclusive orthodoxy no room for the free play of the faculties his Maker gave him, he presently became absorbed in the pomps and vanities by which he was surrounded, like many another disheartened sinner before him, (and one behind him!) When the charms of the yellow rose were exhausted he went plunging into flashing poppies, indigo lilacs, erubescent lilies, and kindred depths of dissipation till the preacher's allotted time of grace was past, and the doxology was being sung; then, in the effort to regain his first estate, his feet tripped on a grass green grape and he came down on the waterfall, where one of his legs caught in the meshes of the enclosing net and he was borne ignominiously dangling, head downwards, from the scene of his sacrilegious trifling. So, through the hardness of the doctrine preached, that grasshopper's last estate was worse than the first.

The Mantes and Phasmidae or Walkingsticks belong to a class of insect monsters unknown in your northern climate. The spectral Walkingsticks look like nothing so much as dead twigs when at rest, and when moving about in their sluggish manner give one a disagreeable feeling as of looking at some dead thing trying to come to life. They are of a dull ash-gray color, with slender bodies from two to three inches in length, and long, spangling legs, thin as threads, on which their wiry bodies are borne high from the ground, so that they seem rightly named Specters, Phasmidae, etc., and like ghostly things in general are very unpleasant for the human eye to dwell upon.

The Mantes sustain about the same relation to the Spectres in regard to personal appearance, as aldermen are supposed to sustain to ordinary human beings. The general outline of the one, enlarged as to circumference in certain regions, and with the addition of official length of coat-tails in the form of wings of a gray-green tint, will answer very well for the other. Add to this that the Mantes have a hinge in the spine by which they are enabled to adapt themselves to circumstances, diplomatically speaking, and the functional correspondence may be more complete. Rearhorse is the common name for these creatures here. I never say anything in animal or insect life so grotesquely and hideously human in gesture and expression as they are. I use the word expression advisedly; there are many human countenances with less of it than is to be seen in the little triangular faces of these insects, with their wide, flat foreheads, prominent eyes and suggestive mouths. They will rear up at you by means of the aforesaid hinge, fold their long, spiny arms akimbo, turn their three-cornered heads wedgewise, lick their jaws, and roll their wicked, round eyes as if daring you to come on and be swallowed without further ceremony. They have a weird, half-human look, that the Scotch would call "uncanny." Being predaceous, and belligerently inclined, they afford much amusement to boys and idlers at street corners, where they are pitted against each other and fight desperately. They devour other insects, and in lack of them, fall upon and eat their own family and kinfolk. So they are classed among the benefactors of the human race for reasons which may bear out the aldermanic comparison still further. They likewise have great respect for religious observances, and spend much of their time in devotional attitudes thus acquiring the common name of "praying Mantis," a misnomer, doubtless for *preying* manthis. The drop upon you from the tree branches, rear up at you from the pavements, say their Pharisaical prayers on your doorsteps, get free rides down the avenue on your unsuspecting shoulders, or perform their grotesque antics on the apex of the bonnet or hat covering our unconscious head. Your neighbor may be laughing in his sleeve at your expense, but you have the consolation of knowing that he is just as liable to have his unseemly mirth capped by the same fearful climax.

The mosquitoes are too well known as universal evils to require words wasted on them here, further than to say that like all great national evils they seem to calumniate at the Capital, living to a very advanced age, attaining an enormous size, and developing their voracious powers to an extraordinary degree. This year a good many have come up from the South, on parole probably, and they are so giant and withal so tough that it is doubtful if the frost can hit them, or harm them if it should. So it is very likely that the Government will have them to winter over.

L.

October 7, 1865, page 4

Letter from Washington

THE STREETS AS THEY WERE AND ARE | OLD RESIDENT | ENTERPRISE AND ITS DOINGS | PUBLIC IMPROVEMENTS | PET INSTITUTIONS

Washington, October 2, 1865

Less than five years ago there was not a street car in Washington, not a foot of track, or ground broken for one—only the lumbering old omnibus to convey passengers to and from the depot, or strangers about the city; but that seemed all-sufficient for the needs of the Capital as it was, and the inhabitants thereof were content. When the war came new necessities sprung up. A new set of people filled the sleepy old place. They had husbands, brothers, sons, and friends in the armies encamped on the surrounding heights and in the hospitals stretched along the distant suburbs. Facilities were demanded for reaching them, and the Avenue and Seventh Street railroads were constructed, but amidst prophetic head-shakings and cautionings of the wise and prudent, who, judging the future by the past, saw only a lack of wisdom and waste of funds in the enterprise. Even less than two years ago, an old resident, and one shrewd enough in business to have known better, asserted that the moment the war was ended there would not be travel enough on these lines to sustain them a week, and that within a month thereafter the cars might be turned into kindling wood, as the rails would be torn up and sold for old iron.

That very "resident" has lived to see the end of the war, but no such consequences as those predicted. On the contrary, there is another extensive line of track laid, and cars are running every five minutes past his own door, through a street handsomely graded and paved, but which six months since was a veritable "Slough of Despond," with its sidelong wagon ruts and bottomless clay mire holes. Now, instead of forebodings for the future, one hears only lamentations for short-sightedess in the past. If they could only have known that real estate would be worth anything when the war was over, how many of these faithless croakers might have made themselves millionaires! They had money, but no confidence, and so did not invest, and can now only look on with astonished and rueful faces at the enormously increased value of real estate and dwellings which but a little while ago were offered for a song and went a-begging for purchasers.

"I would as soon have my son put his money in the fire as invest it in Washington," said a shrewd and careful parent in 1863; today both parent and son are groaning over the high rents they have to pay, and wishing the prices of lots and houses were within their reach once more.

Everywhere about the city improvements are going on. Private enterprise seems wide awake, and is reaping rich rewards for all its outlays of energy and expense. It is not enterprise indigenous to this soil and climate, however. The race that existed here before the war had no such stirring word in its dictionary. That race dozed away summer after summer in supreme content with the low, dingy old dwellings inherited from their ancestors, and built as no dwellings in modern civilized communities are, with the back kitchen doors in front, and the staircases all turned into the streets. Pennsylvania avenue they had paved, because, being a morass naturally, and the only way of passage between the Capitol and the White House, it was found necessary to secure so much of a permanent footing for the Government. The other streets served the pigs better without paving, and the people too, for that matter, as it saved the expense both of first cost and repairs.

The new elements, first drawn and driven here by force, are gathering strength, obliterating the old landmarks, and ushering in a new dispensation for the Capital. One can scarcely turn a corner or pass a square in the city where building or repairing of some sort is not in progress. Piles of brick and beds of mortar are characteristic features of the streets, and pits and dead-falls in the form of cellar holes and scaffoldings everywhere beset the sidewalks. It is anticipated that the crowds of visitors to this city during the coming winter will be unprecedented, and everybody who can is building on an additional room or two to rent; but aside from these, handsome blocks and dwellings are filling up hitherto vacant lots or taking the place of shanties and rubbish that late were a part of Washington.

The public buildings are also in process of completion and renovation; the two operations going on at the same time, as parts of them are so old as to be in need of repairs while other portions are still unfinished. Workmen are busy at the Capitol tearing out partitions for the enlargement of the Congressional library; the Senate chamber and Representatives' Hall with their suites of anterooms are also undergoing repairs, cleansing, and repairing for reception of their winter occupants. At the Patent Office, the great north hall, where the Sanitary and Soldiers' Fair was held two years ago, has been finished, except the frescoes on the paneled ceiling, and is fitted up with double rows of glass cases along the floor and galleries, for the reception of models from the overcrowded cases in the other halls. The north front is also being completed; the masses of brick and stone, and unsightly blocks of marble so long lying about the street in that vicinity, are growing into shape and beauty, and fast taking their places as part of the noble edifice. The south and east fronts, meanwhile, had become so dingy with age and weather stains, that for decency's sake it was found necessary to apply the paint brush, and they are now gleaming white and pure in the light of these splendid October days and dazzling moonlit nights. Work on the Treasury building is also in progress, and the prospect is that some future generation may yet rise up and pronounce all these splendid structures finished.

But there is one subject, a great source of complaint from strangers, one of inspiration inexhaustible from newspaper locals, which Washington enterprise evidently don't intend to meddle with, and that is the street gutters. Now since the abolition of slavery, the street gutter is the peculiar and pet institution of the city. Doubtless if some daring innovator should arise and attempt reform, he would be met by the unbottled wrath and indignation of those who have so long nursed and smelled this institution, and been preserved from the horrors of asphyxia by the exhalations thereof.

The Washington gutter system is nothing to be ashamed of and hidden under ground; it is all above aboard, patent to the eye of the world, and to its nostrils also. Down every street, and checkering every pavement, the green-tinged waters go flowing all abroad through the length and breadth of the city, dispensing their pungent perfumes gratis to citizens and strangers alike. Mondays are especially distinguished by the overflowing of these sluices from the outpourings of washtubs, bathtubs, slop-buckets, etc.; and as washings of this sort are said to be conducive to the health and vigor of grape and pumpkin vines, so it may be that to the same cause this goodly town may attribute its excellent sanitary condition. Fainting is an obsolete word here; ladies don't know how it is done; they never have the trouble of carrying smelling bottles in their pockets, and all on account of the abundance of free ammonia everywhere exhaling from the gutters. Perfumers generally find their business a losing one, owing to the high taxes and small sales; it is said they are going to get up a petition, asking Congress to tax the street smells, so as to put down monopoly and equalize matters; in which case smelling salts in vinaigrette may come in fashion again.

L.

October 12, 1865, page 4

Letter from Washington

THE ENTOMOLOGICAL EXHIBITION IN PARIS AWARD THE GOLD MEDAL TO AN AMERICAN ARTIST | HOW OUR INSTITUTIONS ARE APPRECIATED ABROAD

From Our Own Correspondent
Washington, October 6, 1865

A long and interesting letter has just been received by the Department of Agriculture from Mr. Glover, now in Paris. The entomological exhibition did not close till the 18th September, when it was publicly announced at the distribution of prizes that the highest honor, the "Grande Medaille d'or de S. M. L'Empereur," or the gold medal offered by his Majesty, the Emperor, was awarded to "Townsend Glover, of Washington, U.S.A. for his work on the Insects of America."

This is a recognition of genius and an award of honor highly merited by the recipient thereof, and one which it is to be hoped will be appreciated in this country, and lead our own people to properly esteem the value of Mr. Glover's entomological labors. The plates he exhibited there are duplicates of those which cover the walls of the Agricultural Museum here, and which are daily consulted by visitors to identify their insect enemies, study their habits, and acquaint themselves with the methods of exterminating them. A work with those illustrations and accompanying text, published by Government and distributed as Patent Office reports are, would do for the agriculture of the country more even than those Reports have done for its mechanical development. This will be realized some day, but the appreciation seems very likely to come through "foreign intervention."

An extract from a French paper accompanies Mr. Glover's letter, in which it is stated that the Department of Washington has done great service to the cause of agriculture by having so able a representative at that Exposition; and that the explanation of the system adopted by the Department in reference to its cabinet collection has incited Parisian savans to institute a similar system of agricultural instruction. When the press of our own country, professing to labor for the interests of the farmer, can afford to lay aside groundless prejudices and seed-store partisanship, there will be a truer understanding and appreciation of the good that has already been done by this much-abused and neglected Department, and with a better understanding will come a desire to assist it in the struggle for existence, instead of trying to crush it for the gratification of some petty spite. At present it seems that personalities rule, and the institution must suffer, its influence be depreciated, and the good it has done and is doing be ignored, or worse, misrepresented, to serve individual interests.

Mr. Glover gives a very lengthy and entertaining description of his visit to the Gardens of Acclimatation for animals, birds and domestic fowls. His letter will probably be published entire in the next monthly report of the Department. After the conclusion of the exhibition he left the continent for England, where he will remain two or three weeks, and return to this country early in November. He will be warmly welcomed by his many friends who are now rejoicing at his success and the high honor he has achieved, for himself, for the Department, and for the cause to which he has devoted his life-long labors.

L.

October 19, 1865, page 4

Our Washington Letter

Letter from our Entomologist in Paris | American Feeling and French Appreciation | Notes on the Exhibition | The Old Peanut State | An Oily Suggestion

From Our Own Correspondent
Washington, October 13, 1865

Commissioner Newton has received another letter from Prof. Glover, the entomologist, from which I make a few extracts that may be of interest to the general reader. He writes from Paris under date of Sept. 27, and says in regard to the feeling among American residents there: "Our Minister, Mr. Bigelow, and all the Americans I have seen in Paris appear to be very much pleased that America has come in 'first' in the 'exposition of insects, etc.' I send you several French papers which speak very flatteringly of its utility and efficiency; so that I may hope that my time has not been lost, and that I have done what was desired and expected of me, that is, to show to other nations that although our country has been desolated by war, agriculture has not been neglected. Also that with the Government its interests have been gaining in vigor and efficacy, as even during the war what was once only a dependent bureau of the Patent Office, has been raised to a separate and independent Department, which rank it now holds."

The idea of an agricultural and economic museum, such as Mr. Glover has been engaged in organizing in the Department here during the year past, seems to be highly appreciated by the French naturalists, entomologists, etc., who have not only resolved to adopt the same plan in connection with their own agricultural societies, but will do all in their power to assist him in building up this by valuable donations, and by a system of exchange or interchange of such articles as may be desired to perfect the plan. M. Geurin Menevile has for this purpose presented Mr. Glover with some fine specimens of silk, cocoons, etc.; and Messrs. Vilmorin, Andrieux, & Co. have contributed for the Museum the engravings of the "Album Vilmorin," and for the gardens and greenhouses of the Department packages of the choicest flower and other seeds. "These gentlemen," says Mr. G., "have the highest reputation in France for their flower seeds, and have selected for us only the very best, in order to keep up their reputation in the States, and to show what really good flowers are."

From these seeds others will be raised here and distributed to florists throughout the country.

INSECT POWDERS

Mr. Glover has also procured for propagation the seeds of the true "Pyrethrum," the plant from which the celebrated insect powders are made. He remarks: "I have endeavored to get all the information possible on this subject; and I find that if the dried fresh *flowers* alone are used, and the air excluded from the bottles in which the powder is preserved, the fine dust is a powerful insect destroyer. It is blown and scattered upon the insects by means of a bellows and other instruments made for the purpose, samples of which I shall bring with me. The powder of the flower is at present so much adulterated with the stock and leaf that nine times out of ten the insect powders we get from the shops are of very little value. In the exposition there were several varieties of this plant, of all of which I procured seeds, and hope to be able to experiment and report on their efficacy another year."

MR. LAVERRIER AND SILK RAISING

"M. Jules Laverrier called upon me yesterday. He is, or is about to be, appointed Secretary to the Central Agricultural Society of France, and will be a most useful auxiliary to our Department. He approves highly of the plan of our Museum, and is so much pleased with it that he says he will endeavor to establish one on the same principle in France, and if successful promises to exchange specimens of French grains and other productions for our American kinds.

M. Laverrier has spent several years in Mexico, and wishes to induce Americans to commence the silk culture in that country, which he says is specially adapted to it, both in climate and comparative dryness of the seasons. The inhabitants, he states, are particularly fitted for rearing the silk worm, as their whole attention has been hitherto given to the cochineal insect, which now is of comparatively little value. So many substitutes have been discovered for that valuable dye, the price of cochineal is at present so unremunerative as to almost put a stop to their culture.

"I see by the Lyons papers that complaints are made about Americans taking away their best workmen, in order to commence silk manufacture in the States. If so, perhaps it may prove a good thing for our Southern sisters, if the inevitable and ubiquitous negro can be taught to rear and take care of silkworms. The climate of the Southern States is most favorable to their cultivation, and the *morus multicanius* once planted there grows and flourishes to the greatest luxuriance. The season is also so much longer than in Europe, several crops of worms might be produced in one year. If, however, an effort should be made to carry on this business to any extent in the States, extreme caution should be used in procuring seed or eggs, not to import any from Europe, without being perfectly sure that they come from a healthy stock, as in Italy and elsewhere the silkworms are dying by millions from a peculiar disease, which by many has been attributed to a fungoid origin.

THE COLONIAL MUSEUM

"I visited the permanent exhibition of Algeria and the Colonies, in the Industrial Palace, and was exceedingly pleased with the system and arrangement of the Museum. It approaches nearer than anything I have yet seen to what we are endeavoring to accomplish in our own infant cabinet, and shows what can be done for the public if we are allowed by Congressmen to go on with the useful work we have commenced. In a museum like this not only the farmer, but the manufacturer, the druggist, and indeed almost any man, no matter what his trade or profession, can always learn something new and useful in his business, and frequently find to his astonishment that things he has hitherto looked upon as weeds or mere cumbers of the ground, by science and industry can be made a source of great profit, both to himself and his country. Although the name was attached to each object, I missed our system of references to the different or best works in which a fully detailed account is given of the plant, or seed, or mode of manufacture. In the first place the specimens are divided into series, and secondly with sections, so that any object may be found by referring to the number of the section and series, these being conspicuously printed in golden letters over each glass case."

Here follow tables of the classifications, and a detailed description of the various objects of interest therein. Speaking of the oils, he says: "The oil from our common peanut was extremely fine and clear. A great many of the ground nuts are now imported into France from Algeria, but in former times tons of them were shipped from the Southern States, especially from North Carolina, the oil pressed out and refined in France, and then returned to us, and frequently sold as pure olive oil! If there were more enterprise in the South, a very large business could be done in the oil of peanuts."

Cannot some enterprising Yankee go down on this idea, and lubricate the machinery of the old Peanut State, so as to bring her into running Union order again? So that they "strike oil," what does it matter whether it be peanut or petroleum?

L.

October 26, 1865, page 4

Letter from Washington

How the Carpet-Knights Did in War Times | The Men Who Have Taken Their Places | What They Are and What They May Be | President Johnson's Policy

From Our Own Correspondent
Washington, October 19, 1865

Reconstruction rebels are about as plenty here now as the "carpet-knights," shoulder-strapped, and sometimes otherwise strapped gentry were a few months ago. In the times of war Washingtonians could pretty generally tell when the army was on the eve of a great battle, by the glitter of gilded bands and buttons, and the prodigal display of white-gloved and dainty-livered officials on the hotel steps and about the public buildings. Unlike the times of which Campbell wrote, "coming events" in our day cast their shadows behind, instead of before; it was the substance of the army that went into action; the bone, and nerve, and sinew, animated by patriotism and principle; and it was the shadows who said one to another, "Behold now, if we go up to do battle against this people we shall receive hurt, some by the spear and some by the edge of the sword, and some by the mighty engines of war, whose roaring is very terrible; now therefore let us go up to the chief city, where abide the elders and rulers of the land, and say unto them, 'It is nothing; behold our enemies, the Confederates, will not fight, and we thy servants have come up hither that we may not be a burden and a tax upon our brethren in the field, to eat of their substance and consume their provender.'"

So they made haste and got themselves up to the chief city, and said as they had agreed; and they felt that it was good to be in a safe place; and they stood at the street corners, and sat in public places, and by reason of their goodly raiment they found favor in the eyes of the damsels of the city, and were taken into their houses and made merry with them, saying, "Of the greenbacks which Uncle Sam shall give us for his mark upon our shoulders, each man according to the degree of his value in his own eyes, shall ye not also receive a share, for that ye have taken us in, and your houses have sheltered us, and we are not this day on the field of battle where the whiteness of our gloves would be tarnished with dust, and the smoke of brimstone offend our nostrils."

And they tarried long, and were upon the streets as the frogs of Egypt for multitude. And when the battle was ended, if it were in favor of the enemy, they said, "See, now, it is because they called us not to put us at the head of the hosts." And if it were otherwise they said, "Behold, the victory is ours; let us take unto ourselves the glory, for how should our hosts have triumphed if they had not been men made like unto us, breathing the same air which we also breathe."

Ah, well! those were palmy days for tinsel soldiery. But the soulless ephemeral have fluttered away their little life and gone. May the streets of the Capitol know them no more forever.

But these strange characters hitherto unknown in history, who have taken their places, these quasi-loyalists, these treason-made nondescripts who boast of manliness, and fight against humanity, these aristocrats of physical despotism and plebeians in intellect, these sturdy labor-haters who have wrestled with fate and find themselves worsted, what is to be the result of their pilgrimage to the political Mecca? what its effect upon themselves, upon the Capital, and upon the country, when they shall return, pardoned? They, for the most part at least, have nothing of the ephemeral nature about them. Great, strong-handed, backwoods-looking men, burly and brusque, they seem as if bound to be victorious in any other contest than the wicked, unnatural one in which they have been engaged. With intellect in proportion to their physical girth they might conquer anything short of destroy; or, taking truth and right for their inspiration and allies, they might compel fate and mold destiny to their will. But they are not ready for any such work yet. Work! they hate the very word, and will oppose that most stubborn and unyielding of all fronts, prejudice, to the progress of the times as resolutely as they opposed with their physical force the onward march of Northern arms. And the result will be the same in the end, though they shut their eyes to it now. In another generation, perhaps sooner, they will be deploring the forfeiture of estates of higher value than the acres of corn and cotton lands for which they are bending unwilling knees to Andrew Johnson today.

The *hegira* hither of these men, singly and in crowds, as they are daily coming, will be one means by which their eyes will be opened to the new order of things their wicked attempt to overthrow the Government has brought about. If they do not see and accept the good that is being brought out of evil, the light that is coming out of darkness, it is because they will not, and it will be left for their children to see when they shall come to read the history of these times. One good result of their compulsory visit they cannot avoid, and that is the knowledge they gain of the world outside the limits of their own plantations, and of a race of beings unconnected with "nigger-drivers," slave gangs, and overseers. Hundreds of them have never known any other world, or had any nearer contact with humanity. These were the elements, stubborn and fearless through their very ignorance, on which the leaders of the rebellion relied for success. The open-mouthed astonishment with which they explore this to them new-found world, with its unimagined wonders and phases of existence as strange as if they belonged to another planet, can only be equaled by the surprise with which their whilom political leaders and old habitués of the place witness its growing thrift and prosperity, as compared with what it was when they held the reins of government and blocked the wheels of enterprise with the chief cornerstone of their political heresy. President Johnson could not have devised a more effective lesson initiatory of Southern civilization, than that they have learned by being forced out of their old treadmill routine and thrown in contact with the principles of free labor struggling vigorously for the recognition of their birthright at the Capitol of the nation. The next best thing he could do for them would be to require that, as a preparation meet for his Executive grace, they spend at least one month among the working classes, the well-to-do farmers and mechanics of each of the Northern, Middle and Western States. Free labor, after that, might have a different signification to them from what it does now.

Yesterday three or four of these sturdy penitents, shaggy, bronzed six-footers, each with a cheek full of tobacco, and with hands thrust deep down as ever a Yankee's could get into the pockets of their butternut brown trousers, while exploring some industrial department of the Patent office, were heard deprecating the necessity of labor now threatening themselves and their families.

"It's what I never reckoned would happen in my days," said one, "to have our women doing the work in the place of niggers. But some women, Yankees I reckon, has done all these yer silks and carpets and gowns and things, and it looks like our turn is coming."

"I reckon they'll have to come to worse things than these yet," said another. "Heaps on 'em wont have a nigger to tote the baby or pack a bucket of water—"

"Yes," interrupted a third, "and what's more, we wont git no pity from nobody nuther. I cared more about keeping slaves on' count the women than anything else. I want my wife and children to look at, and not to be made niggers of—blast the war! it's knocked things end-ways; and it looks mightily like the niggers is coming out game in the end—leastways we've lost 'em."

"Yes; but I reckon we'll make a life of it yet, if we get a-goin' wonst; looks like they do here in the old Federal city, enyhow! *and I reckon what they can do in this District we can do in Middle Tennessee,* said the first speaker, with something of triumph in his tone, as they passed out of hearing. That man when he gets back to Tennessee will be a new lump of leaven in the old meal tub. There will be hundreds like him from every State in Dixie, and so by the contagion of ideas and by the pride of the race, the South will be regenerated and redeemed.

The presence of these representative middle men proves better than anything else could do the wisdom of the President's lenient policy towards them, and, hard as the more radical politicians find it to smother the wrath and righteous indignation they have nursed so long, they must in honesty acknowledge that it will be better by gentle measures to mold these rough materials into men, to call out what manhood there may be in their natures, than by revenge, retaliation, or oppression to make them still more animal than they are. I believe our President understands himself, and in doing so he understands the men with whom he is dealing. He knows that upon these men and upon their children, in common with corresponding classes in the Northern States, the future destiny of our country rests; and history can point to no spectacle more sublime that they which Andrew Johnson offers to the world today, standing as he does above all party factions on the broad platform of human rights, at once a mediator, and an example, saying to over zealous friends, "You know not what you ask"; and to those who were as he once was, "Come up higher."
L.

November 16, 1865, page 4

Our Washington Letter

THE GREAT MICHIGAN CABBAGE, AND WHAT CAME OF IT

From Our Own Correspondent
Washington, November 10, 1865

A few weeks ago the Department of Agriculture was astonished by the advent in its midst of a handsome present in the shape of an enormous cabbage from Michigan. It was sent to the Department by the Hon. J. F. Driggs of the Saginaw District, by whom it was raised from seed obtained here last spring. The weight of this monstrous cabbage head was *thirty pounds,* and it just filled the half-barrel plump full!

Notice of its arrival and dimensions was duly given in the city papers, and never did elephant at a circus, or "star" at a theater draw more crowded houses than did this kingly comer from the Northern Peninsula. It was duly installed in the Museum, and held levees and receptions day after day (Sundays excepted,) for more than two weeks. Hour by hour admiring crowds came and made obeisance to it, and touched it, and spoke appreciating words, and often tasted, just to prove their judgment correct. And so it was, that the more they tasted the greater their admiration grew, and the more they desired to taste. Little by little, and leaf by leaf it seemed vanishing away. Decay, too, came and laid its finger upon it, and the odor thereof began to be diffused abroad, and to offend the nostrils of many. Then it was that your scribe begged of the authorities permission to save it from prolonged decline and an inglorious end; and consent was given.

Now it was that in this city there dwelt a man called James, whose surname was Johnson, and he abode in an upper room, he and his wife with him. And in the same house there was a damsel named Julia, a woman of excellent countenance, and of good repute among all the armies of Uncle Sam for the good deeds she did unto the sick and wounded in the field of battle. The same also did James and his wife, and all three are held in honor of their countrymen and their countrywomen for these things unto this day. And all three were from the land of the great cabbage, as was also your scribe. And it seemed good unto me to deliver the cabbage unto their hands, saying, If ye will now make a savory dinner and invite thy servant, and we will eat and be merry together, and they did so. And the wife of James went out into the market places, and bought of the flesh of fat cattle and of swine, tender and good for food, and of the fruits of the earth each after its kind, and she made a savory dinner, and invited thy servant, and behold there was not room on the table for all that she had made. And we four sat upon chairs at the four sides of the table, and the cabbage was in the midst; and about it were the fruits of the earth and the flesh of cattle, and butter and bread with salt and spices and all things desirable to please the eye and to satisfy the appetite withal. But the cabbage was the crowning glory thereof, and we gave thanks and did eat of it, and of all the good things which the wife of James had set before us, and we were glad in our hearts, making merry and speaking the praises of John, whose surname is Driggs, in that it had entered into his heart to send such a mighty cabbage from the home of our fathers to gladden our hearts in this strange land.

And we said one to another, Behold is not this cabbage like unto a man of pure heart, even the man from whose hands it came? For though outwardly it may bear marks of being of the earth, earthy, yet within it is white as snow, tender, and sweet, full of goodness, and giving freely of its substance to satisfy them that are hungry! And we agreed one with another that it was so, for had we not eaten till we were satisfied? And we rose up and went our ways, praying that his cabbages may never be less.

L.

November 17, 1865, page 4

Our Washington Letter
The Department Clerks and their Would-be Reformers | Where the Wrong Lies

From Our Own Correspondent
Washington, November 11, 1865

I see it stated in your paper a few days since, that the Department clerks were indignant at the extra hour of reform, loafing at their desks and doing no more work in seven hours than formerly in six hours.

It is a mistake to style the "extra hour" a reform. The regular business hours for the Departments are from nine to four; the reduction of one hour, making their working time from nine till three, was only temporary during the heat of summer, and was so understood. The return to the regular hours when the summer heats were over, was a matter of course; and if clerks loaf at their desks in consequence, the inference is that loafing is their forte under whatever regulations they may be.

Work in nearly all the Departments has very much decreased with the return of peace to the country, and hence a corresponding reduction of the clerical force employed has taken place. Many of the ladies heretofore engaged at the Treasury have been discharged, and it is announced that some hundreds more will be out of employment by the first of next month. It is anticipated that there will be a great deal of suffering here this winter, among a very worthy class who have heretofore had work from Government, but will now be obliged to seek other ways of living. This change taking place just as the inclement season is setting in will make it very trying, especially as the salaries allowed to women have been so small that it was impossible for them to lay up anything for the future. A bare living is about all they been able to make in many instances, and some who are widows with dependent families have scarcely done that.

The order of the Secretary of the Interior discharging all women employed in his department, will add much to the distress of that class; and a good deal of feeling seems to be aroused against the Secretary for this act, since it is asserted by many that the rooms are not wanted for "other purposes," but will be immediately filled with soldier clerks who will probably receive double the salaries for doing the same work the women have done. It is hinted by friends of women's rights that if lady clerks were entitled to vote, these thing would not be so. Be that as it may, many most excellent, industrious, and deserving women will be deprived of the means of earning a living, and if they happen not to have friends to aid them, as too many have not, Heaven only knows what will become of them. Washington is so filled with dependent people that it is next to an impossibility for all to get work, and so many hundreds being turned out of employment at this trying season must necessarily make matters worse. It is pitiful even now to see the numbers of needy applicants daily turned away from the doors of the public offices, and still others will continue to flock to the city from all quarters, each hoping they may be more successful than the luckless hundreds whose prayers have been denied.

Mrs. Swisshelm, herself a Government employee, recently published a letter in the *Washington Chronicle,* in which she stated that the employment of women as clerks in the Departments, if not already acknowledged as a failure, was very likely to prove so; and gave as a reason for that belief the habit women have of "dragging the drawing-room" into business places and business hours. That may be very true in regard to a certain class, who, unfortunately for the sex, are too much given to "dragging habits" everywhere. It is well known that there are girls or women employed here whose board per month costs more than they receive in salary. How they live and how they dress in such splendor, as some of them do, is a mystery to the honest plodding ones in the same rooms, who board on half the amount, and find it difficult to save a dollar for luxuries. Their presence in the Department at all is one of the evils necessarily arising from the source through which such appointments are made. It is seldom that the head of a department or a bureau has a choice in the matter of selecting his clerks, especially the female portion. They yield to the pressure from members of Congress, and they in turn are governed by personal considerations or by the wishes of constituents whose influence they desire to secure. As a general thing the fitness of an applicant for the duties to be performed never enters into the calculation. A favorite desires an appointment, and the appointment must be made, leaving the matter of fitness to adjust itself as best may be, so that the salary is secured. Thus many frivolous, inefficient and unworthy persons obtain places, and for their sins curses are showered upon female employees indiscriminately.

Some women, like Mrs. S., being neither young nor pretty themselves, cannot seem to forgive others for being so, and slash right and left among those of their own sex who are lucky or luckless enough, either by taste in dress or beauty of form or feature, to attract a passing glance of admiration from one of the opposite gender. Slipshod in habits by nature, and hopeless and unkempt by practice, youth, beauty, and neatness have all one name to these self-elected critics, and that name is "vanity." In denouncing inefficiency, Mrs. S. uses no discrimination, so far as her own sex is concerned, but rates them all alike, and all of very little account because they differ from herself. She has been trying for three or four years past to reform Washington by writing scolding letters for publication in distant cities; and finding that Washingtonians still went on about as they liked, she made an attempt to get a hearing nearer home. The *Chronicle* ventured to publish one letter berating the unfortunate government clerks who happen to be good looking and wear hoops, and then shut down the gate. The ponderous old *Intelligencer* is too prosaic and conservative for her society, and the twinkling *Star* and twittering *Republican* of too little consequence, so it is whispered that she is about to send to Minnesota for her own press, through which she can talk to these impenitent sinners according the dictates of her own heart, and none can molest or say her nay. She has some ideas of practical good sense, which if enforced by attractive personal example, and without the accompanying termagant spirit seemingly inherent in her nature and inseparable from her name, might be of appreciable weight and influence.

In regard to the matter of purity, integrity and efficiency of Government clerks, it is doubtful if either sex would suffer in comparison with the other; and whether such an assertion is complimentary or otherwise the clerks themselves can best judge. At all events there seems little likelihood of reform while the present system of appointing is adhered to.

L.

November 24, 1865, page 4

Our Washington Letter

Indian Summer and Street Shows | Caprices of Fashion | The Coming of Winter and Its Work

Correspondence of the *Advertiser and Tribune*
Washington, D.C., November 10, 1865

The belles of Washington are in their glory during these splendid Indian summer days. If one wants to be delighted with the sight of brilliant colors, gorgeous dresses, forms that defy nature to imitate them, and faces that make art blush for her own boldness, it is only necessary to take a stroll up and down Pennsylvania avenue, on the fashionable north side, at any time between four and six o'clock in the afternoon. There may be seen all the tints of spring, summer, and autumn blended in brilliant confusion, and nature itself "cropping out," as geologists would say, in all the forms of leaf and flower, and fruit and plumage; only nature never dreamed of such combinations of colors, and such an amalgamation of elements aerial and terrestrial as are there displayed. From "Willard's" to somewhere in the vicinity of Third Street, the spectacle is like a showy and crowded panorama, passing and repassing, ever varied and ever dazzling; that is, when the air is of such tempting softness, and the sunshine so warm and golden as it has been for these two weeks past.

It is one of the glories of this capital that it is in a climate where the people can spend so much time with comfort in the open air. Homes, in our Northern acceptation of the term, there are none in the city, taking it in a general sense; the individual exceptions being too few to be appreciable to the mass. Everybody boards out, or takes in boarders; in either case, in the Washington way of doing such things, precluding the possibility of home comfort. Boarders in fact live mostly upon the street, whether there be rain or shine. They sleep in one house, get their meals in another, and do their work someplace else, and get their washing done where they can; a very scattering sort of existence to make the best of it. For the family circle they are forced to substitute the public promenade, and there they are met by the householders who abolished home and thrust themselves and children into back rooms and attics to give place to lodgers. All are glad when pleasant days give them a chance to pass the leisure after dinner hours outside their prison walls. The pretense of shopping is a good thing, inasmuch as something besides the truth must give color to the necessity for these gay excursions. How little shopping is really done at such times may be judged by a glance at the groups of handsome clerks leisurely lounging over their counters or gazing through the show windows at the living, moving rainbow without. Everybody is looking at everybody else, admiring or criticizing; and so these promenades have come to be a sort of carnival for fashionable display.

Fashion is very capricious here; or at least her devotees are. Coming from all parts of the country, and, indeed, from all parts of the world, all bring their own peculiarities of style, and thus make up a most wonderful conglomerate mass. Here is a lady in light silk and summer shawl, and there one in heavy *moiré* with muff and tippet. One wears the inverted sitz bathtub on her head, with a parlor window curtain for a veil; another rejoices under an immense pheasant-tail plume attached to a morsel of straw called a hat. Birds of all sizes, from an owl to a humming bird, are used as ornaments for the head and placed in front as a sort of balance to the waterfall in the rear. Beetles, butterflies, grasshoppers, and other entomological specimens, cunningly counterfeited, may be seen nestling among the locks and about the brows of dainty ladies, who would scream with fright and very likely faint at sight of the originals. Lizards, serpents, young alligators, etc., are coming into fashion in Paris as ornaments, and will doubtless be adopted here to enhance the charms of American ladies.

But these days of sunshine and outdoor show will soon be over now; these living specimens of natural history will be hived up in their garrets and back rooms, and only come out to exhibit their ornamental counterfeits at receptions, levees, and other festive occasions. The strangers fast crowding into the city warn us that winter and the Congressional season are near at hand. Dwellings for rent are scarce and held at the highest rates; lodging rooms are the same, and board keeps pace in price.

The public buildings have generally undergone thorough renovating and cleaning without and within. Many streets have been newly paved during the summer; and advances have been made in many ways towards a more civilized condition of things than has prevailed for the past few years. It only remains for Congress to follow up the reforms in political matters, to make the Capital of the nation what it should be; but Hercules' task at stable cleaning was a mere play-spell to the job they have in hand this winter. The river of purification needs to be turned through every department of Uncle Sam's household; and let the nation pray that the strength and courage of its servants fail not till the work be done.
L.

December 5, 1865, page 4

Our Washington Letter

VISIT FROM GEN. GRANT'S FATHER | AN EXHIBITION IN PROSPECT

From Our Own Correspondent

JESSE ROOT GRANT

The father of Lieut. Gen. Grant was in town yesterday, and among other public buildings and institutions, visited the Patent Office and the Department of Agriculture. He spent an hour or more in the Museum Rooms, but nearly every moment was taken up in introductions and hand shakings between him and members of the different offices in the building; for notice of his presence spread from room to room, and the heads of Departments and Bureaus hastened to pay their respects to him. Clerks followed their superiors and gathered around in groups looking and listening, while messenger boys filled the door with their anxious faces. It was quite an impromptu levee.

The old gentleman is seventy-two years of age, but hale and hearty looking, the most noticeable indications of his years being his slightly defective hearing. The modesty of his honored son is proverbial, and the bearing of the father proves that it is an inherited trait. He received all the deference paid to him in a quiet, gratified way, but as meekly as if he was accepting alms instead of honors. In speaking of the Lieut. General his voice trembled with emotion as he said, "Whatever may have been the experience of others, I am sure my son can never have reason to say that 'Republics are ungrateful.' In every way that a people could show love and gratitude they have been shown to him, and not only in words and actions, but in substantial awards and in ways as honorable and generous in the nation as they were flattering to him. He says these testimonials of affection are often oppressive to him, as it is mortifying to think that others as worthy or worthier than he may be neglected and forgotten."

Mr. Grant is a strongly-built man, a little stooping in the shoulders, has large and pleasant features, a fresh complexion, close trimmed whiskers slightly mixed with gray, blue eyes, and brown hair in which scarcely a touch of silver can be detected, the top of his head is scarcely bald, but with his hat on and only the dark locks beneath it visible around the fresh, unwrinkled, thoughtful face, he does not look as old as many men do at forty. His affability pleases all, he was quite as ready to shake hands with our pretty little messenger boy who begged to be introduced to him, as he was with his Honor, the Commissioner of Patents, or with the stately Marshal of the District who came to escort him over to the Post Office Department. All honor to the good old man, the father of our nation's hero.

"THE RECONSTRUCTIONIST"

Is the title of Mrs. Swisshelm's new paper that is to be born here next week. The occupant of a glass house is going to amuse herself by throwing stones at those who are lucky enough to have more substantial abiding places. It is supposed by many that the Government will survive the peltings of the ancient dame, and that it will go on its way much as the moon did after the night-long baying of a discontented Snarleyow. She begins her prospectus with the startling paradox that "Liberty has been betrayed by her friends," and proposes to take up arms for the Goddess, to let light into the dark places of Government, and do the thinking for the public generally; all of which she can doubtless better afford time for than people can who are more bound by the old-fashioned ideas of domestic obligations. Having such a leader it is to be presumed that progress and reform will make astonishing strides during the coming winter. The belligerent lady requires some such safety valve as a newspaper under her own control will afford. Brawling women have pretty much the same propensities in these days as they had in the times of Solomon, and delight to exhibit themselves on housetops. In this instance, as in many others, doubtless distance will lend enchantment to the view.

L.

Glossary

Aceldana. A field of bloodshed.

Adams, John (1735–1826). Second president of the United States, 1797–1801.

Apollo. In Greek and Roman mythology, the god of the sun, music, poetry, and manly youth and beauty.

Argus-eyed. Argus, in Greek legend, is a giant with one hundred eyes, hence the meaning is an observant or vigilant person.

Augean Stables. *See* Hercules

Aunt Chloe. Wife of Uncle Tom in Harriet Beecher Stowe's book *Uncle Tom's Cabin*.

Aurora. In Greek mythology the Goddess of Dawn.

Baal. In the Bible, the false god of the Phoenicians, generally associated with greed, pestilence, and evil, and the source of many names for devils.

Babel, Tower of. In the Bible, a great tower by means of which men tried to reach Heaven. God destroyed the tower, and, as punishment, gave mankind different languages to create confusion among them.

Baker, Jacob. Enlisted in Company F, 16th Infantry, January 25, 1864, at Detroit, for three years, age 17. Mustered January 25, 1864. Wounded in action May 4, 1864. Discharged on surgeon's certificate of disability August 3, 1865.

Baldwin, Mrs. A. C. Isabella Churchill Baldwin, wife of Augustus C. Baldwin, member of Congress 1863–65, from Michigan.

Barton, Clara (1821–1912). Founder of the American Red Cross. She organized a volunteer service to aid sick and wounded Civil War soldiers on the field.

Bates, Edward (1793–1869). U.S. attorney general 1860–64.

Bigelow, John (1817–1911). U.S. consul in Paris, 1861–64, and minister to France, 1864–67.

Blair, Montgomery (1813–83). U.S. postmaster general from Kentucky, 1861–64.

Bloomer. A costume was named for Amelia Bloomer (1818–94) whose name is associated with a dress reform movement which included full Turkish trousers gathered at the ankles with a dress over it. The style was widely ridiculed.

Blue Beard. A French story in which a rich man, nicknamed Blue Beard because of his hideous blue beard, has had six wives and marries a seventh. He leaves the keys of his castle with her while he goes on a journey, telling her that she may enter any room but one. She disobeys, and enters the forbidden room where she discovers the headless bodies of his former wives.

Bollman, Lewis. Appointed to the statistical branch of the Agriculture Department in 1863.

Booth, John Wilkes (1838–65). Shot and killed President Lincoln at Ford's Theatre in Washington, D.C., April 14, 1865. On April 26, 1865 he was found and shot near Port Royal, Virginia.

Boreas. In Greek mythology, the north wind.

Bowen, Sayles J. Postmaster of Washington, D.C., appointed by Lincoln in 1862. Also served as president of the Freedman's Aid Society.

Briareus. A giant of Greek mythology having a hundred hands.

Broomall, John Martin (1816–94). U.S. representative, Republican of Pennsylvania, 1863–69.

Bryan, John (1794–1864). Lois Bryan Adams's father. An early settler in Michigan.

Buchanan, James (1791–1868). Fifteenth president of the United States, 1857–61.

Bull, John. John Bull was considered to be the typical Englishman.

Bull Run. Two major battles were fought at Bull Run, Virginia. Both battles were Confederate victories. (Also known as Manassas.)

Burnside, Ambrose Everett (1824–81). U.S. general. In the early months of the Civil War he headed successful naval-military expeditions along the southeastern seacoast. He resigned his commission in 1864. He was governor of Rhode Island from 1866–69 and U.S. Senator from 1875–81.

Burroughs, Andrew Jackson. Shot and killed by Mary Harris (see note on Mary Harris).

Butchered braves of Plymouth. Refers to King Philips' War, 1675–78.

Butler, Benjamin Franklin (1818–93). U.S. general. On May 1, 1862 he was head of the U.S. troops who occupied New Orleans. On May 15, 1862 he ordered that "when any female shall, by word, gesture, or movement, insult or show contempt for any officer or soldier of the United States, she shall be treated as a woman of the town plying her avocation."

Carpenter, Francis Bicknell (1830–1900). New York portrait painter. Carpenter painted "Emancipation Proclamation before the Cabinet" based on sittings and on photographs taken for him by cameramen from Mathew Brady's studios. It was ready for viewing in the White House by July 22, 1864. Thereafter it was exhibited in several cities and was copied in 1865 by engraver Alexander Hay Ritchie and made into a popular print.

Carpet-Knights or Carpetbaggers. Northerners who went to the South during the period after the war and came to control many Southern state and municipal governments strictly for their own financial gain. So called because they packed their belongings in the then-popular luggage called carpetbags.

Catron, John (1786?–1865). Supreme Court justice, 1837–65.

Ceres. In Roman mythology, goddess of agriculture.

Chandler, Zachariah (1813–79). U.S. senator, Republican from Michigan 1857–75. Chandler helped organize the Republican party in Michigan. He was a prominent member of the Radical Republicans and opposed the moderate policies of both Lincoln and Johnson. He was secretary of the interior 1875–77.

Channing, Rev. William Henry (1810–84). Pastor of the Unitarian Society, Washington, D.C., 1861–63; chaplain of the U.S. House of Representatives, 1863–65.

Chase, Salmon P (1808–73). U.S. secretary of the Treasury. He resigned his Cabinet position in July 1864 in a dispute with Lincoln. Lincoln appointed him chief justice of the U.S. Supreme Court in October 1864.

Chicago Water Spout. The Democratic Convention was held in Chicago, Illinois, and nominated George McClellan for president and George Pendleton for vice president. The platform adopted reflected the views of the Peace Democrats. The Lincoln administration's

Glossary

conduct of the Civil War was denounced, with particular criticism of the use of martial law and the abridgement of state and civil rights. The platform called for an immediate end to hostilities and a negotiated peace.

Chittenden, Lucius E. Appointed register of the Treasury in 1861; resigned August 10, 1864.

Christian Commission. The United States Christian Commission was organized in New York City on November 15, 1861 to promote the spiritual and temporal welfare of soldiers in the U.S. Army and sailors and marines in the navy, in cooperation with chaplains and others. Its ministrations were conducted chiefly though not entirely by volunteers. It brought together earlier private organizations for such welfare and united them in one agency to collect, receive, and distribute food, clothing, and sundries; to provide religious services for the soldiers without undue regard to particular sects; and to distribute publications, chiefly religious and moral.

Clark, Daniel (1809–91). U.S. senator, Republican from New Hampshire, 1858–66.

Clay, Brutus J. (1808–78). U.S. representative, Democrat from Kentucky, 1863–65.

Clifford, Nathan (1803–81). Justice of the U.S. Supreme Court, 1858–81.

Coal Harbor, Battle of. Probably Cold Harbor fought in Virginia May 30–June 12, 1864.

Cole, Gabriel. Of Salem, Michigan. Enlisted in Company I, 5th Cavalry, August 19, 1862, at Allegan, for 3 years, age 31. Mustered August 30, 1862. Wounded in action and left at Hanover, Pa., July 1863. Promoted corporal. Wounded in action April 6, 1865. Honorably discharged at Annapolis, Md., June 27, 1865.

Colfax, Schuyler (1823–85). U.S. representative, Republican from Indiana, 1855–69; speaker of the U.S. House 1863–69. On April 8, 1864, he left the Speaker's Chair to move the expulsion of Alexander Long of Ohio, who had spoken in favor of recognizing the Confederacy. The resolution was later changed to one of censure. Vice President of the United States, 1869–73.

Colored troops. After the Emancipation Proclamation was issued January 1, 1863 Lincoln called for African-American regiments to help fight the war. By the end of the war there were approximately 300,000 African-American troops in 166 regiments.

Conspiracy trial. On May 1, 1865, President Andrew Johnson ordered the formation of a nine-man military commission to try the conspirators in the assassination of President Lincoln and other government officers. The trial lasted from May 10 to June 30, 1865. The trial was a military one even though the defendants were civilians. The defendants were: George A. Atzerodt, David E. Herold, Lewis Thornton Powell (or Payne) Mary E. Surratt, Samuel B. Arnold, Michael O'Laughlin, Edman Spangler, and Samuel A. Mudd.

On June 30, 1865, the military commission found them all guilty. Powell, Atzerodt, Herold, and Mrs. Surratt were sentenced to death. O'Laughlin, Arnold, and Mudd were sentenced to life imprisonment at hard labor. Spangler was given 6 years hard labor.

On July 5, 1865, sentence was passed on the conspirators, and the same day approved by President Johnson. The execution of the sentence was one of the most summary on record. The sentence was made known to the prisoners on Thursday, the 6th, and the very next day, at half past one o'clock, those sentenced to be hung were executed.

Constitutional Amendment, April 8, 1864. The 13th Amendment abolished slavery in the United States. It passed the Senate, 38–6, on April 8, 1864, but failed in the House, 93–65, on June 15, 1864. On January 13, 1865, the resolution passed the House by more than a two-thirds majority, 119–56, and Lincoln signed it February 1, 1865. It was ratified by three quarters of the states December 18, 1865.

Contraband. A term widely used during the Civil War for a negro slave, especially a fugitive or captured slave, from a decision made by General Butler in 1861 that such slaves were contraband of war. A contraband of war is anything forbidden to be supplied by neutrals to belligerents in time of war, and liable by the law of nations to be captured and confiscated.

Copperheads were those northern Democrats who opposed the Union's war policy and favored a neogiated peace. A copperhead is a poisonous snake akin to a rattlesnake, but without rattles.

Cowper, William (1731–1880). English poet.

Cox, Samuel Sullivan (1824–89). U.S. representative, Democrat from Ohio, 1857–65; Democrat from New York 1869–89.

Crapo, Henry Howland (1804–69). Governor of Michigan, 1865–69.

Crockett, David (1786–1836). U.S. Representative, Democrat from Kentucky 1827–31; Whig of Kentucky 1833–35. The backwoods humor and tall tales of Davy Crockett, the "coonskin congressman" became proverbial.

Custer, George Armstrong (1839–76). Union officer. From the first battle of Bull Run to Lee's surrender, Custer took part in almost every major battle of the Army of the Potomac.

Davis, David (1815–86). U.S. Supreme Court justice 1862–77.

Davis, Garret (1801–72). U.S. senator, Republican from Kentucky, 1861–67.

Davis, Henry Winter (1817–65). U.S. representative, American party from Maryland, 1855–57; Republican from Maryland, 1857–61; Unconditional Unionist party from Maryland, 1863–65.

Davis, Jefferson (1808–89). President of the Confederate States of America, 1861–65. Graduated from the U.S. Military Academy in 1828, and served in the army until 1835. Served in the U.S. Senate representing Mississippi 1847–51. Served as U.S. secretary of war 1853–57. Elected again to the Senate from Mississippi and served 1857–61. When Mississippi withdrew from the Union he resigned his Senate seat. Inaugurated as president of the Confederacy in February 1861. When Richmond, the capital of the Confederacy, fell, Davis and his cabinet fled. Davis was captured in Georgia in May 1865. There are many accounts of his capture and details are contradictory. There were reports of Davis being taken in woman's dress, in various forms of disguise, and of his trying to escape. Many of these stories appear to be exaggerated. Apparently he did wear a waterproof raincoat and had on a shawl due to the rain, and was first found a short distance from his tent in a futile effort to escape. After his capture Davis was confined at Ft. Monroe for two years. He was indicted for treason but never brought to trial.

Day, William Howard (1825–1900). A Massachusetts African-American abolitionist, editor, printer, educator, and clergyman.

DeBow's Review (1846–80). A journal edited by James Dunwoody Brownson DeBow. It presented statistics, news items, and essays to encourage the economic development of the South and the West. It defended slavery, advocated secession, and led the movement to revive the African slave trade.

Defrees, John D. Esq. (1811–82). Superintendent of the Government Printing Office. Appointed by Lincoln, March 23, 1861.

DeKalb, Baron Johann (1721–80). DeKalb was a German officer who served in the American Continental Army in the Revolutionary War. He was a major general in the army and was with Washington at Valley Forge.

Diet of Worms. Diet is a formal public assembly. The Diet of Worms, held at Worms, Germany, in 1521, convened to check the Reformation and condemned Luther as a heretic.

Dix, Dorothea (1802–87). U.S. superintendent of women nurses during the Civil War.

Doane, Dr. Possibly Thomas Doane (1821–97). An engineer from Charleston.

Dodge, Jacob Richards (1823–1902). When the U.S. Department of Agriculture was organized in 1862 he became an editor in the department. In May 1866, he became

Glossary

the department statistician. The Paris Exposition of 1889 awarded him a gold medal for exhibits of graphic illustrations of agriculture statistics.

Doughfaces/Copperheads. Those Northern Democrats who opposed the Union's war policy and favored a negotiated peace. Lincoln assumed strong executive powers in suppressing them, including arrests, suppression of the press, suspension of habeas corpus, and censorship.

Douglas, Mrs. Stephen Douglas. Adele Cutts Douglas (1835–99). Washington society belle and wife of Stephen A. Douglas.

Dow, Neal (1804–97). U.S. general.

Downing, Andrew Jackson (1815–52). Landscape gardener, architect, horticulturist. In 1851, Downing was hired to lay out the grounds for the Capitol, the White House, and the Smithsonian Institution in Washington. As the first great American landscape gardener, Downing created a national interest in the improvement of country houses and estates which made over the face of rural America.

Dumont, Ebenezer (1814–71). U.S. representative, Unionist from Indiana 1863–67.

Edgar, Capt. W. M. Possibly William M. Edgar of the 18th Missouri.

Elder, William Henry (1819–1904). Bishop of Natchez during the Civil War.

Eldridge, Charles Augustus (1820–96). U.S. representative, Democrat from Wisconsin, 1863–75.

Ellsworth, Oliver (1745–1807). Chief justice of the Supreme Court 1796–99.

Ellsworth, Elmer Ephrain (1837–61). First commissioned officer to die in the Civil War. When Virginia seceded from the Union on May 23, 1861, Ellsworth readied his men to take Alexandria, which was just across the Potomac from Washington. It was close enough that a rebel flag could be seen from the White House. On entering Alexandria, Ellsworth removed the flag from the Marshall House hotel. The hotel's proprietor, James W. Jackson, shot him and was shot in turn by Corporal Francis E. Brownell of Ellsworth's unit.

Enri, Dr. Henri. Engaged by the United States Department of Agriculture as chemist to replace Charles W. Wetherill in 1864.

Erysipelas. Also known as St. Anthony's Fire. An acute febrile disease associated with a local, intense, reddish inflamation of the skin and subcutaneous tissue, frequently of the face, caused by streptococcus.

Eugenie, Empress (1826–1920). Wife of French Emperor Napoleon III.

Everett, Edward (1794–1865). Orator and statesman. Everett was a Massachusetts Unitarian clergyman who made many famous speeches in the Union cause, the best known was his two-hour oration preceeding Lincoln's five-minute Gettysburg Address. He also served as U.S. representative 1825–35, as governor of Massachusetts 1836–40, as minister to Great Britain 1841–45, and as president of Harvard University 1846–49.

Ewell, Richard Stoddert (1817–72). Confederate General.

Fair for the Benefit of the Christian Commission. Held in the Patent Office February 29, 1864. The fair netted $25,000 for the Christian Commission and the families of District volunteers.

Father Abraham. A popular name for Abraham Lincoln.

Festus. The title of a poem by Philip James Bailey (1816–1902).

F.F.V.'s. First Families of Virginia.

Field, Stephen Johnson (1816–99). U.S. Supreme Court justice, 1863–97.

Finck, William Edward (1822–1901). U.S. representative, Democrat from Ohio 1863–67, 1874–75.

Floyd, Thompson and Co. John Floyd (1806–63) was the secretary of war in the Buchanan administration. He was accused in the North of concentrating guns in Southern arsenals in anticipation of their capture by Confederate troops. Jacob Thompson (1810–85) was the secretary of the interior in the Buchanan administration. He was accused of fraud in the administration of the Indian Trust Fund.

Ford's Theatre. The theater in Washington, D.C., where Lincoln was shot.

Fort Fisher. A fort in the port of Wilmington, North Carolina. After heavy fighting it was captured by Union forces January 15, 1865.

Fort Pillow. After the battle at Fort Pillow, Tennessee, on April 12, 1864, the Confederates swarmed into the fort with little difficulty. At this point Southern and Northern accounts diverge. Federal losses were approximately 231 killed, 100 seriously wounded, 168 whites and 58 negroes captured. Southern accounts maintain that Federal losses were incurred in fighting their way back to the river's edge and before surrender. Northern accounts maintain that the Federals surrendered as soon as the fort was overrun and were shot in cold blood by the Confederate forces.

Fort Sumter. A fort in Charleston harbor. The firing on Fort Sumter on April 12, 1861 is considered to be the start of the Civil War. The fort was retaken by the Union troops on February 18, 1865, an event of particular significance for the North.

Fox, Henry M. Enlisted in Company M, 5th Cavalry, August 12, 1862, at Coldwater, Michigan, for three years, age 18. Mustered August 30, 1862. Promoted to corporal August 2, 1863; to first sergeant January 1, 1865. Commissioned second lieutenant April 14, 1865. Mustered out at Fort Leavenworth, Kansas, June 19, 1865 as first sergeant.

Franklin, Benjamin (1706–90). Statesman, inventor.

Frauds of New York soldiers. In the 1864 Presidential election some states allowed volunteer soldiers to vote absentee. New York's governor, a leader of the Peace Democrats, sent a delegation to Washington to help Democratic soldiers around Washington cast their vote. The delegation was imprisoned and charged with fraud. After the election they were found not guilty by a military commission.

Fredericksburg. The Battle of Fredericksburg was fought on December 13, 1862 in the wooded heights above Fredericksburg, Va. General Burnside with 113,000 Union troops attacked General Lee's Confederate army of 75,000 troops. In this battle 12,600 Union troops died and the Confederates lost about 6,000 troops.

Freedman. A generic term applied to all ex-slaves after the adoption of the Thirteenth Amendment to the Constitution which abolished slavery.

Freedman's Bureau. In order to protect the interests of the former slaves, Congress established the Bureau as part of the War Department in 1865 for a period of a year. The Bureau was charged with obtaining labor contracts for former slaves, helping them find homes, settling their disputes, and obtaining employment for them. The Bureau sent hundreds of agents throughout the South to facilitate this program and to do additional work in educational facilities, relief, and the administration of justice. During its existence it founded over 100 hospitals, rendered medical aid to 500,000 patients, distributed over 20,000,000 rations, settled thousands of freedmen on abandoned or confiscated lands, and established over 4,000 schools.

Freedman's Fair. A fair organized to raise money for the cause of the Freed slaves. The National Freedman's Relief Association was a private relief organization to provide clothing, temporary homes, and employment for the freed slaves.

Frémont, John Charles (1813–90). Called the "Pathfinder," Frémont explored and mapped the West from 1838–46. He was governor of California in 1847. Frémont served as United States senator from California, 1850–51. In 1856, he was the presidential candidate of the Republican party. During the Civil War he served the Union at a rank of major general.

French, Benjamin B. Clerk in the U.S. House of Representatives 1845–47. He was appointed commissioner of Public Buildings in the District of Columbia September 7, 1861.

Frogs of Egypt. In the Bible, in the Book of Exodus, God sent ten plagues to Egypt when the Pharaoh refused to let the Israelites leave. One of the plagues covered the land with frogs.

Gales and Seaton. Joseph Gales Jr. (1786–1860), and William Winston Seaton (1785–1866) were brothers-in-law who owned and operated a printing business in Washington, D.C. In addition to publishing the *National Intelligencer* 1812–66, they published the *American State Papers* 1832–61 and *A Register of the Debates in Congress* 1825–37. Gales was mayor of Washington, D.C., 1827–30. Seaton was mayor of Washington, D.C. 1840–50.

Garnett, Henry Highland (1815–82). In 1864 he was appointed pastor of the Fifteenth Street Presbyterian Church in Washington, D.C. On February 12, 1865, he preached in the hall of the House of Representatives, the first African-American to do so.

Garrison, William Lloyd (1805–79). A leader of the abolitionist movement in the United States. He edited the *Liberator* from 1831 to 1865.

Gilpin fashion. William Cowper's *The Diverting History of John Gilpin, Showing How He Went Further Than He Intended and Came Home Safe Again,* was a humorous poem written in 1783 in which Gilpin borrows a horse that, once started, cannot be stopped.

Glover, Townsend (1813–83). The first man to hold an official entomological position for the United States government.

Gold Hoax. On May 18, 1864, the *New York World* and the *Journal of Commerce* printed a false statement that Lincoln had asked for another 400,000 troops. The stock market reacted by sending the price of gold up 10 percent. When the hoax was revealed it was discovered to be the plot of Joseph Howard Jr., who had purchased gold and wished to advance its price on the market.

Goodyear, Charles (1800–60). Invented ways to use rubber for garments and shoes for protection from the weather.

Grand Review. Parade of the Armies in Washington, D.C., on May 23 and 24, 1865. An estimated 150,000 men marched in review before the president and the commanding generals. The volunteer army was then disbanded.

Grant, Jesse (1794–73). Father of Ulysses S. Grant.

Grant, Ulysses Simpson (1822–85). Became general in chief of the armies of the United States on March 12, 1864, and took over the strategic direction of the war. After the war he remained as head of the army. He was named secretary of war by President Johnson. He was elected president of the United States as a Republican in 1868, and reelected for a second term in 1872.

Greenbacks. The popular name for U.S. government legal tender notes irredeemable in coins which were first issued in 1862. They were made a permanent part of currency in 1878.

Gregory, Edgar M (–1871). Breveted general of the U.S. Army. Brevet rank was an honorary rank awarded for gallant or meritorious action in time of war.

Grier, Robert Cooper (1794–1870). Supreme Court justice 1846–70.

Grinnel, Josiah Busnell (1821–91). U.S. representative, Republican from Iowa, 1863–67.

Hair styles. "A la Ramshorn" or like a Ram's horn. "A la Medusa" or like Medusa in the Greek legend who had snakes for hair.

Hale, John Parker (1806–73). From New Hampshire he served as a Democratic representative 1843–45. He served in Senate as a Democrat from 1847–53, and as a Republican from 1855–64.

Halleck, Henry Wager (1815–72). U.S. general. In 1861, he was placed in charge of the Department of the Missouri. In 1862, he was appointed general in chief of the Union forces. In 1864 he was replaced by Grant and became Grant's chief of staff.

Haln, Georg Michael Decker (1830–86). Governor of Louisiana 1864–65. Haln actively opposed secession and refused to support the Confederacy.

Haman (as in "hang him high as Haman"). In the Bible, Haman planned to kill all the Jews until the plot was exposed by Esther, and he was himself killed.

Hamlin, Hannibal (1809–91). Vice president of the United States 1860–64.

Hancock, Winfield Scott (1824–86). Union general. During the war Hancock was chief of the military department of Louisiana and Texas. Because of his outstanding military record the Democrats made him their presidential candidate in the 1880 election which he lost to Garfield.

Hardtack. A kind of hard biscuit usually baked in a large round cake, without salt.

Harlan, James (1820–99). Republican from Iowa. U.S. senator, 1855–65; secretary of the interior, 1865–66. Harlan was appointed by Lincoln as secretary of the interior but did not assume the duties of the office until after Lincoln's death. He broke with Johnson over Reconstruction and resigned his Cabinet post in July 1866.

Harper Brothers of New York. A publishing firm established in 1817. Harper's was the first publishing firm to use steam run presses and the first to introduce electrotyping on a large scale.

Harrington, Henry William (1825–82). U.S. representative, Democrat from Indiana 1863–65.

Harris and Fitch. Thaddeus William Harris (1795–1856) was author of *A Treatise, Some of the Insects of New England which are Injurious to Vegetation*, 1842. Asa Fitch (1809–79) was a New York State entomologist.

Harris, Benjamin Gwinn (1805–95). U.S. representative, Democrat from Maryland 1863–67.

Harris, Mary. "On the 30th of January a clerk in the Finance Department at Washington, Mr. Andrew Jackson Burroughs, came to his death in a singularly tragical manner at the hands of Miss Mary Harris, a former lover. Mr. Burroughs occupied a desk in a room near the principal passage on the second floor of the Department. About midway to this passage there was a clock fixed, and at four o'clock P.M., a young lady who had been noticed sauntering about the hall during a good part of the day took her position in a doorway by the clock. It was the hour of closing business, and the passage was thronged with the retiring employees. She was waiting for Mr. Burroughs, and as the latter came from his room and passed by where she stood she shot him dead.

The lady give her name as Mary Harris. She had resided in Chicago. She seemed about twenty years of age, was quite pale and delicate in complexion, with dark hair and eyes and an aquiline nose. The reason which she gave for committing the crime was that Burroughs had violated his promise of marriage to her, and had married another lady. Except in the simple violation of his word it seems he had done her no harm. She had met Burroughs in Burlington, Iowa, where her parents resided. Her parents had objected to her receiving his addresses, he being fifteen years her senior. But an attachment grew up between them, and they appear to have kept up a pretty regular correspondence. Their affair was broken off by Burrough's marriage to another lady. On the 5th of July Miss Harris instituted against Mr. Burroughs an action for breach of promise of marriage. At the close of the year she went to Washington to carry on the prosecution, and the sequel of the painful story is given in the tragic event which we have related" (*Harper's Weekly*, March 4, 1865, 140–41).

Harris, Thomas Maley (1817–1906). U.S. general.

Hartshorn. Used as a lightner of dough. Hartshorn is ammonium carbonate or Sal volatile.

Henry, Joseph (1797–1878). First Secretary of the Smithsonian Institution 1846–78.

Henry, Patrick (1736–99). Statesman and orator. First governor of Virginia. He is best known for his oratory and the famous "Give me liberty or give me death" speech.

Glossary

Hercules. A Greek hero who possessed great physical strength and courage, and performed twelve extraordinary tasks, one of which was to clean the Augean stables. These stables contained an enorous number of oxen, and remained uncleaned for many years. Hercules cleaned them in a day by diverting two rivers through them.

Hood, John Bell (1831–79). Confederate general.

Hooker, Joseph (1814–79). U.S. general.

Hooper, Samuel (1808–75). U.S. representative, Republican from Massachusetts, 1861–75. While Mrs. Lincoln remained in the White House after the death of her husband President Johnson resided with the Hoopers.

Housewives. Small kits for soldiers that contained thread, needles, and buttons.

Howard, Jacob (1805–71). U.S. representative, Whig from Michigan. 1841–43; U.S. senator, Republican from Michigan, 1862–71.

Hutchinson Family Singers. A very popular family singing group from New Hampshire.

Intelligencer. See *National Intelligencer.*

Invalid Corps. A great number of Civil War soldiers were disabled by wounds, disease, and accidents. Initially the permanently disabled received medical discharges from the army, but later they remained in the service and performed noncombat duties, relieving other soldiers to fight.

Irish Brigade. 1st Division, II Corps, Army of the Potomac. Each regiment of the brigade, made up primarily of Irish immigrants, carried a green flag with the harp, the symbol of Ireland, in addition to the national colors.

Iron Mills of the Gods. From a poem by Longfellow "The mills of the gods grind slowly yet they grind exceeding small." This means that the ways in which reforms are brought about, crime is punished, and so on, are often slow, but the end result may be perfectly achieved.

Jackson, Thomas Jonathan (1824–63). Confederate general. His nickname was "Stonewall" because his unit withstood heavy attacks at First Bull Run like a stone wall and could not be moved. He was killed at the Battle of Chancellorsville.

Jay, John (1745–1829). First chief justice of the U.S. Supreme Court, 1789–95.

Jefferson, Thomas (1743–1826). Third president of the United States, 1801–09.

Jeremiah. In the Bible Jeremiah is a great prophet, particularly noted for the grieving poems about the destruction of Jerusalem in the book of Lamentations, which is associated with him.

John Brown's Body. A song often performed in the North. In 1862, Julia Ward Howe (1819–1910) put new words to the music and it became "Battle Hymn of the Republic." The words begin "Mine eyes have seen the glory of the coming of the Lord."

Johnson, Andrew (1808–75). Seventeenth president of the United States, 1865–69; governor of Tennessee, 1853–57; U.S. senator, 1857–62. When Tennessee seceded from the Union he remained in the Senate and supported Lincoln. He was Lincoln's vice president in the second term and became president when Lincoln was assassinated.

Johnson, James. Possibly James E. Johnson of Alpine. Entered service September 6, 1862, age 23. Sergeant Company B, 6th Cavalry. Commissioned 2nd Lieutenant, December 4, 1864. Mustered out November 24, 1865.

Johnson, Reverdy (1796–1876). U.S. senator from Maryland. He was elected to the Senate as a Whig, 1845–49. He was U.S. attorney general, 1849–50; Democratic senator from Maryland, 1863–68. In the 1864 presidential election he supported McClellan since he felt the Emancipation Proclamation was unwise and resented Lincoln's interference in the Maryland and Kentucky elections.

Juggernaut. An object or belief calling for blind obedience or ruthless sacrifice from the Hindu religion. A Hindu ceremony has an image of Visnu drawn on a car, and it was formerly erroneously supposed that devotees allowed themselves to be crushed under the wheels of the car.

Kanoch. I.e., Canuck, a term referring to Canadians.

Kellogg, Mrs. Francis W. The wife of a U.S. representive from Michigan.

Kernam, Francis (1816–92). U.S. representative, Democrat from New York 1863–65. U.S. senator from New York, 1875–81.

Ladies' National Covenant. The trade deficit was large during the war and various ways of reducing it were tried. "Congress temporarily raised duties fifty per cent in hopes of stemming the tide of importation. The patriotic women of the nation, ever on the alert for methods of aiding the country, early in 1864 called a meeting of the loyal women of Washington, at which time an association, pledging women to the use of home manufactures, was formed under the name of "Ladies' National Covenant," with offices in every State and Territory within the national lines" (Elizabeth Cady Stanton, et al., *History of Woman Suffrage.* [New York: Fowler and Well, 1882], 39–40).

Lane, Mrs. The wife of a Kansas senator originally from Indiana.

Lafayette, Marie Joseph Paul, Marquis de (1757–1834). Lafayette came to the United States from France to fight in the Revolutionary War in 1777. He was commissioned a major general in the American army.

Lee, Robert Edward (1807–70). Confederate general in Chief. Lee graduated from the U.S. Military Academy in 1829. He was the Superintendent of West Point from 1852–55. Lee was offered positions as general for both the North and the South at the start of the Civil War and went with his home state of Virginia and fought for the Confederacy.

Legree, Simon. The villian in *Uncle Tom's Cabin* by Harriet Beecher Stowe. He is the brutal plantation owner who has Uncle Tom beaten to death; synonymous with all the evil of the Southern slave system and one of the most widely known villians in literature.

Leutze, Emanual (1816–68). Painter. His work was in the nineteenth-century German tradition.

Lincoln, Abraham (1809–65). Sixteenth president of the United States, 1861–65.

Lincoln, Mary Todd (1818–82). Wife of Abraham Lincoln, married in 1842.

Little Mac. Nickname of McClellan.

Livingston, John. Enlisted in Company A, First Sharpshooters, December 25, 1862, at Battle Creek, for 3 years, age 18. Mustered March 20, 1863. Died June 17, 1864, of wounds received in action at Spottsylvania, Va., May 12, 1864.

Loan, Mrs. Wife of Benjamin Franklin Loan, Congressman from Missouri.

Long, Alexander (1816–86). U.S. representative, Democrat from Ohio, 1863–65. Long spoke for the Peace Democrats stating that the law was on the side of the Confederates and the Union cause was not defensible. Speaker Colfax presented a motion for expelling Long from the House for favoring recognition of the Confederacy. Long was censured by a vote of 80 to 69 and declared an unworthy member of the House of Representatives.

Lovejoy, Owen (1811–64). U.S. representative, Republican from Illinois 1856–64. He introduced the bill to abolish slavery in all territories of the United States.

Manna. A food dropping from heaven, miraculously supplied to the children of Israel in the wilderness when they were following Moses (Exodus 16:14–36).

McClellan, George Brinton (1826–85). Commander of the Union Army of the Potomac, 1861–62. He was the Democratic party's nominee for president in 1864. He was governor of New Jersey 1878–81.

McConnell, Joseph E. Enlisted in Company B, 24th Infantry, April 1, 1863, at Detroit for 3 years, age 18. Mustered April 1, 1863. Discharged at Detroit September 12, 1865, on account of wounds received in action June 18, 1864.

McDougall, James Alexander (1817–67). U.S. senator, Democrat from California, 1861–67.

Glossary

McReynolds, Andrew Thomas (1806–98). Organized and led into the field the first regiment of cavalry for the Union Army. Enlisted as a colonel, June 1861. Honorable discharge, August 1864.

Market in Washington. Center market was an agglomeration of sheds and shacks which backed on the sewer of the canal.

Marshall, John (1755–1835). Third chief justice of the U.S. Supreme Court, 1801–35.

Mason, traitor. Possibly James Murray Mason (1798–1871). President Davis appointed Mason commissioner of the Confederacy to Great Britian and France. Federal officials seized Mason from the British steamer Trent while he was enroute to Europe.

Miller, Samuel Freeman (1816–90). Justice of the U.S. Supreme Court, 1862–90.

Mitts. Mittens made with one finger on the right hand and thumb neatly laced with leather that enabled soldiers to fire their weapons while wearing their mitts.

Molock. The name of a Semitic deity whose worship was marked by the sacrifice by burning of children offered by their parents; hence, anything conceived as requiring frightful sacrifice.

Monroe Doctrine. The doctrine, proclaimed December 2, 1823, by President James Monroe, that the interposition of any European power to control the destiny of a Latin-American state would be looked on as an unfriendly act toward the United States, and that the American continents should no longer be subjects for any new European colonial settlement.

More, Thomas (1478–1535). English poet.

Morrill, Anson Peaslee (1803–87). U.S. representative, Republican from Maine 1861–63; governor of Maine 1855–56.

Morris, Mary. Wife of Commodore Henry W. Morris.

Mudsills. A term from the Southern United States which means, figuratively, a person of the lowest stratum of society.

Multitudes (like those who came up from the Sea of Galilee). An episode from the Bible: "But Jesus withdrew himself and his disciples to the sea: and a great multitude from Galilee followed him, and from Judea, and from Jerusalem, and from beyond Jordan; and they about Tyre and Sidon, a great multitude, when they had heard what great things he did, came unto him" (*Mark* 3:7–8).

Myers, Amos (1824–93). U.S. representative, Republican from Pennsylvania, 1863–65.

Nadal, Bernard Harrison (1812–?). Minister of a Methodist church in the Baltimore conference; chaplain of the House of Representatives.

National Freedman's Relief Association of New York. Formed in 1862 and dedicated to assisting black slaves in making the transition to freedom.

National Intelligencer. A Washington newspaper published by Gales and Seaton. A staunch Whig supporter. The paper backed McClellan in the 1864 campaign and lost much of its reputation in the process.

Negroes used by Southern Armies. The Confederate army used many negro servants and laborers, but did not employ negro combat troops. A regiment was organized in New Orleans but not accepted into service. In 1863, a proposal to arm slaves was briefly considered. In November 1864, Davis considered the limited use of negro troops, and Robert E. Lee agreed that the idea had merits. In May 1865, the Confederate congress passed a law authorizing that up to 300,000 slaves be called for military service, but there was no mention of their being freed in connection with this duty. The next month a few companies were organized, but the surrender came before any of them were used.

Nelson, Samuel (1792–1873). U.S. Supreme Court justice 1845–72.

Nemesis. The personification of retributive justice in Greek literature.

Newton, Isaac (1800–67). First U.S. commissioner of the Agriculture Department.

Nichols, Clara Irene Howard (1810–85). A newspaper editor and women's rights leader. She worked in the Quartermaster's Office December 1863–March 1866.

Odd Fellows. Independent Order of Odd Fellows was founded in 1819. It is a fraternal benefit society.

Old Capitol. The Old Capitol prison was used mainly for prisoners of war, deserters, suspected spies, and persons awaiting trial. The Washington prison was housed in a temporary and hastily built substitute for the United States Capitol burned by the British in the War of 1812. The building was later used for a hotel but had fallen on hard times and was dilapidated and run down when pressed into use by the government for a prison.

Old Dominion. The nickname for Virginia.

Old Point Comfort. A prison in Virginia.

Orth, Godlove Stein (1817–82). U.S. representative, Republican from Indiana 1863–71, 1873–75, and 1879–82.

Pardoning of Southerners. Part of the Reconstruction plan of President Johnson. Based on Lincoln's policies, this involved an amnesty to all former Rebels with the exception of certain prominent former Confederates in the army and the government. After military governors were appointed for the Southern states, constitutional conventions were to be held, and after ratification of the Thirteenth Amendment (abolishing slavery) and the acceptance in Congress of the new legislators, the states were to be readmitted to the Union.

Parole. Lacking a means for dealing with large number of captured troops early in the Civil War, the U.S. and the Confederate governments relied on the traditional European system of parole and exchange of prisoners. The terms called for prisoners to give their word not to take up arms against their captors until they were formally exchanged for an enemy captive of equal rank.

Partington, Mrs. Humorous character created by Benjamin P. Shillaber in a book published in 1854, *The Life and Sayings of Mrs. Partington and Others of the Family*.

Patent Lock Case. Argued March 16,1864. Decided April 4, 1864 (68 US 662–64)

Peirce, Henry Augustus (1808–85). Merchant and diplomat associated with California and Hawaii.

Pendleton, George Hunt (1825–89). U.S. representative, Democrat from Ohio 1857–65; U.S. senator 1879–85. He was the vice presidential candidate of the Democratic party in 1864, running with McClellan as a Peace Democrat.

Phillips, Wendell (1811–84). A leader of the American Anti-Slavery Society.

Pierian Spring. A fountain in Pieria, sacred to the muses, and believed to communicate poetic inspiration.

Pierce, Franklin (1804–69). Fourteenth president of the United States, 1853–57.

Pike, Mrs. Wife of Frederick Pike, congressman from Maine

Pioneer Corps. Pioneers were skilled soldiers detached from their regular units to clear roads, construct bridges, dig trenches, and erect fortifications.

Pleiad. A group or cluster of illustrious or brilliant persons or things, usually seven. The name comes from a Greek myth when the seven daughters of Atlas and the nymth Pleione are transformed into a group of stars—the Pleiades.

Plumb, J. C. of Ypsilanti Seminary. The Plumbs went to Washington as volunteers to the Christian Commission.

Pomona. The Roman goddess of fruit.

Powell, Lazarus Whitehead (1812–67). U.S. senator, Democrat from Kentucky 1859–65; governor of Kentucky 1851–55.

Powers, Hiram (1805–73). American sculptor.

Proclamation of May 2, 1865. President Andrew Johnson issued a proclamation accusing

Glossary

Jefferson Davis and others of inciting the murder of Lincoln and procuring the actual perpetrators. A $100,000 reward was offered for the arrest of Davis.

Public Functionary. Term of derision referring to President Buchanan.

Rail-splitter. Lincoln's nickname.

Randolph, John (1773–1833). U.S. representative from Virginia, 1799–1825, 1827–29; U.S. senator 1825–27.

Revenue cutters. Boats belonging to the U.S. Revenue Service, the forerunner of the Coast Guard. The boats were used to help blockade Confederate ports.

Rice, Hon. Mrs. The wife of John H. Rice, representative from Maine, 1860–67.

Rip van Winkle. A short story by Washington Irving. Rip van Winkle meets a group of trolls whose drink puts him to sleep for twenty years. When he awakes, not knowing he has been asleep for so long, he finds a changed world.

Rochambeau, Jean Baptiste Donatien de Vimeur, Count (1725–1807). Sent by Louis XVI to head French forces aiding Washington in the Revoluntary War.

Rogers, Andrew Jackson (1828–1900). U.S. representative, Democrat from New Jersey 1863–67.

Rollins, James Sidney (1812–88). U.S. representative, Conservative from Missouri, 1861–65.

Rutledge, John (1739–82). Chief justice of the U.S. Supreme Court, August term 1795.

Samson. Biblical character purported to have great strength, which came from his vow never to cut his hair. Delilah, on finding out the source of his strength, cut his hair while he slept and delivered him to his enemies. (*Judges* 8–16)

Sanitary Commission, United States. The object of the organization was to do for soldiers what the government did not do, including raising the hygienic standards of the camps and diet, caring for the wounded, coordinating the program to send food and supplies to the soldiers, and compiling a directory of the sick and wounded in army hospitals. They also provided a home in Washington for discharged soldiers and lodges near railroad stations for transients. This volunteer organization had branches in all Northern states.

Sanitary Fairs. Fund raising activities for the United States Sanitary Commission held in many towns and cities in the North. The fairs raised large amounts of money for the work of the commission.

Saulsbury, Willard (1820–92). U.S. senator, Democrat from Delaware, 1859–71.

Saunders, William (1822–1900). In 1862, Saunders was appointed superintendent of the experimental gardens of the newly created Department of Agriculture. He designed the grounds of the Department at Washington and had charge of their development until his death in 1900. In 1863, he designed the national cemetery at Gettysburg.

Schenck, Robert Cumming (1809–90). U.S. representative, Republican from Ohio, 1863–71; Whig from Ohio 1843–51.

Scott, A. H. Possibly Gustavus Hall Scott (1812–82) a U.S. naval officer from Virginia.

Seward, William Henry (1801–72). U.S. secretary of state, 1861–69; U.S. senator 1849–61; governor of New York 1839–42. When Booth shot Lincoln, a co-conspirator forced his way into Seward's home, assaulted Seward's family and stabbed Seward. Seward recovered.

Seymour, Horatio (1810–86). Governor of New York (1853–55; 1863–65). He was the national leader of Lincoln's opposition. He opposed the Emancipation Proclamation and opposed filling New York state's draft quotas for the Union Army.

Sheridan, Philip Henry (1831–88). U.S. general.

Sherman, William Tecumseh (1820–91). U.S. general; commander of the U.S. Army, 1869–84.

Shoddy family. Shoddy was the name of the material for making uniforms at the beginning of the war. It was very poor material which could not stand up to military conditions. Hence, the name refers to anything cheaply made.

Siege of the Capital. The only serious threat to the capital occurred in July 1864, when Lt. General Jubal A. Early's Confederates invaded Maryland and arrived opposite the capital's defenses. Early attacked the works near Fort Stevens, but when veterans of the VI Corps arrived to fill the entrenchments, the Confederates withdrew to Virginia.

Sigel, Franz (1824–1902). U.S. general from Germany. A popular song of the Civil War is based on Sigel:

> I've come shust now to tells you how
> I goes mit regimentals,
> To schlauch dem voies of liberty,
> Like dem old continentals
> Vot fights mit England long ago
> To save der Yankee eagle;
> Und now I gets my soldier clothes,
> I'm going to fight mit Sigel.

Sisters in hospitals. Nuns served as nurses in hospitals during the Civil War.

Slavery. Was abolished in the District of Columbia by Act of Congress, in a bill signed April 16, 1862.

Smith, Caleb (1808–64). Secretary of the interior, 1860–62.

Smith, Green Clay (1826–95). U.S. representative, Unionist from Kentucky 1863–66; governor of Montana Territory 1866–69.

Smithson, James (1765–1829). Donated money for the establishment of an institution for the increase and diffusion of knowledge among men, which was opened as the Smithsonian Institution in Washington in 1846.

Smithsonian fire. "On the afternoon of January 24, at about three o'clock, a fire broke out in the Smithsonian Institute building in the loft area above the picture-gallery, between the ceiling and the roof. The fire is supposed to have been occasioned by a defective flue. It was not long before the ceiling fell in, and the picture gallery was in a sheet of flame. The conflagration was nearly altogether confined to the main building and above the first story, in which was the museum. Unfortunately, the latter was considerably damaged by water. The wings were not much burned, and the library in the west wing, containing over one hundred thousand volumes, was uninjured.

The loss by the fire includes the lecture room, the philosophical laboratory with most of the instruments, the originals of private records, and the archives of the institution, together with the destruction of the pictures in the gallery. About two hundred of Stanley's pictures were here, of which only five or six were saved" (*Harper's Weekly* February 11, 1865, 94).

Soldiers' Rest. At a large building near the depot, the Soldiers' Rest and the Soldiers' Retreat, the men were fed and lodged, efficiently policed and forwarded. As the troop trains neared the capital, the commissary department was notified, and gangs set to work cutting meat, cooking, and laying the tables. Promptly on their arrival, the men sat down to a hot meal. If their orders were to leave at once for the field, a day's ration for each was cut and cooked while they ate.

"Sound and fury, signifying nothing." A quotation from MacBeth Act V, Scene 5.

Southern Literary Messenger (1835–64). The literary repository for the Virginia Historical and Philosophical Society. The *Messenger* printed travelogues, biography, translations, poetry, book reviews, and fiction.

Southworth, Emma Dorothy Eliza Neville (E. D. E. N.) (1819–99). Popular novelist. She wrote between 50–60 novels and made as much as $6,000 a year from her writing at the height of her career. She has been identified as the greatest publishing success in nineteenth-century America. Southworth also served as a volunteer in a hospital near her home during the Civil War.

Spalding, Rufus Paine (1798–1886). U.S. representative, Democrat from Ohio, 1863–69.

Spottsylvania, Battle of. May 1–12, 1864 in Virginia. It was the first modern trench warfare battle.

Stagg, Peter. Entered service in Company K, First Cavalry, at organization, as Second Lieutenant, August 22, 1861 at Trenton, for 3 years, age 25. Commissioned August 22, 1861. Mustered September 26, 1861. Reported as captain, Company E. Commissioned major November 12, 1862. Mustered November 12, 1862. Commissioned lieutenant colonel, December 7, 1862. Mustered January 1, 1863. Commissioned colonel August 17, 1864. Mustered September 26, 1864. Brevet brigadier general, U.S. Volunteers, March 1, 1865, for gallant and distinguished services. Mustered out at Salt Lake City, Utah Territory, March 10, 1866.

Stanley, John Mix (1814–72). Artist. After living and painting in other places Stanley and his family moved to Detroit, Michigan, in 1864, where he spent the rest of his life.

Stanton, Edwin McMasters (1814–69). U.S. secretary of war 1862–68.

Stanton, Elizabeth Cady (1815–1902). A pioneer in the women's suffrage movement.

Stephens, Ann Sophia (1810–86). Popular author. During the Civil War Stephens served as vice-president of the Ladies' National Covenant, a society for the suppression of extravagance.

Stephens, Thaddeus (1792–1868). U.S. representative, Republican from Pennsylvania 1859–68; Whig 1849–53.

Substitutes. A man subject to military service could avoid it by supplying an able-bodied replacement. Supply and demand determined fees for substitutes. Newspaper advertisements early in the war offered a few hundred dollars for a service-worthy male.

Sumner, Charles (1811–74). U.S. senator, Republican from Massachusetts 1857–74; Democrat 1851–57. In May 1856 Sumner made a speech critical of slavery and the Kansas-Nebraska Act. He was beaten senseless on the floor of Senate by South Carolina Senator Preston Brooks. Sumner had a large part in the organization of the Republican party. At the end of the Civil War it was said that the two most influential men in public life were Abraham Lincoln and Charles Sumner.

Sunderland, Byron (1819–1901). Pastor of the First Presbyterian Church of Washington, D.C., 1853–98; chaplain of the U.S. Senate 1861–64.

Surratt, Mary (1817–65). A widow from Maryland, she moved to Washington around the beginning of the war and ran a boardinghouse. Her eldest son was in the Confederate army and her youngest son was a Confederate spy and dispatch carrier. She was arrested after Lincoln's assassination for her alleged part in the plot. She was found guilty and hanged.

Swain, Noah Haynes (1804–84). Justice of the Supreme Court, 1862–81.

Swisshelm, Jane Grey (1815–84). Journalist and reformer. Editor of the Pittsburgh *Sunday Visiter,* [sic] 1847, a weekly advocating abolition, temperance, and women's suffrage. Editor of the *St. Cloud Democrat,* a Minnesota Republican newspaper 1858–63; contributor to the *New York Tribune.* Worked in the federal civil service during the Civil War. As a result of her attack on President Johnson in the *Reconstructionist,* a newspaper she established in Washington, D.C., Johnson had her dismissed from her federal position in 1866.

Taney, Roger Brooke (1777–1864). Chief justice of the U.S. Supreme Court, 1836–64.

Tasistro, Louis Fitzpatrick (1808–68). He was born in Ireland, and came to the United States as a young man. He edited newspapers in New York City and Boston, wrote for periodicals, and was on the stage. He later settled in Washington, D.C., where he was for several years a translator for the State Department.

Terry, Alfred Howe (1827–90). U.S. general.

Thomas, George Henry (1816–70). U.S. general.

Thompson, George (1804–78). English abolitionist. In September 1834 Thompson came to the United States to work with members of the American Anti-slavery movement. On his speaking tours his life was often in danger. At the end of 1835 he had to escape from Boston on an open boat to catch a ship going to England. He revisited America in 1851, and again during the Civil War. When he visited during the Civil War a public reception was given for him in the House of Representatives, in the presence of President Lincoln and most of the Cabinet.

Tilton, Theodore (1835–1907). Editor of the *New York Independent* and advocate for women's rights. He was a strong abolitionist.

Toombs, Robert Augustus (1810–85). Secretary of state of the Confederacy, 1861–65. U.S. representative from Georgia, 1845–53; U.S. senator. 1853–61.

Tophet. A place in the Valley of Hinnom, near Jerusalem, where the Jews made human scarifices, esp., to Moloch, later used as a dumping ground for refuse and regarded as symbolic of the place of torment in a future life; hence, the place of punishment for the wicked after death, or hell.

Tunnicliffe, Joseph, Jr (1818–81). Entered service in 4th Infantry, as surgeon, June 20, 1861, at Adrian, age 42. Commissioned to date May 16, 1861. Mustered June 20, 1861. Transferred to 1st Infantry, at organization, August 17, 1861. Mustered October 31, 1861. Resigned and honorably discharged on surgeon's certificate of disability, December 10, 1862. Served as assistant state military agent until the close of the war.

Uncle Sam. The popular nickname for the United States.

Union League. Clubs that were among the score of patriotic clubs established throughout the North during the Civil War. The Union Leagues took part in state and local Republican politics. The headquarters were in Washington, D.C.

Varden, John. A Washington, D.C., citizen who had established a small museum in the capital in 1829. His collection became a part of the art holdings of the National Institute and was exhibited in the Patent Office building before it was moved to the Smithsonian Institution in 1862.

Victoria, Queen (1819–1901). Queen of England who reigned from 1837–1901.

Voorhees, Daniel Wolsey (1827–97). U.S. representative, Democrat from Indiana 1861–66, 1869–73; U.S. senator 1877–97. He defended Mary Harris at her murder trial.

Warder, John Aston (1812–83). Promoted landscape gardening. Editor of the *Flax and Hemp Commission Report* published by the government in 1865; publisher of *Western Horticulture Review* 1850–54.

Washington, George (1732–99). First president of the United States 1789–97.

Washington, Martha (1732–1802). Wife of George Washington.

Waterloo and Belgium gaiety. The Battle of Waterloo, June 18, 1815, took place twelve miles south of Brussels, Belgium, and about two miles south of the village of Waterloo, Belgium.

Watts, Isaac (1674–1748). English hymn writer.

Wayne, James Moore (1790–1867). Justice of the U.S. Supreme Court, 1835–67.

Webster, Daniel (1782–1852). Orator. U.S. senator from New Hampshire 1827–41, 1845–50; secretary of state 1841–43, 1850–52.

Weitzel, Godfrey (1835–84). U.S. general.

Welles, Gideon (1802–78). U.S. secretary of the Navy 1861–69.

Glossary

Wesley, John (1703–91). The founder of Methodism. His brother, Charles (1708–88) worked with him in the ministry and wrote over 7,000 hymns.

Whaley, Kellian Van Rensalear (1821–76). U.S. representative, Republican from Virginia 1861–63; West Virginia 1863–67.

Wheelock, Susan (1833–?). Agent of the Michigan Soldiers Relief Association. She wrote a book about her experiences, *The Boys in White: The Experience of a Hospital Agent in and around Washington* (New York: Lange and Hillman, 1870).

Wilderness, Battle of. May 5–6, 1864. The battle took place in Virginia. The effective strength of the Army of the Potomac was 115,000; it suffered 17,500 casualties (15 percent). The effective strength of the Army of Northern Virginia was 60,000; its casualties have been estimated at 7,500 (12 percent). The battle ended in a tactical draw, but it was a strategic victory for Grant, who turned south May 7th, unimpeded by Lee.

Willards. A famous hotel in Washington.

Willcox, Orlando Bolivar (1823–1907). U.S. general from Detroit.

Willey, Waitman Thomas (1811–1900). U.S. senator, Republican from Virginia 1861–63; Republican from West Virginia 1863–71.

Wilson, Henry (1812–75). U.S. senator from Massachusetts, 1855–73. Republican vice president 1873–75.

Wilson, Harriet Malvina. Wife of Henry Wilson.

Wilson, William. Enlisted in Company I, 11th Infantry, August 24, 1861, at Monroe, for three years, age 19. Mustered August 24, 1861. Taken prisoner at Chattanooga, Tennesee, September 20, 1863. Died June 17, 1864. Buried in National Cemetery at Andersonville, Georgia.

Winfield, Charles Henry (1822–88). U.S. representative, Democrat from New York, 1863–67.

Wood, Fernando (1812–81). Mayor of New York City 1854–57; U.S. representative, Democrat from New York 1841–43, 1863–65, 1867–81. One of the organizers and leaders of the Peace Democrats.

Yankee Doodle. A popular song of uncertain origin, was known in England in the mid eighteenth century, and was perhaps introduced in America by British soldiers during the French and Indian War (1755–63) in derision of provincial troops.

Zouaves. One of a body of infantry in the French service, originally Algerians. They wear a peculiar and brillliant uniform of gaiters, baggy trousers, short and open fronted jacket and, usually a tasseled cap or turban. Their drill is quick and spirited and the corps has been noted for dash and valor. Hence, one of a body of soldiers adopting the dress and drill of the Zouaves, as was done by a number of volunteer regiments in the Civil War.

BIBLIOGRAPHY FOR GLOSSARY

African American Almanac. Detroit: Gale Research, 1994.
Ames, William E. *A History of the National Intelligencer.* Chapel Hill: University of North Carolina Press, 1972.
Appleton's Cyclopedia of American Biography. 6 vols. New York: D. Appleton, 1888–91.
Bailey, L. H. *Standard Cyclopedia of Horticulture.* 3 vols. New York: Macmillan Co., 1935.
Boatner, Mark Mayo. *Civil War Dictionary.* New York: D. McKay, 1959.
Bryan, Wilhelmus B. *A History of the National Capital. Volume 2: 1815–1878.* New York: Macmillan, 1914.
Burr, C. B. *Medical History of Michigan.* 2 vols. Minneapolis: Bruce Publishing Co., 1930.
Congressional Quarterly. *Members of Congress Since 1789.* Washington, D.C.: Congressional Quarterly, 1977.
Congressional Quarterly. *National Party Conventions, 1831–1972.* Washington, D.C.: 1976.
Dictionary of American Biography. 22 vols. New York: Charles Scribner's Sons, 1928–58.
Dictionary of National Biography. 22 vols. London: Oxford University Press, 1949–50.
Faust, Patricia. ed. *Historical Times Illustrated Encyclopedia of the Civil War.* New York: Harper and Row, 1986.
Fischer, Carolyn, and Carol Schwartz, eds. *Encyclopedia of Associations.* Detroit: Gale Research, 1995.
Green, Constance M. *Washington: Village and Capital, 1800–1878.* Princeton: Princeton University Press, 1962.
Grote, David. *Common Knowledge: A Reader's Guide to Literary Allusions.* New York: Greenwood Press, 1987.
Harper's Weekly. 1863–65.
Heaps, Willard A., and Porter W. Heaps. *The Singing Sixties.* Norman: University of Oklahoma Press, 1960.
Johnson, Thomas H. *Oxford Companion to American History.* New York: Oxford University Press, 1966.
Jolly, Ellen R. *Nuns of the Battlefield.* Providence, R.I.: Providence Visitor Press, 1927.
Kinietz, Vernon. *John Mix Stanley and His Indian Paintings.* Ann Arbor: University of Michigan Press, 1942.

Larsen, Arthur J., ed. *Crusader and Feminist: Letters of Jane Grey Swisshelm, 1858–1865.* St. Paul: Minnesota Historical Society, 1934.

Leech, Margaret. *Reveille in Washington, 1860–1865.* New York: Harper and Brothers, 1941.

Logan, Rayford, and Michael Winston, eds. *Dictionary of American Negro Biography.* New York: Norton, 1982.

Long, E. B. *The Civil War Day by Day: An Almanac, 1861–1865.* Garden City, N.Y.: Doubleday, 1971.

Michigan. Adjutant-General's Department. *Record of Service of Michigan Volunteers in the Civil War, 1861–1865.* 46 vols. Kalamazoo: Ihling Bros. and Everard, Printers, 1905.

Munden, Kenneth. *The Union: Guide to the Federal Archives Relating to the Civil War.* Washington, D.C.: Published for the National Archives and Records Administration by the National Archives Trust Fund Board, 1986.

Murray, James, ed. *A New English Dictionary on Historical Principles.* 10 vols. Oxford: Clarenden Press, 1888–1928.

National Cyclopedia of American Biography. 62 vols. Clifton, N.J.: J. T. White, 1898–1984.

Neely, Mark E. *Abraham Lincoln Encyclopedia.* New York: McGraw-Hill, 1982.

New Century Cyclopedia of Names. 3 vols. New York: Appleton-Century-Crofts, 1954.

New Century Dictionary of the English Language, Based on Matter Selected from the Original Century Dictionary. New York: Appleton-Century, 1936.

Notable American Women, 1607–1950. 3 vols. Cambridge, Mass.: Belknap Press of Harvard University Press, 1971.

Oehser, Paul H. *The Smithsonian Institution.* New York: Praeger, 1970.

Oxford Companion to Women's Writing in the United States. New York: Oxford University Press, 1995.

Rees, Nigel. *Brewer's Quotations: A Phrase and Fable Dictionary.* London: Cassell, 1994.

Robertson, John, comp. *Michigan in the War.* Lansing: W. S. George and Co., 1880.

Stanton, Elizabeth Cady, et al. *History of Woman Suffrage.* New York: Fowler and Well, 1882.

Supreme Court Justices: A Biographical Dictionary. New York: Garland, 1994.

United States War Department. 70 vols. *The War of the Rebellion: A Compilation of Official Records of the Union and Confederate Armies.* Washington, D.C.: GPO, 1880–1901.

Warner, Ezra J. *Generals in Blue: Lives of the Union Commanders.* Baton Rouge: Louisiana State University Press, 1964.

―――. *Generals in Grey: Lives of Confederate Commanders.* Baton Rouge: Louisiana State University Press, 1959.

Who Was Who in America, 1607–1896. Chicago: Marquis Who's Who, 1963.

Index

abolitionism, 96–97, 102, 119. *See also* slavery; 13th Amendment
Adams, Abigail, 250–51
Adams, James R., 13
Adams, Lois Bryan, 10–11, 13–22; business manager, 16–17; camp visits, 268–70; civil service appointment, 18; columns, 9–10, 25–26; death, 22; editorial voice, 15–16, 22–23; education, 12, 13; government employees, reflections on, 291–94; health, 277; hospital volunteer, 10, 22; "L," 10; *Michigan Farmer,* 14–17; social encounters, 49–51; social issues, 16; *Sybelle and Other Poems,* 17–18; train trip, 207–8; Washington reflections, 37, 181, 190; weather reflections, 99–101, 177–78, 246–47; White House receptions, 78–80; writer, 10, 13, 17–18. *See also* Agriculture, Department of; hospital visits
African-Americans. *See* blacks
agricultural periodicals, household departments, 15–16
Agriculture, Department of, 55–64, 172–73; cabbages, 337–38; description of, 57–58, 192; employees, 20; establishment of, 20, 55, 62–64; Museum, 71–74, 172–73, 192–93, 332; newspaper articles, 282–83; reports, 64, 70–71, 288; seed rooms, 59–60; seeds, 57, 60–61, 67, 173, 290–91; Statistical Bureau, 68–71
Alcott, Louisa May, 22
Alexandria, Virginia, 132–33
antislavery. *See* abolitionism
anti-Union sentiments. *See* secessionists
Arlington Heights, cemetery, 183
artificial fruit, 72–73
assassination trial. *See* conspiracy trial

Baker, Jacob, 154–55, 160, 187–88
Barrett, Michael, 161
Barton, Clara, 22
Barton, Mrs., 135–36, 140–41
battle flags, 197–98; Stonewall Jackson, 198
bee hives, 323
blacks, 234, 253; conditions of, 239; education of, 296–97; 4th of July celebrations, 171, 275–77; Odd Fellows, 35; soldiers, 148–49, 255. *See also* contrabands; slavery; 13th Amendment
Bloomer, Amelia, 345
Bollman, Lewis, 69, 75
Bowen, Sayles J., 95
brevet rank, 351
Briggs, Emily, 24–25
Brooks, Preston, 359
Broomall, John Martin, 142
Bryan, John, 11–13, 205–7
Bryan, Sarah, 11

camp life, 268–70
Capitol building: construction of, 36; description of, 42–45; Rotunda, 43
Carpenter, Francis Bicknell, 179
Catron, John, 95
cattle diseases, 321
China tea plants, 45, 65–66
Chittenden, Lucius E., 84
Christian Commission, 83, 165, 211–17, 349; delegates, 214–15
clerks, government: hours, 291, 339; reflections on, 291–94; salaries, 19, 81, 217, 219, 245; women, 19–20, 24, 339–41. *See also* government employees
Clifford, Nathan, 94–95
Colfax, Schulyer, 120
colored cars. *See* street cars, segregation
Colored Sabbath Schools, picnics, 171
Congressional Library, 43
congressmen, 240–41
conspiracy trial, 274–75, 277, 280
construction, Washington, 182, 328–29
contrabands, 51, 295–96
Copperheads, 111, 112–13, 349
Cox, Samuel Sullivan, 109
Crapo, Henry Howland, 267
Culver, Charles, 150

Davis, David, 95
Davis, Garrett, 104, 106
Davis, Henry Winter, 116
Davis, Jefferson, 356–57
Day, William Howard, 276
Democratic Convention, 346–47
Detroit, description of, 18
Doane, Dr., 120–21
Dodge, Jacob Richards, 75–76
domestic manufacturing, 139, 143
dress reform movement. *See* Ladies' National Covenant
Dumont, Ebenezer, 117
dyes, 191–92

Early, Jubal A., 358
economy, United States, 142–43
editorial voice, 15–16, 22–23
election, presidential. *See* presidential election; voting
"Emancipation Proclamation before the Cabinet," 179–80, 346

employment, women. *See under* women
Entomological Exhibition (1865), 286–87, 322–24, 330–31
entomology, museum, 333. *See also* Agriculture, Department of, Museum
Erol, Henry, 191–92

fair, Washington's birthday, 83–85
fashions, 35, 279, 342; hair, 245; makeup, 241; promenading, 203, 341; rainwear, 127–28
Fern, Fanny, 25
Field, Stephen Johnson, 95
Finck, William Edward, 116
Finley Hospital, 164–65. *See also* hospitals
1st Michigan Sharpshooters, 161
Fitch, Asa, 352
flowers, 145–46
food, 34, 190–91, 273, 294–95
Ford's Theatre, 281–82
foreign goods, importation, 134–38
4th of July celebrations, 169–71, 275–77
Franklin, Benjamin, 51
Freedman's Bureau, 238
French, Benjamin B., 84
fruit, 190–91. *See also* food
fruit trees, 67

Garnett, Henry Highland, 233, 238
Geisboro, 131
Georgetown, 39
Gibbs, T. H., 143–44
Glover, Townsend, 194–95, 330–34; artificial fruit, 72–73; award, 330; Entomological Exhibition (1865), 287, 320–24, 330–31; entomologist, 72, 76; museum, 172, 192. *See also* Agriculture, Department of, Museum
Goddess of Liberty, 36
government employees, 289, 294; vacations, 189. *See also* clerks, government; women, working conditions
Government Printing Office, 80–82
Grant, Jesse Root, 343–44
greenhouses, Washington, 45
Grennell, James S., 75
Grier, Robert Cooper, 95

Hale, Sarah Josepha, 25
Hall, J. W., 160

Index

Hall of Relics, 46–49
Harris, Benjamin Gwinn, 115
Harris, Mary, 281, 283–85
Henry, Joseph, 227
Holcomb, J. W., 160
Horen, James P., 150
hospitals, 150–51, 164–65, 210; regimental, 269
hospital visits, 151–53; aid, 156–57; Finley Hospital, 164–65; German soldiers, 163; Michigan soldiers, 160–62, 187–88; Scottish soldiers, 152, 159; story of, 167–69; volunteers, 21, 183. *See also* soldiers, wounded
House of Representatives, 170; antislavery speeches, 233
housing, Washington, 34, 36, 88–90, 184, 219, 247
Howard, Joseph, Jr., 351
Howe, Julia Ward, 353

inauguration balls, 241, 245
insect powders, 332
insects, 194–95, 322–23, 325–27
Intelligencer, 254–55, 272
Invalid Corps, 171
Irish Brigade, 267

Jackson, James W., 349
Johnson, Andrew, 95, 336, 337, 356
Johnson, Reverdy, 102–3
Johnstone, Robert F., 14, 17, 27n. 16
journalists, women, 15–16, 22–23, 25
July 4th celebrations. *See* 4th of July celebrations

Kernam, Francis, 115

"L." *See* Adams, Lois Bryan, "L"
Ladies' National Covenant, 25–26, 134–41
Ladies' Union League, 127. *See also* Ladies' National Covenant
Lee's surrender, celebrations, 253–54
letter writing, 153–54, 166
Leutze, Emanual, 50
levy, 89
Library of Congress, 43
lilacs, 145–46
Lincoln, Abraham: applications for favors, 224–25; assassination, 256; concerts, 146; conspiracy trial, 274–75, 277, 280; fair, Washington's birthday, 84; inauguration, 242–44; public receptions, 79, 223–24; war's end, 254. *See also* White House: public receptions
Lincoln, Mary Todd, 80
living conditions, women. *See under* women
Livingston, John, 168
Long, Alexander, 118, 347; expulsion case debates, 108–14, 114–20
loyalists, 98, 262–63

McClellan, George Brinton, 193
McConnell, Joseph E., 188
McDougall, James Alexander, 106
McNesbit, William, 166
Michigan Farmer, 14–17; "Household Department," 15–16
Michigan Sharpshooters, 1st. *See* 1st Michigan Sharpshooters
Michigan soldiers. *See* soldiers: Michigan; soldiers, wounded, Michigan
Michigan Soldiers Relief Association, 10, 21–22, 157, 165, 212
Michigan Territory, 12
military parades, 171, 263–67, 268
Miller, Samuel Freeman, 95
Montgomery, Colonel, 121–25
Morrill, Anson Peaslee, 93
Museum of the Department of Agriculture. *See* Agriculture, Department of, Museum

National Freedman's Relief Association, 350
National Freedmen's Relief Association of New York, 238–39
Nelson, Samuel, 94
newspaper publishing, 13
Newton, Isaac, 20, 74–75, 172
Niagara Falls, 208–9

Oak Hill Cemetery, 40
Odd Fellows, 35
office holders. *See* clerks, government; government employees
Olmstead, E., 160
Orth, Godlove Stein, 115

parks, Washington, 126–27, 249–50

Parton, Sarah Willis, 25
passports, 321–22
Patent Office, 46
Patent Office seeds, 173
patriotic sentiments, 98, 262–63
patronage, government, 289–90, 295, 339, 340. *See also* clerks, government; government employees
pay inequities, 19, 219. *See also under* women
Peace Democrats, 346. *See also* War Democrats
peaches and milk, 190–91
Petersburg occupation, celebrations, 252–53
Plumb, Mrs. J. C., 160–61
Potomac Ferry, crossings, 131
poverty, Washington, 247–48
Powell, Lazarus Whitehead, 104, 106
presidential election: voter sentiments, 193–94, 205; voting, 350
prisoners, conditions of, 128–30
"Prisoner's Refrain, The," 129
Proclamation of May 2, 1865, 261
propagating garden, government, 65–68
public goose, 282–83
public speaking, women, 135, 136, 137

racial prejudice, 97, 255
rebels, paroled, 257–58
receptions, public, White House, 78–80, 223, 244
reconstruction rebels, 334–36. *See also* secessionists
Richmond occupation, celebrations, 252–53
Rollins, James Sidney, 119–20

salaries. *See* clerks, government: salaries; pay inequities; women, salaries
sanitation, Washington, 36–37, 185–86, 274, 329–30
Saunders, William, 66, 67, 76–77
Schenck, Robert Cummings, 111–14
Scott, A. H., 142–43
Seaton, William Winston, 351
secessionists, 37–38, 91–92, 261–62, 271, 272; anti-Union sentiments, 176–77; arrests, 204; *Intelligencer,* 254–55; women, 176–77, 280–81
seed rooms, 59–60

seeds, 57, 60–61, 67, 173, 290–91
Seymour, George, 154
Sheridan, Philip Henry, 264
Sherman, William Tecumseh, 231, 266
sidewalks, Washington, 36–37. *See also* sanitation, Washington
Sigel, Franz, 163–64
silk production, 290, 323–24, 332–33
slaveholders, 89–90, 104, 239; story of, 298–320
slavery, 119, 121, 233, 255; amendment to abolish, 102, 105–7; sentiments, 38, 239; story of, 298–320. *See also* contrabands
Smith, Green Clay, 118–19
Smithson, James L., 230
Smithsonian Institution, 45–46; fire, 227–29; mission, 230
soldiers: black, 148–49, 255; camp life, 270; description of, 265; Michigan, 129–30, 154–55, 160, 161, 168, 187–88; New York, 204–5; on leave, 231–32
soldiers, wounded, 151–52, 156–57, 159–61; Canadian, 160; German, 163; lengthy hospitalization, 210–11; Michigan, 148, 149–50, 153, 154–55, 157–58, 162–63, 165–66, 187–88; rebel, 155; Scottish, 151, 159; Union meeting, 196–97; visits, 147–48. *See also* hospital visits
Southworth, Emma Dorothy Eliza Neville, 40–41
souvenirs, White House, 225–26
Stagg, Peter, 267
Stanley, John Mix, 227–28, 229
Stanton, Elizabeth Cady, 140
Statistical Bureau, Department of Agriculture, 68–71
Stephens, Ann Sophie, 134–35, 140
Stephens, Thaddeus, 109
Stowe, Harriet Beecher, 354
street cars, segregation, 234–36; Washington, 204, 297, 327–28
suffrage, 272
Supreme Court, 93–94
Surratt, Mary, 280
Swain, Noah Haynes, 95
Swisshelm, Jane Grey, 24, 340–41, 344
Sybelle and Other Poems, 17–18

sympathizers. *See* secessionists

13th Amendment, 102, 105–7
Thomas, George, 148
Thompson, George, 103
Thompson, Jacob, 350
Tilton, Theodore, 238–39
Tompkins, Dr., 239
Toombs, Robert Augustus, 112
travel, Europe, 321–22
Tunnicliffe, Joseph, Jr., 197, 199

Uncle Sam, 155
Union, opinion on, 38
Union League, meetings, 120–25, 141–44
Union meetings, 196–97
United States Christian Commission. *See* Christian Commission
United States Department of Agriculture. *See* Agriculture, Department of

Vicksburg, escape: story of, 122–25
Voorhees, Daniel Wolsey, 114–15

War Democrats, 111, 113, 346
War Department, 237
Warder, John Aston, 173
war reporters, 23
war's end, celebrations, 253–54
Washington: concerts, 277–80; description of, 19, 35–37, 199–202; dust, 86–88; in mourning, 258–59; siege, 174–75; social life, 126–27, 156, 285–86; swampland, 249; visitors to, 182–83.
See also White House: concerts, public receptions; 4th of July celebrations
Washington, George, 47; birthday celebrations, 236–37; fair, 83–85
Washington Young Men's Association, 103
Wayne, James Moore, 94
weather, reflections on, 99–101, 246–47; Washington, 177–78, 231, 248–49
weevils, 194–95
Whaley, Kellian Van Rensalear, 116–17
White House: concerts, 146, 278, 279–80; description of, 78, 200–201, 250–51; grounds, 201–2, 278–80; in mourning, 259; levee, 244; public receptions, 78–80, 223, 244; thefts, 225–26
Whitman, Walt, 22
Willey, Waitman Thomas, 96–97
Wilson, William W., 129–30
women, 176–77, 280–81; employment, 19–20, 24, 339–41; fashion (*see* fashions); journalists, 15–16, 22–23, 25; living conditions, 219; public speaking, 135, 136, 137; salaries, 19, 81, 219 (*see also* clerks, government: salaries); secessionists, 176–77, 280–81; working conditions, 19–20, 60, 81, 82. *See also* Ladies' National Covenant
women's rights, employment, 16
women writers, editorial voice, 15–16, 22–23
Wood, Fernando, 109, 111, 112–13
working conditions. *See under* women

Titles in the Great Lakes Books Series

Freshwater Fury: Yarns and Reminiscences of the Greatest Storm in Inland Navigation, by Frank Barcus, 1986 (reprint)
Call It North Country: The Story of Upper Michigan, by John Bartlow Martin, 1986 (reprint)
The Land of the Crooked Tree, by U. P. Hedrick, 1986 (reprint)
Michigan Place Names, by Walter Romig, 1986 (reprint)
Luke Karamazov, by Conrad Hilberry, 1987
The Late, Great Lakes: An Environmental History, by William Ashworth, 1987 (reprint)
Great Pages of Michigan History from the Detroit Free Press, 1987
Waiting for the Morning Train: An American Boyhood, by Bruce Catton, 1987 (reprint)
Michigan Voices: Our State's History in the Words of the People Who Lived It, compiled and edited by Joe Grimm, 1987
Danny and the Boys, Being Some Legends of Hungry Hollow, by Robert Traver, 1987 (reprint)
Hanging On, or How to Get through a Depression and Enjoy Life, by Edmund G. Love, 1987 (reprint)
The Situation in Flushing, by Edmund G. Love, 1987 (reprint)
A Small Bequest, by Edmund G. Love, 1987 (reprint)
The Saginaw Paul Bunyan, by James Stevens, 1987 (reprint)
The Ambassador Bridge: A Monument to Progress, by Philip P. Mason, 1988
Let the Drum Beat: A History of the Detroit Light Guard, by Stanley D. Solvick, 1988
An Afternoon in Waterloo Park, by Gerald Dumas, 1988 (reprint)
Contemporary Michigan Poetry: Poems from the Third Coast, edited by Michael Delp, Conrad Hilberry and Herbert Scott, 1988
Over the Graves of Horses, by Michael Delp, 1988
Wolf in Sheep's Clothing: The Search for a Child Killer, by Tommy McIntyre, 1988
Copper-Toed Boots, by Marguerite de Angeli, 1989 (reprint)
Detroit Images: Photographs of the Renaissance City, edited by John J. Bukowczyk and Douglas Aikenhead, with Peter Slavcheff, 1989
Hangdog Reef: Poems Sailing the Great Lakes, by Stephen Tudor, 1989
Detroit: City of Race and Class Violence, revised edition, by B. J. Widick, 1989
Deep Woods Frontier: A History of Logging in Northern Michigan, by Theodore J. Karamanski, 1989

Orvie, The Dictator of Dearborn, by David L. Good, 1989
Seasons of Grace: A History of the Catholic Archdiocese of Detroit, by Leslie Woodcock Tentler, 1990
The Pottery of John Foster: Form and Meaning, by Gordon and Elizabeth Orear, 1990
The Diary of Bishop Frederic Baraga: First Bishop of Marquette, Michigan, edited by Regis M. Walling and Rev. N. Daniel Rupp, 1990
Walnut Pickles and Watermelon Cake: A Century of Michigan Cooking, by Larry B. Massie and Priscilla Massie, 1990
The Making of Michigan, 1820–1860: A Pioneer Anthology, edited by Justin L. Kestenbaum, 1990
America's Favorite Homes: A Guide to Popular Early Twentieth-Century Homes, by Robert Schweitzer and Michael W. R. Davis, 1990
Beyond the Model T: The Other Ventures of Henry Ford, by Ford R. Bryan, 1990
Life after the Line, by Josie Kearns, 1990
Michigan Lumbertowns: Lumbermen and Laborers in Saginaw, Bay City, and Muskegon, 1870–1905, by Jeremy W. Kilar, 1990
Detroit Kids Catalog: The Hometown Tourist by Ellyce Field, 1990
Waiting for the News, by Leo Litwak, 1990 (reprint)
Detroit Perspectives, edited by Wilma Wood Henrickson, 1991
Life on the Great Lakes: A Wheelsman's Story, by Fred W. Dutton, edited by William Donohue Ellis, 1991
Copper Country Journal: The Diary of Schoolmaster Henry Hobart, 1863–1864, by Henry Hobart, edited by Philip P. Mason, 1991
John Jacob Astor: Business and Finance in the Early Republic, by John Denis Haeger, 1991
Survival and Regeneration: Detroit's American Indian Community, by Edmund J. Danziger, Jr., 1991
Steamboats and Sailors of the Great Lakes, by Mark L. Thompson, 1991
Cobb Would Have Caught It: The Golden Age of Baseball in Detroit, by Richard Bak, 1991
Michigan in Literature, by Clarence Andrews, 1992
Under the Influence of Water: Poems, Essays, and Stories, by Michael Delp, 1992
The Country Kitchen, by Della T. Lutes, 1992 (reprint)
The Making of a Mining District: Keweenaw Native Copper 1500–1870, by David J. Krause, 1992
Kids Catalog of Michigan Adventures, by Ellyce Field, 1993
Henry's Lieutenants, by Ford R. Bryan, 1993
Historic Highway Bridges of Michigan, by Charles K. Hyde, 1993
Lake Erie and Lake St. Clair Handbook, by Stanley J. Bolsenga and Charles E. Herndendorf, 1993
Queen of the Lakes, by Mark Thompson, 1994
Iron Fleet: The Great Lakes in World War II, by George J. Joachim, 1994
Turkey Stearnes and the Detroit Stars: The Negro Leagues in Detroit, 1919–1933, by Richard Bak, 1994
Pontiac and the Indian Uprising, by Howard H. Peckham, 1994 (reprint)
Charting the Inland Seas: A History of the U.S. Lake Survey, by Arthur M. Woodford, 1994 (reprint)
Ojibwa Narratives of Charles and Charlotte Kawbawgam and Jacques LePique, 1893–1895. Recorded with Notes by Homer H. Kidder, edited by Arthur P. Bourgeois, 1994, co-published with the Marquette County Historical Society
Strangers and Sojourners: A History of Michigan's Keweenaw Peninsula, by Arthur W. Thurner, 1994

Win Some, Lose Some: G. Mennen Williams and the New Democrats, by Helen Washburn Berthelot, 1995
Sarkis, by Gordon and Elizabeth Orear, 1995
The Northern Lights: Lighthouses of the Upper Great Lakes, by Charles K. Hyde, 1995 (reprint)
Kids Catalog of Michigan Adventures, second edition, by Ellyce Field, 1995
Rumrunning and the Roaring Twenties: Prohibition on the Michigan-Ontario Waterway, by Philip P. Mason, 1995
In the Wilderness with the Red Indians, by E. R. Baierlein, translated by Anita Z. Boldt, edited by Harold W. Moll, 1996
Elmwood Endures: History of a Detroit Cemetery, by Michael Franck, 1996
Master of Precision: Henry M. Leland, by Mrs. Wilfred C. Leland with Minnie Dubbs Millbrook, 1996 (reprint)
Haul-Out: New and Selected Poems, by Stephen Tudor, 1996
Kids Catalog of Michigan Adventures, third edition, by Ellyce Field, 1997
Beyond the Model T: The Other Ventures of Henry Ford, revised edition, by Ford R. Bryan, 1997
Young Henry Ford: A Picture History of the First Forty Years, by Sidney Olson, 1997 (reprint)
The Coast of Nowhere: Meditations on Rivers, Lakes and Streams, by Michael Delp, 1997
From Saginaw Valley to Tin Pan Alley: Saginaw's Contribution to American Popular Music, 1890–1955, by R. Grant Smith, 1998
The Long Winter Ends, by Newton G. Thomas, 1998 (reprint)
Bridging the River of Hatred: The Pioneering Efforts of Detroit Police Commissioner George Edwards, 1962–1963, by Mary M. Stolberg, 1998
Toast of the Town: The Life and Times of Sunnie Wilson, by Sunnie Wilson with John Cohassey, 1998
These Men Have Seen Hard Service: The First Michigan Sharpshooters in the Civil War, by Raymond J. Herek, 1998
All-American Anarchist: Joseph A. Labadie and the Labor Movement, by Carlotta R. Anderson, 1998
A Place for Summer: One Hundred Years at Michigan and Trumbull, by Richard Bak, 1998
Michigan in the Novel, 1816–1996: An Annotated Bibliography, by Robert Beasecker, 1998
"Time by Moments Steals Away": The 1848 Journal of Ruth Douglass, by Robert L. Root, Jr., 1998
Early Midwestern Travel Narratives: An Annotated Bibliography, 1634–1850, by Robert R. Hubach, 1998
The Detroit Tigers: A Pictorial Celebration of the Greatest Players and Moments in Tigers' History, updated edition, by William M. Anderson, 1999
Letter from Washington, 1863–1865, by Lois Bryan Adams, edited and with an introduction by Evelyn Leasher, 1999